Contemporary Tourism Reviews

Volume 1

Edited by Chris Cooper

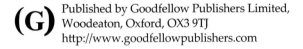 Published by Goodfellow Publishers Limited,
Woodeaton, Oxford, OX3 9TJ
http://www.goodfellowpublishers.com

British Library Cataloguing in Publication Data: a catalogue record for
this title is available from the British Library.

Library of Congress Catalog Card Number: on file.

ISBN: 978-1-910158-05-0

 Design and typesetting by P.K. McBride, www.macbride.org.uk

Cover design by Cylinder, www.cylindermedia.com

Printed by Marston Book Services, www.marston.co.uk

Contents

Introduction

Chris Cooper

In 1989 I launched a research review series titled *Progress in Tourism, Recreation and Hospitality Management* (Cooper, 1989). *Progress* was one of the first attempts to draw together synoptic reviews of research in tourism and allied subjects, even though it was relatively early days for the field. Twenty-five years on, as the subject has matured and grown, it is appropriate to return to the *Progress* format of an annual book series drawing together cutting-edge research reviews. However, this new series demonstrates a number of differences from the original *Progress* series. Not the least of these is in the use of technology. This annual book series of *Contemporary Tourism Reviews* comprises reviews that are individually downloadable and include hyperlinks and interactive web features. This allows the reader to access multiple layers of information and references using the concept of the 'page as portal'.

Tourism research too, has changed and developed considerably over the last twenty-five years. It has expanded and splintered into many different sub-fields as the subject has matured, journals have been launched (estimates suggest the number approaches 300), increasing numbers of texts have been written and research centres established. This growing body of work is evidenced by the many subsequent published reviews, readers and handbooks summarising research themes, often with 'progress' in the title. These include thematic reviews in the leading journals such as *Annals of Tourism Research* and *Tourism Management*. These reviews too, cover the major sub-fields of tourism and are beginning to prompt a new generation of thinking. Examples here include Lynch et (2011) for hospitality; Eagles (2014) for research priorities in park management; Standing et al (2014) for a review of tourism and technology; and Xin et al (2012) for a review of research methodologies applied to tourism. Similarly, we have seen the emergence of challenges to conventional views in the form of the 'critical turn' on tourism studies and the reconceptualization of tourism as a 'mobility'. Nor is the field immune from major new ideas and thinking from other fields – here the influence of marketing concepts (Dolnicar and Ring, 2014) and the 'service dominant logic' is clearly important for tourism (Shaw et al, 2011). Given the contributions of other fields, it is important that tourism researchers recognise these varied disciplinary roots (Botterill, 2001).

Subject maturity has prompted the perennial debate about whether tourism is a discipline. Applying the tests used by Harland et al (2006), tourism fails to meet the criteria of a discipline – it has neither the field coherence nor quality of theoretical development required. But does this really matter? More useful perhaps is the discussion about inter-disciplinarity, multi-disciplinarity or indeed, the view of Coles et al (2006) that such debates do not lead anywhere and that in fact we are in a 'post disciplinary' period.

At the end of the day, tourism research delivers tourism knowledge stocks for use in teaching, further research, policy formulation and practice (Cooper, 2006). These tourism knowledge stocks continue to grow, facilitated by subject maturity, technology and the revolution in digital publishing. New tourism knowledge is constantly being generated by researchers, consultants, the industry and government (see for example Echtner and Jamal, 1997; Jafari, 1990). The majority of this tourism knowledge generation has occurred since 1970, with the early work summarised in the original *Progress* series. Over the years, the growing number of tourism researchers has effectively created a community of practice (COP) or 'academic tribe' for tourism with common publications and language (Tribe, 1997). In terms of tourism knowledge stocks, Tribe (1997) identifies two distinct sources: firstly, 'mode 1 knowledge' is created in higher education institutions based upon disciplines and fields'; whilst 'mode 2 knowledge' is generated outside higher education and traditional disciplines by industry, government, and consultants. This knowledge tends to be problem-based and set within a specific context. Yet, tourism knowledge stocks are dominated by work written in English and it is only in recent years that work in other languages, notably Spanish and Mandarin, is being made available to non-native speakers (see for example, Leunga et al, 2014).

Despite the growth of tourism knowledge, many argue that the tourism sector has not engaged with tourism researchers and their generation of new knowledge: indeed the sector could be seen as a research-averse (Cooper and Ruhanen, 2002). This issue is not new and has been identified by a number of authors who argue that there is a gap between tourism research generation and its utilisation (see for example Hudson, 2013; Pyo, 2012; Thomas, 2012; Tribe, 2008). This is an important issue for tourism as it is also clear that the generation and use of new tourism knowledge for innovation and product development is critical for competitiveness.

There are however, signs that this situation is changing. Leading companies in the sector are overtly engaging with sustainability and climate change issues, providing role models for the rest of the sector - and SMEs in particular. Companies such as Accor, Tui and P&O are examples here. International agencies in the government sector are also engaging with researchers, notably the OECD's tourism unit and the UN World Tourism Organization.

This underscores the fact that tourism research does not take place in an institutional or policy vacuum. Policy relevant to tourism also concerns the importance given to research and development within economies and the positioning of tourism in higher education by national governments. Here, there is clear need for leadership and advocacy from the academy (Dredge and Schott, 2013). The

Tourism Education Futures Initiative is a good example here (www.tourismeducationfutures.org/). Tourism higher education and research is part of national systems and a clear trend is for a more utilitarian tone to the bidding for research funds (Thomas, 2012), the increasing importance of the research 'impact' agenda, the growing influence of biblio-metrics and the juggernaut of research selectivity exercises (Hall, 2011). This direction of travel should be good news for tourism researchers who will be able to demonstrate the impact of their work on the sector, but the key to success will still be the response of research users. Nonetheless, this shifting policy environment is impacting upon how researchers are assessed, how their careers develop and the future direction of tourism research itself. Here, it is imperative that tourism research is seen to be relevant and engaging with the bigger picture issues in the world such as climate change and poverty reduction to counter Tribe's (2006) view that tourism research is unpredictable and fickle in its coverage.

I hope that this volume will contribute to tourism knowledge stocks and to the increasing relevance of tourism research. The invited reviews in this first volume have been written to provide critical, state of the art and authoritative coverage of the sub-fields and related topics of tourism, written by leading thinkers and academics in the field. Each review is a critical, readable and sometimes controversial account of the development of the literature in sub-fields of tourism. The reviews cover the development of the field - the key milestones, literature, events and writers to deliver the reader with the current state of the art and a clear legible map of the field, emerging issues and a future focussed agenda as well as an extensive reference list. In this volume I have included both thematic reviews (economics, history, transport, event management, the tourism area life cycle and forecasting) as well as applied reviews (policy, services management, city branding and accounting). I am grateful to the authors of these reviews – all acknowledged leaders in the field - and to Sally North and Tim Goodfellow for their support for this volume.

Chris Cooper, Oxford, November 2014

References

Botterill, D. (2001) The epistemology of a set of tourism studies, *Leisure Studies*, **20**, 199–214

Coles, T., Hall, C.M. and Duval, D. T. (2006) Tourism and post-disciplinary enquiry, *Current Issues in Tourism* **9**, (4&5), 235-319

Cooper, C. P. (1989) *Progress in Tourism Recreation and Hospitality Management* I, Belhaven, London

Cooper, C. (2006). Knowledge management and tourism, *Annals of Tourism Research* **33** (1) 47–64.

Cooper, C. and Ruhanen, L. (2002) *Best Practice in Intellectual Property Commercialization*, CRCST: Brisbane

Dolnicar, S and Ring, R. (2014) Tourism marketing research: Past, present and future, *Annals of Tourism Research*, July, 31–47

Dredge D. and Schott, C. (2013) Academic agency and leadership in tourism higher education, *Journal of Teaching in Travel & Tourism*, **13** (2), 105-129

Eagles, P. F. J. (2014) Research priorities in park tourism, *Journal of Sustainable Tourism*, **4**, 528-549

Echtner, C. and T. Jamal (1997) The disciplinary dilemma of tourism studies, *Annals of Tourism Research*, **24**, 868–883

Hall, C. M. (2011) Publish and perish? Bibliometric analysis, journal ranking and the assessment of research quality in tourism, *Tourism Management*, **32**, 16-27

Harland, C.M., Lamming, R.C., Walker, H., Phillips, W.E., Caldwell, N. D., Johnsen, T.E., Knight, L.A., and J. Zheng, (2006) Supply management: is it a discipline? *International Journal of Operations & Production Management*, **26** (7), 730-753

Hudson, S. (2013) Knowledge exchange: A destination perspective, *Journal of Destination Marketing and Management*, **2**, 129-131

Jafari, J. (1990) Research and scholarship: the basis of tourism education, *Journal of Tourism Studies*, **1** (1) 33- 41

Leunga, D., Lib, G., Hoc Nang Fonga, L., Lawa, R., and Loa, A. (2014), Current state of China tourism research, *Current Issues in Tourism*, **17** (8) 679-704

Lynch, P. Molz, J.P. Mcintosh, A. Lugosi, P. and Lashley, C (2011) Theorizing hospitality, *Hospitality & Society*, **1** (1), 3-24

Pyo, S. (2012) Identifying and prioritizing destination knowledge needs, *Annals of Tourism Research*, 39 (2), 1156-1175

Shaw, G., Bailey, A., and Williams, A. (2011) Aspects of service-dominant logic and its implications for tourism management: Examples from the hotel industry, *Tourism Management*, **32**, 207-214

Standing, C., Tang-Taye, J-P., and Boyer, M. (2014) The impact of the internet in travel and tourism: A research review 2001-2010, *Journal of Travel & Tourism Marketing*, **31** (1), 82-113

Thomas, R. (2012) Business elites, universities and knowledge transfer in tourism, *Tourism Management*, **33**, 553-561

Tribe, J.(1997) The indiscipline of tourism, *Annals of Tourism Research*, **24**, 638–657

Tribe, J. (2006) The truth about tourism, *Annals of Tourism Research*, **33**(2) 360–381

Tribe, J. (2008) Tourism: A critical business, *Journal of Travel Research*, **46**, 245-255

Xin, S., Tribe, J., and Chambers, D. (2012) Conceptual research in tourism, *Annals of Tourism Research*, **41**, 66–88

Economics of Tourism

Larry Dwyer, Peter Forsyth, Andreas Papatheodorou

Contents

Dr. Larry Dwyer is Professor of Travel and Tourism Economics in the School of Marketing, Australian School of Business at the University of New South Wales, Australia. Larry is a founding member and President of the International Association for Tourism Economics. In 2007, Larry was appointed as a Fellow of the International Academy for Study of Tourism, the world's peak academic tourism association.

Dr. Peter Forsyth is Professor of Economics in the Department of Economics at Monash University, Australia. Most of his research has been on transport economics and especially the economics of air transport, and tourism economics. Peter maintains close links with the German Aviation Research Society.He has been a frequent speaker at the Hamburg Aviation Conference, and in 2005 he delivered the Martin Kunz Memorial Lecture.

Dr Andreas Papatheodorou is an Assistant Professor in Industrial Economics with Emphasis on Tourism at the University of the Aegean, Greece. He is a Fellow of the UK Tourism Society and a member of the Executive Board of the International Association for Tourism Economics. In 2009 he was recognized as an Emerging Scholar of Distinction by the International Academy for the Study of Tourism.

A hyperlinked PDF version of this review is available for download from the CTR area of Goodfellow Pubishers' website: http://www.goodfellowpublishers.com/ctr

Introduction

Tourism has been a major growth industry globally for over five decades. Factors underpinning this growth include the growth of incomes and wealth, improvements in transport, changing lifestyles and consumer values, increased leisure time, international openness and globalization, immigration, special events, education, information and communication technologies, destination marketing and promotion, improved general and tourism infrastructure and so on (Matias et al 2007). Since there are economic consequences to all of these factors it is not surprising that research in the area of tourism economics has increased substantially during the same period. At the same time, the study of tourism economics has attracted relatively few research economists compared to other topics, such as energy and transport economists, within the mainstream discipline.

Although indirectly related to tourism economics, we may argue that the serious study of the field began in the mid 1960s with the seminal book produced by Clawson and Knetsch (1966) on the *Economics of Outdoor Recreation*. Rather prophetically, the book dealt in detail with environmental issues, which are now considered of crucial importance in tourism economics. Four years later, Gray (1970) published a very enlightening book on the interrelation between international travel and trade. From then onwards, tourism gradually gained momentum among economists; interestingly, however, it was not until 1995 that *Tourism Economics*, i.e. the first academic journal dedicated to the study of tourism economics, emerged. As a complementary development it is also worth noting the establishment of the International Association for Tourism Economics in 2007.

Four major observations can be made about the state of research in tourism economics.

First, there are ongoing areas of research very much within the single disciplinary mainstream economic methodological framework. Obvious topics include demand modelling, forecasting, economic impact and industry analysis (Stabler et al., 2010). Second, several areas of research in economics have emerged that were either non-existent two decades ago or were in their infancy. These include Game Theory, Chaos Theory and climate change economics. These have been applied to tourism. Third, there are several research areas relevant to the wider context of tourism studies, that tourism economists have virtually ignored, or have relatively neglected. These relate to themes and issues and methodologies of analysis that have been recognized in other fields of the subject. These include ecological economics, poverty alleviation, and sustainable development.

Fourth, tourism economics has become increasingly quantitative over time, paralleling developments in the economics literature. Critics have argued that the emphasis on 'positivist/post positivist' epistemologies renders the economics of tourism less relevant than it might otherwise be in addressing real world issues and problems. As Jennings (2007) has argued, quantitative based research has become the 'orthodoxy' for tourism economists and has prevented them from addressing tourism problems in a more holistic, interdisciplinary way appropriate to the complexity of tourism phenomena. Jennings's view is that new and different methodologies and methods must be employed by tourism economists for theory development, to better serve the industry, and for policy formulation. Jennings' review reflects the debate in the wider tourism literature concerning the continued unwarranted adherence to positivist, quantitative oriented orthodoxy in the face of tourism's complexity, rapidly changing characteristics and instability, quite different from its nature in the 1960s.). For some years now geographers (and new economic geographers) have taken up a political economy stance. Williams (2004), advocates a political economy perspective wherein theoretical developments in the approach have relevance to issues in tourism as illustrated by issues such as commodification in the sector's markets, its labour structures and processes and its regulation.

A discussion of the issues that have been addressed in tourism economics for the past 50 or so years reveals that the range of issues addressed is perhaps much wider than the criticisms might imply. We highlight several topics for discussion below.

Developments and Current Issues in Tourism Economics

Tourism Demand and Forecasting

Demand modelling, one of the most developed and rigorous areas of the economic analysis of tourism, is a long-established area of economic research and continues to be so. Research over the past four decades suggests that the range of factors affecting the demand for tourism is very large. The more prominent factors that have been included in destination demand modeling are income, (exchange rate adjusted) relative prices, transport costs, marketing and promotion activity, migration levels and qualitative factors time available for travel, trade and ethnic ties between the countries; destination attractiveness (for example, culture, climate, history, natural resources, tourism infrastructure; special events taking place at the destination; natural disasters; and social threats such as political instability, health issues or terrorism) (Crouch 1994a, Lim 2006, Saymaan et al 2008). Of these factors, the bulk of studies indicate that income, and to a lesser extent price, are the most important (Crouch 1992). Still, the focus on income as an influence on tourism flows has been associated with a relative neglect of wealth as a determining factor (Alperovich and Machnes 1994). Thus, while the Global Financial Crisis (GFC) certainly reduced incomes on average for millions of people, perhaps the greatest effect was on their level of wealth due to the decline in value of their assets including superannuation payouts. While there has always been some recognition that wealth is important for some tourism markets eg. Seniors' tourism, the issue needs more research (Sheldon and Dwyer 2010).

An additional variable that affects tourists' decisions is the marketing expenditure of the tourism product/service provider (at both destination level and firm level). Recent research has sought to estimate marketing elasticities and the return to destinations from their marketing investment (Dwyer, Pham, Forsyth, and Spurr, 2014). Marketing expenditures are important in that they are one of the few direct ways in which a destination can influence the demand for its products. Recent demand studies have also affirmed the importance of migration stocks and flows as affecting inbound and outbound travel numbers, expenditure and economic impacts on destinations (Seetaram, 2012).

There has also been some questioning of the best proxy for price in demand equations. For a large number of cross country studies, researchers have used the real exchange rate. Depending on the context this may not be a good proxy. As a result, researchers are using competiveness indices (Dwyer and Forsyth, 2011; Dwyer, Seetaram, Forsyth and King 2014).

Demand analysis has recently taken new directions, with greater attention being increasingly paid to the characteristics framework of demand (Lancaster 1966). This is also associated with the development of the hedonic pricing method (Rosen 1974, Sinclair et al 1990, Clewer et al 1992, Papatheodorou 2001, 2002, Papatheodorou et al., 2012) and discrete choice analysis (Louvier, 2000). More recent studies evaluating a variety of tourism markets are using panel data techniques (Naudé and Saayman 2005, Van Der Merwe et al 2007, Saayman and Saayman 2008). When cross-sectional and time series data are combined, as in panel data analysis, greater insights are gained from the data. Panel studies offer all the advantages of a larger number of observations; that is, more informative data, less multicollinearity, more degrees of freedom and more efficient estimates. In tourism demand studies, panel data techniques allow the inclusion of the variables that are mostly static for one region (such as distance), but which differ between regions, which is not possible with time series data only. Panel data is expected to play an increasingly important role in tourism demand analysis.

Over time, the modeling of tourism demand has become more sophisticated and more complex and different contexts of study, different data sets, use of different variables and different modeling techniques preclude generalizations (Crouch 1994a, 1995; Lim 1999, 2006). Given the importance of a better understanding of demand for destination management, marketing and policy purposes tourism demand modeling may be expected to continue to be refined with more input from the econometrics literature (Song and Witt 2000, Li et al 2005, Song and Li 2008).

Forecasting is especially important in tourism because it aids long term planning and is fundamental to the conduct of modern business and destination management. It is particularly challenging because: the tourism product is perishable; tourism behaviour is complex; people are inseparable from the production-consumption process; customer satisfaction depends on complementary products and services; and tourism demand is extremely sensitive to natural and human-made disasters (Archer 1980, 1994). In a changing global tourism environment it is important, for both government policy development and business planning, to have reliable short-term and long term forecasts of tourism activity (Frechtling 2001).

1 There are two broad approaches to tourism forecasting: qualitative tourism forecasting and quantitative tourism forecasting (Sheldon and Var 1985). The same as for the area of demand modeling the forecasting literature is increasingly incorporating 'state of the art' statistical techniques that are new to tourism research (Song and Turner 2006). Song and Witt (2000) were the first researchers to systematically introduce a number of modern econometric methods to tourism demand analysis. More recently, modern econometric methods, such as the autoregressive distributed lag model (ADLM), the error correction model (ECM), the vector autoregressive (VAR) model, the almost ideal systems approach (AIDS and the time varying parameter (TVP) models, have emerged as the main forecasting methods in the current tourism demand forecasting literature.. The technical illustration of these methods is in Song and Witt (2000) and Li, Song and Witt, 2006; Song and Li 2008). There is no single quantitative technique that gives best forecasting results in all contexts (Song and Li 2008).

2 Qualitative tourism forecasts are based on the judgments of persons sharing their experience, practical knowledge and intuition. These judgments are found through polling, expert opinion, panel consensus, surveys, Delphi technique and scenario writing and are often used to moderate or "second guess" quantitative forecasts (Frechtling 2001). Qualitative forecasting is best applied when facing insufficient historical

data; unreliable time series; rapidly changing macro environments; major disturbances; and when long term forecasts are desired.

The choice of forecasting method depends on several considerations including: the level of accuracy required; the ease of use of the forecasting technique; the cost of producing the forecasts compared with the potential gains from their use; the speed with which the forecasts can be produced; the time frame of the forecast; the quality and availability of data on which the forecast is to be made; and the complexity of the relationships to be forecast. Recently, attempts have been made to enhance tourism forecasting accuracy through forecast combination and forecast integration of quantitative and qualitative approaches (Faulkner and Valerio 1995; Blake et al. 2004). Forecasts need to be justifiable with the forecasting process transparent and open to all to question and challenge. Combined forecasts tend to have greater explanatory power than single approach forecasts and tend to be more accurate and future research in this area should reflect an understanding of this (Song and Li 2008).

At bottom, we simply do not know enough about consumer travel behaviour to give definite forecasts in many circumstances. No single model consistently outperforms others in all contexts (Song & Li, 2008). Recent literature thus suggests combining the forecasts from different models with a view to improving forecasting accuracy (Shen, Li, & Song, 2011).Since tourism is subject to volatility, exogenous events of considerable magnitude and sudden changes in consumer behaviour, we can expect a continuing emphasis on consumer behaviour as a topic in tourism research generally and tourism economics in particular (Sheldon and Dwyer 2010).

Supply and Pricing

The price that a tourism firm sets for its supplied products depends on the interplay of a number of factors that are internal and external to the firm. These include the firm's objectives and ownership pattern, the market structure in which it operates, the degree of competition within the market and the firm's position within the market, seasonality, government policy, the macroeconomic environment, the price of other goods, capacity constraints, the degree of perishability of its products and so on (Fyall and Garrod 2005). In the wider economics literature, competitive profit maximizing firms are acknowledged to apply a variety of pricing strategies including uniform pricing, price discrimination, bundling, tying, peak load pricing, and two part tariffs as well as non-marginal pricing strategies involving penetration pricing, markup pricing, non-profit goals, as necessary. Marginal pricing approaches of the type most used in economic analysis work best when the firm is well informed and able to make effective use of the information available to it. Moreover, in the tourism industry generally, some firms may be less focused on maximizing profits than in achieving other objectives. Tourism firms can potentially adopt different pricing strategies according to their objectives (which may emphasize market share or lifestyle objectives). The pricing strategies adopted will have different implications for firm output, sales and profits. There is a real issue of whether firms can be characterised as profit maximisers. The issue is important since small businesses of the type that comprise the global tourism industry historically have operated with low profitability - many may seek lifestyle as well as profit objectives.

While firms can compete through the use of pricing strategies they can also improve the quality of the characteristics of goods and services. Such quality improvements often enable the products to be sold for higher prices, effectively by making the demand curve more inelastic. Determining the importance of quality in firms pricing strategies is important (Mangion et al 2005). The hedonic pricing method has been used by tourism researchers to show how various supply- related factors explain the variation in overall accommodation and package tour prices, presenting tourism managers with an opportunity to enhance their strategic pricing through quality improvements and innovation (Sinclair et al 1990, Papatheodorou, 2002; Monty and Skidmore 2003).

In general, the economic analysis of the structure of tourism supply is founded in industrial economics. Issues concerning tourism supply cover economic efficiency (mainly relating to productivity), employment, industrial structure, entrepreneurship and management and information communication technologies (ICT). The traditional approach of market competitive structures and pricing has not figured strongly in tourism research until recently, particularly the concepts of oligopoly, duopoly and contestable markets that characterize certain tourism sectors (Papatheodorou, 2004; Stabler et al 2010). There has been research recently on tourism sectors within the Structure-Conduct-Performance (SCP) paradigm, in particular the travel trade. The structure prevailing in any tourism market depends on numerous interlocking characteristics, amongst them: the number of sellers; the existence and extent of product differentiation; the cost structure; the presence of barriers to entry; and the extent of vertical and horizontal integration. The SCP paradigm is useful for gaining an overall picture of tourism markets, highlighting key features and capturing essential relationships (Davies and Downward 1998, 2006). Within this framework, the market structure within which a tourism firm operates is held to affect the firm's conduct (decision-making processes), which, in turn, is held to affect the firm's performance (potential to make profit, increase its market share and achieve efficiency). This linearity may also work in reverse. Public policy (government involvement and influence in the marketplace) affects basic demand and supply conditions in the market, influencing market structure, rewarding or disparaging conduct and, ultimately, conditioning performance. Important ways through which government may differentially affect tourism markets include taxes and subsidies, regulation, price controls, competition laws, and information provision to tourism stakeholders (Lei 2006).

A good example of the above is provided by air transport. Over time, governments have chosen to implement less restrictive regulation of air transport, and this has led to more competition, lower fares (especially as a result of the development of low cost carriers such as Southwest and Ryanair), and more travel (Papatheodorou, 2008). This provides a policy dilemma for governments in their regulation and/or support of both industries (i.e. transport and tourism). For example does a country wish to encourage tourism, and maximize economic benefits of tourism, by keeping taxes, on both aviation and ground tourism, low? Or does it wish to make use of its market power, and use foreign tourists as a source of revenue (as well as protecting its own airlines)? Whichever of these options it chooses, it will need to determine at which level –aviation or ground tourism- such taxes are best levied. This issue has been coming to a head in the growing debate on whether or not a country gains from air (and other mode) passenger duties, as implemented by the UK, Germany and Australia (see Forsyth et al, 2014). Furthermore, if there is already general taxation of tourism and aviation services, it will need to determine how best to counteract these if it wishes to keep taxes low. Aviation and tourism taxation need to be considered jointly- though they often are not (Forsyth, 2006).

Research on the supply of tourism products has benefitted from attention to the supply side of tourism products and industries, which is documented in the Recommended Methodological Framework (TSA-RMF) (UNWTO 2008). The recommended framework for tourism statistics identifies tourism's component products and industries through the concepts of Tourism Characteristic and Tourism Connected products and industries. Many countries are documenting their tourism industries through the use of tourism satellite accounts (TSAs). Progress made in the development of the recommended framework of statistics has now opened up a suite of research opportunities for tourism economists (Frechtling 1999). These include measuring tourism's interrelationship with other industries as well as comparison of tourism activity with other major industries in terms of size, economic performance, employment, and contribution to the national and regional economy, and comparisons between regions, countries or groups of countries. Researchers now have a better opportunity to help tourism stakeholders to better understand the economic importance of tourism activity; and by extension its role in all the industries producing the various goods and services demanded by tourists. In this way tourism economics can better serve as a tool for enhanced strategic management and planning for the tourism industry to achieve enhanced destination competitiveness in the context of broader policy agenda.

Among others, the framework should consider the effect of the continuing development of Information Technology (IT) on the structure of supply, particularly the intermediaries, determining their competitiveness, efficiency, innovation and productivity. IT is essentially about such matters as competitiveness, efficiency, innovation diffusion, marketing and productivity, each of which is capable of being informed by economics. The oligopolistic nature of various tourism sectors shows that firms seek to control their supply chains through vertical and horizontal integration and through the formation of strategic alliances (Howarth and Kirsebom 1999, Morley 2003). By introducing game theory to the study of the firm and the market, 'new industrial economics' has provided a powerful tools for analysing behaviour and strategies of tourism suppliers in different tourism sectors, and destinations particularly in the context of a supply chain (Song, 2011).

The tourism industry has experienced many financial crises over the years, yet there remain large knowledge gaps about the behaviour and strategies of firms under financial stress especially in the aftermath of the great recession in the late 2000s (Papatheodorou et al., 2010). The implications for new product development, investment, marketing, and staffing are not well understood. Likewise, the strategic options to help firms remain viable during economic downturns are not well researched. Additionally, little is known about the impacts of financial and economic crises on event sponsorship, business meetings and corporate travel. Historical accounts and case studies of tourism stakeholder responses to previous economic recessions may also provide valuable lessons for the future (Smeral 2010).

Measuring Tourism's Economic Contribution, Impacts and Net Benefits

It is widely acknowledged that both domestic and international tourism make an 'economic contribution' to a destination, that tourism has positive and negative 'economic impacts' and that it brings 'benefits and costs' to a destination. While often used in the literature, these terms are generally not well understood by researchers.

The economic contribution of tourism refers to tourism's economic significance - to the contribution that tourism related spending makes to key economic variables such as Gross Domestic (Regional) Product, household income, value added, foreign exchange earnings, employment, and so on. Given the development of Tourism Satellite Accounts (TSAs) worldwide it can be expected that more research will be undertaken on tourism's economic contribution to a destination. TSA allow the tourism industry to be better included in the mainstream of economic analysis. Tourism's total economic contribution (both direct and indirect) measures the size and overall significance of the tourism industry within an economy. The research literature may now be expected to contain more studies that compare and analyse the contributions that tourism and its component industries make to key variables such as GDP, value added and employment. TSAs provide policy makers with insights into tourism and its contribution to the economy providing an instrument for designing more efficient policies relating to tourism and its employment aspects. As a result of basing more of their research in analysing data from TSA, the outputs of tourism economists should become even more relevant to the information needs of destination managers (Frechtling 1999, Jones, Spurr 2006, Jones and Munday 2007).

TSAs can also be used to develop performance indicators such as measures of productivity, prices and profitability for the tourism industry as a whole as well as performance in individual sectors (Dwyer, Forsyth and Spurr 1997), measures of tourism yield, and also estimates of tourism's carbon footprint (Dwyer et al 2010). Tourism researchers now have the data to explore the performance of individual tourism sectors or of the entire tourism industry relative to that of other industries, domestically and internationally. TSAs are not in themselves modeling tools for economic impact assessment. Tourism economists have a role to play in keeping other researchers and destination managers aware of the distinction between 'economic contribution' and 'economic impact'. *Economic contribution* measures the size and overall significance of the industry within an economy, while e*conomic impact* refers to the *changes* in the economic contribution resulting from specific events or activities that comprise 'shocks' to the tourism system.

Over the past four decades a substantial number of economic impact studies have been published based on multipliers estimated from input-output models. These have generally focussed on the effects of tourism demand shocks to nations (Archer 1977, Archer and Fletcher 1996), subregions (Archer 1973), and special events (Burns et al 1986, Crompton et al 2001). However, researchers, destination managers and tourism policy makers often ignore the limitations of multipliers based on Input Output (I-O) modelling, despite their limited policy relevance for tourism (Briassoulis1991). Economy wide effects must be taken into account in determining the impacts of increased tourism expenditure on a destination. An expanding tourism industry tends to 'crowd out' other sectors of economic activity. The extent of these 'crowding out' effects depends, in turn, on factor constraints, changes in the exchange rate, the workings of labour markets and the macroeconomic policy context (Copeland 1991). The study of the economic impacts of tourism shocks has recently undergone a 'paradigm shift' as a result of the use of CGE models in place of I-O models. CGE models can be tailored to allow for alternative conditions such as flexible or fixed prices, alternative exchange rate regimes, differences in the degree of mobility of factors of production and different types of competition. Thus, a number of useful papers have been published using CGE modelling to estimate the economic impacts of shocks associated with inbound tourism (Adams and Parmenter 1995, 1999; Dwyer et al. 2003); the economic impacts of tourism crises (Blake et al. 2003a; Pambudi et al. 2009); the economic impacts of special events (Dwyer, Forsyth and Spurr 2005; Blake 2005); destination marketing (Dwyer, et al. 2014); carbon taxes (Dwyer, Forsyth, Spurr, and Hoque, 2013); evaluation of economic policy (Blake and Sinclair 2003); and tourism effects on income distribution and poverty reduction (Blake, Arbache, Sinclair and Teles 2008;Wattanakuljarus and Coxhead 2008). Recently, interesting studies have used general equilibrium analysis to explore the effects of tourism growth on other sectors (Nowak and M. Sahli 2007) as well as the effect of a booming sector on tourism growth (Forsyth, Dwyer and Spurr 2014).

While CGE models are particularly helpful to tourism policy makers who seek to use them to provide guidance about a wide variety of 'what if?' questions, arising from a wide range of domestic or international expenditure shocks or alternative policy scenarios, there are several situations where economic impact analyses do not provide the right information for policy formulation. The measured impacts on economic activity of most tourism shocks, such as increases in tourism expenditure, may normally be expected to be much greater than the net benefits which they generate for the community (or in other words, the measure of the extent to which they make the community better off). Recognizing this, some CGE models (Blake 2005, Blake et al. 2008, Dwyer et al, 2006) are explicitly designed to include a measure of resident welfare. Consistent with economic theory, Blake et al (2008) measure a change in welfare by equivalent variation (EV), which indicates how much the change in welfare is worth to the economy at the pre-simulation set of prices. This measure takes the results from what may be quite complex effects of a simulation on a household and produces a single value to describe how much better (or worse) off the economy is as a result of such effects. Tourism economists now have an added opportunity to inform tourism stakeholders on the net benefits associated with tourism development. Surprisingly, perhaps, despite the progress in concepts and applications of cost benefit analysis in the economics literature, this area is relatively neglected in tourism economics.

Investment and Innovation

Strong, continuing tourism investment is vital to a strong, successful tourism industry. Apart from the increase in capacity and profits that accrue to individual firms and the tourism sector in general from successful investment, the perceived national and regional benefits that come from a more favourable tourism investment climate include economic growth; job creation; utilisation of domestic resources, particularly renewable resources; skills acquisition; expansion of exports; development of remote areas of the country; and facilitation of increased ownership of investment by the nation's citizens. Unfortunately these outcomes of investment are often taken for granted by researchers and insufficiently examined in particular cases.

The importance of tourism investment became particularly evident during the recent Global Financial Crisis. Declining asset values impacted on the ability of firms to fund debt or invest and many capital projects (including fleet expansion, hotel projects, attractions etc) were shelved due to financing difficulties. Credit availability and de-risking of bank balance sheets stifles the volume of tourism investment needed to support tourism growth over time with its attendant economic effects. The source of capital financing is an important issue in tourism investment decision-making, since it can substantially affect a tourism project's overall costs. We need greater understanding of the sources of finance available to support tourism investment including the extent of distortions that exist in different economies to restrict its volume. Various theories of the basis of firms financing decisions have been proposed in the wider finance literature. These include the Pecking Order and Trade-off theories as well as right- financing and the Market Timing Hypothesis (Frank and Goyal 2008). There are opportunities for tourism economists to explore the implications of these different perspectives to increase our understanding of the conditions that support successful tourism investment.

Tourism industries worldwide (eg, airlines, rail services, public transport) display the problems associated with regulated infrastructure such as inadequate investment, excessive investment, poor service quality, over servicing, high cost operation, and ineffective use of available capacity. These problems also appear with tourism infrastructure. The positive side is that in many destinations the problems are being diagnosed, and regulation is being better designed to take account of the problems that have developed... The extent of environmental constraints on the development of tourism infrastructure is an area in need of the attention of researchers. Consideration of the trade-offs that must be made between economic and environmental attributes is a crucial task to achieve sustainable development of the tourism industry.

Infrastructure industries are often complex ones which pose a number of public policy problems which need to be addressed- for example, they are often monopolies, and governments will wish to limit the use of their market power. Infrastructure projects, which often involve large, capital intensive investments, often have large environmental impacts, (for example airports) which mean that obtaining approval for them is a drawn out process. There are various economic problems associated with ensuring the supply of tourism infrastructure, These include investigation of the changes that have been taking place in the institutional structure of infrastructure- the move from public to private provision; the congestion problem which impedes the efficiency of infrastructure provision; problems in government regulation of tourism infrastructure; the effects of environmental constraints on infrastructure; how provision of good infrastructure can stimulate tourism; and the particular problems that developing countries face in ensuring that their infrastructure helps their tourism development. Moves to privatization appear to have resulted in improved performance of infrastructure generally, including tourism oriented infrastructure. The establishment of public private partnerships, and an increasing emphasis on 'user pays are two initiatives that hold out the promise of further improvements over time.

Provision of tourism infrastructure and its maintenance is a particular problem for developing countries given lack of local investment, limitations on local legal systems and pressure from donor countries. While researchers have addressed these issues, very often the type of economic modelling that has been employed will not give accurate results on the extent to which investment in tourism infrastructure will benefit a destination nor does it lead to a better understanding of who gains and who loses within the destination. As some researchers have shown (eg. Blake 2008, Wattanakuljarus and Coxhead 2008), it cannot be assumed that investment in infrastructure to develop the tourism industry will reduce poverty within a destination. The GFC has reminded us that public sector investment in 'tourism and community infrastructure' may have both counter-cyclical and longer-term merits in the current and prospective environment, provided its social return justifies the use of taxpayer funds involved. However, little effort seems to have been devoted to investigate the 'returns' to destinations from provision of infrastructure that is used by tourists, especially when tourist use is subsidized by resident ratepayers and taxpayers. Infrastructure provision also increases the efficiency of privately producing and distributing tourism services, facilitating the supply of tourism services at competitive prices.

Productivity measurement is an emerging research area in tourism and this has given rise to increased research on investment, innovation, labour skills, enterprise and competition. While there is a large research literature concerned with developing productivity measures in hospitality (Barros and Alves 2004, Barros 2005, Assaf 2008) and in aviation (Barbot et al 2008) the relative productivity performance of different countries' tourism industries is a relatively neglected research area. A fundamental problem in deriving tourism production functions is the difficulty of establishing what constitutes the sector's inputs and outputs.

Taxation

Tourism economists have argued that there are sound economic reasons for taxing tourism beyond simply collecting revenues to provide public services to tourists and their suppliers. A well designed system of tourist taxation can benefit the residents of destinations in several ways (Mak 2006).At the heart of it, there is the exportability of tourism taxes. Much or all of the tax burden can be paid by tourists who are not resident in the country in which the taxes are levied (Mak 2006). On the other hand, tourism taxes can impose costs on a destination. They can result in a contraction of economic activity with adverse effects on Gross Domestic Product, employment and foreign exchange earnings. The reduced price competitiveness of a tourism destination following the imposition of general or specific taxes may be such as to reduce the economic contribution of tourism to the wider economy. Additionally, taxes result in deadweight losses to destinations that impose them, reducing the welfare of resident consumers and producers. Taxes can also lead to retaliation by other destinations resulting in a lose-lose situation for the residents of each country. Furthermore, 'tourism tax exporting' may result in inefficiently high tourism taxes that may well be rational from the viewpoint of the individual country or jurisdiction, but too high from a more general, worldwide welfare perspective (Forsyth and Dwyer 2002).

Given the increasing importance of tourism taxation in both developed and developing countries, greater understanding of the economic underpinnings of tourism taxation and its effects is necessary, so that appropriate policies for tourism taxation can be formulated.

The great bulk of research has involved partial equilibrium analysis of specific sectors of the economy (Spengler and Uysal 1989, Fujii, Khaled and Mak (1985), Sakai (1985), Mak (1988, 1996, 2008) and Hiemstra and Ismael (1992, 1993). A tax that directly affects tourism flows will have impacts across the entire economy as the reduced demand impedes employment growth in tourism and related industries. To understand the full implications of any tourism shock it is necessary to move beyond partial equilibrium analysis to consider the general equilibrium (economy wide) effects (Gooroochurn and Sinclair 2005). It is necessary to use CGE models of the economy, with all direct and indirect linkages between sectors, to explore this issue and tourism economists can be expected to undertake more research along these lines (Dwyer, Forsyth, Spurr and Hoque, 2013; Forsyth, Dwyer, Pham and Spurr, 2014).

The net benefit from tourism development depends critically on how a destination designs its public finance/revenue system to tax travel and tourism.Given the increasing importance of tourism taxation in both developed and developing countries, greater understanding of the economic underpinnings of tourism taxation and its effects is necessary, so that modelling of tourism taxation can be undertaken and appropriate policies for tourism taxation can be formulated.

Environment and Sustainability

The importance of environment to sustainable tourism development is widely acknowledged. At the same time, much of the discussion of the interaction between the two has been uninformed by economic analysis. It is the "public good" aspect of many environmental resources that leads to their under-provision (Tisdell 2006). Given the progress made in the environmental economics literature tourism economists have the opportunity to make greater contributions to our understanding of how to preserve valued natural environments in the context of tourism development.

Tourism economists have emphasised that the total economic value of a tourism environmental amenity is composed of its use value (actual use value) and non-use value. Components of non use value are option, quasi-option, existence, bequest, and vicarious value. Within this framework of thinking, the environmental impacts of tourism activity may be measured either directly (through their obvious price effects in the marketplace) or indirectly (through the construction of proxy prices) (Tisdell 2006).

The various measurement techniques available for valuing environments in tourism contexts and which can be used to inform policy making have been much discussed. The techniques available to measure the non use of an environmental amenity include: stated preferences (for example, contingency valuation (Lockwood & Tracy 1995; Lockwood et al 1996); and contingent choice (Louvier et al 2000, Hanley et al 2001); revealed preferences (for example, hedonic pricing (Espey and Lopez 2000, Monty and Skidmore 2003) and travel cost (Carr and Mendelson 2003,Chen et al 2004); and imputed valuation (for example, replacement cost, damage cost avoided and production factor method).

There has been a gradual trend towards the use of market-based instruments for environmental policy. Tourism economists have the opportunity to meet the challenge of addressing the issues that attend the use of economic instruments in their protection of the environment from any adverse effects of tourism, including: uncertainty; boundary problems; transaction costs; and public good considerations (Dwyer et al 1995, Tisdell 2001).

A topic which is expected to increasingly engage the attention of tourism economists is that of mitigation of, and adaptation to, climate change. The climate is a public good. Human-induced climate change is an externality on a global scale which, in the absence of policy intervention, is not 'corrected' through any institution or market. Climate change is argued to be the greatest market failure the world has seen (Stern 2006). Markets for relevant goods and services (energy, land use, innovation, and so on) do not reflect the full costs and benefits of different consumption and investment choices for the climate (Tol 2008).The same as for other industries, the tourism industry contributes to climate change through its generation of greenhouse gas emissions to meet tourist needs. Tourism generates a carbon footprint both directly (through emissions associated with production of a tourism service) and indirectly (through emissions associated with the supply of inputs into tourism production). Climate change, in turn will directly impact on a country's tourism industry and the benefits it creates through loss or degradation of attractions, the costs of adaptation and replacement of capital infrastructure. Climate also has a major influence on destination choice. Tourism is a footloose export industry, and both suppliers and consumers will cross borders to the extent that a destination becomes less attractive due to climate change (Berrittellaa 2006, Bosello et al 2007). Tourism will be affected by the different types of climate change mitigation policies, all of which will increase the cost base of tourism firms. Since climate change generates both negative and positive impacts in the tourism sector and these impacts will vary substantially by market segment and geographic region, there are 'winners and losers' at the business, destination and nation level. There is thus substantial scope for tourism economists to investigate these issues, including the effects on the tourism industry of different policy measures to mitigate climate change and achieve development on a sustainable basis.

Destination Competitiveness

Destination competitiveness is linked to the ability of a country or region to deliver goods and services that perform better than other destinations on those aspects of the tourism experience considered to be important by tourists. Recognizing this, researchers have developed indices of both general and price competitiveness. If the limitations of the various competitiveness indices are recognized, they can be valuable tools for policy formulation for any tourism destination to achieve and maintain competitive advantage over competitors, as well as empirical studies of tourism demand. The outcomes will be more informed policy making regarding the type of tourism development most likely to enhance resident quality of economic and social life. Tourism economists can contribute to our understanding of how these goals can be achieved, most effectively and efficiently. It has proved difficult, however, to develop an integrated model of destination competitiveness comprising both quantitative and qualitative variables (Crouch and Ritchie 1999, Dwyer and Kim 2003).

With some exceptions (Dwyer et al 2000) tourism researchers generally appear to have placed greater effort on developing models of overall destination competitiveness rather than on price competitiveness. Factors that impinge on price competitiveness include: exchange rates; inflation; the price of labour; productivity; export booms; tax structures and levels; infrastructure charges; fuel prices; and environmental charges. There is substantial opportunity to undertake further research on the determinants of price competitiveness of different sectors of the tourism industry as well as the price competitiveness of the destination as a whole (Dwyer and Forsyth,2011). The type of price competitiveness index employed depends on the research or policy needs at a given time. In some situations, quickly calculated, simple measures are most useful, while in others, more detailed and accurate measures are required. Tourism economists can help to refine the existing price indicators or develop new ones while assessing their relevance to the different research needs in different destinations. Since 2007, the World Economic Forum (WEF) has been publishing its annual Travel and Tourism Competitiveness Index (TTCI) to compare the tourism performance of different countries (140 in 2013) .The TTCI is composed of 14 "pillars" of T&T competitiveness. The pillars are organized into three sub indexes capturing broad categories of variables that facilitate or drive Travel and Tourism competitiveness. These categories are (1) T&T regulatory framework, (2) T&T business environment and infrastructure, and (3) T&T human, cultural, and natural resources (World Economic Forum, 2009). Issues neglected by economists include links between destination competitiveness and national and sectoral productivity and the role that tourism destination competitiveness plays in the wider public policy domain of national competitiveness. The TTCI provides tourism economists with a rich database to explore demand and competiveness issues.

Tourism and the Way Forward

Like other areas of economics, tourism economics is a mixture of areas which are at different stages of development. Some areas are well developed, others are newer, and possibly controversial, and some are newly emerging.

Some areas which are relatively established are: demand analysis and forecasting; pricing and firm strategies; and destination competitiveness. In these areas, research will take the form of applying new techniques (such as panel studies in demand or more rigorous measurement of indices with destination competitiveness).

Some of the newer and possibly more challenging areas include: the use of CGE models to develop policy; exploring the boundaries of tourism taxation; and the use of CGE models in tourism policy work is becoming established, though controversies remain. On the other hand, the taxation of tourism is an old issue, but there are still questions about how it should be used. In particular, the use of CGE models can be used to measure what the costs in terms of foregone economic activity might be.

Finally, there are some areas which have not yet been given much attention, though they could become big issues of the future – these include: climate change and how it is addressed and mitigated; risk and investment, and trade and location.

There is already a lot of interest in climate change issues, and this is likely to be an area which blossoms. The GFC has highlighted the risks that tourism firms operate under, and thus the importance of research in risk mitigation. Finally, tourism is very much an industry which has strong spatial dimension. In spite of this, explosion of interest in geography and trade has made little impact on tourism economics so far.

Tourism economists, like their mainstream colleagues, largely continue to work within the traditional positivist paradigms of micro and macroeconomics, emphasizing the attainment of equilibrium outcomes. Mainstream economics has long been criticised for its restrictive assumptions that have narrowed the accepted orthodoxy. Critics claim that this divorces the discipline from real world issues and problems. The range of different approaches in the discipline suggests that a pluralistic attitude is required, with cross-fertilization of concepts, theories and methods, both within and from outside the subject. As pointed out by Stabler et al (2010) within the mainstream discipline there are signs of pressure to broaden its perspective coming from psychology, social psychology and sociology which can inform tourism demand modelling the newer fields of ecological and environmental economics. In particular, the ecological research field has widened the scope of economics by acknowledging the relevance of and embracing the natural sciences, sociology, cultural, ethical and political studies and welfare economics, which recognizes the normative elements of the subject. By implication, tourism economists will need to better embrace mixed (quantitative and qualitative) methodologies within interdisciplinary research agenda to advance knowledge in tourism (Jennings 1997, Stabler et al 2010). This has already happening with the boom in behavioural and experimental economics in mainstream economics, though it has yet to have a large impact on tourism economics.

In addition to some of the under-researched issues as noted above, we can identify other areas that tourism economists have relatively neglected. New Economic Growth theories, which have helped to bring spatial issues more into the agenda of mainstream economics, have been relatively neglected in tourism economics. With some exceptions Labour market theories and tourism employment are also under-researched (Baum 1996, Dwyer and Forsyth 1998). There is also a lack of attention to the contribution that growth theories can make to our understanding of tourism development (Stabler 2010). In particular, insufficient attention has been paid to issues of how international trade, both in goods and services, coupled with globalization, affects the structure, development and growth of destinations and consequently their natural, human-made and human environments. Drawing on examples concerning branding, niche and segmentation marketing, Stabler et al (2010) argue that the Ricardian and Ohlin–Hecksher theories applied in mainstream economics do not fully accord with what is required to analyse tourism. In particular, there are problems in relating them to how trade influences infrastructural investment and strategies, The theories of Linder (1961) and Porter (1998) that concern market structures, emphasizing the relevance of inter-industry trade that is a feature of tourism have not received sufficient attention from tourism economists.

The directions for further research highlighted above are just some of those that arise in the topics covered in the wider literature. Changing global trends (economic, social, demographic, political, technological and environmental) will continually pose challenges to economic theory and policy and the ways we analyze tourism activity. Whatever the specific topics that researchers will address in the coming years it is clear that tourism economics provides a fertile ground for research with the potential to inform policy making to improve socio-economic prosperity in all destinations worldwide.

References

Adams, P D and Parmenter, B R (1995), An applied general equilibrium analysis of the economic effects of tourism in a quite small, quite open economy, *Applied Economics*. **27**(10), 985-994.

Alperovich, G and Machnes, Y (1994), The role of wealth in the demand of international air travel, *Journal of Transport Economics and Policy*, **28**, 163-173.

Archer, B (1973) *The Impact of Domestic Tourism*. Bangor Occasional Papers in Economics No.2.Cardiff: University of Wales Press.

Archer, B (1977) Tourism in the Bahamas and Bermuda: Two Case Studies, Occasional Papers in Economics No. 10, Bangor: University of Wales Press.

Archer, B (1980), Forecasting demand, quantitative and intuitive techniques, *International Journal of Tourism Management*, March, pp 5-12.

Archer, B and Fletcher, J (1996), The economic impact of tourism in the Seychelles, *Annals of Tourism Research*, **23**, 1: 32-47.

Archer, B (1994), Demand forecasting and estimation, in *Travel, Tourism, and Hospitality Research: A Handbook for Managers and Researchers*. J R Brent Ritchie and Charles R Goeldner (ed.), Second Edition: 105-114. New York, John Wiley and Sons Ltd.

Assaf, A and Matawie, K (2008) Cost efficiency modeling in health care foodservice operations, *International Journal of Hospitality Management*, **27** (4), 604-613.

Barbot, C, Costa, A and Sochirca, E (2008) Airlines' performance in the new market context: A comparative productivity and efficiency analysis, *Journal of Air Transport Management* **14** (5), 270-274

Barros, C, and Alves, F (2004), Productivity in the tourism industry, *International Advances in Economic Research*, **10**, 215–225.

Barrowclough, D (2007) Foreign investment in tourism and small island developing states, *Tourism Economics*, **13** (4), 615–638.

Baum, T (1996) *Managing Human Resources in the European Tourism and Hospitality Industry. A Strategic Approach.* London: Chapman and Hall.

Berrittellaa, M, Bigano, A, Rosona, R and Tol, R S J (2006), A general equilibrium analysis of climate change impacts on tourism, *Tourism Management*, **27**, 913–924.

Blake, A (2005), *The Economic Impact of the London 2012 Olympics, Research Report 2005/5*, Christel DeHaan Tourism and Travel Research Institute, Nottingham University Business School,

Blake, A, Arbache, J S, Sinclair, M T and Teles, V (2008), Tourism and poverty relief, *Annals of Tourism Research*, **35** (1), 107-126.

Blake, A, Durbarry, R, Eugenio-Martin, J L , Gooroochurn, N, Hay, B, Lennon, J, Sugiyarto, G, Sinclair, M T and Yeoman, I (2004) *Tourism in Scotland: The Moffat Model for Forecasting and Policy in Complex Situations*, Tourism and Travel Research Institute.

Blake A, Gillham, J and Sinclair, M T (2006) CGE tourism analysis and policy modeling, in L. Dwyer and P. Forsyth (eds) *International Handbook of Tourism Economics*, London: Edward Elgar.

Blake, A T and Sinclair, M T (2003), Tourism crisis management: US response to September 11, *Annals of Tourism Research*, **30**(4), 813-32.

Blake, A T, Sinclair, M T and Sugiyarto, G (2003a), Quantifying the impact of foot and mouth disease on tourism and the UK economy, *Tourism Economics*, **9**(4), 449-465.

Blake A, Sinclair, M T and Sugiyarto, G (2003b), Tourism and globalisation: economic impact in Indonesia, *Annals of Tourism Research*, **30**(3):683-701.

Bosello, F, Roson, R and Tol, R S J (2007), Economy-wide estimates of the implications of climate change: sea level rise, *Environmental and Resource Economics*, **37**, 549-571.

Briassoulis, H (1991), Methodological issues: tourism input-output analysis, *Annals of Tourism Research*, **18**, 435-449.

Burns, J, Hatch, J and Mules, T (eds) (1986), *The Adelaide Grand Prix: the impact of a special event*, The Centre for South Australian Economic Studies, Adelaide, South Australia.

Carr, L and Mendelsohn, R (2003), Valuing coral reefs: A travel cost analysis of the Great Barrier Reef, *Ambio*, **32**(2) 353-357

Chen, W, Hong, H, Liu, Y, Zhang L, Hou, X and Raymond, M (2004) Recreation demand and economic value: an application of travel cost method for Xiamen Island, *China Economic Review*, **15**, 398-406.

Clarke, H, and Ng, Y (1993), Tourism, economic welfare and efficient pricing, *Annals of Tourism Research* **20**, 613–632.

Clawson, M and Knetsch, J L (1966) *Economics of Outdoor Recreation*, Baltimore: Johns Hopkins University Press.

Clewer, A, Pack, A and Sinclair, M T (1992). Price competitiveness and inclusive tour holidays, in *Choice and Demand in Tourism*, edited by P. Johnson and B. Thomas. London: Mansell, pp. 123-43.

Copeland B R (1991), Tourism, welfare and de-industrialization in a small open economy, *Economica*, **58**, 515-29.

Crompton, J L, Lee, S and Shuster, T (2001), A guide for undertaking economic impact studies: the Springfest Festival, *Journal of Travel Research*, **40** (1): 79–87.

Crouch, G I, (1992), Effects of income and price on international tourist demand, *Annals of Tourism*, **19**(4), 643–664.

Crouch, G I (1994a), The study of international tourism demand: a review of findings, *Journal of Travel Research*, **33**, 12-23.

Crouch, G I (1994b), The study of international tourism demand: a review of practice, *Journal of Travel Research*, **33**, 41–54.

Crouch, G I (1995), A meta-analysis of tourism demand, *Annals of Tourism Research*, **22** (1), 103-118.

Crouch, G I and Ritchie, J R (1999) Tourism, competitiveness, and societal prosperity, *Journal of Business Research* 44, 137-152.

Davies, B and Downward, P (2006), Structure conduct performance and industrial organisation in tourism, in L Dwyer and P Forsyth (eds) (2006) *International Handbook on the Economics of Tourism*, Edward Elgar, UK.

Davies, B and Downward, P (1998) Competition and contestability in the UK package tour industry: some empirical observations, *Tourism Economics*, **4**, 241–51.

de Mello, M, Pack, A and Sinclair, M T (2002), A system of equations model of UK tourism demand in neighbouring countries, *Applied Economics* **34**, 509-521 de Melo, J (1988), SAM-based models: an introduction, *Journal of Policy Modelling* **10**, 321-325.

Dixon, P and Parmenter, B (1996) Computable general equilibrium modelling for policy analysis and forecasting, in H Aman, D Kendrick and J Rust (eds), *Handbook of Computational Economics, Vol. 1*, pp. 4–85. Melbourne: Elsevier Science B.V.

Dwyer, L, Duc Pham, T, Forsyth, P, Spurr, R (2014) Destination marketing of Australia: return on investment, *Journal of Travel Research*, **53** (3) 281 – 295

Dwyer L, and Forsyth, P (1993) Assessing the benefits and costs of inbound tourism, *Annals of Tourism Research*, **20** (4), 751-768.

Dwyer, L and Forsyth, P (1993a), Government support for inbound tourism promotion: some neglected issues, *Australian Economic Papers*, **32**, 355–373. (Also in C A Tisdell, ed (2000), *The Economics of Tourism*, Vol II, International Library of Critical Writings in Economics, Edward Edgar, UK)

Dwyer, L and Forsyth, P (1994), Motivation and impacts of foreign tourism investment, *Annals of Tourism Research*, **21** (3), 512-537.

Dwyer L and Forsyth, P (1998) Estimating the employment impacts of tourism to a nation, *Tourism Recreation Research*, **23** (2), 3-12.

Dwyer, L and Forsyth, P (2008) Economic measures of tourism yield: what markets to target? *International Journal of Tourism Research* **10**, 155-168.

Dwyer L and Forsyth, P (2011) Methods of estimating destination price competitiveness: a case of horses for courses? *Current Issues in Tourism* **14** (8), 751-777

Dwyer L, Forsyth, P and Clarke, H (1995) Problems in the use of economic instruments to reduce adverse environmental impacts of tourism, *Tourism Economics* **1** (3), 265-282.

Dwyer, L, Forsyth, P, Fredline, L, Jago, L, Deery, M and Lundie, S (2007) Yield measures for Australia's special interest inbound tourism markets *Tourism Economics* **13** (3), 421–440.

Dwyer, L, Forsyth, P, Madden, J and Spurr, R (2000), Economic impacts of inbound tourism under different assumptions regarding the macroeconomy, *Current Issues in Tourism*, **3**(4), 325-363.

Dwyer, L, Forsyth, P and Spurr, R (2004) Evaluating tourism's economic effects: new and old approaches, *Tourism Management*, **25**, 307- 317.

Dwyer, L, Forsyth, P and Spurr, R (2005), Estimating the Impacts of Special Events on the Economy, *Journal of Travel Research*, 43 (May):351–59.

Dwyer, L, Forsyth, P and Spurr, R (2006) Assessing the economic impacts of events: a computable general equilibrium approach, *Journal of Travel Research* **45**, 59-66.

Dwyer, L, Forsyth, P and Spurr, R (2007) Contrasting the uses of TSAs and CGE models: measuring tourism yield and productivity *Tourism Economics* **13** (4) 537-551.

Dwyer, L, Forsyth, P and Spurr, R (2007b) Productivity and yield measurement in Australian inbound tourism using tourism satellite accounts and computable general equilibrium models in J. Tribe and D. Airey (eds) *Advances in Tourism Research*, University of Surrey, UK.

Dwyer, L, Forsyth, P, Spurr, R and Van Ho, T (2006) Economic effects of the World tourism crisis on Australia, *Tourism Economics* **12** (2) 171-186.

Dwyer, L, Forsyth, P, Spurr, R and Hoque, S (2013) Economic impacts of a carbon tax on the Australian tourism industry, *Journal of Travel Research*, **52** (2) 143-155

Dwyer, L and Kim, C W (2003), Destination competitiveness: a model and indicators, *Current Issues in Tourism*, **6** (5), 369-413.

Dwyer, L, Seetaram, N, Forsyth, P and King, B (2014) Is the migration-tourism relationship only about VFR? *Annals of Tourism Research*, **46** 130-143

Espey, M and Lopez , H(2000), The impact of airport noise and proximity on residential property values, *Growth and Change*, **31** (22) 408-419.

Faulkner, B and Valerio, P (1995), An integrative approach to tourism demand forecasting, *Tourism Management*, **16** (1) 29-37.

Faulkner, B and Russell, R (1997) Chaos and complexity in tourism: in search of a new perspective, *Pacific Tourism Review*, **1**, 93–102.

Fletcher, J and Westlake, J (2006), Globalisation, in L. Dwyer and P Forsyth (eds) (2006), *International Handbook on the Economics of Tourism*, Cheltenham, UK and Northampton, MA, USA: Edward Elgar.

Forsyth, P and Dwyer, L (2002), Market power and the taxation of domestic and international tourism, *Tourism Economics*, **8** (4) 377-399.

Forsyth, P and Dwyer, L (2010) Exchange Rate Changes and the Cost Competitiveness of International Airlines: The Aviation Trade Weighted Index, *Research in Transport Econom*ics **24**, 12-17

Forsyth, P, Dwyer, L, Duc Pham, T and Spurr, R (2014) The impacts of Australia's passenger movement charge on tourism and the economy, *Tourism Management* **40**, 126-136

Forsyth, P, Dwyer, L and Spurr, R (2014) Is Australian tourism suffering Dutch disease? *Annals of Tourism Research* **46**, 1–15

Frank M Z and Goyal, Vidhan K (2008) Trade-off and pecking order theories of debt in B Espen Eckbo (ed.) (2008) *Handbook of Corporate Finance: Empirical Corporate Finance, Volume 2* (Handbooks in Finance Series, Elsevier/North-Holland), Ch. 12.

Frechtling, D (1999) The tourism satellite account: foundations, progress and issues, *Tourism Management* **20** 163-170.

Frechtling, D C (2001). *Forecasting Tourism Demand: Methods and Strategies.* Oxford, UK: Butterworth-Heinemann.

Fujii, E, Khaled, M and Mak, J (1985), The exportability of hotel occupancy and other tourist taxes, *National Tax Journal*, **38**, 169–177.

Fyall, A and Garrod, B (2005), *Tourism Marketing: A Collaborative Approach*, Channelview Publications.

Gooroochurn N and Sinclair, T (2005), The economics of tourism taxation: evidence from Mauritius, *Annals of Tourism Research*, **32** (2), 478–498.

Gray, H P (1970) *International Travel—International Trade*, Lexington, Mass.: D.C. Heath.

Hanley N, Maurato, S and Wright, R (2001) Choice modelling approaches: a superior alternative for environmental valuation? *Journal of Economic Surveys* **15** (3), 435-462.

Hiemstra, S J, and Ismail, J A (1992), Analysis of room taxes levied on the lodging industry, *Journal of Travel Research*, **31**(1):42–49.

Hiemstra, S J and Ismail, J A (1993), Incidence of the impacts of room taxes in the lodging industry, *Journal of Travel Research*, **31** (4), 22–26.

Howarth, G and Kirsebom, T (1999), *The Future of Airline Alliances: Current thinking, strategic directions and implications*, Gemini Consulting and Reed Business Information, Sutton UK.

Jago, L and Dwyer, L (2006), *Economic Evaluation of Special Events: A Practitioner's Guide*, Common Ground Publishing Pty. Ltd., Altona, Australia.

Jennings, G R (2007), Advances in tourism research: theoretical paradigms and accountability, in A Matias, P Nijkamp and P Neto (eds) *Advances in Modern Tourism Research: Economic Perspectives*, Heidelberg: Physica-Verlag, 9–35.

Jones C and Munday, M (2007) Exploring the environmental consequences of tourism: a satellite account approach, *Journal of Travel Research*, **46**,164.

Jones, C, Munday, M and Roberts, A (2003) Regional tourism satellite accounts: a useful policy tool? *Urban Studies*, **40** (13) 2777–2794.

Lancaster, K J (1966), A new approach to consumer theory. *Journal of Political Economy*, **74**: 132-57.

Lei, Z (2006), Theoretical pillars of industrial organization in tourism in A Papatheodorou, (ed.) *Corporate Rivalry and Market Power: Competition Issues in the Tourism Industry*, London: I.B. Tauris, pp. 20-34

Li, G, Song, H, and Witt, S F (2005), Recent developments in econometric modeling and forecasting, *Journal of Travel Research*, **44**, 82–99.

Lim, C (1999), A meta analysis review of international tourism demand. *Journal of Travel Research*, **37**, 273–284.

Lim, C (2006), Tourism demand modelling: issues and implications, in L Dwyer and P Forsyth (eds) *International Handbook of Tourism Economics*, Edward Elgar, London.

Lockwood, M and Tracy, K (1995), Nonmarket economic valuation of an urban recreation park, *Journal of Leisure Research* **27**(2), 155-167.

Lockwood, M, Tracy, K and Klomp, N (1996), Analyzing conflict between cultural heritage and nature conservation in the Australian Alps: A CVM approach, *Journal of Environmental Planning and Management* **39**(3), 357-370.

Louvier J, Henscher, D and Swait,J (2000) *Stated Choice Methods: Analysis and Applications*, Cambridge, UK, Cambridge University Press.

Madden J (2006), Economic and fiscal impacts of mega sporting events: a general equilibrium assessment, *Public Finance and Management* 6(3) 346-394

Mak J (1988), Taxing hotel room rentals in the US, *Journal of Travel Research*, **27**,(1) 10–15.

Mak J (2006), Taxing travel and tourism, in L Dwyer and P Forsyth (eds) *International Handbook of Tourism Economics*, Edward Elgar, UK.

Mak, J (2008), Taxing cruise tourism: Alaska's head tax on cruise ship passengers, *Tourism Economics*, **14** (3), 599–614

Mangion, D, Durbarry, R and Sinclair, T (2005), Tourism competitiveness: price and quality, *Tourism Economics*, **11**(1), 45-68.

Monty, B and Skidmore, M (2003), Hedonic pricing and willingness to pay for bed and breakfast amenities in Southeast Wisconsin. *Journal of Travel Research*, **42**, 195-99.

Morley, C L (2003), Impacts of international airline alliances on tourism, *Tourism Economics*, **9**, pp 31–51.

Morley, C.L. (2006), Airline alliances and tourism, in L Dwyer and P Forsyth, eds, *International Handbook on the Economics of Tourism*, Edward Elgar, UK.

Matias, A, Nijkamp, P and Neto, P (eds) (2007) *Advances in Modern Tourism Research: Economic Perspectives*, Heidleberg: Physica-Verlag.

Narayan, P and Prasad, B C (2007) The long-run impact of coups on Fiji's economy: evidence from a computable general equilibrium model, *Journal of International Development*, **19** (2), 149-160.

Naude, W A and Saayman, A (2005), Determinants of tourist arrivals in Africa: A panel data regression analysis, *Tourism Economics*, **11**, 365–391.

Nowak J J and Sahli, M (2007) Coastal tourism and Dutch disease in a small island economy, *Tourism Economics*, **13** (1), 49–65

O'Connell, J F and Williams, G (2005) Passengers' perceptions of low cost airlines and full service carriers: A case study involving Ryanair, Aer Lingus, Air Asia and Malaysia Airlines, *Journal of Air Transport Management* **11** (2005) 259–272.

Oum, T H, Waters, W G and Yong, J S (1992), Concepts of price elasticities of transport demand and recent empirical estimates, *Journal of Transport Economics and Policy* **26** (2), 139–154.

Pambudi, D, McCaughey, N and Smyth, R (2009), Computable general equilibrium estimates of the impact of the Bali bombing on the Indonesian economy, *Tourism Management* **30**.

Papatheodorou, A (1999). The demand for international tourism in the Mediterranean region. *Applied Economics*, **31**, 619–630.

Papatheodorou, A (2002), Exploring competitiveness in Mediterranean resorts, *Tourism Economics*, **8**: 133-50

Papatheodorou, A (2004) Exploring the evolution of tourist resorts. *Annals of Tourism Research*, **31**(1): 219-237

Papatheodorou, A (2008) The impact of civil aviation regimes on leisure markets, in A Graham, A Papatheodorou, A. and P Forsyth, (eds) *Aviation and Tourism: Implications for Leisure Travel*, Aldershot: Ashgate, 49-57

Papatheodorou, A, Lei, Z and Apostolakis, A (2012) Hedonic price analysis. In L Dwyer, A Gill and N Seetaram (eds.) *Handbook of Research Methods in Tourism: Quantitative and Qualitative Approaches*, Cheltenham: Edward Elgar, 170-182.

Papatheodorou, A, Rossello, J, and Xiao, H (2010) Global Economic Crisis and Tourism: Consequences and Perspectives. *Journal of Travel Research*, **49** (1): 39-45.

Rosen, S (1974), Hedonic prices and implicit markets: product differentiation in pure competition. *Journal of Political Economy*, **82**, 34-55.

Saayman, A and Saayman, A (2008), The determinants of inbound tourism to South Africa, *Tourism Economics*, **14**(1):81-96.

Sheldon, P J (1990) A review of tourism expenditure research, in C P Cooper, (ed.) *Progress in Tourism, Recreation and Hospitality Management, Vol 2*, London: Belhaven, 399–403.

Sheldon P and Dwyer, L (2010) The global financial crisis and tourism: perspectives of the Academy, *Journal of Travel Research* **49** (3)

Sheldon, P J and Var, T (1985). Tourism forecasting: A review of empirical research, *Journal of Forecasting*, **4**(2), 183-195.

Seetaram, N (2012). Immigration and tourism demand: empirical evidence from Australia, *Tourism Management*, **33**(6) 1535-1543

Shen, S, Li, G and Song, H (2011). Combination forecasts of international tourism demand, *Annals of Tourism Research*, **38**(1), 72–89.

Sinclair M T (1998), Tourism and economic development: a survey, *Journal of Development Studies* **34** (5), 1-51.

Sinclair, M T, Clewer, A and Pack, A (1990), Hedonic prices and the marketing of package holidays: the case of tourism resorts in Malaga in G Ashworth and B. Goodall (eds), *Marketing Tourism Places*, London, Routledge, 85-103.

Song, H (2011). *Tourism Supply Chain Management*. London: Routledge.

Song, H and Li, G (2008). Tourism demand modelling and forecasting- a review of recent research. *Tourism Management*. **29** (2), 203-220.

Song, H and Turner, L (2006). Tourism demand forecasting in L Dwyer and P Forsyth (eds.), *International Handbook on the Economics of Tourism*. Cheltenham: Edward Elgar.

Song, H and Witt, S F (2000). *Tourism Demand Modelling and Forecasting: Modern Econometric Approaches*. Cambridge: Pergamon.

Song, H, Witt, S F and Jensen, T C (2003) Tourism forecasting: Accuracy of alternative econometric models. *International Journal of Forecasting*, **19**(1), 123-141.

Spurr, R (2006). Tourism satellite accounts. In L Dwyer and P Forsyth (eds.), *International Handbook on the Economics of Tourism*. Cheltenham: Edward Elgar.

Stabler M, Papatheodorou, A and Sinclair, T (2010) *The Economics of Tourism*, Second Edition, London: Routledge.

Stern, N (2006) *Stern Review. The Economics of Climate Change*, UK Treasury, London.

Sugiyarto, G, Blake, A and Sinclair, M T (2003), Tourism and globalization: economic impact in Indonesia, *Annals of Tourism Research*, **30**(3), 683-701.

Tisdell, C A (1983), Public finance and the appropriation of gains from international tourists: some theory with ASEAN and Australian illustrations, *Singapore Economic Review*, **28**, 3-20.

Tisdell C A (1987) Tourism, the environment and profit, *Economic Analysis and Policy* **17** (1), 13-20

Tisdell, C A (2001), *Tourism Economics, the Environment and Development: Analysis and Policy*, UK: Edward Elgar.

Tisdell, C A (2006) Valuation of tourism's natural resources in L Dwyer and P Forsyth (2006) *International Handbook on the Economics of Tourism*. Edward Elgar, Cheltenham, UK and Northampton, MA. USA, pp. 359-378

Tol, R S J (2008), Why worry about climate change? a research agenda, *Environmental Values*, **17** (4), 437-470.

UNWTO (2008), *2008 International Recommendations for Tourism Statistics*, UNWTO, New York, NY and Madrid

Van Der Merwe, P, Saayman, M, and Krugell, W F (2007), The determinants of the spending of biltong hunters, *South African Journal of Economics and Management Sciences*, **10**(2) 184–194.

Wagner, J (1997), Estimating the economic impacts of tourism, *Annals of Tourism Research*, **24**(3) 592-608.

Wattanakuljarus, A and Coxhead, I (2008) Is tourism-based development good for the poor? A general equilibrium analysis for Thailand. *Journal of Policy Modeling*, **30** (6), 929-955.

World Economic Forum (2009) *Travel and Tourism Competitiveness Report 2009*. Geneva: World Economic Forum.

Zhou, D, Yanagida, J F, Chakravorty, U and Leung, P (1997), Estimating economic impacts of tourism, *Annals of Tourism Research*, **24**(1), 76-89.

Glossary

CGE models: A mathematical specification of key relationships within an economy (what determines levels of demand, supply, etc). A model is calibrated to real data to ensure that it provides a good representation of the economy. It treats the economy as a whole, allowing for feedback effects of one sector on another, and represents it as a system of flows of goods and services between sectors.

Climate change economics: examines the impact of climate change in relation to the economy.

Delphi technique: A forecasting method reliant on a panel of experts. It is a questionnaire-based system in which the panel answer a series of questions over the course of two or more rounds. After each questionnaire the answers are summarised and the panel are encouraged to refine their answers to the next based on the answers from the last. It is a way of bringing experts' opinions together without bringing the people together face to face. The experts also remain anonymous throughout the process.

   http://is.njit.edu/pubs/delphibook/

Discrete choice analysis: Discrete choice involves a choice between two or more discrete alternatives. Discrete choice analysis examines these situations and choices in which the optimum is not characterised by "standard first order conditions", looking at a number of alternatives.

Economic impact: An economic impact is the change that takes place in an economy due to some existing or proposed project, action, event or policy.

Ecological economics: "Ecological Economics is the science of sustainability. It brings together academics and practitioners from a variety of science and social science disciplines including biology, ecology, chemistry, computer science, economics, management, sociology and philosophy. The common goal of ecological economists is to improve theoretical models and practical solutions to achieving long term economic and social well-being without undermining the absorptive, regenerative and resource capacity of the natural environment."

   "The United States Society for Ecological Economics" http://www.ussee.org/ v2/about.php

Forecasting: Making statements estimating the outcome of events before they occur, often using techniques such as qualitative research and quantitative methods. Delphi is a popular qualitative technique in forecasting.

Foreign exchange earnings: Proceeds from the export of goods and services of a country, and the returns from its foreign investments

Gross Domestic Product: The measure of the total economic activity of one country or the value of the economy's output. This includes the income on production of goods and services and takes into account the consumer, investment and government spending, and the value of exports minus the value of imports.

   http://www.hm-treasury.gov.uk/data_gdp_backgd.htm

Hedonic pricing method: A system used to estimate the price of a good using both factors and characteristics relating to the product itself and external factors. The most common example is the housing market, where the price is based on factors within the house and external factors (such as area, proximity to amenities). The method is used to determine how much each factor contributes to or affects the price of the house.

Income: On an individual level this is earnings through employment or investment. On a company level it equals to total revenue over costs, including taxes.

Input-Output models: I–O models comprise tables that are a set of accounts relating the components of final demands to the various industrial sectors, the interaction between industrial sectors and the relationship between the industrial sectors and the primary inputs.Using a matrix representation, a nation or regions' economy the model is used to predict the effects of changes in an industry will have over others. As well as the effect by the government, consumers and foreign suppliers and business on the economy in general.

http://www.sjsu.edu/faculty/watkins/inputoutput.htm

Modern econometric methods: The use of statistics and mathematical approaches to the economy and problems within it, analysis and development.

Multipliers: "Applies to the changes in exogenous demand for any industry's output, and is thus not solely related to tourism activity. Within the context of tourism multiplier effects are those economic impacts brought about by a change in the level or pattern of tourism expenditure. The term 'multiplier' is derived from the fact that the value of expenditure is multiplied by some estimated factor in order to determine the total economic impact."

John Fletcher. *Encyclopaedia of Tourism*

Panel data techniques: Panel data is multi-dimensional data, which examines observations and occurrences over long or multiple time periods.

Poverty alleviation: Strategies and policies aimed at reducing the amount of poverty in anything from a small community to the wider world.

Price: The published or negotiated terms of the transaction of goods or a service between those who produce the product and the consumer.

Richard Teare, Haydn Ingram and Gavin Eccles. *Encyclopaedia of Tourism*

Pricing strategies: The different methods of pricing a product. Price must reflect the supply and demand and take into account a number of factors including competition and fixed and variable costs.

'Public good': Within economics a 'public good' is a non-rivalrous good, one that if consumed by one individual does not reduce its availability to others. It is also non-excludable, thus no one can be excluded from consuming the good.

Public policy: Action taken by government on a particular issue or set of issues, this can take the form of laws, funding, legislative acts or judicial decisions.

Scenario writing: "A description of variables related to sectoral developments, e.g. the energy scenarios of the International Institute for Applied Systems Analysis (IIASA) in which the variation range of the scenarios is determined by the world energy-consumption. Variables consist of low, high or average energy consumption, and from that the consequences for the availability of energy sources are considered. For each scenario the geo-political and the ecological consequences are discussed.

The second way in which scenarios are used is less common but in my opinion more important. In this category scenarios provide alternatives of societal developments with regard to one another.

The third form in which scenarios are presented encompasses all scenarios with two, or more, differing parameter values of the same variable:"

> Jozef W. M. van Doorn. "Scenario writing: A method for long-term tourism forecasting?" *Tourism Management.* **7** (1), March 1986, 33-49

Structure-Conduct-Performance (SCP) paradigm: Based on the idea that market performance is controlled by the conduct of firms which in turn depends on market structure. These three factors, conduct, performance and structure are interconnected through the characteristics of the structure of the market. The connection between these factors turns on 'matching' the structural characteristics against models of perfect competition, monopoly, monopolistic competition and oligopoly.

> Ferguson, Paul R and Glenys J. Ferguson. *Industrial economics: issues and perspectives.* NYU Press, 1994.

Sustainable development: A form of development that does not compromise the ability of future generations to meet their needs but at the same time meeting the needs of the present. Sustainable development would at least maintain ecological integrity and diversity, meet human needs.

> Geoffrey Wall, *Encyclopaedia of Tourism*

Tourism infrastructure: The facilities and services that form the underlying base for the tourism industry (link to def) on both the small scale in a resort and the larger scale for a country.

Tourism Satellite Accounts (TSA): "A Tourism Satellite Account (TSA) is a statistical accountant framework in the field of tourism and measures the goods and services according to international standards of concepts, classifications and definitions which allow valid comparisons from country to country in a consistent manner. A complete TSA contains detailed production accounts of the tourism industry and their linkages to other industries, employment, capital formation and additional non-monetary information on tourism."

> http://ec.europa.eu/enterprise/sectors/tourism/cooperation/tourism-satellite-account/index_en.htm

Tourist taxation: The taxes that fall on tourists and tourism businesses.

Tourism and History

John K. Walton

Contents

John K. Walton, a graduate of Merton College, Oxford and the University of Lancaster, is an Ikerbasque Professor in the Department of Contemporary History, University of the Basque Country UPV/ EHU. He has worked for many years on themes in the history of tourism, especially coastal resorts, and especially in Britain and Spain, and he edits the *Journal of Tourism History* for Routledge. His most recent books are (edited, with Patrick Browne) *Coastal Regeneration in England - 2010* (Lincoln: Coastal Communities Alliance), and (with Keith Hanley) *Constructing Cultural Tourism: John Ruskin and the Tourist Gaze* (Bristol: Channel View, 2010).

Introduction

The relationships between researchers and teachers in Tourism Studies and History have until recently been intermittent and remote. Tourism Studies, as it has emerged as an academic discipline, has been dominated by economics, and by business and management studies. It has had little time for the humanities, although it has accommodated important perspectives from geography, sociology and anthropology. The important developments in the academic study of travel writing in the past, often with a strong gender dimension, have tended to remain within their own (highly productive) silo, although some contributions from literary historians have made a sustained impact. (Fussell, 1980: Buzard, 1993) I have discussed the enduring, but eroding, resistance of Tourism Studies to the recognition of History, and of the humanities more generally, in recent publications, which also explore the varieties, ramifications, themes and geographical spread of work in the history of tourism (Walton, 2009a, 2009b).

Tourism and the Culture of the Historical Profession

Historians, on the other hand, have been very slow to recognise the potential significance of tourism's past for their discipline. They have failed to recognise the global (and globalising) importance of tourism as a transforming set of economic activities as it has emerged as the largest and most pervasive international industry of the new millennium, feeding off and into transport innovation, inter-cultural contact, social transformation and environmental impact, and linking up with traditional historians' concerns such as politics, empires and diplomacy as well as economic development. The enduring preoccupation of British economic historians with the now defunct or moribund industries of the first Industrial Revolution, in the form of cotton, coal, iron and steel, and shipbuilding, or (of much greater current relevance) with the financial services industries, has pre-empted any widespread recognition of the importance of tourism, or the opportunities it presents. Even the economic historians' turn from supply to demand, to consumption and consumerism, has concentrated attention more on retailing and the supply of tangible goods than on the consumption of experiences; and where this has gained ground, the dominant focus has been on entertainment, shows and audiences rather than tourism as a theme in itself. This has been a general pattern: it has not been confined to the British historical profession.

Over the last few years, however, significant changes have been gathering momentum. Isolated works on tourism history go back more than half a century, although three of the pioneering British productions came from a civil servant, a geographer and a poet. (Pimlott, 1947; Gilbert, 1953; Nicholson, 1955) British professional historians began to take an interest during the 1970s, but the publications that began to appear towards the end of the decade were slow to gain recognition outside a small niche area, and this was also the case with the similarly emerging field of leisure history (Walvin, 1978; Walton, 1978; Bailey, 1978; Cunningham, 1980). The growing visibility of tourism as a dynamic and economically significant set of phenomena was also sufficient, by this time, to encourage the writing of overviews from outside the historical academy, some of which proved to be of lasting value, such as Turner and Ash's (1975) coinage of the 'pleasure periphery'. Gaviria's (1974) contemporary history of the rapid growth of tourism in Spain under the sponsorship of the Franco regime, relating it to the developing literature on neo-colonialism, was also a landmark publication. Over the following two decades outputs began to multiply with gathering momentum, especially on British themes and on what might be labelled 'destination' rather than 'tourism' history(Walton, 1983; Ward and Hardy, 1984; Morgan and Pritchard, 1993). But British historians also began to tackle themes in European tourism (a notable example being John Pemble's (1987) *The Mediterranean Passion*), French, Swiss and German historians joined the emergent collective enterprise, and interest began to spread to North America, while in 1996 the historical geographer John Towner pulled together an overview of tourism history across the 'Western world', building on his earlier work on the Grand Tour (Haug, 1982; Désert, 1983; Chadefaud, 1987; Corbin, 1994; Walton and Smith, 1996; Towner, 1996; Aron, 1999; Koshar, 2000; Tissot, 2000).

The European Grand Tour has, indeed, been one of the few themes in tourism history to receive a regular mention in tourism textbooks, and it has long attracted attention from historians(Black, 2003). The other consistent ingredient has been the story of Thomas Cook, often represented as the inventor of the package tour and of 'modern' 'mass tourism', and sustained by a series of in-house histories using the company archives (Pudney, 1953; Swinglehurst, 1974; Brendon, 1991). As in this case, the history of tourism has continued to attract writers from outside the academy, as well as academics based outside the imagined frontiers of 'History', which may have helped to lower its status within university history departments. Why this should apply to tourism rather than war or monarchs, where the same issues apply, must remain an open question (Blume, 1992; Withey, 1997; Lencek and Bosker, 1998; Bray and Raitz, 2001). After all, writers on (recognisably) tourism history from related disciplines, such as sociology, geography or anthropology, sometimes produce important insights or excellent overviews that provide material assistance to historical understanding (Shields, 1991; Löfgren, 1999). The paucity of source material (until comparatively recently) in 'respectable' sources such as national government archives, and the limited amount of consolidated, dedicated sources to work through, may also have contributed to the marginal status of the theme, alongside the shortage of trustworthy quantifiable data and the enduring sense that anything connected with leisure and pleasure is by definition frivolous and beneath the notice of the serious historian. The history of tourism has followed a similar trajectory to that of sport, with a time-lag of a few years: a fecund and proliferating sub-discipline has been slow to gain acceptance outside its own imagined boundaries. Dominant voices within the historical profession have remained unwilling to embrace or even accept the legitimacy of histories of tourism, leisure, enjoyment and 'popular culture' (Walton, 1995), even as the volume of excellent work in these fields continues to expand and connect with 'legitimate' themes such as politics, government and diplomacy (Chaplin, 2009, pp. 9-17; Endy, 2004; Merrill, 2001; Pack, 2006; Hazbun, 2008).

Recent Developments in Tourism History

The most sustained and significant developments in tourism history on a broad front have arisen in the early twenty-first century. The geographical coverage of work on tourism history has extended from Europe to the United States, Australasia and Latin America, and international comparative tourism histories have begun to appear (Dubinsky, 1999; Sterngass, 2001; Shaffer, 2002; Chambers, 2003; Davidson and Spearritt, 2000; White, 2005; Pastoriza, 2002; Berger, 2006; Cross and Walton, 2005). Alongside the gathering momentum of new publications on a broadening front, several edited collections of essays have pulled ideas together on national and international stages, from classical antiquity to the post-Second World War period. Most of them have been the products of international gatherings of tourism historians, or historians with an interest in tourism (Baranowski and Furlough, 2001; Berghoff *et al.*, 2002; Tissot, 2003; Walton, 2005a; Gorsuch and Koenker, 2006; Battilani and Strangio, 2007; Grandits and Taylor, 2010).

Meanwhile a professional infrastructure has been laid down, with the foundation in 2003 of the International Commission for the History of Travel and Tourism (ICHTT), which is affiliated to the global International Commission for the Historical Sciences, and has provided a regular forum through conferences and symposia. Dedicated tourism history sessions have been held (for example) at the global economic history conference in Buenos Aires and the International Commission for the Historical Sciences at Sydney in 2005. Another is planned for the Amsterdam conference of ICHS in 2010. An international conference at Blackpool on 'Resorting to the Coast' in 2009, attracted 160 papers from literally all over the world, most of them on historical themes, indicating the development of interest in this aspect of tourism history (and by implication others) in (for example) China, Vietnam and Turkey. Significantly, this involved cross-disciplinary collaboration between the ICHTT and the Centre for Tourism and Cultural Change at Leeds Metropolitan University.

Occasional, isolated articles on historical themes related to tourism have long been appearing in historical, geographical and sociological outlets, as well as in *Annals of Tourism Research*, but tourism history has also developed its own dedicated outlets. The pioneer was the Italian journal *Storia del Turismo*, edited by Annunziata Berrino and published from Naples (mainly in Italian) since 2000 by the Istituto per la Storia del Risorgimento Italiano (*Storia del Turismo*, 2000-). The German journal travel and tourism journal *Voyage*, founded soon afterwards and edited by Hasso Spode, has recently produced a special issue dedicated entirely to the history of tourism (*Tourismusgeschichte(n)*, 2009). The foundation of the international *Journal of Tourism History* in the same year, published by Routledge through Taylor and Francis and supported by the ICHTT, marks the coming of age of tourism history as an academic entity (*Journal of Tourism History*, 2009-). Running parallel to this are the efforts of Conrad Lashley and colleagues to extend the remit of Hospitality Studies from narrow practical professional concerns to embrace a broad spectrum of the social sciences, including History (Lashley and Morrison, 2000; Walton, 2003). Tourism history is now a force to be reckoned with. How should its relationship with Tourism Studies and cognate disciplines develop?

Why Tourism Needs History

The first point to emphasize is that Tourism Studies needs to take proper account of the history of tourism, rather than leaving it to the token reiteration of myths and over-simplified 'facts' in brief introductions. It is significant that a recent publication on tourism studies and the social sciences deals with every social science except History (Holden, 2005); and there is no similar work on Tourism Studies and the Humanities, although historians can sometimes be found working in the same university faculties as Tourism Studies academics . It is important for a discipline, especially a hybrid one of relatively recent emergence, to understand its themes and preoccupations over time, to be able to chart trends and variations, and to identify changes in assumptions and patterns of thought, recognising that current versions of 'common sense' are neither universal nor inevitable, but the products of particular historical conjunctures. This is, then, not just a matter of antiquarian interest or the accumulation of 'knowledge' for its own sake, although such motives should never be discounted. Such recognition enables current practitioners to look critically at their own assumptions, at where they have come from in terms of intellectual genealogies, and at whether the circumstances under which they were generated still (or ever did) hold good.

Well-documented historical awareness also provides resources for challenging the myths of history as progress, and the validity of selected exemplary stories that may otherwise become 'truths universally acknowledged' and distort understanding, such as the many that surround Thomas Cook (Walton, 2010a). Access to critical historical perspectives underpinned by systematic evidence-based research should also give pause for thought about the validity of assumptions and expectations based on growth and gigantism as the only determinants of 'success'. A large number of publications are available on the methodologies and uses of history, and this is not the place to rehearse their arguments (Appleby, Hunt and Jacob, 1994; Evans, 1997; Tosh, 2008). But there is no doubt that the incorporation of historical concepts, approaches and evidence opens out opportunities for making comparisons over time as well as between places, countries and sectors, and expands the contextual understanding of researchers beyond the mechanistic, the narrow, the path-dependent and the silo. History, with its discursive writing styles and concern for context, depth of field and recovering the texture of diverse cross-currents of experience, also has the power to enrich and (usefully) complicate what might otherwise be narrow and reductive projects and expositions.

Bringing History into Tourism Studies

These claims can be supported convincingly by examining what historical research can bring to the well-established trope of the Tourism Area Life Cycle (TALC) (Butler, 2005). This approach, based on the idea of the product cycle, should be inherently an historical concept, addressing as it does the assumed evolution over time of tourist destinations from 'discovery' to 'consolidation', 'stagnation', over-development, and decline or 'rejuvenation'. But most TALC-based analyses focus overwhelmingly on the recent past and on the later stages of the 'cycle', presenting the earlier stages schematically and with little attention to the interaction of variables in the processes (note the plural) at work, or the individuality of particular experiences within wider grammars of development. The work of Gale and Botterill (2005) on the North Wales resort of Rhyl has provided a useful corrective, with its emphasis on the careful analysis and triangulation of a range of recent sources; but there is no substitute for the examination of a range of processes from a variety of perspectives over a longer period. A further problem with TALC is a tendency to work backwards from a predetermined perception of a current situation, which tends to foreshorten processes and to concentrate the attention on destinations that appear to have gone through all the stages of the cycle, setting aside the many cases in which development is partial or limited, and a state of sustainable equilibrium, often relatively environmentally friendly, can be achieved without arriving at a crisis of over-development, stagnation or the need to rejuvenate. A thorough histori-cal approach would complicate the processes, increase the range of variables and deepen the analysis of their interaction. In many cases it would also challenge the highly schematic assumptions behind the original approach.

The incorporation of historical approaches and contextual understanding into Tourism Studies would ideally form part of a wider 'cultural turn' embracing the humanities as well as a wider range of social sciences, and incorporating qualitative as well as quantitative methodologies in more systematic ways. This is a tall order, but the first signs of change are appearing. Tourism Studies is not the only policy-oriented discipline to have remained inhospitable to History, of course: even the well-established sub-discipline of business history has strug-gled to penetrate the inner workings of business schools, and its pattern of cita-tions has only a limited (though not insignificant) level of interaction with the 'mainstream' economics, business and management studies literature, despite the high status accorded to journals such as *Business History*. Historians remain corrosively sceptical about the principle as well as the practices of ranking out-puts though journal citation indices, and very worried about its implications for diversity, originality and interdisciplinary developments, and this divergence of values and attitudes will also get in the way of building bridges (Di Vaio and Weisdorf, 2009; Walton, 2010b; Lee, 2007; Gingras, 2008; Clark and Rowlinson, 2004). Here we find strong evidence of contrasting assumptions between disci-plines, of course; but if historical approaches to the analysis of issues in tourism are to be incorporated into the discipline, the mutual suspicions will have to be overcome or at least suspended.

How Tourism Can Use History: the Imagined Past and its Ambiguities

Over and above these arguments, there are various ways in which Tourism Studies, and indeed the businesses of tourism, can make use of academic his-tory. Most obvious is the appropriation of historical research in the develop-ment of the kind of heritage tourism that requires a genuine, grounded appre-ciation of the legacies of the past, in the form of associations with events and stories, the built environment and the 'cultural landscape' of custom and past practices that live on, however hybridised and reinvented, in the marketable present. Peter Borsay's (2000) work on Bath is an excellent example of a his-torical analysis of the development, successive mutations, protection, negotia-tion, reiterated reinvention and marketing of images and visions of an endur-ing past. There is an important difference between the pastiche and invention of the Disney version of 'heritage' and the representation and re-presentation of 'real people, real places and real things', however such endeavours may be compromised and negotiated through problems of health and safety, practicality, availability and conservation needs, leading to (for example) the display and especially the use of replicas rather than originals (Cross and Walton, 2005, Chapters 5-6; Wallace, 1989; Moore, 2000). Tourists do not necessarily require an informed understanding of the detailed historical associations of a location in order to appreciate the atmosphere and patina of a site whose core is authentically historic, however 'staged' that 'authenticity' may be on the ground, whether by an overarching organisation or by a congeries of actors working independently alongside each other in a 'historic' urban centre that lives by tourism even as it celebrates the surviving traces of its 'quaint' or 'interesting' industrial or commercial past (MacCannell, 1976; Bann, 1990, pp. 125-6). The presentation for tourist purposes of historical survivals from a more distant past raises even more complex issues of choice, selection, presentation and re-creation, and makes even more demands on historical scholarship and the historical imagination in tension with the commercial need o present attractive structures and a compelling story (Berger, 2006). The ability to communicate an understanding of historical processes, and to incorporate this into redevelopment and regeneration projects so as to refresh the offer without destroying its essential appeal, requires the recruitment of historical expertise and ethics in support of a discerning, evocative and educative tourism aimed at well-informed and up-market visiting publics.

Corporate interests have long been alert to the value of ownership of their history, in the sense of controlling and orchestrating the display and communication of artefacts and archives, and the power it provides for public relations and advertising purposes. Thomas Cook's use of a unique archive, to promote a strong view of the firm's founder as innovator and pioneer in the classic Victorian tradition of the self-made man and heroic entrepreneur and present a romantic image of the firm's history, is a case in point, although the value of Brendon's (1991) history of the firm as a piece of scholarly research in its own right should not be understated. Business uses of corporate 'heritage' to attract tourists (and school parties) have not always been as (relatively) reputable, as (for example) Rowlinson's (2002) study of the attitudes to history displayed at Cadbury World has demonstrated very effectively (Delahaye et al. 2009)..

In spite of attempts to argue the contrary from relativist and 'post-modern' perspectives, it is clear that public museums, even as they tread the difficult line between 'education' and 'entertainment' and strive to meet the expectations of their visitors without distorting their presentation and interpretation, offer a very different kind of product; and historical understanding, by various routes, can empower customers to engage actively and critically with what they see, to make choices and to draw informed conclusions (Moore, 2000). The open-air industrial museum is a useful case in point: ventures such as Beamish in County Durham and the Ironbridge Gorge museum in Shropshire have been criticised for lack of authenticity in bringing houses, businesses and artefacts together from a variety of sites as if they formed a unified settlement, for airbrushing social conflict out of the picture, for giving insufficient attention to gender issues, and for incorporating what they show into conventional, dominant historical narratives; but they have emerged from such critiques with resilience, and the value of their own collections and archives for serious historical research helps to underpin an underlying integrity (Cross and Walton, 2005, Chapter 6; West, 1988). This is not to suggest that the situation is always clear-cut: on North Yorkshire's Captain Cook heritage trail in the early twenty-first century, for example, it was the official birthplace site museum at Marton (Middlesbrough) that presented an imagined version of the interior of the vanished cottage where the explorer was born, the schoolroom museum at nearby Great Ayton that offered the visitor a complete but imagined reconstruction of Cook's childhood schoolroom, and 'Captain Cook's House', overseen by the Whitby Literary and Philosophical Society, that represented itself as the place where Cook lived as an apprentice, when the evidence for this was extremely scanty (Walton, 2009c). But even this is better than complete fabrication or propaganda.

The History and Heritage of Tourism

Tourism, as an industry of long standing, also has its own histories, heritage and industrial archaeology, and its sites of historical memory and significance deserve to stand alongside those more conventional Industrial Revolution locations, such as Ironbridge, Saltaire, Blaenavon and New Lanark (to name four of Britain's eight), or Essen (Germany), or Pulacayo (Bolivia), that are already inscribed as UNESCO World Heritage Sites and participate in the tensions between tourist exploitation, historical authenticity, and in some cases (such as Liverpool's waterfront) urban regeneration and contemporary architectural interventions, that are characteristic of such places (ICOMOS, 2009; Barber, 2002). As the importance of the 'heritage of the recent past' and of 'cultural landscapes' are increasingly being recognised, so the history of tourist sites *as* tourist sites, the architecture and practices of persisting past pleasure environments, becomes a marketable proposition and a legitimate object of preservationist intervention (Gibson and Pendlebury, 2009). Hence, for example, the promotionof UNESCO World Heritage Site status for those parts of Blackpool that express its status as the world's first working-class seaside resort, and the parallel celebration in the early twenty-first century of Blackpool's popular entertainment heritage. These and related initiatives depend on informed understandings of

Blackpool's past, while remaining clear-eyed about the changes and replace-ments that have taken place in the fabric of all the sites in question, and rec-ognising the need for sustained negotiation between preservation, celebration, imagination and necessary innovation as historical interests collide with the well-funded energies of regeneration (Walton and Wood, 2008, 2009). A related development is the campaign to save Margate's Dreamland cinema and amuse-ment park, and to establish a working museum of amusement park rides on the Dreamland site, appealing (as all such initiatives must) to a potentially powerful combination of history and nostalgia, to the re-creation of happy memories of past pleasures, in marked contrast with that darker side of historically-fuelled tourism that finds expression in slave castles and concentration camp museums (Dreamland Trust, 2009; Lennon and Foley, 2000).

Broadening the Curriculum

Tourism and history are thus, in many cases, necessary and potentially mutual-ly supportive companions, although often in complex and therefore interesting ways. The temptation to over-simplify should always be resisted in interpret-ing and communicating processes: respect for consumers of 'the past' should always be encouraged, and the development of assorted historical enthusiasms and hobbies, especially the kind of historical genealogy that goes beyond family trees to look carefully at context, makes this requirement all the more pressing (Samuel, 1994; Carter, 2008; Gelber, 1999). But over and above these ambiguous relationships between history, 'heritage' and tourism, there are more direct and obvious uses for tourism history. As it continues to develop, and to multiply examples of past processes through the case-studies from which historians like to build (enabling as they do richness of texture and depth of field), it provides a quarry of examples from which current practitioners can learn and perhaps avoid repeating earlier mistakes. More basically still, some knowledge of his-torical development, historians' thought-processes, and even dates and events enables the avoidance of embarrassing errors in the presentation of descrip-tive or promotional material, and especially of committing unwanted anach-ronisms. A surprising amount of tourism activity will be found to rely on the presentation of historical material, and the cultural capital that accrues from familiarity with relevant historical issues, biographies and debates will enhance this dimension of working with tourism. So what this adds up to, of course, is a call for a broadening of the Tourism Studies curriculum to take account of what history in particular, but the humanities in general, have to offer, going beyond the narrowly practical and economic, and perhaps adding additional spice to the learning process.

impact the railways had on Victorian culture (and, it might be added, tourism); and interest in railways has always had a strong historical component, no doubt reinforced by growing awareness of, and pride in, Britain's status as the originator of railways and the radiating point for their global spread (Freeman, 1992; Carter, 2001). But the preservation movement emerged from a uniquely high peak of popular railway enthusiasm, especially among boys and young men, during the generation after the Second World War, fuelled by a very effective commercial press (especially the almost eponymous firm of Ian Allan) which developed the enthusiast market, and a proliferation of clubs for 'trainspotters' and the more up-market category of 'railway enthusiasts' (Dickinson, 2007). The sheer scale of the railway system, and the variety of its locomotives, trains, services, stations and paraphernalia, inherited not only from the 'Big Four' companies that were produced by the forced amalgamations of 1923 but also from their multifarious forebears (Simmons, 1986), provided sustenance for the craze, which was also fed by the new locomotive movements that were facilitated by the nationalised system from 1948 onwards. Within a few years, however, this seemingly permanent source of pleasure and interest came under threat through the switch to diesel traction signalled by the Modernisation Plan of 1955 and the contraction of the system in face (mainly) of road competition, culminating in the closures of the mid to late 1960s that were promoted by the Beeching Report (Gourvish, 1986; Thomas, 1976; White, 1986). This environment of threat and decline nurtured a romantic determination to save what could be saved, and a tremendous volume of financial resources and goodwill was made available for the expensive and time-consuming tasks of preservation and restoration, some of which were very demanding in terms of skills and expertise. Significantly, much of this was supplied by current and former railway workers themselves, taking 'busmen's holidays' in support of this idealised supplement to an everyday working environment in which they took pride and a sense of responsibility. The movement was helped by the coincidence in time between the scrapping of steam locomotives and the contraction and transformation of railway freight services: one of the biggest scrapyard operators, at Barry in South Wales, preferred to concentrate on the easier task of scrapping wagons, leaving an extensive pool of slowly decaying locomotives which became available for purchase for preservation projects (Dickinson, 2007; Whittaker, 1995).

It is clear that this important branch of the heritage tourism industry cannot be understood in its present form without a grasp of its own history, and those of the businesses that it celebrates and commemorates. Its enthusiast participants have a very strong and well-informed sense of the past they celebrate and try to re-create, nurtured by book and video nostalgia publishing industries (from Oakwood Press and David and Charles to Silver Link), an astonishing proliferation of websites offering precise data and scholarly detail on rolling stock, liveries and past practices (often aimed at the numerous railway modelling community), and histories of almost every company and route that ever existed. They have been helped by the wider development of open-air industrial museums, such as Beamish in County Durham (some of which incorporate small railway and electric tramway operations of their own), as part of the rise of that particular branch of the 'heritage industry', which reached a peak during the 1980s and about which the eminent Ruskin scholar and cultural historian Robert Hewison wrote a famous polemic (Hewison, 1987; Cross and Walton, 2005; Harvie, 2002). The National Railway Museum, especially since its establishment in York, has been willing to lend exhibits in working order to appropriate 'heritage' railways, and a whole supporting industry offering certificated repairs and even new construction has sprung up even as most of the 'main-line' manufacturers were driven to the wall by the policies of the Thatcher and Major governments (Gourvish, 2008).

Curiously, perhaps, the popularity and success of 'heritage' railways has coincided with deeply ambivalent attitudes towards their progenitors and their distinctive enthusiast culture. There is a deep reservoir of affection and nostalgia towards old trains, especially steam trains, even among those who never saw them in routine action on the main railway system. The enduring success, and adaptability to new media, of the children's *Thomas the Tank Engine* series plays an obvious part here, and the role of the steam locomotive in the *Harry Potter* novels has given the theme a new lease of life for teenagers and young adults. 'Heritage' railways have been nimble in taking advantage of this. At the same time, 'trainspotter' has become a term of denigration and abuse, although the concept seems to have become effectively divorced from the 'heritage' railways sector (Carter, 2008; Whittaker, 1995). The establishment of preserved railways was also marked by obstruction and often hostility on the part of British Railways, which was unwilling to sell trackbeds or make withdrawn locomotives available, in its managerial concern to modernise its image and divest itself of an unwanted past. This ambivalence towards survivals from an industrial past is part of a widespread pattern in modern British culture: it applies, for example, to the seaside holiday and its paraphernalia (Walton, 2000). Tourism professionals need to be aware of it.

Enthusiasts and the Problems of 'Authenticity'

For many of the promoters of preserved and revived railways, generating tourism traffic was almost a necessary evil: what they really wanted was to run, and experience, the trains. They succeeded in attracting rich and influential patrons and supporters, such as (in the early stages) the flamboyant Conservative MP Sir Gerald Nabarro, and until the early 1990s Robert Adley, the Conservative

MP for Christchurch, a member of various parliamentary transport and tourism committees (Nabarro, 1971). There is, indeed, a populist, militaristic conservative tone to many of the preservation movement's activities, though it has never been strong enough to deter (for example) active trade unionists and socialists such as the historian and transport campaigner Paul Salveson. The naming of locomotives in preservation continues a tendency to celebrate stately homes, regiments and other aspects of aristocracy that was already apparent before the Second World War (Walton, 2005b). Wartime week-ends and similar commemorations are common, and attractive, features of special promotions. The important thing is that they positively attract some constituencies while not excluding others.

The staging of authenticity in these settings is enduringly, and increasingly, difficult, however. There is bound to be an artificial element to the operation of isolated, often self-contained lines without the satisfying scale, complexity and element of unpredictability that the full steam railway system had provided (Whittaker, 1995; Dickinson, 2007). Purists can argue over details of presentation and livery, but commercial considerations (like the requirements of film-makers regarding the livery of the 'Harry Potter' locomotive) trump authenticity when necessary, and they have had to accept the impossibility of matching the distribution of preserved locomotives to the lines on which they ran, especially as the availability of types has been distorted by the importance of the pool of survivors at Barry. 'Wartime Week-ends' sometimes have to be run using post-war locomotives and other rolling stock. The need to attract large volumes of non-enthusiast customers has led to the proliferation of Thomas week-ends, Santa Specials, murder mystery trains (paying direct or indirect homage to Agatha Christie and the Orient Express) and other 'inauthentic' money-spinners. Then there are vexed questions, common to the presentation of all 'heritage' sites: what period do you adopt when restoring a station, and do you pick a particular year, or provide a palimpsest? What is particularly interesting is that conflicts over such issues never seem to have escalated to the point of damaging the core relationships between preservation, presentation and tourist revenue that are at the heart of these, ultimately, tourism businesses.

But the enthusiasts themselves have been flexible, not least in pursuing their enthusiasms. They have repatriated examples of 'lost' British locomotive classes from distant overseas sidings, and restored them to working order with numbers that extend the original British series. More ambitious still have been the recent projects to provide representatives of classes that were completely lost to scrapping, most famously the *Tornado* A1 Pacific project, which has attracted a great deal of favourable publicity. Several others are now in the pipeline. The adoption of new technologies and materials, whether to re-create a locomotive as it might have been modernised during a longer career, or to make construction less expensive, or (as at Beamish) to create a 'replica' that meets Health and Safety standards, is a further potential (and sometimes actual) source of conflict. And, of course, the extensive 'heritage diesel' enthusiast group has to be fitted in alongside the steam fans. Fortunately for the railways in their endless search for volunteers, for every requirement there seems to be an enthusiast (Gelber, 1999).

The Future of Heritage Railways?

Can this continue? How do you find workers for all roles, given the bias towards locomotives and the footplate? One of the prime causes for the rapid decline of the steam railway was the difficulty of recruiting to the really dirty jobs such as engine cleaners, ash-shovellers and carriage cleaners (Dickinson, 2007). How do you sustain enthusiasm, and a sufficient number of skilled people, into the generation that follows the last original train-spotters? How do you keep up with the increasingly expensive demands of Health and Safety, and with the high cost of necessarily customised repairs in the absence of the economies of scale of the original workshops? What is the future for 'heritage' railways? (Carter, 2008, Chapter 10).

Tourism planners and promoters will need to keep these issues in mind, whether they run 'heritage' railways, provide financial support for them, administer and respond to their lottery and other charitable bids, or wish to support such railways among the assets and attractions of their resorts, as at (for example) Whitby, Swanage or Minehead, or in various National Parks. At every level and in every respect, the relationships between tourism and history are crucial to effective decision making, conflict resolution and executive action. This is a particular illustration of a general truth.

Tourism and History: Looking Forwards

The prospects for tourism history are lively and encouraging. Historical evidence on a broad front is now being taken seriously into consideration, not only where traces, survivals and associations from the past are part of the tourism offer, but also where destinations are refreshing and regenerating themselves. This can be seen along the English coastline, for example, where the Coastal Communities Alliance is producing a regeneration handbook which gives due weight to the contribution of an understanding of historical processes to the construction of current policies, including historical approaches to planning, environment and entertainment as well as architecture, public art and the built environment (Lincolnshire Coastal Action Zone, 2006; Gray, 2006; Brodie and Winter, 2007). Such innovations (looking backward in order to move forward more satisfyingly and convincingly) do not command universal assent, especially when the 'heritage of the recent past' is at issue, and this process is generating its own historical processes of conflict and debate, of thesis, antithesis and shifting synthesis, as it moves along (Walton and Wood, 2009). Debates over the future of Prora, the Baltic resort built by the Nazis' Strength through Joy (KdF) organisation on the eve of the Second World War, provide an extreme example of the sort of conflicts that can emerge (Baranowski, 2004; Semmens, 2005). But an awareness of the value and utility of history, like the humanities in general, should continue to become more deeply embedded in tourism practice. This in turn will help to make the case for expanding the role of historical understanding in Tourism Studies, albeit from small origins, as the discipline moves outwards from the practical, instrumental and narrowly business-oriented to realize the global importance of the phenomena it studies by extending its field of engagement to develop fuller understandings of background, context and influences. Such a development is, of course, greatly to be encouraged.

References

Appleby, J.O., Hunt, L. and Jacob, M. (1994) *Telling the Truth About History.* New York: Norton.

Aron, C. (1999) *Working at Play.* New York: Oxford University Press.

Bailey, P. (1978) *Leisure and Class in Victorian England.* London: Routledge and Kegan Paul.

Bann, S. (1990) *The Inventions of History.* Manchester: Manchester University Press.

Baranowski, S. (2004) *Strength through Joy: Consumerism and Mass Tourism in the Third Reich.* Cambridge: Cambridge University Press.

Baranowski, S. and Furlough,E. (eds.) (2001) *Being Elsewhere: Tourism, Consumer Culture and Identity in Modern Europe and North America.* Ann Arbor: University of Michigan Press.

Barber, C. (2002) *Exploring Blaenavon Industrial Landscape World Heritage Site.* Llanfoist: Bolrenge Books.

Battilani, P. and Strangio, D. (eds.) (2007) *Il Turismo e le Citta tra XVIII e XXI Secolo.* Milan: FrancoAngeli.

Berger, D. (2006) *The Development of Mexico's Tourism Industry: Pyramids by Day, Martinis by Night.* London: Palgrave Macmillan.

Berghoff, H., Korte, B. and Schneider, R. (eds.) (2002) *The Making of Modern Tourism: the Cultural History of the British Experience, 1600-2000.* London: Palgrave.

Black, J. (2003) *The British Abroad: the Grand Tour in the Eighteenth Century*. Stroud: Sutton.

Blume, M. (1992) *Cote d'Azur: Inventing the French Riviera*. London: Thames and Hudson.

Borsay, P. (2000) *The Image of Georgian Bath, 1700-2000*. Oxford: Oxford University Press.

Bray, A. and Raitz, V. (2001) *Flight to the Sun: the Story of the Holiday Revolution*. London: Continuum.

Brendon, P. (1991) *Thomas Cook: 150 Years of Popular Tourism*. London: Secker and Warburg.

Brodie, A. and Winter, G. (2007) *England's Seaside Resorts*. Swindon: English Heritage.

Butler, R.W. (ed.) (2005) *The Tourist Area Life Cycle*. Vols. 1 and 2, Clevedon: Channel View.

Buzard, J. (1993) *The Beaten Track*. Oxford: Clarendon.

Carter, I. (2001) *Railways and Culture in Britain*. Manchester: Manchester University Press.

Carter, I. (2008) *British Railway Enthusiasm*. Manchester: Manchester University Press.

Chadefaud, M. (1987) *Aux Origines du Tourisme dans les Pays de l'Adour*. Pau: Université de Pau.

Chambers, T. (2003) *Drinking the Waters: Creating an American Leisure Class at Nineteenth-Century Mineral Springs*. Washington, D.C.: Smithsonian Institution.

Chaplin, P. (2009) *Darts in England, 1900-39: a Social History*. Manchester: Manchester University Press.

Clark, P. and Rowlinson, M. (2004) The treatment of history in organizational studies: towards an "historic turn"? *Business History* **46**, pp. 331-52.

Corbin, A. (1994) *The Lure of the Sea*, Cambridge: Polity.

Cross, G. and Walton, J.K. (2005) *The Playful Crowd: Pleasure Places in the Twentieth Century*. New York: Columbia University Press.

Cunningham, H. (1980) *Leisure and the Industrial Revolution*. London: Croom Helm.

Davidson, J. and Spearritt, P. (2000) *Holiday Business: Tourism in Australia since 1870*. Carlton: Miegunyal Press.

Delahaye, A., Booth, C., Clark, P., Procter, S. and Rowlinson, M. (2009) The genre of corporate history. *Journal of Organizational Change Management* **22**, 27-48

Désert, G. (1983) *La Vie Quotidienne sur les Plages Normandes du Second Empire aux Années Folles*. Paris: L'Harmattan.

Di Viao, G. and Weisdorf, J.L. (2009) Ranking economic history journals: a citation-based impact-adjusted analysis. *Cliometrica*, published online 29 March.

Dickinson, W.E. (2007) *A Friend in Steam: One Man's Lifelong Passion for the Steam Railway*. Kettering: Silver Link.

Dreamland Trust (2009), www.savedreamland.co.uk accessed 7 September 2009.

Dubinsky, K. (1999) *The Second Greatest Disappointment: Honeymooning and Tourism at Niagara Falls*. New Brunswick, NJ: Rutgers University Press.

Endy, C. (2004) *Cold War Holidays: American Tourism in France*. Chapel Hill: University of North Carolina Press.

Evans, Richard J. (1997) *In Defence of History*. London: Granta.

Freeman, M. (1992) *Railways and the Victorian Imagination*. New Haven: Yale University Press.

Fussell, P. (1980) *Abroad: British Literary Travelling between the Wars*. Oxford: Oxford University Press.

Gale, T. and Botterill, D. (2005) A realist agenda for tourism studies. *Tourist Studies* **5**, 151-74.

Gaviria, A. (1974) *España a Go-go*. Madrid: Turner.

Gelber, S.M. (1999) *Hobbies: Leisure and the Culture of Work in America*. New York: Columbia University Press.

Gibson, L. and Pendlebury, J. (eds.) (2009) *Valuing historic environments*. Aldershot: Ashgate.

Gilbert, E.W. (1954) *Brighton: Old Ocean's Bauble*. London: Methuen.

Gingras, Y. (2008) Du mauvais usage de faux indicateurs. *Revue d'Histoire Moderne et Contemporaine* **55-4** bis, special issue on 'La fiebre de l'évaluation', 67-79.

Gorsuch, A.E. and Koenker, D.P. (eds.) (2006) *Turizm: the Russian and East European Tourist under Capitalism and Socialism*. Ithaca: Cornell University Press.

Gourvish, T.R. (1986) *British Railways, 1948-73: a Business History*. Cambridge: Cambridge University Press.

Gourvish, T.R. (2008) *Britain's Railways 1997-2005*. Oxford: Oxford University Press.

Grandits, H. and Taylor, K. (eds.) (2010) *Yugoslavia's Sunny Side: A History of Tourism in Socialism (1950s-1980s)*. Budapest: Central European University Press.

Gray, F. (2006) *Designing the Seaside*. London: Reaktion.

Hardy, D. and Ward, C. (1984) *Arcadia for All*. London: Mansell.

Harvie, C. (2002) Engineer's holiday: L.T.C. Rolt, industrial heritage and tourism, in Berghoff *et al.* (eds.), *The Making of Modern Tourism*.

Haug, C.J. (1982) *Leisure and Urbanism in Nineteenth-Century Nice*. Lawrence: Regents Press of Kansas.

Hazbun, W. (2008) *Beaches, Ruins, Resorts: the Politics of Tourism in the Arab World*. Minneapolis: University of Minnesota Press.

Hewison, R. (1987) *The Heritage Industry*. London: Methuen.

Holden, A. (2005) *Tourism Studies and the Social Sciences*. London: Routledge.

Journal of Tourism History (2009-, in progress). London: Routledge/ Taylor and Francis.

Koshar, R. (2000) *German Travel Cultures*. Oxford: Berg.

ICOMOS (2009) *Industrial and Technical Heritage in the World Heritage List*. Paris: UNESCO-ICOMOS Documentation Centre, July.

Lashley, C. and Morrison, A. (eds.), (2000) *In Search of Hospitality: Theoretical Perspectives and Debates*. London: Butterworth Heinemann.

Lee, F.S. (2007) The Research Assessment Exercise, the state and the dominance of mainstream economics in British universities. *Cambridge Journal of Economics* **31**, 309-25.

Lencek, L. and Bosker, G. (1998) *The Beach: The History of Paradise on Earth*. Harmondsworth: Penguin.

Lennon, J.J. and Foley, M. (eds.) (2000) *Dark Tourism*. London: Continuum.

Leon, W. and Rosenzweig, R. (eds.) (1989), *History Museums in the United States*. Urbana: University of Illinois Press.

Lincolnshire Coastal Action Zone (2006) *National Coastal Futures*, Report of Symposium at the Royal Renaissance Hotel, Skegness, 18-19 July.

Löfgren, O. (1999) *On Holidays: a History of Vacationing*, Berkeley: University of California Press.

MacCannell, D. (1976) *The Tourist*. London: Macmillan.

Merrill, D. (2001) Negotiating Cold War paradise: United States tourism, economic planning and cultural modernity in twentieth-century Puerto Rico. *Diplomatic History* **25**, 179-214.

Moore, K. (2000) *Museums and Popular Culture*. London: Continuum.

Morgan, N. and Pritchard, A. (1993) *Power and Politics at the Seaside*. Exeter: University of Exeter Press.

Nabarro, Sir G.D.N. (1971) *Severn Valley Steam*. London: Routledge and Kegan Paul.

Nicholson, N. (1955) *The Lakers: the Adventures of the First Tourists*. London: Robert Hale.

Pack, S.D. (2006) *Tourism and Dictatorship: Europe's Peaceful Invasion of Franco's Spain*. Basingstoke: Palgrave Macmillan.

Pastoriza, E. (ed.) (2002) *Las puertas al mar*. Buenos Aires: Biblos.

Pemble, J. (1987) *The Mediterranean Passion*. Oxford: Clarendon Press.

Perkin, H.J. (2002) *The Making of a Social Historian*. London: Athena.

Pimlott, J.A.R. (1947) *The Englishman's Holiday: a Social History*. London: Faber.

Pudney, J. (1953) *The Thomas Cook Story*. London: Michael Joseph.

Rowlinson, M. (2002) Cadbury World. *Labour History Review* **67**, 101-19.

Samuel, R. (1994) *Theatres of Memory*, Vol. 1. London: Verso.

Semmens, K. (2005) *Seeing Hitler's Germany: Tourism in the Third Reich*. Basingstoke: Palgrave Macmillan.

Shaffer, M.S. (2002) *See America First: Tourism and National Identity 1880-1940*. Washington DC: Smithsonian Institute.

Shields, R. (1991) *Places on the Margin*. London: Routledge.

Simmons, J. (1986) *The Railway in Town and Country, 1830-1914*. Newton Abbot: David and Charles.

Sterngass, J. (2001) *First Resorts: Pursuing Pleasure at Saratoga Springs, Newport and Coney Island*. Baltimore: Johns Hopkins University Press.

Storia del Turismo (2000-, in progress) Milan: FrancoAngeli.

Swinglehurst, E. (1974) *The Romantic Journey: the Story of Thomas Cook and Victorian Travel*. London: Pica Editions.

Thomas, D. St J. (1976) *The Country Railway*. Newton Abbot: David and Charles.

Thompson, E.P. (1972) Anthropology and the discipline of historical context. *Midland History* **1**, 41-55.

Tissot, L. (2000) *Naissance d'une Industrie Touristique: les Anglais et la Suisse au XIXe Siecle*. Lausanne: Payot Lausanne.

Tissot, L. (ed.) (2003), *Construction of a Tourism Industry in the 19th and 20th century: international perspectives*. Neuchatel, Switzerland: Alphil.

Tosh, J. (2008) *Why History Matters*. Basingstoke: Palgrave Macmillan.

Towner, J. (1996) *An Historical Geography of Recreation and Tourism in the Western World, 1540-1940*. Chichester: Wiley.

Turner, L. and Ash, F. (1975) *The Golden Hordes: International Tourism and the Pleasure Periphery*. London: Constable.

Tourismusgeschichte(n) (2009) special issue of *Voyage. Jahrbuch fur Reise- & Tourismusfurschung*, Band 8.

Wallace, M. (1989) Making Mickey Mouse history: portraying the past at Disney World, in Leon and Rosenzweig (eds.), *History Museums in the United States*.

Walton, J.K. (1978) *The Blackpool Landlady: a Social History*. Manchester: Manchester University Press.

Walton, J.K. (1983) *The English Seaside Resort: a Social History 1750-1914*. Leicester University Press.

Walton, J.K. (1995) The lion and the newt: a British view of American conservatives' fear of social history. *Journal of Social History* **29**, special supplement, 73-84.

Walton, J.K. (2000) *The British Seaside: Holidays and Resorts in the Twentieth Century*. Manchester: Manchester University Press.

Walton, J.K. (2003) Hospitality and history, *The Hospitality Review* **5**, 40-44.

Walton, J.K. (ed.) (2005a) *Histories of Tourism: Representation, Identity and Conflict*. Clevedon: Channel View Press

Walton, J.K. (2005b) Power, speed and glamour: the naming of express steam locomotives in inter-war Britain, *Journal of Transport History*, third series, **26**, 1-19.

Walton, J.K. (2008) New directions in British historiography: the emergence of cultural history? *Revue Francaise de Civilisation Britannique* **14**(4), 19-30.

Walton, J.K. (2009a) Prospects in tourism history: evolution, state of play and future developments. *Tourism Management* **30**, 783-93.

Walton, J.K. (2009b) Histories of tourism, in T. Jamal and M. Robinson (eds.), *The Sage Handbook of Tourism Studies*. London: Sage Publications, pp. 115-29.

Walton, J.K. (2009c) Marketing the imagined past: Captain Cook and cultural tourism in North Yorkshire, in R. Thomas (ed.), *Managing regional tourism: a case study of Yorkshire, England*. Ilkley: Great Northern Books, pp. 220-32.

Walton, J.K. (2010a) Thomas Cook, in R. Butler and R. Russell (eds.), *Giants of Tourism*. Wallingford: CABI.

Walton, J.K. (2010b) New directions in business history: themes, approaches and opportunities, *Business History*.

Walton, J.K. and Smith, J. (1996) The first century of beach tourism in Spain: San Sebastián and the "playas del norte" from the 1830s to the 1930s, in J. Towner, M. Barke and M.T. Newton (eds.), *Tourism in Spain: Critical Issues*. Wallingford: CAB Publications, pp. 35-61.

Walton, J.K., and Wood, J. (2008) La station balnéaire comme site du Patrimoine mondial? Le cas de Blackpool, in Y. Perret-Gentil, A. Lottin and J.-P. Poussu (eds.), *Les villes balnéaires d'Europe occidentale du XVIIIe siecle a nos jours*. Paris: Presses de l'Université Paris-Sorbonne, pp. 423-52.

Walton, J.K., and Wood, J. (2009) Reputation and regeneration: history and the heritage of the recent past in the re-making of Blackpool, in L. Gibson and J. Pendlebury (eds.), *Valuing Historic Environments*, pp. 115-37.

Walvin, J. (1978) *Beside the Seaside*. London: Allen Lane.

Ward, C. and Hardy, D. (1986) *Goodnight Campers*. London: Mansell.

West, B. (1988) The making of the English working past: a critical view of the Ironbridge Gorge Museum, in R. Lumley (ed.), *The Museum Time Machine*. London: Routledge, pp. 36-61.

White, H.P. (1986) *Forgotten Railways*. Newton Abbot: David and Charles.

White, R. (2005) *On Holidays: a History of Getting Away in Australia*. North Melbourne: Pluto Press.

Whittaker, N. (1995) *Platform Souls: the Trainspotter as Twentieth-Century Hero*. London: Victor Gollancz.

Wilson, A. (ed.) (1993) *Rethinking Social History*. Manchester: Manchester University Press.

Withey, L. (1997) *Grand Tours and Cook's Tours*. New York: Morrow.

Glossary

Annals of Tourism Research: Journal published by Elsevier a "social sciences journal focusing upon the academic perspectives of tourism. While striving for a balance of theory and application, *Annals* is ultimately dedicated to developing theoretical constructs. Its strategies are to invite and encourage offerings from various disciplines; to serve as a forum through which these may interact; and thus to expand frontiers of knowledge in and contribute to the literature on tourism social science." www.elsewview.com

Authenticity: Introduced by MacCannell (1973) as a research programme in tourism social sciences, it relates to the sociology of motivations. It tends to relate to the products of tourism such as cuisine or festivals and whether they are carried out traditionally and by the correct custom by locals.

Ning Wang in J Jafari (2003). *Encyclopaedia of Tourism*. Taylor & Francis

MacCannell, D. (1973) "Staged Authenticity: arrangements of social space in tourist settings" *American Journal of Sociology* **79** (3): 589-603

Business History: Journal published by Routledge through Taylor & Francis. The journal "is an international journal concerned with the long-run evolution and contemporary operation of business systems and enterprises. Its primary purpose is to make available the findings of advanced research, empirical and conceptual, into matters of global significance, such as corporate organization and growth, multinational enterprise, business efficiency, entrepreneurship, technological change, finance, marketing, human resource management, professionalization and business culture." www.tandf.co.uk

Centre for Tourism and Cultural Change at Leeds Metropolitan University: "Through academic research, collaborative projects, consultancy, conferences, publications, professional development and postgraduate programmes, we aim to contribute to a more comprehensive understanding of the complexities of tourism as a global phenomenon at different social and political scales. We are interested in the theoretical and political issues related to tourism/tourist culture, tourism development, and the mobilisation of cultural resources by, and for, the tourism sector." www.tourism-culture.com

Coastal Communities Alliance: A network of over 40 local authorities and coastal organisations in the UK "who seek to promote best practice in coastal regeneration and to inform policy and funding by providing local evidence and local solutions for the distinctive socio-economic problems of coastal towns." www.coastalcommunities.co.uk

Grand Tour: Emerging from the tradition in Europe from the early modern period in which the sons of the upper classes were sent abroad on a Grand Tour as a means of completing his education, the Grand Tour saw other parts of society and many of the upper classes toured around Europe in search of cultural heritage. Over the course of the sixteenth, seventeenth and eighteenth centuries thousands of Britons, Germans, French and Russians travelled around the Continent, principally to France, Italy, Switzerland and Germany in search of culture and the arts. Inspired by the aesthetic principles of the picturesque and Edmund Burke's concept of the sublime, wealthy Britons moved between the mountainous regions and the major places of cultural importance as ascribed by the many guidebooks published in the period.

Heritage: The word heritage refers to inheritance, thus in terms of national heritage this could mean landscape, natural resources, built environment etc. This is also linked to cultural heritage which refers to the inherited physical and intangible features of a society, nation or group of people.

Industrial Heritage Tourism: Industrial heritage include the "material remains of industry, such as sites, buildings and architecture, plants, machinery and equipment. Industrial heritage also refers to housing, industrial settlements, industrial landscapes, products and processes and documentation of the industrial society." Thus industrial heritage tourism sees "the development of touristic activities and industries on man-made sites, buildings and landscapes that originated with industrial processes of earlier periods".

P. F. Xie. Developing industrial heritage tourism: A case study of the proposed jeep museum in Toledo, Ohio. *Tourism Management* 27: 6 (2006), pp 1321-1330

Edwards & Llurdes. "Mines and quarries: Industrial heritage tourism." *Annals of Tourism Research* **23** (1996), pp. 341–363.

Industrial Revolution: Usually linked to the industrial and mechanical innovation of the 18th and 19th centuries, first in Britain and then in the rest of Europe, particularly referring to the method of production or mechanisation of a process of production in an industry, for example mass production. The industrial revolution saw the shift from a agricultural economy to an industrialised one in Britain. This trend is also linked with mass urbanisation as the population moved into cities to work in the new industries.

P. Mathias (2001). *The First Industrial Nation: The Economic History of Britain 1700-1914*. Routledge

International Commission for the History of Travel and Tourism (ICHTT): Affiliated to the International Commission for the Historical Sciences and founded at the '"Tourisms: Identities, Environments, Conflicts and Histories" Conference (University of Central Lancashire, Preston, UK, 21-23 June 2001).

"The Commission represents all scholars interested in the history of travel and tourism, promotes research in these rich and rapidly-expanding fields of interest, and is working on creating an effective network and profitable exchange of information, ideas and research projects between historians of different countries." www.ichtt.org

International Commission for the Historical Sciences: Also known as le Comité International des Sciences Historiques (CISH) was founded in Geneva on May 15, 1926. The organisation unites and organises intellectuals in the historical sciences from around the world. www.cish.org

Journal of Tourism History: Journal published by Routledge through Taylor & Francis, founded in 2009, the *Journal of Tourism History* is supported by the International Commission for the History of Travel and Tourism.

Mass tourism: Refers to the steady stream of tourists to holiday destinations that has been developing since the 1960s. This is linked to the cheaper transport and affluence in industrialised countries.

Jeremy Boissevain, in J Jafari (2003). *Encyclopaedia of Tourism*. Taylor & Francis

National Railway Museum: Located in York, UK the museum is the largest railway museum in the world.

Open Air Industrial Museum: A museum that recreates a historic buildings, a town or section of a town in order for the visitor to move around and experience travelling through a historical setting. Volunteers and employees in costume from the historical period demonstrate and guide visitors around. They are also known as 'living museums' for this reason.

Post-modern: Linked strongly to critical theory. In terms of tourism, the growth of mass tourism is linked to postmodernism as tourists travel on known and well trodden paths with little knowledge or understanding on the regions and places they visit.

Dean MacCannell in J Jafari (2003). *Encyclopaedia of Tourism*. Taylor & Francis

Railway preservation: Usually linked to railway heritage. Railway perseveration looks at conserve the railway equipment and technology, including locomotives, carriages, track and stations no longer used.

Storia del Turismo: Italian journal edited Annunziata Berrino and published from Naples (mainly in Italian) since 2000 by the Istituto per la Storia del Risorgimento Italiano.

Thomas Cook: In 1841 Thomas Cook arranged an excursion from Leicester to Loughborough (UK) on the newly extended Midland Counties Railway on the first advertised privately chartered trip. Cook continued these excursions, including organised trips to the Great Exhibition in London in 1851. In the mid-1850s he started to take groups abroad, first to Europe and then further afield in the 1860s. Thomas Cook and Son was set up as a travel agency, set up branches across the world and produced guidebooks. The company was sold in the 1920s but continues as a travel agency to this day.

Tourism Area Life Cycle (TALC): Created by Richard Butler, TALC is based on the product cycle concept, sales starting off slowly, rapid growth, stability followed by decline. Visitors to a area will start off small, limited by access, facilities and knowledge, as facilities increase as will visitor numbers, then with marketing and further facilities the number of visitors will grow rapidly and then eventually decline as carrying capacity is reached.

UNESCO World Heritage Sites: UNESCO is a specialised agency of the United Nations and covers education, science, culture and communication. "Its aim is to build peace in the world through knowledge, social progress, exchange and mutual understanding among peoples." www.unesco.org

Voyage: German travel and tourism journal founded and edited by Hasso Spode.

Volunteers: Persons working on behalf of others or for a cause without payment for time and services.

Tourism Policy

Noel Scott

Contents

Noel Scott is Professor at Griffith Institute for Tourism, Griffith University, Australia, and the author of several books and over 150 academic papers. He has extensive experience as a senior tourism manager and researcher and over 25 years in industry research positions. His research interests involve aspects of destination policy, planning, management and marketing. He is on the editorial boards of three journals: *Service Industries Journal*, *Current Issues in Tourism* and *Revista Academica do Observatorio de Inocacao do Turismo* (Brasil).

A hyperlinked PDF version of this review is available for download from the CTR area of Goodfellow Pubishers' website: http://www.goodfellowpublishers.com/ctr

Introduction

The study of government policy seeks to understand how policy decisions are created, the information, interests and values involved in policy processes and what their impacts are (Hall, 2008). Tourism policy is an important area for study because of its practical and theoretical importance. Tourism policy studies of *practical significance* to government may be in relation to bilateral airline negotiations (Elliott, 1997), decisions about provision of facilities and services and land use planning (Kerr, 2003), interactions with other economic sectors such as agriculture and mining, publicly 'owned' resources such as national parks as attractions, the issuing of tourist visas and in the funding of destination marketing (Ahmed & Krohn, 1990). Government develops policy to address market failure in destination marketing (Smeral, 1998) and to mitigate the cultural, social and environmental effects of tourism (Kerr, 2003). Governments control the amount of paid holidays (York & Zhang, 2010), currency movements (Wanhill, 1987), international affairs, border security, and social and community development. Governments policy in areas such as agriculture (Leslie & Black, 2005; Williams & Ferguson, 2005), security (Blake & Sinclair, 2003), and health (Zeng, Carter, & De Lacy, 2005) can have a profound effect on tourism flows. This government involvement is pervasive and is at national, provincial and local levels (Kerr, 2003) requiring center and region to coordinate their policies (OECD, 2012). Tourism provides around 10% of the world's economy on average but varies in its impact in particular countries with consequent effects on the communities and natural environments with which it interacts.

Tourism is an open system where the potential for collateral impact and damage from external shocks, crises and disasters is significant (B. Ritchie, Crotts, Zehrer, & Volsky, 2014). Despite the pervasive government involvement in tourism, it is only recently that formally stated and publicly accessible national tourism policies have become common (Bhanugopan, 2001; Buhalis, 2001; Reid & Schwab, 2006). Tourism may be affected indirectly by government policy in a related area; or directly through active pursuit of a policy objective. In many countries, tourism policy is directed to achieving regional economic development (Harrison & Schipani, 2007).

Tourism policy, explicitly or implicitly involves beliefs and values, about what is good and bad, providing the basis for allocation of resources. However in many cases, the lack of a clear answer to the problem being addressed, has led such policy issues to be called 'wicked' problems (Rittel & Weber, 1973). An example from Eritrea is the trade-off between the 'social and ecological dangers posed by large-scale development', and a 'desperate need of foreign investment and the foreign exchange earnings some of which could be generated through tourism' (Burns, 1999, p. 343). This means that it is unlikely for there to be positive-sum outcomes for all participants resulting in 'winners and losers (Hall & Jenkins, 2004). Thus, policy development is seen as complex (McDonald, 2009), and may be best dealt with as a complex adaptive system (Farrell & Twining-Ward, 2005).

Tourism also provides an interesting context in which theories developed in more traditional areas may be tested. Tourism provides a complex bundle of hedonic and mostly discretionary services, that is distinct from the agricultural, resource extraction, or manufacturing sectors that have traditionally been the focus of government economic policy. Operationally it involves an ill-defined heterogeneous set of stakeholders in often simultaneous cooperative and competitive behavior at both destination and global scales. These stakeholders include tourism operators, cooperative organizations, government bodies, networks of people and organizations, the community, non-government organizations, and so on. Therefore tourism policy may be a domain for examination of concepts such as trust, competition and collaboration, social identity, power; and viewed through disciplinary and ideological 'lenses', and at different levels (macro, meso, micro) of analysis (Jenkins, 2001).

Therefore we may discern an industry policy and academic policy literature. Tourism policy research may seek to provide advice to government, or it may see policy as the object of study. An industry perspective would look to change policy to secure a competitive edge in increasingly global consumer markets (Ritchie & Crouch). Bramwell and Lane (2006, p. 1) characterise this approach as 'distinctly positivist and empirical in outlook; it leaves the impression that it is dealing with objective, value-free or neutral knowledge'. The global expansion of tourism has provided need for policy advice and academics have recorded instances of policy in case studies leading to an unconsolidated literature dominated by 'policy led and industry sponsored work so the analysis tends to internalize industry led priorities and perspectives' (Franklin & Crang, 2001, p. 5).

This review of the academic tourism policy literature attempts to organize a 'diverse and fragmented literature' (Coles, Hall, & Duval, 2006, p. 296) about which there is 'little agreement about how [it] should be studied and the reasons underpinning such studies' (Hall & Jenkins, 1995, p. 2). The paper builds on the work of Ambrosie (2010) who allocated categorized papers on a rational to social paradigm continuum, as well as the numerous books on 'tourism policy' and 'tourism policy and planning'. Other papers have reviewed a particular topic in a focused way such as urban tourism competitiveness policy (Connelly, 2007, p. 85). This paper analyses the literature using the concept of the policy cycle, ideology and values implicitly or explicitly adopted, level of policy and methodology.

The Literature of Tourism and Policy

Reviewing and integrating such an unconsolidated literature is a daunting task and studies of policy, planning, and analysis of tourism are difficult to delineate. Many journal articles include 'policy' in their list of keywords on the basis that their findings may be of interest to policymakers, and papers may discuss the policy implications of their work in the conclusions section. The inclusion or exclusion of papers that provide policy implications in a discussion that is otherwise about marketing, consumer behavior, economics, sociology, biology, and so on, may explain why there is disagreement over the size of the tourism policy literature. Some authors have argued that the tourism policy literature is limited (Ballantyne, Packer, & Axelsen, 2009), while a recent review using 'public' and 'policy' as search terms in a search of 18 journals over the period 1980-2007 has identified over 400 articles (Ambrosie, 2010). Indeed, based on the pervasive government involvement in tourism, and its interest in the impacts of tourism, it is arguable that all tourism research is policy research.

The concept of policy has no accepted definition (Airey & Chong, 2011). 'Policy' is derived from the word 'polis', denoting a city-state of ancient Greece, from which the terms 'politics', 'polity' and 'police' are also derived (Colebatch, 2009, p. 63). One way of defining policy is as a 'handle on the way we are governed, a concept which we use to make sense of what we do' (Colebatch, 2009, p. 63) or 'whatever governments choose to do or not to do' (Dye, 1992, p. 2). In this sense policy is a name to describe the general actions and outcomes of government. However, as governments are complex and produce many outcomes, such a definition may be considered summative only (Dubin, 1976), useful as an intro-duction to a complex phenomenon but which requires further elaboration.

Analysis of the definitions of policy used in the literature suggests that it involves some sort of decision, either expressed through a process or an outcome. Thus policy is a 'web of decisions and actions that allocate values' (Easton, 1953, p. 128). Alternatively tourism policy includes government action, inaction, deci-sions, and non-decisions as these all imply a deliberate choice between alterna-tives (Richter, 1983). The notion that public policy involves choices about both whether to develop a policy and what type of policy choices need to be made suggests that developing public policy is a political activity, influenced by the characteristics of a particular society, the formal structures of government, and the local political system (Hall, 2000), and 'political debate about what the agenda is' (D. Dredge & Jenkins, 2007, p. 10). Extensive private sector involve-ment in tourism means this debate extends beyond government and includes national tourist organizations, consumer associations, pressure groups, hotels, restaurants, tour operators, travel agencies (Van Doorn, 1982, p. 155).

This leads to a study of tourism policy from the perspective of political economy (Britton, 1982; Elliott, 1997; Mosedale, 2011), where ideology affects tourism policy and the degree of development reached (Sessa, 1976). Swain (1999, p. 1008) suggests that the study of policy and power in tourism 'includes a broad range of concepts from ideology to exchange rates and visa control'. An increasingly important view associated with the ideology of neo-liberalism is that policy communities or networks of interested stakeholders play an important part in the development of issues and policy formulation processes. Thus policy and the policy process will change over time, and what is 'good' policy must be determined by argument not scientific information although science has an important role to play in policy development.

The rational approach to policy is therefore contrasted with policy as a social process (Lawrence & Dredge, 2007) involving communication (Stevenson, Airey, & Miller, 2008), and importantly that policy cannot be separated from implementation (Greenwood, Williams, & Shaw, 1990). The policy implementation process may also require a number of other steps such as administrative coordination and policy coordination (Elliott, 1997; Hall, 1999), and the exercise of power (Marzano & Scott, 2009). In summary then, there are a broad range of characteristics which identify policy. Policy involves actions, decision, politics, values and ideological beliefs, social processes involving communication, and outcome such as legislation and implementation.

One area of dispute in tourism is the extent to which policy and planning overlap and indeed much tourism policy development occurs in the context of the planning processes. Some authors separate planning from policy development, where planning … 'is a process that occurs up to the point of decision making. Policy denotes the formal adoption of a position by government' (Dredge & Jenkins, 2007, p. 10), and is the basis of policymaking (Van Doorn, 1982). Other authors consider that the output of the policy process is an overall strategy for tourism development (Ritchie & Crouch, 2003) that presumably leads to development of a plan; and that policy may not be stated separately but must be inferred from plans developed, often at national level. Again, some consider policy and planning overlapping where policies are ongoing principles and broad goals while planning overlaps and 'is the process by which decisions are made as to the optimum way to implement policies and achieve goals' (Veal, 2002, p. 5). In the tourism literature policy is often considered different from politics and is the outcome of some political process (Altinay & Bowen, 2006). Thus politics has a formative impact on tourism policies (Matthews & Richter, 1991; Richter, 1983) but is a distinct process (Henderson, 2003). We may conclude that policy and planning overlap in tourism. This may be due to assumptions among governments that tourism will happen, and is a form of development that requires planning and implementation rather that serious ideological and political debate.

This section has highlighted the need for this review, some limitations of the literature relating to policy, the scope of this review, definitions of policy and how policy overlaps with planning and politics. In the next section, this review looks at the creation of public policy using an adopted similar to that of the policy cycle model as a structure. The policy cycle model is an analytical perspective which simplifies the tourism policymaking process by segregating it into formal stages (Pforr, 2001), typically agenda setting, formulation, decision making (grouped here as development of the aim), implementation, and evaluation. In addition the section will examine 'development' as one dominant aim of tourism policy.

Creating Public Policy

Many factors affect the development of policy. In this section we analyse policy firstly in terms of a government's aims or objectives and in particular tourism *development*. This is pervasive in the literature of tourism, and we find it in other terms, such as sustainable development, alternative development (Weaver, 1995), and so on. After discussing the concept of development, this review examines a range of other policy objectives found in the tourism literature.

Policy Aims, Objectives and Ideologies

Government policy objectives reflect its responsibilities and ideology. Objectives can be formal or informal, stated or unstated (Elliott, 1997). *Formal* objectives are normally consistent with the aims laid down in the national constitution or in the party policy documents or manifesto. The dominant *informal* objectives may be to achieve certain stakeholder aims, or simply to hold on to power and stay in office. Jenkins and Henry (1982, p. 501) describes government involvement in tourism as active; a deliberate action 'introduced to favour the tourism sector'; or *passive* 'an action which may have implications for tourism, but is not specifically intended to favour or influence tourism'. Traditionally, government involvement in tourism has largely been a product of wider policy aims such as the national balance of payments, or regional economic development targets (Kruczala, 1990; Smyth, 1986).

Early reasons for government involvement in developing countries in the post second world war period were development of foreign exchange earnings; foreign investment; employment in tourism; land use policies; and air transport and tourism (Jenkins & Henry, 1982). These objectives may be distinguished from the means of achieving these objectives; Richter and Richter (1985) list five *policy options* for South Asian countries (in 1985): public versus private tourism development; domestic versus international tourism; class versus mass tourism; centralization versus decentralization; and integrated versus enclave tourism.

A central theme in the literature concerns development of tourism as an instrument of economic development and as a tool developing countries - a focus of research in tourism studies since the 1970s (Hall, 2007). Numerous books and journal articles have examined tourism development (Aramberri & Butler, 2005; Burns & Novelli, 2008; Telfer & Sharpley, 2008), and papers (Bhanugopan, 2001; Gartner, 2004; Hall & Michael, 2007; Khadaroo & Seetanah, 2007; Lindberg, Andersson, Dellaert, & Dellaert, 2001; Nilsson, 2001; Puppim de Oliveira, 2003; Reid & Schwab, 2006; Rosentraub & Joo, 2009; Sharpley, 2009; Telfer, 2002; Tosun, 2001; Tsartas, 2003; Turegano, 2006; Wilkinson, 2001). Development theories 'consciously or unconsciously express a preferred notion of what development is and these preferences, in turn, reflect values' (Sharpley & Telfer, 2002, p. 13) and ideology.

Despite its centrality and importance however, the concept of development appears to defy definition (Whitford, 2009). In the early policy literature, tourism was seen uncritically as a form of economic development that sought to improve the living conditions of people (Tosun, 2001, p. 290). Wight (2002), in the context of sustainability, distinguishes between growth and development. Economic growth is an increase in quantity, while economic development is an improvement in the quality of life without necessarily causing an increase in quantity of resources consumed, but instead an increase in self-reliance (Lepp, 2008). Goldsworthy (1988) considers that development is usually considered a purely good outcome but in fact there is no likelihood of positive-sum outcomes with gains to all participants. Development involves policy choices and some stakeholders may benefit from it while others lose.

Early attempts at proactive development intervention were subject to criticism by dependency theory authors. Britton (1982, p. 334) defines dependency as 'involv[ing] the subordination of national economic autonomy to meet the interests of foreign pressure groups and privileged local classes rather than those development priorities arising from a broader political consensus'. It has been claimed that the outcome of the race to modernize results in internal elites and leads to concentration of power and dependency (Steiner, 2006), and the erosion of 'political and social autonomy' (Macnaught, 1982, p. 377). A more sophisticated view is that dependency results from the failure to improve the social and political institutions as modernization occurs (Dieke, 1993) and Turegano (2006) rejects dependency as inevitable in favour of path dependency.

Based on the 'failure' of early tourism in developing countries and the lessons learned, a number of other development theories evolved. Azcairate (2006) lists these as modernization, dependency theory, human development and post-development. Harrison and Schipani (2007) provide a historical sequence of the changes from 'simplistic models of modernization', to the reaction evident in dependency theory, to alternative tourism, the inclusion of social and environmental protection, and community based approaches (Hawkins & Mann, 2007). A similar sequence is found in the four platforms of Jafari (1989) - (advocacy, cautionary, adaptancy and knowledge based) that reflect ideological and policy changes (Swain et al., 1999). Weaver (2001) has summarised the relationship between tourism platforms, paradigm shifts, tourism structure and ecotourism status in Western societies.

Along with these successive changes in development paradigm, the focus of tourism policy has changed from pure promotion, to product development, to maintaining competitiveness (Fayos-Sola, 1996). Most recently, post-development studies have understood development as a global discourse resisted by local 'Others' although this discourse may be considered a two way process mediated by powerful local actors (Azcairate, 2006). Each paradigm emphasises different aims and roles for tourism that represent 'the substance of policy' (Kerr, 2003). Each is connected with or emphasises functional roles for government such as: coordination, planning, legislation, entrepreneurial support, stimulation, promotion, social tourism, and public interest protection (Hall, 2000).

We may also characterize policy based on the problem it addresses. Tourism is a complex domain (Grant, 2004, p. 221) that touches upon a wide ranges of 'problem areas' such as aboriginal rights, aviation, biodiversity, disability and access, domestic tourism, events, health, innovation, knowledge and learning, development/land use, national parks, place identity, political legitimacy, regional development, rural tourism, safety/crisis management, training and human resources, recreation, urban development. Each of these numerous related domains is the subject of a specific literature and various policy prescriptions leading to a view of policy as 'an outcome' rather than 'a process' (Colebatch, 2009). From an outcome perspective each of the problem areas is subject to expert opinion on the best 'solution', a view that diminishes the political debate and ideological beliefs.

As discussed above, policies are influenced by ideological arguments about tourism, especially in developing states (Mathews, 1975), and it is important to understand the ideological basis for policy development in order to obtain insight into workings of government (Whitford, 2009). Many different ideological positions are available such as liberalism, social democracy, communism and mercantilism (O'Neil, 2007, p. 47). These differ in terms of the role of the state in the economy (i.e. liberalism: little involvement; minimal welfare state, social democracy some state ownership and regulation; large welfare state); the relative importance of the market; how policy is made, and the type of policies that are acceptable. In many countries one ideology may be dominant, and may vary over time. Tourism policy in Australia (Airey & Ruhanen, 2014) and New Zealand (Shone & Ali Memon, 2008) has increasingly been underpinned by a neo-liberalist ideology. Indeed, this ideology has been suggested as influencing development policy in provincial rural communities in Canada (Mair, 2006, p. 39) and in Peru (Desforges, 2000) and many other countries.

Neo-liberalism is 'a theory of political economic practices which proposes that human well-being can best be advanced by the maximization of entrepreneurial freedoms within an institutional framework characterized by private property rights, individual liberty, free markets and free trade' (Harvey, 2006, p. 145). Duffy (2008, p. 329) considers it a 'process by which market-based regulation is expanded, the role of the state is reduced, and a complex array of public–private networks operate'. Neo-liberalism has been associated with the commodification of nature (Duffy, 2008) and emphasises deregulation and a strong interest in the concept of governance as will be discussed later in this paper.

Geographic Level of Policy

Tourism policy has been studied at a number of geographic levels ranging from global, multi-country national, regional, to local government and may be multi-level. Many of the issues that affect tourism transcend borders: Wheatcroft (1988) examined aviation policy in the expanded European Union. Globalization is a factor that has influenced the development of multi-country policy (Hannam, 2002; Hjalager, 2007; Sugiyarto, Blake, & Sinclair, 2003) and requires coordination across national boundaries. The development of the General Agreement on Trade in Services (GATS) is an example of how transnational policy and processes are affecting tourism (Edgell, 1995). Dredge has conducted a body of research on the subnational level in Australia, (2001). At the local authority level, policy making is often constrained by higher levels of government (Human, 1994). Tovar and Lockwood (2008) examines local attitudes to the effect of tourism on community in Tasmania. There is often also an interaction between levels of policy due to the need for collaborations between levels of government policy makers, such as Federal and State governments in Australia (D. Dredge & Jenkins, 2003). Greenwood (1990, pp. 55-56) argues that there may be "distortion of policy objectives as it passes through implementing agencies could be regarded, at a crude level of abstraction, as akin to a process of 'Chinese Whispers'". In the European Union, policy is needed at three levels,

European Union, national and local that should be compatible with a degree of consultation if not cooperation, between the levels (Greenwood et al., 1990).

A 'whole-of-government' approach to tourism policy adopted in New Zealand is discussed by Zahra and Ryan (2005). In general this approach is difficult to implement as the broad inputs and effects of tourism policy leads to conflicts between government departments. Pearlman (1990) for example discusses macro-policy conflicts between social tourism subsidised by the state for domestic tourists and international tourism as well as difficulties with central planning of the economy. Richter (2003) notes that there is a lack of coordinated policy making in the area of health and tourism across countries. Pearce (1998) discusses the development of tourism in Paris as significantly related to urban planning and policy. Tourism policy is often driven by a broad policy agenda and action in other spheres rather than particularly targeted at tourism (Church, Ball, Bull, & Tyler, 2000, p. 316). Tourism policy also may in turn affect other policy domains with Expo events policy affecting housing (Olds, 1998). It is also used to rationalise other interests, such as a desire amongst enthusiasts to see trams in Christchurch, New Zealand (Pearce, 2001).

Policy Making Process

The policy cycle approach examines the process of making policy, hence moving the focus from particular policy aims, ideology, outcomes, countries and levels of government, and towards recognition of the complexity of policymaking. Hall (2002) suggests that a five stage pattern of policy attention to emergent issues will be followed: pre-problem stage, alarmed discovery and euphoric enthusiasm, realisation of the cost of significant progress, gradual decline of intense public interest and the post-problem stage. However this can only be a first approach as it does not recognise the complexity of policy development. Instead policy making is a complex process of identification and attention; a "continuing iterative process" in which ...factors are interpreted and reinterpreted, thus further influencing the perceptions of policy makers (Weed, 2006, p. 238); and a 'process of issue identification and management where multiple issues are being simultaneously identified, framed, prioritised and de-prioritised' (Wray, 2009, p. 675).

Issues can be further influenced by events, personalities, pressures groups and institutional failure, as well as scale and time (Lawrence & Dredge, 2007). McCoy (1982, p. 277) considers "public policy formulation is a process of conflict and compromise; a matter of mediating between competing factions with 'private interests' and defining the 'public interest' or the 'national interest'," which Bramwell considers path dependent (2009). It is essentially a social process, involving communication and negotiation between people in the context of wider change (Stevenson et al., 2008). Thus there is general agreement that policy making is complex and more of an art that a science, involving communication, negotiation, interests and issue framing.

The issues considered in policy may be 'national' interests and important to all the population. Ritchie (1988) argues for consensus policy formulation in tourism through surveys of resident attitudes. However policy development is often considered as controlled by elites (Yasarata, Altinay, Burns, & Okumus, 2010) or power blocs; with a dominance of dominance of close business-government ties (Craik, 1990; Hall, 1999). There has been increasing examination of the effectiveness of tourism policies in achieving their stated aim (Andriotis, 2001). Policy implementation can be considered part of the policy process, and requires the development of skills and competences (Henry & Jackson, 1996), and may involve vested interests (Thomas & Thomas, 1998). Barriers to implementation of sustainable tourism policy include; economic priority (short term economic focus wins over long term social and environmental concerns); lack of planning (too much damage was already done and initiatives were not strong enough to apply to already damaged areas); lack of stakeholder involvement; lack of integration with regional and national frameworks and policies; lack of accountability of politicians (lack of political will); and lack of coordination with other government parties (political clash) (Dodds, 2007). Dodds and Butler (2010) indicate that self-interest is a barrier to implementing sustainable tourism policies. Ioannides (1995, p. 591) found that to avoid a failure of sustainable policy implementation, it is important to maintain effective dialogue between communities and policy makers, and that one way to achieve this is through community visioning workshops whereby different interest groups in the host locality express their fears and aspirations. Means to avoiding conflict in tourism development may be grouped into three main categories: power-coercive; empirical-rational; and normative-educative (Prunier, Sweeney, & Geen, 1993). Backward mapping (Greenwood et al., 1990, p. 55) is another technique for policy implementation.

A policy output may be a statement on an issue, a non-decision, or the creation and use of an instrument. Logar (2010) discusses the effects of policy instruments for sustainable tourism on identified tourism impacts and issues in Crikvenica, Croatia. Policy outputs should be distinguished from policy outcomes, which may be unintended (Hall & Jenkins, 2004). There are a range of instruments to implement policy (Puppim de Oliveira, 2003) including government legislation, directives and guidance, fiscal and monetary measures, to the creation of special bodies (Airey, 1983); investment incentives (Ward, 1989, p. 241) and eco-taxes (Cantallops, 2004). Government intervention in tourism includes the regulation of tourist guiding in terms of licensing, certification, training, pay and benefits, marketing and conducting tours, and the organization and professional ethics of guides (Dahles, 2002). There may be as many 'instruments as there are targets of policy' (Kerr, 2003, p. 33). Another instrument is a non-decision (Reed, 1997, p. 572) where no decisions are taken or necessary, as well as when conscious choices are made to do nothing, to thwart demands for change, or to adopt plans that are imperfectly implemented.

Governments and their critics have become more aware of and interested in the study of the process, outcomes, and impacts of tourism public policies. Deegan (2000) reviews successes of tourism in Ireland and considers there is a need to study the causal links between policy and performance. Baretje (1982) suggests that tourism's outcomes should be measured properly to ensure correct policy decisions. Hence, the evaluation of government decisions, actions, and programs, and therefore of tourism public policies, is receiving growing recognition (Hall & Jenkins, 2004). However, this may be difficult 'because of the influence of a number of other factors, chief among which are external issues such as the economic climate in the major source markets' (Chambers & Airey, 2001, p. 95). Odularu (2008) uses economic analysis to understand the outcomes of tourism in Africa. He concludes that economic performance in West Africa can be enhanced through sound tourism development policies that support economic openness with greater emphasis on liberalization policy. Bull (1990) evaluates different policies for foreign investment on Australia tourism.

Policy outcomes for various types of tourism have also been evaluated. Ecotourism has become an important means of tourism development, protected area management and community development. Its success is mixed however, and probably most successful as a political process (Buckley, 2009). While outcomes may be measured in terms of economic growth (Lee & Chang, 2008) other measures such as protection of public interest have also been discussed (Dredge & Thomas, 2009). Castellani and Sala (2010) have discussed measures of policy outcomes for sustainable performance.

Analysing Policy

The approaches to analyzing public policy have been grouped into four types; rational choice, socioeconomic, institutionalism and networks (John, 1998; Tyler & Dinan, 2001). The rational choice or scientific approach focuses on providing factual knowledge and analysis rather than an intrinsically political view, and in the same way, each approach is based on a particular view of the world and how it operates, and incorporates theories and concepts, but which may overlaps with other approaches.

A number of researchers claim that dominant approaches to understanding public policy have developed from the rational paradigm (Farrell & Twining-Ward, 2004; Kerr, Barron, & Wood, 2001; Pforr, 2005; Stevenson et al., 2008). Early tourism policy was developed at a time when no strong evidence base existed for the dilemmas caused by tourism or indeed any recognition that negatives existed. Tourism was seen as a source of development "The challenge facing tourism planners in Zambia is the optimum development of the industry …" (Teye, 1988). Much criticism is done with the benefit of hindsight. Examples of a scientific approach include satellite accounts used for sustainable tourism policy development (Pham, Dwyer, & Spurr, 2009), CGE modelling for policy formulation (Dwyer, Forsyth, & Spurr, 2004), and public choice analysis as a model to analyse government policy decisions (O'Fallon, 1993), and to investigate calls for market intervention (Michael, 2001). Treuren and Lane (2003) discuss the difference between rational versus contingent planning. Araña (2013) has sought to ask tourists to valuation of climate change policy.

The scientific choice model has been used to analyse; the effect of state subsidization of small tourism businesses (Fleischer & Felsenstein, 2000), and policy alternatives for access to private land in Sweden (Mortazavi, 1997). Policy design is an associated term and is used by Blake and Sinclair (2003) for analyzing the effect of September 11. A similar approach is taken by Sugiyarto, Blake and Sinclair (2003) in looking at the effects of globalization on Indonesia. Cohen (1988) adopts a rational approach to the study of policy dilemmas posed by AIDS in Thailand, a major tourism destination with a developed sex industry. The use of rational models for policy design has been criticised due it ignoring politics (Tosun, 2001).

Critics claim that a scientific approach is "reductionist, producing thin description that ignores the dynamics within the environment and have not provided the analytical tools to investigate context" (Stevenson et al., 2008, p. 733). Policies are subject to ideologies (Hall & Jenkins, 2004). The rational choice model is based on the concepts of personal choice and maximisation of individual benefits as basis of policy action or inaction (Tyler & Dinan, 2001). It appears that this approach provides inputs into policy development but does not analyse policy development and does not address the issue of politics and 'win-lose'. An institutional approach focuses on the organizational powers, rules, investment incentives and constraints that influence policy development and implementation (Dieke, 1993; Sofield, 1993). The term institution refers to many different types of entities, as well as the rules used to structure patterns of interaction within and across organisations (Kerr, 2003). This highlights that tourism is strongly influenced by (reliant on) government and therefore highly institutionalised, for example in examining public policy for tourism in Northern Island (Smyth, 1986, p. 126).

Institutional analysis considers that public policy is predominantly made within political and public institutions, and has been criticized for underplaying the political and social processes (Stevenson et al., 2008). Institutional approaches have been used by Dredge and Jenkins (2003) in studying Australia State – Federal relationships, and by Zahra (2005) discussing National Tourism Organizations. The development of policy and changes to their roles and responsibilities can have 'profound influences on the NTO and the development of the tourism industry in that country' (Zahra & Ryan, 2005, p. 22). Hannam (2004) studied the power relationships of Indian State organizations and how this affects tourism policy.

A number of theories are related to the institutional approach including regime theory (Russo & Segre, 2009), city/urban growth machine (Molotch, 1976), and regulation theory (Mair, 2006). The regime framework (Stone, 1989) considers that property regimes (institutions) affects tourism development options (Russo & Segre, 2009). Healy (1994, p. 59) describes "three property rights regimes for managing such resources: privatization, management by government, and common property regimes".

The urban growth machine theory developed by Molotch (1976) and the urban regime seek to understand "the power and role of business interests in urban policy, and the emergence of coalitions involving business and other interests" (Church, 2004, p. 562). This theoretical framework discusses the idea of local groups that vie with each other as determining policy towards tourism in a city (Madrigal, 1995). Most recently, there has been renewed interest in institutions through the work of Ostrom's theory of collective action (Ostrom, 1990), and especially the design principles for robust management of common pool resources (Haase, Lamers, & Amelung, 2009). Community based tourism may be considered a form of institution theory as it examines the importance of addressing host community interests and involving host communities in public policy decision making (Thyne & Lawson, 2001). Murphy (1985) discusses involvement in community planning on the basis that the community should decide how tourism will be developed, as it may be an instrument for dispute between local people and central authority as in South America (Kent, 2006).

Non-governmental organizations (NGOs) and interest groups are other types of institutions that have been found to influence tourism policy (Lovelock, 2003). Lovelock (2003) discusses the tactics NGOs use to gain legitimacy such as media, advocacy and litigation. NGOs are also seen to be important stakeholders in policy development (Jamal & Getz, 1999; Kousis, 2000). In many countries the open nature of tourism leads to a number of interest groups that seek to "contribute to public policy-making and implementation in the tourism domain" (Greenwood, 1992, p. 255). Interest groups are associated with client politics "typical of policies with diffuse costs and concentrated benefits. An identifiable group benefits from a policy, but the costs are paid by everybody or at least a large part of society and that tourism policy is one such area" (Hall, 1999).

The application of ethics to policy can be considered as fitting into a number of perspectives but here is considered as exemplifying a particular type of shared value or institution. Early interest in ethics is embodied in a study of development of tourism (Lea, 1993). A broader interest in ethics has been stimulated by the need to implement sustainable development principles (Bramwell & Lane, 2008; Macbeth, 2005). Environmental ethics are an important requirement for policy (Holden, 2003) and need to be embedded in the market economy (Holden, 2009). Further Bramwell and Lane (2008, p. 1) argue that there is a move to focus on 'just sustainability', and involve concerns about social justice. Corruption leads to a deterioration of social justice and is a failure of ethics (Church, 2004). It is argued that the legacy of uneven development, and the entrenched power of regional economic and political elites, is likely to undermine the prospects for a just model of sustainable tourism (Bianchi, 2004).

The social approach includes a focus on the arrangement, actions and interactions of individual people or organizations. "Tourism policy-making is seen as a social activity with the focus being placed on examining how actors (institutions, groups, organizations, individuals) relate to each other, or on the factors that influence perceptions of policies" (Bramwell & Lane, 1999). Collaborative policy development may involve conflict resolution, problem solving and capacity building processes (Lovelock, 2001, 2002). Some authors have a more holistic approach and focus attention on the collaborative environment, the interaction between different initiatives, the networks and communications between the people involved in the process and the political nature of policy making (D. Dredge, 2006a; Laing, Lee, Moore, Wegner, & Weiler, 2009; Stevenson et al., 2008).

There is an evolving body of theory of collaboration and partnerships, along with criteria for assessing the effectiveness of collaborative projects and practical guides for their initiation and management. Collaboration involves a number of stakeholders working interactively on a common issue or 'problem domain' through a formal cross-sector approach. Typically, this process involves an exchange of ideas and expertise and/or pooling of financial resources (Vernon, Essex, Pinder, & Curry, 2005). Yasarata, Altinay, Burns, and Okumus (2010) highlight how elite controlled networks and access to power lead to control of politicians who create a favourable investment climate policy that leads to planners implementing physical planning and activities. Collaboration involves the concept of power, social exchange theory and resource dependency (Jamal & Getz, 1995).

Relational approach

The relational approach emphasizes increased participation by 'stakeholders' in the planning and operation of tourism organizations (Hall 2000). Long (2001) adopts an actor-oriented approach to examine agency, structures and social change. Bramwell (2006), and Bramwell and Myer (2007) adopt this actor oriented/relational approach to study power, policymaking, and related debates associated with tourism development. The later paper focuses on relations between actors and structures using an island in former East Germany as their case. Dredge (2006b) adopts a network to examine the development and delivery of policies.

Network approaches to policy development focus on 'policy communities' made up of people who interact within networks. Here 'policy emerges as a result of informal patterns of association' considering the dynamics of 'complex relationships' by examining them 'as they shift and change'' (John, 1998, p. 1; Stevenson et al., 2008). Policy networks have, therefore, emerged as powerful organising perspectives to understand relational conceptions of policymaking (Wray, 2009). Networks have been used to examine environmental governance (Erkuş-Öztürk & Eraydin, 2010), interest groups in England (Tyler & Dinan, 2001), public-private partnerships, stakeholder's involvement and the role of networking and collective learning (Vernon et al., 2005). Denicolai, Cioccarelli and Zucchella (2010) interpret the tourism network approach by analysing four dimensions: knowledge sharing, formal agreements, degree of integration of local services, and trust. Scott, Cooper and Baggio (2008a) discusses the structure of networks. One feature of networks are bridging organizations (Jamal & Getz, 1995, p. 191), which span the social gaps among organizations and constituencies to enable coordinated actions.

The concept of governance has been used to study regional institutions (Church, 2004; Church et al., 2000; Reed, 1997, p. 570; Timothy, 2003), decentralization in Turkey (Yuksel, Bramwell, & Yuksel, 2005), networks (Yuksel et al., 2005), develop principles of good governance (Eagles, 2009), and to examine protection of the public interest (D. Dredge & Thomas, 2009). Attempts to clarify types of governance include a typology of governance (Hall, 2011b), governance comparisons (Derco, 2012), and identification of governance archetypes (d'Angella, Carlo, & Sainaghi, 2010). Studies have examined governance for sustainable tourism development (Erkuş-Öztürk & Eraydın, 2010), complexity (Baggio, Scott, & Cooper, 2010a) and local governance (Beaumont & Dredge, 2010). In a neo-liberal world, boundaries are dissolving between public and private sectors and there is greater interdependency of actors in policymaking (Dianne Dredge & Jenkins, 2012). Two recent reviews of tourism governance are available (Ruhanen, Scott, Ritchie, & Tkaczynski, 2010; Zhang & Zhu, 2014).

Social capital, power, narratives and learning

A number of concepts from the social sciences have been applied in policy studies. Social capital refers to the bank of resources built up through interpersonal networks and associations upon which individual members of a community can draw. While there is some disagreement about the origin of the term 'social capital', there is no doubt that it is a concept which has gained prominence over the last decade. Social capital is about networks, about relationships and about reciprocity (Macbeth, Carson, & Northcote, 2004).

A number of studies aim to study who tourism power-holders are, the sources of their power, the values and interests that are served by the exercise of power (Church, 2004; Hannam, 2002). As Richter (1983, p. 318) writes "tourism development, then, is a policy area only if political elites decide it will be". Marzano and Scott (2009) examine the exercise of power in destination branding, while Church (2007) discusses the power of the military in Panama. Doorne (1998) argues that the study of power should be contextualised within particular environments and from particular perspectives, and acknowledges that there is no singular objective 'truth' in the analysis of politics, policies and power. Bianchi (2004) argues that the entrenched power of regional economic and political elites, is likely to undermine the prospects for a just model of sustainable tourism, and to consolidate inequalities across the region. Findings of research by Airey and Ruhanen (2014) provide evidence for what Dredge (2011) describes as the industry capture of the policy space.

Attempts to influence growth policies have also examined their discourses, knowledge frameworks, and relative influence on the government (Bramwell, 2006). The precise agendas and discourses adopted by the various interest groups, amidst contemporary concerns about sustainability, would appear to be crucial to the success, or otherwise, of their arguments (Markwick, 2000). Cousin (2008) notes that the discourse of tourism has symbolic value and can act as a means of unifying elites. A recent strand of research has focused on policy analysis and learning in policy networks (Schianetz, Kavanagh, & Lockington, 2007), and identified three different types of learning: instrumental or technical, conceptual or social policy, and political (Hall, 2011a). A recent book examines knowledge management in tourism (Fayos-Sola, Da Silva, & Jafari, 2012).

Methodology for Policy Studies

Compared to the theoretical discussion of policy, there is only a small methodological literature concerning tourism policy. There is some agreement that the study of tourism policy involves complexity, dynamism and change, and as a result Stevenson, Airey and Miller (2008) recommend the use of multiple approaches to understand policy making, and the use of grounded theory development. There is a need for awareness of the researcher's ideological beliefs and values as these may direct or constrain information sources, methodology, analysis, and findings.

The case-study approach is the predominant research strategy used in studies of tourism policy is and indeed Hall and Jenkins (1995) consider this overused. They recommend use of thick description to improve understanding of policy in a specific context rather than attempting to develop universal models. Such an approach can consider the wider political context within which decisions are made (Stevenson et al., 2008). Jenkins (1996) discusses interviewing and data collection for policy studies.

A number of methods have been used to examine tourism policy mainly concerning identifying and analyse the relationships and interactions between stakeholders. Stakeholder mapping considers these relationships as well as differing interests and powers, and has been used for planning strategies and establishing political priorities in terms of managing stakeholder relationships (Markwick, 2000). Greenwood, Williams and Shaw (1990) discuss backward mapping as a data collection approach.

Social network analysis (SNA) methods are increasingly being adopted to study policy networks (Pforr, 2002). SNA involves collecting data concerning relationships between stakeholders (termed nodes). These are mapped using mathematical techniques with results displayed visually in network diagrams and network attributes quantitatively measured (Scott et al., 2008a; Scott, Cooper, & Baggio, 2008b). Such a quantitative approach has been criticised as positivist and ignoring the changing nature of relationships (Rhodes, 2002). SNA provides information on structural properties of the network as a whole that supplements the study of the relationships among individual stakeholders. A second differentiating characteristic is that it does not a priori define groups and structures within the destination (Scott et al., 2008a). Baggio, Scott, and Cooper (2010b) have further developed these methods and the techniques for the study of complex adaptive systems and provided an example of their application, the case of a tourism destination. Use of futures studies for developing longer term policies has also been recommended (Van Doorn, 1982).

Conclusions

This review of the study of tourism policy in tourism is based on the policy cycle as well as the analysis approach used. These two classificatory dimensions appear useful for seeking to integrate and synthesize a complex and fragmented literature. The review has highlighted the importance of the concept of development to tourism policy; in fact they are almost synonymous. The academic literature of tourism has over time moved from a simplistic view of tourism development based on contribution to central government macroeconomic policy to embrace sustainable development. It is arguable however that the practice of policy development in many countries has not followed the same pattern. Based on an examination of the literature, policy has been characterized as involving actions, decision, politics, values and ideological beliefs, social processes involving communication, outcomes such as legislation and implementation. Tourism policy involves collective action and how collective choices are made, implemented and enforced in and for a society (Buhrs, 2000).

It also appears that policy research has moved from particular political or ideological perspectives to a more sociological perspective looking at concepts like power, collaboration, and governance. Thus, generalist theories have been replaced with development of policy in the context of local actors' power. That said tourism policy seems set within ideologies (mostly) with little questioning of boundaries. It seems to be about optimization of a particular approach or choice of policy options within a policy ideology. Additionally public tourism policy is increasingly seen as the study of parts of governments – rather than government as a whole.

Overall, we may conclude that contrary to the findings of Ballantyne, Packer, and Axelsen (2009) the tourism policy literature is not limited and indeed is a vibrant and active area for research. That said the tourism policy field does have area where improvements may be made. In particular, policy studies would benefit from comparative studies at a national or regional level. Some authors may say that such an approach ignores the complexity of policy contexts that frustrate comparisons between regions, countries or policy areas. However, it does appear that, for example, there is some commonality of policy instruments used around the world and thus comparison between their implementation and outcomes may prove useful, for examples in development of regions. Recently, there have been a number of such studies (Almeida García, 2014; Derco, 2012; OECD, 2012). In particular cross-country comparisons using examples of non-Western policy development may be useful. Certainly there is a need for monitoring and evaluation of policy after implementation (Bramwell & Lane, 2006). Policy evaluation studies are a possible short cut to information about the effects and efficiency of various specific interventions (Hjalager, 2010). A conclusion of some studies is that government tourism plans have little probability of influencing market forces to achieve economic success in destination areas and some indication of the effect of government policies would be extremely useful (Choy, 1991).

Areas for further research also include tourism laws - in countries such as Vietnam Cambodia and Laos – a tourism law is being developed and this holds interesting policy implications for its study. Perhaps there is a need for separate discussions about implications of industrialized and non-industrialized country destination planning, in that residents from the former have more flexibility in responding to development pressures than residents of the latter countries (Burns, 1999, p. 344).

A second developing areas found in the literature is the adoption and examination of the sociological perspective and concepts, such as the use of power (Bramwell & Meyer, 2007; Cheong & Miller, 2000), tourism policy networks, knowledge management (Cooper, 2006), tourism destinations as a commons (Ostrom, 1998, 2005) and especially the design principles for robust management of common pool resources (Connelly, 2007; Haase et al., 2009). Hall and Jenkins (2004) suggest a need examination of the linkage between power, ideology, values, and institutions. Another area is the interaction of policy from other sectors on tourism, such as between terrorism and tourism (Richter & Waugh Jr, 1986). It would also be of interest to study the transfer of policy around the world and the role of various types of organizations in doing this (Hawkins & Mann, 2007).

Clearly the domain of sustainability is of critical importance but there is a need to distinguish between policy ideal and practice. For example Ioannides and Holcomb (2003, p. 40) consider that upmarket tourism an 'unrealistic long-term option for sustainable tourism development' and that there is a need to determine how to create sustainable tourism when it is dependent on an unsustainable transportation system. Policy research remains a critical area for further research.

References

Ahmed, Z. U. and Krohn, F. B. (1990). Reversing the United States declining competitiveness in the marketing of international tourism: a perspective on future policy. *Journal of Travel Research*, **29**(2), 23-29.

Airey, D. (1983). European government approaches to tourism. *Tourism Management*, **4**(4), 234-244.

Airey, D. and Chong, K. (2011). *Tourism in China: Policy and development since 1949*. London: Routledge.

Airey, D. and Ruhanen, L. (2014). Tourism policy-making in Australia: A national and state perspective. *Tourism Planning & Development*, **11**(2), 149-162.

Almeida García, F. (2014). A comparative study of the evolution of tourism policy in Spain and Portugal. *Tourism Management Perspectives*, **11**, 34-50.

Altinay, L. and Bowen, D. (2006). Politics and tourism interface. The case of Cyprus. *Annals of Tourism Research*, **33**(4), 939-956.

Ambrosie, L. (2010). Tourism policy research: avenues for the future. *International Journal of Tourism Policy*, **3**(1), 33-50.

Andriotis, K. (2001). Tourism planning and development in Crete: Recent tourism policies and their efficacy. *Journal of Sustainable Tourism*, **9**(4), 298-316.

Aramberri, J. and Butler, R. (2005). *Tourism development: issues for a vulnerable industry*: Multilingual Matters Ltd.

Araña, J. E., León, C. J., Moreno-Gil, S. and Zubiaurre, A. R. (2013). A comparison of tourists' valuation of climate change policy using different pricing frames. *Journal of Travel Research*, **52**(1), 82-92. doi: 10.1177/0047287512457260

Azcairate, M. C. (2006). Between local and global, discourses and practices: rethinking ecotourism development in Celestan (Yucatan, Mexico). *Journal of Ecotourism*, **5**(1/2), 97-111.

Baggio, R., Scott, N. and Cooper, C. (2010a). Improving tourism destination governance: a complexity science approach. *Tourism Review*, **65**(4), 51-60.

Baggio, R., Scott, N. and Cooper, C. (2010b). Network science – a review with a focus on tourism. *Annals of Tourism Research*, **37**(3), 802-827.

Ballantyne, R., Packer, J. and Axelsen, M. (2009). Trends in tourism research. *Annals of Tourism Research*, **36**(1), 149-152.

Baretje, R. (1982). Tourism's external account and the balance of payments. *Annals of Tourism Research*, **9**(1), 57-67.

Beaumont, N. and Dredge, D. (2010). Local tourism governance: a comparison of three network approaches. *Journal of Sustainable Tourism*, **18**(1), 1-22.

Bhanugopan, R. (2001). Tourism development in Papua New Guinea: Strategies for success. *Asia Pacific Journal of Tourism Research*, **6**(2), 65 - 73.

Bianchi, R. V. (2004). Tourism restructuring and the politics of sustainability: A critical view from the European periphery (The Canary Islands). *Journal of Sustainable Tourism*, **12**(6), 495-529.

Blake, A. and Sinclair, M. T. (2003). Tourism crisis management - US response to September 11. *Annals of Tourism Research*, **30**(4), 813-832.

Bramwell, B. (2006). Actors, power, and discourses of growth limits. *Annals of Tourism Research*, **33**(4), 957-978.

Bramwell, B. and Cox, V. (2009). Stage and path dependence approaches to the evolution of a national park tourism partnership. *Journal of Sustainable Tourism*, **17**(2), 191-206.

Bramwell, B. and Lane, B. (1999). Collaboration and partnerships for sustainable tourism. *Journal of Sustainable Tourism*, **7**(3/4), 179-181.

Bramwell, B. and Lane, B. (2006). Editorial: Policy relevance and sustainable tourism research: liberal, radical and post-structuralist perspectives. *Journal of Sustainable Tourism*, **14**(1), 1-5.

Bramwell, B. and Lane, B. (2008). Priorities in sustainable tourism research. *Journal of Sustainable Tourism*, **16**(1), 1 - 4.

Bramwell, B. and Meyer, D. (2007). Power and tourism policy relations in transition. *Annals of Tourism Research*, **34**(3), 766-788.

Britton, S. (1982). The political economy of tourism in the third world. *Annals of Tourism Research*, **9**(3), 331–358.

Buckley, R. (2009). Evaluating the net effects of ecotourism on the environment: a framework, first assessment and future research. *Journal of Sustainable Tourism*, **17**(6), 643-672.

Buhalis, D. (2001). Tourism in Greece: Strategic analysis and challenges. *Current Issues in Tourism*, **4**(5), 440-480.

Buhrs, T. (2000). The environment and the role of the state in New Zealand. In P. A. Memon & H. Perkins (Eds.), *Environmental Planning and Management in New Zealand* (pp. 27-35). Palmerston North: Dunmore Press.

Bull, Λ. (1990). Australian tourism. Effects of foreign investment. *Tourism Management*, **11**(4), 325-331.

Burns, P. (1999). Paradoxes in planning: Tourism Elitism or Brutalism? *Annals of Tourism Research*, **26**(2), 329-348.

Burns, P. and Novelli, M. (2008). *Tourism development: growth, myths, and inequalities*: CABI Publishing.

Cantallops, A. S. (2004). Policies supporting sustainable tourism development in the Balearic Islands: The Ecotax. *Anatolia*, **15**(1), 39-56.

Castellani, V. and Sala, S. (2010). Sustainable performance index for tourism policy development. *Tourism Management*, **31**(6), 871-880. doi: http://dx.doi.org/10.1016/j.tourman.2009.10.001

Chambers, D. and Airey, D. (2001). Tourism policy in Jamaica: A tale of two governments. *Current Issues in Tourism*, **4**(2-4), 94-120.

Cheong, S.-M. and Miller, M. L. (2000). Power and tourism: A Foucauldian observation. *Annals of Tourism Research*, **27**(2), 371-390.

Choy, D. J. L. (1991). Tourism planning: The case for market failure. *Tourism Management*, **12**(4), 313-330.

Church, A. (2004). Local and regional tourism: policy and power, in A. Lew, C. M. Hall and A. Williams (Eds.), *A companion to tourism* (pp. 555-568). Oxford: Blackwell.

Church, A., Ball, R., Bull, C. and Tyler, D. (2000). Public policy engagement with British tourism: the national, local and the European Union. *Tourism Geographies*, **2**(3), 312–336.

Church, A. and Coles, T. (2007). *Tourism, Power and Space. (Contemporary Geographies of Leisure, Tourism and Mobility)*. Routledge.

Cohen, E. (1988). Tourism and AIDS in Thailand. *Annals of Tourism Research*, **15**(4), 467-486.

Colebatch, H. (2009). *Policy*. Maidenhead, UK.: McGraw-Hill.

Coles, T., Hall, C. M. and Duval, D. T. (2006). Tourism and post-disciplinary enquiry. *Current Issues in Tourism*, **9**(4/5), 293-319.

Connelly, G. (2007). Testing governance - a research agenda for exploring urban tourism competitiveness policy: the case of Liverpool 1980-2000. *Tourism Geographies*, **9**(1), 84-114.

Cooper, C. (2006). Knowledge management and tourism. *Annals of Tourism Research*, **33**(1), 47-64.

Cousin, S. (2008). The nation state as an identifying image. *Tourist Studies*, **8**(2), 193-209.

Craik, J. (1990). A classic case of clientelism: The Industries Assistance Commission inquiry into travel and tourism. *Culture and Policy*, **2**(1), 29-45.

d'Angella, F., Carlo, M. D. and Sainaghi, R. (2010). Archetypes of destination governance: a comparison of international destinations. *Tourism Review*, **65**(4), 61-73.

Dahles, H. (2002). The politics of tour guiding: Image management in Indonesia. *Annals of Tourism Research*, **29**(3), 783-800. doi: 10.1016/s0160-7383(01)00083

Deegan, J. and Dineen, D. A. (2000). Developments in Irish tourism, 1980-96. *International Journal of Tourism Research*, **2**(3), 163-170.

Denicolai, S., Cioccarelli, G. and Zucchella, A. (2010). Resource-based local development and networked core-competencies for tourism excellence. *Tourism Management*, **31**(2), 260-266. doi: 10.1016/j.tourman.2009.03.002

Derco, J. (2012). Destination governance in the Czech Republic, Slovakia and Poland. *Tourism Planning & Development*, **10**(3), 354-364. doi: 10.1080/21568316.2012.747987

Desforges, L. (2000). State tourism institutions and neo-liberal development: a case study of Peru. *Tourism Geographies: An International Journal of Tourism Space, Place and Environment*, **2**(2), 177-192.

Dieke, P. U. C. (1993). Tourism and development policy in the Gambia. *Annals of Tourism Research,* **20**(3), 423-449.

Dodds, R. (2007). Sustainable tourism and policy implementation: Lessons from the case of Calvia, Spain. *Current Issues in Tourism,* **10**(4), 296-322.

Dodds, R. and Butler, R. (2010). Barriers to implementing sustainable tourism policy in mass tourism destinations. *Tourismos,* **5**(1), 35-54.

Doorne, S. (1998). Power, participation and perception: An insider's perspective on the politics of the Wellington waterfront redevelopment. *Current Issues in Tourism,* **1**(2), 129-166.

Dredge, D. (2001). Local government tourism planning and policy-making in New South Wales: institutional development and historical legacies. *Current Issues in Tourism,* **4**(2-4), 355-380.

Dredge, D. (2006a). Networks, conflict and collaborative communities. *Journal of Sustainable Tourism,* **14**(6), 562–581.

Dredge, D. (2006b). Policy networks and the local organisation of tourism. *Tourism Management,* **27**(2), 269-280.

Dredge, D. (2011). Tourism reform, policy and development in Queensland 1989–2011. *Queensland Review,* **18**(2), 62–84.

Dredge, D. and Jenkins, J. (2003). Federal-State relations and tourism public policy, New South Wales, Australia. *Current Issues in Tourism,* **6**(5), 415-443.

Dredge, D. and Jenkins, J. (2007). *Tourism Planning and Policy.* Brisbane: John Wiley and Sons.

Dredge, D. and Jenkins, J. (2012). Australian national tourism policy: influences of reflexive and political modernisation. *Tourism Planning & Development,* **9**(3), 231-251. doi: 10.1080/21568316.2012.678379

Dredge, D. and Thomas, P. (2009). Mongrel management, public interest and protected area management in the Victorian Alps, Australia. *Journal of Sustainable Tourism,* **17**(2), 249-267.

Dubin, R. (1976). *Theory Building in Applied Areas.* Chicago, Illinois: Rand McNally.

Duffy, R. (2008). Neoliberalising nature: global networks and ecotourism development in Madagasgar. *Journal of Sustainable Tourism,* **16**(3), 327-344.

Dwyer, L., Forsyth, P. and Spurr, R. (2004). Evaluating tourism's economic effects: New and old approaches. *Tourism Management,* **25**(3), 307-317.

Dye, T. (1992). *Understanding Public Policy* (7th ed.). Englewood Cliffs: Prentice Hall.

Eagles, P. (2009). Governance of recreation and tourism partnerships in parks and protected areas. *Journal of Sustainable Tourism,* **17**(2), 231-248.

Easton, D. (1953). *The Political System.* New York: Knopf.

Edgell, D. (1995). A barrier-free future for tourism? *Tourism Management,* **16**(2), 107-110.

Elliott, J. (1997). *Tourism, Politics and Public Sector Management.* London: Routledge.

Erkuş-Öztürk, H. and Eraydin, A. (2010). Environmental governance for sustainable tourism development: Collaborative networks and organisation building in the Antalya tourism region. *Tourism Management*, **31**(1), 113-124.

Farrell, B. and Twining-Ward, L. (2004). Reconceptualizing tourism. *Annals of Tourism Research*, **31**(2), 274-295.

Farrell, B. and Twining-Ward, L. (2005). Seven steps towards sustainability: Tourism in the context of new knowledge. *Journal of Sustainable Tourism*, **13**(2), 109-122.

Fayos-Sola, E. (1996). Tourism policy: a midsummer night's dream? *Tourism Management*, **17**(6), 405-412.

Fayos-Sola, E., Da Silva, J. A. M. and Jafari, J. (2012). *Knowledge Management in Tourism: Policy and Governance Applications*: Emerald Group Publishing.

Fleischer, A. and Felsenstein, D. (2000). Support for rural tourism: Does it make a difference? *Annals of Tourism Research*, **27**(4), 1007-1024.

Franklin, A. and Crang, M. (2001). The Trouble with Tourism and Travel Theory? *Tourist Studies*, **1**(1), 5-22.

Gartner, W. C. (2004). Rural tourism development in the USA. *International Journal of Tourism Research*, **6**, 151–164.

Goldsworthy, D. (1988). Thinking politically about development. *Development and Change*, **19**(3), 505-530.

Grant, M. (2004). Innovation in tourism planning processes: action learning to support a coalition of stakeholders for sustainability. *Tourism and Hospitality Planning & Development*, **1**(3), 219–237.

Greenwood, J. (1992). Producer interest groups in tourism policy : case studies from Britain and the European Community. *American Behavioral Scientist*, **36**(2), 36-256.

Greenwood, J., Williams, A. M. and Shaw, G. (1990). Policy implementation and tourism in the UK. Implications from recent tourism research in Cornwall. *Tourism Management*, **11**(1), 53-62.

Haase, D., Lamers, M. and Amelung, B. (2009). Heading into uncharted territory? Exploring the institutional robustness of self-regulation in the Antarctic tourism sector. *Journal of Sustainable Tourism*, **17**(4), 411 - 430.

Hall, C. M. (1999). Rethinking collaboration and partnership: a public policy perspective. *Journal of Sustainable Tourism*, **7**(3/4), 274-289.

Hall, C. M. (2000). *Tourism Planning: Policies, Processes and Relationships*. Harlow: Pearson Education.

Hall, C. M. (2002). Travel safety, terrorism and the media: The significance of the issue-attention cycle. *Current Issues in Tourism*, **5**(5), 458-466.

Hall, C. M. (2007). Pro-Poor Tourism: Do tourism exchanges benefit primarily the countries of the South? *Current Issues in Tourism*, **10**(2&3), 111-118.

Hall, C. M. (2008). *Tourism Planning: Policies, Processes and Relationships* (2nd ed.). Harlow: Pearson Education.

Hall, C. M. (2011a). Policy learning and policy failure in sustainable tourism governance: from first- and second-order to third-order change? *Journal of Sustainable Tourism*, **19**(4-5) 649-671.

Hall, C. M. (2011b). A typology of governance and its implications for tourism policy analysis. *Journal of Sustainable Tourism*, **19**(4-5) 437-457.

Hall, C. M. and Jenkins, J. (2004). Tourism and public policy. In A. Lew, C. M. Hall and A. Williams (eds.), *A Companion to Tourism* (pp. 425-540). Oxford: Blackwell.

Hall, C. M. and Jenkins, J. M. (1995). *Tourism and Public Policy*: Routledge.

Hall, C. M. and Michael, E. J. (2007). Issues in regional development. In E. J. Michael (ed.), *Micro-clusters and Networks: The Growth of Tourism* (pp. 7-20). London: Elsevier.

Hannam, K. (2002). Tourism and development: globalisation and power. *Progress in Development Studies*, **2**(3), 227-234.

Hannam, K. (2004). Tourism and forest management in India: The role of the state in limiting tourism development. *Tourism Geographies*, **6**(3), 331-351.

Harrison, D. and Schipani, S. (2007). Lao tourism and poverty alleviation: community-based tourism and the private sector. *Current Issues in Tourism*, **10**(2/3), 194-230.

Harvey, D. (2006). Neoliberalism as creative destruction. *Geografiska Annaler, Series B: Human Geography*, **88**(2), 145-158.

Hawkins, D. and Mann, S. (2007). The world bank's role in tourism development. *Annals of Tourism Research*, **34**(2), 348-363.

Healy, R. G. (1994). The 'common pool' problem in tourism landscapes. *Annals of Tourism Research*, **21**(3), 596-611.

Henderson, J. C. (2003). The politics of tourism in Myanmar. *Current Issues in Tourism*, **6**(2), 97-118.

Henry, I. P. and Jackson, G. A. M. (1996). Sustainability of management processes and tourism products and contexts. *Journal of Sustainable Tourism*, **4**(1), 17 - 28.

Hjalager, A. M. (2007). Stages in the economic globalization of tourism. *Annals of Tourism Research*, **34**(2), 437-457.

Hjalager, A. M. (2010). A review of innovation research in tourism. *Tourism Management*, **31**(1), 1-12.

Holden, A. (2003). In need of new environmental ethics for tourism? *Annals of Tourism Research*, **30**(1), 94-108.

Holden, A. (2009). The environment-tourism nexus. Influence of market ethics *Annals of Tourism Research*, **36**(3), 373-389. doi: 10.1016/j.annals.2008.10.0

Human, B. (1994). Visitor management in the public planning policy context: A case study of Cambridge. *Journal of Sustainable Tourism*, **2**(4), 221 - 230.

Ioannides, D. (1995). A flawed implementation of sustainable tourism: the experience of Akamas, Cyprus. *Tourism Management*, **16**(8), 583-592.

Ioannides, D. and Holcomb, B. (2003). Misguided policy initiatives in small-island destinations: why do up-market tourism policies fail? *Tourism Geographies*, **5**(1), 39-48.

Jafari, J. (1989). An English-language literature review. In J. Bystrzanowski (ed.), *Tourism as a factor of change: the sociocultural study* (pp. 17-60). Vienna: Centre for Research and Documentation in Social Sciences.

Jamal, T. and Getz, D. (1995). Collaboration theory and community tourism planning. *Annals of Tourism Research*, **22**(1), 186-204.

Jamal, T. and Getz, D. (1999). Community roundtables for tourism-related conflicts: the dialectics of consensus and process structures. *Journal of Sustainable Tourism*, **7**(3), 290-313.

Jenkins, C. L. and Henry, B. M. (1982). Government involvement in tourism in developing countries. *Annals of Tourism Research*, **9**(4), 499-521.

Jenkins, J. (1996). Interviews and interviewing: a case study in geography and public policy. *Australian Geographical Studies*, **34**(2), 261-266.

Jenkins, J. (2001). Editorial. *Current Issues in Tourism*, **4**(2), 69-77.

John, P. (1998). *Analysing Public Policy*. London: Pinter.

Kent, M. (2006). From reeds to tourism: the transformation of territorial conflicts in the Titicaca National Reserve. *Current Issues in Tourism*, **9**(1), 86-103.

Kerr, W. (2003). *Tourism Public Policy, and the Strategic Management of Failure*. New York: Pergamon.

Kerr, W., Barron, G. and Wood, R. C. (2001). Politics, policy and regional tourism administration: a case examination of Scottish Area Tourist Board funding. *Tourism Management*, **22**, 649-657.

Khadaroo, J. and Seetanah, B. (2007). Transport infrastructure and tourism development. *Annals of Tourism Research*, **34**(4), 1021-1032.

Kousis, M. (2000). Tourism and the environment: a social movements perspective. *Annals of Tourism Research*, **27**(2), 468-489.

Kruczala, J. (1990). Tourism planning in Poland. *Annals of Tourism Research*, **17**(1), 69-78.

Laing, J. H., Lee, D., Moore, S. A., Wegner, A. and Weiler, B. (2009). Advancing conceptual understanding of partnerships between protected area agencies and the tourism industry: a postdisciplinary and multi-theoretical approach. *Journal of Sustainable Tourism*, **17**(2), 207-229.

Lawrence, M. and Dredge, D. (2007). Tourism planning and policy processes. In D. Dredge & J. A. Jenkins (Eds.), *Tourism Planning and Policy* (pp. 191-224). Milton: John Wiley & Sons.

Lea, J. (1993). Tourism development ethics in the Third World. *Annals of Tourism Research*, **20**, 701-715.

Lee, C. C. and Chang, C. P. (2008). Tourism development and economic growth: A closer look at panels. *Tourism Management*, **29**(1), 180-192.

Lepp, A. (2008). Tourism and dependency: An analysis of Bigodi village, Uganda. *Tourism Management*, **29**(6), 1206-1214.

Leslie, D. and Black, L. (2005). Tourism and the impact of the foot and mouth epidemic in the UK: reactions, responses and realities with particular reference to Scotland. *Journal of Travel & Tourism Marketing*, **19**(2/3), 35-46.

Lindberg, K., Andersson, T. D., Dellaert, B. G. C. and Dellaert, B. G. C. (2001). Tourism development: assessing social gains and losses. *Annals of Tourism Research*, **28**, 1010-1030.

Logar, I. (2010). Sustainable tourism management in Crikvenica, Croatia: An assessment of policy instruments. *Tourism Management*, **31**(1), 125-135.

Long, N. (2001). *Development Sociology: Actor Perspectives*. London: Routledge.

Lovelock, B. (2001). Interorganisational relations in the protected area – tourism policy domain: the influence of macro-economic policy. *Current Issues in Tourism*, **4**(2-4), 253-274.

Lovelock, B. (2002). Why it's good to be bad: The role of conflict in contributing towards sustainable tourism in protected areas. *Journal of Sustainable Tourism*, **10**(1), 5-30.

Lovelock, B. (2003). A comparative study of environmental NGOs' perspectives of the tourism industry and modes of action in the South and South-East Asia and Oceania regions. *Asia Pacific Journal of Tourism Research*, **8**(1), 1-14.

Macbeth, J. (2005). Towards an ethics platform for tourism. *Annals of Tourism Research*, **32**(4), 962-984.

Macbeth, J., Carson, D. and Northcote, J. (2004). Social capital, tourism and regional development: SPCC as a basis for innovation and sustainability. *Current Issues in Tourism*, **7**(6), 502-522.

Macnaught, T. J. (1982). Mass tourism and the dilemmas of modernization in Pacific Island communities. *Annals of Tourism Research*, **9**(3), 359-381.

Madrigal, R. (1995). Residents' perceptions and the role of government. *Annals of Tourism Research*, 22(1), 86-102.

Mair, H. (2006). Global restructuring and local responses: Investigating rural tourism policy in two Canadian communities. *Current Issues in Tourism*, **9**(1), 1-45.

Markwick, M. C. (2000). Golf tourism development, stakeholders, differing discourses and alternative agendas: The case of Malta. *Tourism Management*, **21**(5), 515-524.

Marzano, G. and Scott, N. (2009). Power in destination branding. *Annals of Tourism Research*, **36**(2), 247–267.

Mathews, H. G. (1975). International Tourism and Political Science Research. *Annals of Tourism Research*, **2**(4), 195-203.

Matthews, H. G. and Richter, L. K. (1991). Political science and tourism. *Annals of Tourism Research*, **18**(1), 120-135.

McCoy, P. (1982). The new national tourism policy act the state role in implementation. *Annals of Tourism Research, 9*(2), 276-279.

McDonald, J. R. (2009). Complexity science: an alternative world view for understanding sustainable tourism development. *Journal of Sustainable Tourism, 17*(4), 455 - 471.

Michael, E. J. (2001). Public choice and tourism analysis. *Current Issues in Tourism, 4*(2-4), 308-330.

Molotch, H. (1976). The city as growth machine. *American Journal of Sociology, 82*(3), 483-499.

Mortazavi, R. (1997). The right of public access in Sweden. *Annals of Tourism Research, 24*(3), 609-623.

Mosedale, J. (2011). Re-introducing tourism to political economy, in J.Mosedale (Ed.), *Political economy of tourism. A critical perspective* (pp. 1-13). London: Routledge.

Murphy, P. E. (1985). *Tourism: A Community Approach.* New York: Metheun.

Nilsson, P. A. (2001). Tourist destination development: The Are Valley. *Scandinavian Journal of Hospitality and Tourism, 1*(1), 54-67.

O'Fallon, C. (1993). Government involvement in New Zealand tourism: A public choice perspective. *GeoJournal, 29*(3), 271-280.

O'Neil, P. (2007). *Essentials of Comparative Politics* (2nd ed.): Norton.

Odularu, G. O. (2008). Does tourism contribute to economic performance in West Africa? *Anatolia: An International Journal of Tourism & Hospitality Research, 19*(2), 340-345.

OECD. (2012). Tourism governance in OECD countries. In OECD (Ed.), *OECD Tourism Trends and Policies 2012.* Paris: OECD.

Olds, K. (1998). Urban mega-events, evictions and housing rights: The Canadian case. *Current Issues in Tourism, 1*(1), 2-46.

Ostrom, E. (1990). *Governing the commons: The evolution of institutions for collective action.* New York: Cambridge University Press.

Ostrom, E. (1998). A behavioral approach to the rational choice theory of collective action. *The American Political Science Review, 92*(1), 1-22.

Ostrom, E. (2005). *Understanding Institutional Diversity.* Princeton: Princeton University Press.

Pearce, D. G. (1998). Tourism development in Paris: public intervention. *Annals of Tourism Research, 25*(2), 457-476.

Pearce, D. G. (2001). Tourism, trams and local government policy-making in Christchurch, New Zealand. *Current Issues in Tourism, 4*(2-4), 331-354.

Pearlman, M. V. (1990). Conflicts and constraints in Bulgaria's tourism sector. *Annals of Tourism Research, 17*(1), 103-122.

Pforr, C. (2001). Tourism policy in Australia's Northern Territory: a policy process analysis of its tourism development masterplan. *Current Issues in Tourism, 4*(2-4), 275-307.

Pforr, C. (2002). The 'makers and shapers' of tourism policy in the Northern Territory of Australia: A policy network analysis of actors and their relational constellations. *Journal of Hospitality and Tourism Research,* **9**(2), 134-151.

Pforr, C. (2005). Three lenses of analysis for the study of tourism public policy: a case from Northern Australia. *Current Issues in Tourism,* **8**(4), 323-343.

Pham, T. D., Dwyer, L. and Spurr, R. A. Y. (2009). Constructing a regional tourism satellite account: The case of Queensland. *Tourism Analysis,* **13**(5/6), 445-460.

Prunier, E. K., Sweeney, A. E. and Geen, A. G. (1993). Tourism and the environment: the case of Zakynthos. *Tourism Management,* **14**(2), 137-141.

Puppim de Oliveira, J. A. (2003). Governmental responses to tourism development: three Brazilian case studies. *Tourism Management,* **24**(1), 97-110.

Reed, M. G. (1997). Power relations and community based tourism planning. *Annals of Tourism Research,* **24**(3), 566-591.

Reid, M. and Schwab, W. (2006). Barriers to sustainable development: Jordan's sustainable tourism strategy. *Journal of Asian & African Studies,* **41**(4), 439-57.

Rhodes, R. (2002). Putting people back into networks. *Australian Journal of Political Science,* **37**(3), 399–416.

Richter, L. (1983). Tourism politics and political science : A case of not so benign neglect. *Annals of Tourism Research,* **10**(3), 313-335.

Richter, L. (2003). International tourism and its global public health consequences. *Journal of Travel Research,* **41**(4), 340-347.

Richter, L. and Richter, W. (1985). Policy choices in South Asian tourism development. *Annals of Tourism Research,* **12**(2), 201-217.

Richter, L. and Waugh Jr, W. L. (1986). Terrorism and tourism as logical companions. *Tourism Management,* **7**(4), 230-238.

Ritchie, B., Crotts, J. C., Zehrer, A. and Volsky, G. T. (2014). Understanding the effects of a tourism crisis: the impact of the BP oil spill on regional lodging demand. *Journal of Travel Research,* **53**(1), 12-25. doi: 10.1177/0047287513482775

Ritchie, J. R. B. (1988). Consensus policy formulation in tourism. Measuring resident views via survey research. *Tourism Management,* **9**(3), 199-212.

Ritchie, J. R. B. and Crouch, G. I. (2000). The competitive destination: A sustainability perspective. *Tourism Management,* **21**(1), 1-7.

Ritchie, J. R. B. and Crouch, G. I. (2003). *The Competitive Destination: A Sustainable Tourism Perspective*: CABI.

Rittel, H. and Weber, M. (1973). Dilemmas in a general theory of planning. *Policy Sciences,* **4**(2), 155-169.

Rosentraub, M. S. and Joo, M. (2009). Tourism and economic development: Which investments produce gains for regions? *Tourism Management,* **30**(5), 759-770.

Ruhanen, L., Scott, N., Ritchie, B. and Tkaczynski, A. (2010). Governance: a review and synthesis of the literature. *Tourism Review,* **65**(4), 4-16.

Russo, A. P. and Segre, G. (2009). Destination models and property regimes: An exploration. *Annals of Tourism Research,* **36**(4), 587-606.

Schianetz, K., Kavanagh, L. and Lockington, D. (2007). The learning tourism destination: The potential of a learning organisation approach for improving the sustainability of tourism destinations. *Tourism Management,* **28**(6), 1485-1496.

Scott, N., Cooper, C. and Baggio, R. (2008a). Destination networks: Four Australian cases. *Annals of Tourism Research,* **35**(1), 169–188.

Scott, N., Cooper, C. and Baggio, R. (2008b). *Network Analysis and Tourism: From Theory to Practice.* London: Multilingual Matters & Channel View Publications.

Sessa, A. (1976). The tourism policy. *Annals of Tourism Research,* **3**(5), 234-247.

Sharpley, R. (2009). Tourism and development challenges in the least developed countries: The case of The Gambia. *Current Issues in Tourism,* **12**(4), 337-358.

Sharpley, R. and Telfer, D. J. (2002). *Tourism and Development : Concepts and Issues.* Buffalo: Multilingual Matters.

Shone, M. C. and Ali Memon, P. (2008). Tourism, public policy and regional development: A turn from neo-liberalism to the new regionalism. *Local Economy,* **23**(4), 290-304.

Smeral, E. (1998). The impact of globalization on small and medium enterprises: new challenges for tourism policies in European countries. *Tourism Management,* **19**(4), 371-380.

Smyth, R. (1986). Public policy for tourism in Northern Ireland. *Tourism Management,* **7**(2), 120-126.

Sofield, T. H. B. (1993). Indigenous tourism development. *Annals of Tourism Research,* **20**(4), 729-750.

Steiner, C. (2006). Tourism, poverty reduction and the political economy: Egyptian perspectives on tourism's economic benefits in a semi-'rentier' state. *Tourism and Hospitality Planning & Development,* **3**(3), 161 - 177.

Stevenson, N., Airey, D. and Miller, G. (2008). Tourism policy making: the policymakers' perspectives. *Annals of Tourism Research,* **35**(3), 732-750.

Stone, C. (1989). *Regime Politics: Governing Atlanta 1946-1988.* Lawrence: University Press of Kansas.

Sugiyarto, G., Blake, A. and Sinclair, M. T. (2003). Tourism and globalization: economic impact in Indonesia. *Annals of Tourism Research,* **30**(3), 683-701.

Swain, M., Brent, M. and Long, V. (1999). Annals and tourism evolving: indexing 25 years of publication. *Annals of Tourism Research,* **25**(Index to Volume 25), 991-1014.

Telfer, D. (2002). The evolution of tourism and development theory, in R. Sharpley & D. J. Telfer (eds.), *Tourism and Development: Concepts and Issues* (pp. 35–78). Clevedon: Channel View.

Telfer, D. and Sharpley, R. (2008). *Tourism and Development in the Developing World*. London: Routledge.

Teye, V. (1988). Geographic factors affecting tourism in Zambia. *Annals of Tourism Research*, **15**(4), 487-503.

Thomas, H. and Thomas, R. (1998). The implications for tourism of shifts in British local governance. *Progress in Tourism and Hospitality Research*, **4**(4), 295-306.

Thyne, M. and Lawson, R. (2001). Addressing tourism public policy issues through attitude segmentation of host communities. *Current Issues in Tourism*, **4**(2-4), 392-400.

Timothy, D. (2003). Supranationalist alliances and tourism: insights from ASEAN and SAARC. *Current Issues in Tourism*, **6**(3), 250-266.

Tosun, C. (2001). Challenges of sustainable tourism development in the developing world: the case of Turkey. *Tourism Management*, **22**, 289-303.

Tovar, C. and Lockwood, M. (2008). Social impacts of tourism: an Australian regional case study. *International Journal of Tourism Research*, **10**(4), 365-378.

Treuren, G. and Lane, D. (2003). The tourism planning process in the context of organised interests, industry structure, state capacity, accumulation and sustainability. *Current Issues in Tourism*, **6**(1), 1-22.

Tsartas, P. (2003). Tourism development in Greek insular and coastal areas: sociocultural changes and crucial policy issues. *Journal of Sustainable Tourism*, **11**(2), 116-132.

Turegano, M. Ã. S. (2006). Dependency and development patterns in tourism: A case study in the Canary Islands. *Tourism and Hospitality Planning & Development*, **3**(2), 117 - 130.

Tyler, D. and Dinan, C. (2001). The role of interested groups in England's emerging tourism policy network. *Current Issues in Tourism*, **4**(2-4), 210-252.

Van Doorn, J. W. M. (1982). Can futures research contribute to tourism policy? *Tourism Management*, **3**(3), 149-166.

Veal, A. J. (2002). *Leisure and Tourism Policy and Planning*. Wallingford, Oxon: CABI Publishing.

Vernon, J., Essex, S., Pinder, D. and Curry, K. (2005). Collaborative policymaking: local sustainable projects. *Annals of Tourism Research*, **32**(2), 325-345.

Wanhill, S. (1987). UK: politics and tourism. *Tourism Management*, **8**(1), 54-58.

Ward, T. (1989). The role of government incentives. *Tourism Management*, **10**(3), 240-241.

Weaver, D. B. (1995). Alternative tourism in Montserrat. *Tourism Management*, **16**(8), 593-604.

Weaver, D. B. (2001). *Ecotourism*. Milton, Queensland: John Wiley & Sons.

Weed, M. (2006). The Influence of Policy Makers' Perceptions on Sport Tourism Policy Development. *Tourism Review International*, **10**(4), 227-240.

Wheatcroft, S. (1988). European air transport in the 1990s. *Tourism Management*, **9**(3), 187-198.

Whitford, M. (2009). A framework for the development of event public policy: Facilitating regional development. *Tourism Management*, **30**(5), 674-682.

Wight, P. A. (2002). Supporting the principles of sustainable development in tourism and ecotourism: government's potential role. *Current Issues in Tourism*, **5**(3), 222-244.

Wilkinson, P. (2001). Tourism development in Anguilla. *Tourism Recreation Research*, **26**(3), 33-41.

Williams, C. and Ferguson, M. (2005). Biting the hand that feeds: the marginalisation of tourism and leisure industry providers in times of agricultural crisis. *Current Issues in Tourism*, **8**(2), 155-164.

Wray, M. (2009). Policy communities, networks and issue cycles in tourism destination systems. *Journal of Sustainable Tourism*, **17**(6), 673-690.

Yasarata, M., Altinay, L., Burns, P. and Okumus, F. (2010). Politics and sustainable tourism development - can they co-exist? Voices from North Cyprus. *Tourism Management*, **31**, 345-356.

York, Q. Y. and Zhang, H. Q. (2010). The determinants of the 1999 and 2007 Chinese Golden Holiday System: A content analysis of official documentation. *Tourism Management*, **31**(6), 881-890. doi: http://dx.doi.org/10.1016/j.tourman.2009.10.003

Yuksel, F., Bramwell, B. and Yuksel, A. (2005). Centralized and decentralized tourism governance in Turkey. *Annals of Tourism Research*, **32**(4), 859-886.

Zahra, A. and Ryan, C. (2005). National Tourism Organisations -- Politics, Functions and Form: A New Zealand Case Study. *Anatolia*, **16**(1), 5-26.

Zeng, B., Carter, R. W. and De Lacy, T. (2005). Short-term perturbations and tourism effects: The case of SARS in China. *Current Issues in Tourism*, **8**(4), 306-322.

Zhang, H. and Zhu, M. (2014). Tourism Destination Governance: A Review and Research Agenda. *International Journal of e-Education, e-Business, e-Management and e-Learning*, **4**(2), 125-128.

Glossary

Community based approaches: The involvement and empowerment of the destination community in the planning and management of tourism in their community.

Dependency Theory: A theory from the social sciences that states that resources flow from the underdeveloped countries to the wealth of the Western world. The countries are kept in dependency due to power structures and systems.

Market Failure: The failure of market forces to account for the total costs and/ or benefits of an economic activity.

Non-Governmental organisations (NGOs): Organisations that are not affiliated or connected with the government.

Organization stakeholders: Individuals, groups, companies or individuals that have a direct or indirect stake in a particular organisation. Stakeholders can include owners, investors, employees, the community and unions.

Policy: A plan of action by an individual, group, company or government that guides decisions.

Policy Cycle: A conceptual tool used to identify and trace the development of a piece of policy. It assists in the understanding of the shaping of policy decisions and their impacts.

Policy communities: Small networks consisting of governments, pressure groups, and other experts that are involved in shaping policy.

Policy implementation: The practical realisation of policy through legislation, planning and the involvement of non-state actors.

Policy instruments: The regulatory and economic tools used to measure policy

Public Good: A public good is a non-rivalrous good, one that if consumed by one individual the availability of that good to others is not reduced. It is also non-excludable, thus no one can be excluded from consuming the good.

Public/private partnerships: Public-private partnerships (or PPP, P3 or P³) refer to a government service or private venture that is a partnership (funded and operated) between a government and a company in the private sector.

Tourism Development: An increase in material prosperity due to tourism. This usually refers to some country or region.

Tourism Policy: Policy involves actions, decision, politics, values and ideological beliefs, social processes involving communication, outcome such as legislation and implementation carried out under the coordination of public administrations related to the processes of analysis, attraction, reception and evaluation of the impacts of tourism flows in a tourism system or destination.

Service Management and Tourism

David Solnet

Contents

David Solnet is a Senior Lecturer in Service Management at the University of Queensland in Australia. Prior to his academic career, David enjoyed a successful 18-year career in the hospitality industry where he held senior management roles in the USA and Australia. David has authored over 20 peer-reviewed articles principally in hospitality and service industry journals.

A hyperlinked PDF version of this review is available for download from the CTR area of Goodfellow Pubishers' website: http://www.goodfellowpublishers.com/ctr

Introduction

We live in a radically different world than that of even 20 years ago. From a business and economic perspective, perhaps the most significant change in the world has been a change from a product, or *manufacturing-orientation* to a *service-orientation*. Most economic consumption today involves processes, activities and personal interaction, rather than simply a purchase of a 'thing'. Economic exchange and therefore business management was developed based on the product orientation; of manufacturing 'things' which were shipped to a retailer who sold them to a consumer at a retail outlet. Many of our management and marketing principles were based on this basic pathway – production, inventory, purchase, consumption. As the world has changed to be more service oriented, management and marketing scholars have failed to keep pace.

The purpose of this review is to introduce the service management paradigm in the context of tourism. This is done via an explanation of the evolution from a product to a service management orientation and an evolutionary mapping of management thought. Then, an overview of relevant service management topics is provided followed by a Case Example of service management principles in action. Finally, an overview of the emerging issues and future focused agenda in the field of service management is provided.

Background

What do we mean when we refer to the evolution of management thought? How is it that the world can evolve, but academic terminology and theory does not, or does so but much more slowly? This delay is evident by the simple example of the traditional 4 Ps of the 'Marketing Mix' (McCarthy, 1960). These Ps' (Product, Price, Place, Promotion) were taken for granted for years as the necessary recipe for successful marketing. When taking an item to market, it was thought, one must consider *what* to sell (Product), *how much* to sell it for (Price), *where* to sell it (Place), and how to *promote* its sale (Promotion).

When service managers and marketers tried to use these 4 Ps for marketing services (e.g., what you 'buy' at a bank), they found this mix insufficient. Subsequently, researchers sought to expand the marketing mix with a series of proposed additions (see Rafiq & Ahmed, 1995). Of these, the most frequently utilised and accepted mix is the revised 7 Ps (or the 'extended marketing mix') (Booms & Bitner, 1981), which takes into account People (all people who directly or indirectly influence the perceived value of the product or service, including knowledge workers, employees, management and consumers), Processes (procedures, mechanisms and flow of activities which lead to an exchange of value) and Physical Evidence (environment in which the service is delivered and in which the service provider and consumer interact).

Why is it important to understand the evolution of management thought? Let us think metaphorically for a moment. Anthropologists in Ethiopia recently unearthed pieces of bones and other fossilised fragments. This discovery provided a series of new clues in the understanding of the development of mankind. In fact, the skeletons found have now been dated as being 4.4 million years old – and have led to a dramatic rethinking about the development of man and the 'family tree' which distinguishes man from chimp-like animals. This recent discovery has elucidated the history of man's development, and has inspired many scientists to enter or re-enter the discourse about mankind's evolutionary history. Learning about our history, clarifying old and new thought, inciting enthusiasm amongst scholars and scientists – all of these things are helpful to the research and scholarly communities. These discoveries and the corresponding papers and discourse help us think, criticise, rethink, communicate, test, retest and advance knowledge! Similarly, as we understand the progression of management thinking – its evolution and consequences – we advance our field and improve research, theory and practice in management!

Terminology and Definitions

What exactly do we mean by 'service' and 'services'? In fact, what seems on the surface as such simple words are anything but! Service is simply an act (a verb), or a process which represents or facilitates the basis of economic exchange (Vargo & Akaka, 2009); whereas services can be defined as *intangible units of output, or activities* (a noun) which in a commercial sense are offered for sale or as part of a sale (for example, restaurant service accompanies the food to form a total experience; both food and service are critical to the value perception of the customer).

Vargo and Lusch (2004) discuss the definition of services, suggesting that the continued debate over its definition was more abandoned than resolved. They argue that this is a reflection of the difficulty in attempting to make goods and services mutually exclusive. They propose a more integrated framework for understanding services and offer a slightly different definition of services as the "application of specialized competences (skills and knowledge), through deeds, processes and performances for the benefit of another entity or the entity itself" (Vargo & Lusch, 2004, p. 326).

The sale of a service often consists of many parts, including activities, processes and interactions (tangible and intangible aspects). Take a hotel as an example. What is a guest buying? Is it a bed? Or is it the temporary use of a bed? Are they buying food? Beverage? The use of a meeting room? Or, are they buying a *total experience* which ideally includes a seamless check-in by friendly, welcoming, knowledgeable staff, a clean, safe and comfortable room and the convenience to eat in a restaurant or have food and beverage delivered to their room? A customer would view the entire offering as a *series of service encounters*. So it is useful to commence this review by ensuring that you are thinking about tourism in the context of service. For example, be clear that the hotel industry is not so much about buildings, beds and food, but rather about service, and about the complexity of creating, selling and managing customer experiences.

From the outset, it is important to note that the terms service 'marketing' and 'management' are often used interchangeably. This review takes the position that management is a more holistic term, incorporating *all* management functions, *including* marketing. This review will use the term 'management' throughout. This review also makes frequent mention of the term 'customers'. It is important, in the context of tourism, to view 'tourists' or 'visitors' in the exact same context as 'customers'. Therefore these terms are used interchangeably.

Tourism and Service Management

Let us quickly reflect upon the concept of 'tourism' as it relates to this review of service. Tourism is often described not so much as an industry, but rather as is a 'complex system' – a combination of interrelated elements forming a unitary whole. Underlying this tourism system is a need to understand how to best manage the tourist experience in order to reach satisfying outcomes for tourists, individual businesses and destinations. The total tourist experience encompasses many aspects, but the primary aim of a tourism system should be tourist 'satisfaction'. Evaluation of satisfaction is usually made as a tourist's overall appraisal of the total destination experience, rather than of one single business. As a result, the management of each component of the tourism system by tourism businesses either individually or as part of organisational networks is particularly important.

Destination and tourism managers must have a watchful eye on all aspects of the *system* to ensure the wider destination performs well for the tourist / visitor, and then each individual business must strike the balance of satisfying tourists / visitors whilst operating profitably. A delicate balance indeed! In fact, tourism systems would be well served to rely on the Latin phrase 'E Pluribus Unum' (out of many, one), thus ensuring that individual participants understand their role in the system of individual aspects / businesses within a larger destination unit.

Before progressing into the key concepts of service management, it would be helpful to first reflect about how tourists evaluate their tourism experiences.

- Think about a tourist's first encounter with a tourism destination. It might be an advertisement for that destination on television or in a newspaper. Or it could be on a website (e.g., Tripadvisor.com). Destination websites often contain many links to travel packages, accommodation choices, car rental business, places to visit and things to do within that destination. Nested within these destination-marketing activities is a reliance on the individual performance of each organization promoted through destination marketing offers.

- Do you think that your impressions of Singapore as a satisfying tourism destination can be influenced by your trip to Singapore on Singapore Airlines? Or a first visit to Australia on Qantas? The UK on British Airways?

- What if the person you speak to on the phone regarding destination services on a toll-free number is less than friendly or enthusiastic?

- How would a tourist react upon stopping at a Visitor Information Centre and finding that the employees (often volunteers) are indifferent or apathetic about the region's tourism activities?

- What if the reservation desk in the hotel, where you plan on spending your first night at the destination, has no sign of your reservation – and they have no rooms available?

As you can see, the experience of the tourist is dependent on many component parts, many of which exist before someone ever becomes a tourist at a destination, and destination marketers hope that none of these links will lead to dissatisfaction with the overall tourist experience.

Evolution of the 'Service' discipline

By all accounts, the economic output of most developed countries today is dominated by 'services', with a generally accepted assumption that between 75-80% of gross domestic 'product' (GDP) is comprised of services (interesting that GDP is predominately comprised of services!). This seems very large, until one reflects upon how and where they spend their money. The basic categories of services are government, tourism, retail trade, healthcare, transport, utilities, communications, finance, insurance and real-estate (Lovelock, Wirtz and Chew, 2009). Services were formerly named the 'miscellaneous' (non-goods) economic category in the 19th century, but have now more appropriately been labelled the 'new economy' (Albrecht & Zemke, 2002) and is dominant across much of the developed and developing world.

Much discourse has taken place over the differentiation of the terms 'goods' and 'services'. Some (e.g., Kotler, 1997) suggest that nearly any business transaction would be either a purely tangible good, a tangible good with accompanying intangible service, a primarily intangible service with accompanying tangible good, or a purely intangible service. Others argue that the service and non-service distinction has become less meaningful and there are only industries, the service components of which are greater or less than those of other industries. Many years ago Marshall (1929) suggested that all industries provide some kind of service, although he pointed out that there was no specific literature which addressed the management of service.

The current service management discipline is often attributed to a seminal paper (Shostack, 1977) in which the author called for services marketing to 'Break Free' from product marketing. Shostack, a senior vice president of Marketing at Citibank, came to realise that the marketing paradigms (such as the 4 Ps mentioned above) taught at university did not adequately apply to what customers 'buy' at banks.

More recently, a series of articles and books by Vargo and Lusch, (see references below) have questioned this call to 'break free', proposing the need for *all marketing and management* to break free of the manufacturing/production orientation, by adopting instead a service orientation. The original call for services to 'break free' from goods included a movement by service management scholars to find a way to make service 'distinct' or unique from more traditional management. As such, a number of generally accepted characteristics were touted as 'unique' to service. While these characteristics may no longer be accepted as 'unique' it is important to be familiar with these concepts because they are still relevant to service management. The four most commonly cited 'distinctive features' of services are:

- ◆ **Intangibility** – services cannot be seen, felt, tasted or touched; they are performances rather than objects;

- ◆ **Inseparability** – goods are often produced, sold and then consumed, whereas services are usually produced and consumed at the same time;

- ◆ **Heterogeneity** – people play a critical role in service delivery; service and people are generally inextricably linked; this creates variability between service providers *and customers* which makes managing service so difficult; and

- ◆ **Perishability** – services cannot be stored; once a service is gone, it can never be sold again – e.g., airline seat, a dinner reservation.

(adapted from Kandampully, 2002)

Notes:

♦ For a critique of these four unique characteristics, see Vargo and Lusch (2004).

♦ For further reading regarding the intangibility of service see Bowen and Ford (2002).

The term 'Service Management' was not actually introduced into mainstream scholarship until the early 1980s (Fisk, Brown and Bitner, 1993; Gronroos, 1993). One of the earliest, yet still often cited definitions of service management is that it is a total organisational approach that makes quality of service, as perceived by the customer, the primary driving force for the operation of any business (Albrecht, 1988).

Another founding scholar in the service management arena, Christian Gronroos, suggested in the mid-1990's that "service management is not a well-delineated concept…It is however used more and more by academics as well as by practitioners…. and is more a perspective than one discipline or one coherent area of its own…" (Gronroos, 1993, p. 5). Gronroos highlights four fundamental shifts in thinking between a product/goods approach and a service approach, proposing that service management move from:

1 a product-based utility (referring to satisfaction received) to total utility.

2 short-term transactions to long-term relationships.

3 core product 'technical' quality to total customer – perceived quality.

4 production quality to total utility quality as *the* key process in management.

The reasons for the growth in services (and subsequent need for management theory) are well defined by Gronroos (1990). He attributes the growth to increasing affluence, more leisure time, a higher percentage of women joining the workforce, greater life expectancy, greater complexity of products that require a service aspect, increasing complexities of life, greater concern about ecology and resource scarcity, and an increased number of new products. Figure 1 provides a summary of the forces that have shaped services marketing and management over the past 20 years.

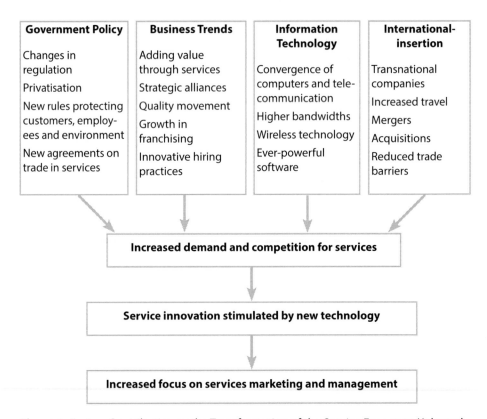

Figure 1: Factors Contributing to the Transformation of the Service Economy. (Adapted from Lovelock & Wirtz, 2004, p. 7)

Is Service Management and Marketing Really 'Unique'?

As mentioned earlier, the most current thinking about whether or not service management should be separated as a distinct field of study (e.g., should it 'break free' from product management?) has been significantly advanced by a number of scholars, led by Robert *Lusch* and Stephen *Vargo*. These authors propose a new 'logic' (S-D, or Service Dominant) – suggesting that it is inaccurate and counterproductive to ask for service marketing and management to "break free" from goods marketing. Rather, they suggest, marketing and management should break free from the goods and manufacturing-based model—that is, goods-dominant (G-D) logic.

Vargo and Lusch commenced the discourse questioning the 'dominant logic' of basing all marketing and management concepts on a 'goods' paradigm and terminologies (see for example, Lusch, Vargo and O'Brien, 2007; Vargo & Akaka, 2009; Vargo & Lusch, 2004, 2008). They argued that the notion of separating goods from service management is grounded in a flawed perspective – one that defines service residually (i.e. once goods are categorized, then services are anything that do not fit into the goods category).

Further information on the Vargo and Lusch 'Service-Dominant Logic' discourse can be found on http://www.sdlogic.net/publications.html

The evolution of service management as an academic discipline was detailed by Fisk, Brown and Bitner (1993) and Berry and Parasuraman (1993). These two works explain how an academic field does not magically appear one day. Rather, researchers make decisions about what to study based on how institutions and industry agree to fund projects and conference attendance. Collaboration and networks develop and over time, with exponential interest from a range of related areas, a field starts to develop. Fisk et al. (1993) proposed the following analogy for the evolution of a new discipline, in this case, services marketing.

- **Crawling out period** (pre-1980), a time of discovery and risk taking, capturing the embryonic beginnings of the service literature; scholars chose to pioneer this blossoming area, however they put themselves into a difficult position of developing new knowledge with no research model or framework; mainly conceptual works, with minimal opportunities to publish in top journals.

- **Scurrying about period** (1980-1985), a time period where interest and enthusiasm for service and services marketing was gaining significant momentum; during this period, the debate between 'services' and 'goods' began to wane, which paved the way for the next stage; a major growth in academic publications around service management and marketing, including top journals.

- **Walking erect period** (1986 – present), this period is marked by explosive growth in numbers of publications as well as corresponding growth in empirical and theoretical rigor in the content; research and discourse on managing quality, designing and controlling service processes, managing supply and demand, and many others; the focus by now had become increasingly cross-functional, as many issues being researched have roots and solutions that span across many boundaries.

To highlight the growth of the Service Management discipline, the list below provides a sample of the journals which publish substantially in service management and marketing.

Table 1: Sample list of key journals and texts in Service Marketing and Management

Specifically service-related academic journals

Journal of Service Research (jsr.sagepub.com)

Journal of Service Management (info.emeraldinsight.com/products/journals/journals.htm?id=josm)

Managing Service Quality (info.emeraldinsight.com/products/journals/journals.htm?id=msq)

Journal of Services Marketing (info.emeraldinsight.com/products/journals/journals.htm?id=jsm)

Service Industries Journal (www.tandf.co.uk/journals/titles/02642069.asp)

Other academic journals which regularly publish service research

Journal of Retailing (www.elsevier.com/wps/find/journaldescription.cws_home/620186/description#description)

Journal of the Academy of Marketing Science (JAMS) (jam.sagepub.com/)

Journal of Business Research (www.elsevier.com/wps/find/journaldescription.cws_home/505722/description#description)

European Journal of Marketing (info.emeraldinsight.com/products/journals/journals.htm?id=ejm)

Sample of service management / marketing textbooks

Fitzsimmons, J.A., Fitzsimmons, M.J. (2008). *Service Management: Operations, Strategy, Information Technology.* McGraw-Hill/Irwin, Boston (6th ed).

Gronroos, C. (2007). *Service Management and Marketing: Customer Management in Service Competition.* John Wiley & Sons, Ltd. West Sussex. (3rd ed.).

Johnston, R. (2008). *Service Operations Management: Improving Service Delivery.* Prentice Hall, New York (3rd ed).

Kandampully, J. (2007). *Services Management: The New Paradigm in Hospitality.* Prentice Hall, New Jersey (2nd ed).

Lovelock, C., Wirtz, J., Chew, P. (2009). *Essentials of Services Marketing.* Prentice Hall, Singapore.

Mills, P. K. and Snyder, K. M. (2010). *Knowledge Services Management: Organizing Around Internal Markets.* New York: Springer.

Parker, David (2012). *Service Operations Management: The Total Experience.* Retrieved from http://www.eblib.com

Rust, R. T., Huang, M. and Edward Elgar Publishing. (2014). *Handbook of Service Marketing Research.* Cheltenham: Edward Elgar Pub. Ltd.

Schultz, M., Doerr, J. E. and Frederiksen, L. W. (2013). *Professional Services Marketing: How the Best Firms Build Premier Brands, Thriving Lead Generation Engines, and Cultures of Business Development Success.* Hoboken, NJ: John Wiley & Sons, Inc.

Zeithaml, V.A., Bitner, M.J. (2009). *Services Marketing: Integrating Customer Focus Across the Firm.* McGraw-Hill Irwin, Boston.

Important Concepts in Service Management

As discussed above, the service management mindset is relatively new, and integrates a number of interrelated concepts in order to create a service perspective. These topics are generally categorised as:

♦ Service operations management;

♦ Service human resource management; and

♦ Service marketing.

This section identifies a number of the more important concepts which underpin service management and which are particularly useful in understanding service related issues in a tourism context. These concepts are:

1 Service Quality

2 Customer Centricity

3 Service Encounter / Customer Contact Employees

4 Tourist / Customer Satisfaction

5 Service Failure / Recovery

6 Linking Employees, Customers and Firm Performance

7 Organisational Culture / Climate for Service

8 Employee Engagement

9 Balanced Scorecard (with a Case Example)

Service Quality

One of the prominent themes in service management centres on the idea of quality. Quality in a business context, before the mid 1980s tended to be geared toward product or manufacturing quality – that which could be checked prior to delivery (e.g., checked in the factory). However, because of the frequent (as mentioned earlier) inseparability between service provider and service receiver, the paradigms in existence to understand and measure service quality were either non-existent, hypothetical and/or conceptual.

Until the middle 1980s little work had been done to define service quality and identify those elements that determine how service quality could be delivered or measured. In a series of seminal papers on service quality, Parasuraman, Zeithaml and Berry (1985) identified quality as an elusive and notably indistinct construct, with its requirements and descriptions not easily articulated by consumers of the day. Given the challenge of articulating the concept, these researchers suggested that measuring such a construct was equally difficult. Nonetheless, it was becoming clear that whilst the substance of service quality was unclear, its importance to consumers was not. These authors commenced a series of papers that are still generally accepted today as a baseline for understanding and articulating service quality (Parasuraman, 1996; Parasuraman, Berry and Zeithaml, 1988; Parasuraman, Berry and Zeithaml, 1991; Parasuraman, Zeithaml and Berry, 1985; Zeithaml, Berry and Parasuraman, 1996).

This seminal research argued that before management could realistically call for improved service quality – it was vital to:

a   Clarify the strategic position and objectives of the organization (quality ambitions would be very different for a fast food restaurant versus a 5-star hotel); and

b   Identify the relevant dimensions of service quality.

Parasuraman and his colleagues (1985) first sought to identify the initial determinants of service quality. The initial list of determinants was narrowed down to ten, and whilst these ten items were later refined through subsequent research and statistical modelling, it is instructive (from an academic and from an industry perspective) to view and have a basic understanding of these determinants (see Table 2).

Table 2: The Original Ten Service Quality Factors from Parasuraman et al. (1985).

Reliability- consistency of performance and dependability.

Responsiveness - willingness or readiness of employees to provide service.

Competence- possession of the required skills and knowledge to perform the service.

Access - approachability and ease of contact.

Courtesy - politeness, respect, consideration, and friendliness of contact personnel

Communication - keeping customers informed in language they can understand

Credibility - trustworthiness, believability, and honesty

Security - freedom from danger, risk, or doubt.

Understanding / knowing the Customer - making the effort to understand the customer's needs.

Tangibles - physical evidence of the service.

For a comprehensive overview of these ten factors and insight into the development of their service quality measures, see the following references:

Parasuraman, A., Zeithaml, V. and Berry, L. (1985). A conceptual model of service quality and its implications for future research. *Journal of Marketing,* **49**(Fall), 41-50.

Parasuraman, A., Berry, L. and Zeithaml, V. (1988). SERVQUAL: A multiple-item scale for measuring consumer perceptions of service quality. *Journal of Retailing*, **64**(1), 12-40.

Parasuraman, A., Berry, L. and Zeithaml, V. (1991). Understanding customer expectations of service. *Sloan Management Review* (Spring), 39-48.

Conceptualizing and measuring service quality has not been easy! There is still no fundamental agreement on the most accurate, appropriate way to measure it. There are however, a number of generally accepted frameworks for understanding and measuring service quality. While debate continues, the following three frameworks provide a general overview of ways and approaches of measuring service quality and are useful for understanding service management.

1 SERVQUAL

The first of these frameworks is known as SERVQUAL and has five dimensions, which were drawn from the ten shown in Table 2 (Parasuraman, Berry and Zeithaml, 1988):

1 **Reliability** – accurate and dependable service;

2 **Responsiveness** – prompt and helpful service;

3 **Empathy** – caring and personalised attention;

4 **Assurance** – knowledge and trust; and

5 **Tangibles** – appearance of physical facilities.

These dimensions are used in a pre- and post- evaluation of a service in order to compare the variance between a consumer's expectation of a service and actual performance.

The SERVQUAL model is known as a 'gaps' model because it measures the variance between expectations and performance. It has been used extensively in the services literature, and to a lesser extent in the tourism literature (Kvist & Klefsjo, 2006) although it is not without significant criticism (Morrison-Coulthard, 2004). Some of the primary criticisms of SERVQUAL include:

1 Concerns with the disconfirmation paradigm (asking a person to compare a service against their expectations for that service);

2 The lack of evidence as to the validity of the 'gaps' type model;

3 The lack of consistent dimensionality with the five-factor scale; and

4 Its failure to work as an effective measure across different service industries.

2 SERVPERF

In response to SERVQUAL, Cronin & Taylor (1992, 1994) argue that there was little if any theoretical or empirical evidence supporting the relevance of the expectations-performance gap as the basis for measuring service quality. They argue that there are critical limitations with SERVQUAL due to the fact that the disconfirmation paradigm does not perform well statistically. They presented a performance-based alternative method called the SERVPERF, which some argue performs better and explains more of the variation in the global measure of service quality in four service industries examined: banks, pest control, dry cleaning, and fast food services.

3 THE NORDIC MODEL

The third framework, developed by Gronroos in the early 1980s, is known as the two-factor Nordic framework. This model has two dimensions, a *technical* or *outcome* dimension, which might be referred to as the 'what'; and a *functional* or *process-related* dimension, which might be referred to as the 'how.'

As an example, a hotel guest will be provided with a hotel room, an airline passenger will be provided with transport, or a tourist - with a coach tour of a city. All of these 'outcomes' of the service process are part of the perceived quality experience. However, a tourist's overall determination of quality is not based solely on the room, the arrival at the destination or the ride in the touring coach. There will be many interactions, or service encounters, between a service provider and a customer, which will influence the tourist's overall impressions of quality. The friendliness and professionalism of the front desk employee, the airline cabin crew and the tour coach operator, for example, will all influence the tourist's perceptions of quality. In other words, a tourist is influence by the actual service (the 'what') and the way in which the service was performed (the 'how').

The Nordic model also proposes other factors such as expectations versus performance and company image which may influence or impact upon perceived service quality. It is therefore important for tourism operators to carefully manage their brand or market image, as this can influence quality perceptions. If, for example, a firm has a favourable image, minor mistakes are more likely to be forgiven. Conversely, if the image is negative, the impact of any mistake will often be considerably greater (Gronroos, 2000).

Customer centricity

At the centre of the service management paradigm is the idea that all decisions made by the firm must be made with the customer as the focal point (Kandampully, 2006). This might seem a logical idea, but businesses for many years often made decisions based on internal motivations – such as cost savings, ease of distribution or convenience for employees. Customer centricity, or even *obsession* must be central to a service management paradigm.

The idea of customer centricity is not a new one. In 1954 Drucker proposed that it is customers who ultimately define what a business is, what it actually produces and whether or not it will prosper (Drucker, 1954). Five trends, still relevant today, have been identified in today's marketplace which reinforce the need for tourism firms to make a transformation from a product to a customer-centric focus (Sheth, Sisodia and Sharma, 2000). These trends are:

♦   Intensifying pressures to improve marketing productivity;

♦   Intensifying competition;

♦   Increasing market diversity;

♦   Demanding and better informed consumers; and

♦   Advances in technology.

Clearly, tourism operates within an environment where all of these trends exist. Successful tourism firms have realised that the best means to develop long-term customer relationships is to place the customer squarely in the middle of all efforts. This is very difficult to do however, and many companies today across all industries struggle with this as an underlying concept despite its logic and seeming simplicity.

For a comprehensive overview of customer centricity, see Shah, Rust, Parasuraman, Staelin and Day (2006).

Customer centricity differs from previous product centric models on a number of dimensions. Table 3 summarizes some of the key differences and distinguishing features of product and customer centricity. The product-centric approach is drawn from the early years of marketing where scholars and industry directed their attention toward the exchange of goods, and where the prime function of marketing was to find ways to bring its products to the market. Customer centricity should be at the heart of the strategy of any tourism business, and because of the high customer contact nature of most tourism businesses, must predominate in the culture of a tourism business.

Table 3: Comparison of the Product-Centric and Customer-Centric Approaches (adopted from Shah et al., 2006)

	Product-Centric Approach	Customer-Centric Approach
Basic philosophy	Sell things to whoever will buy	All decisions start with the customer and are focused on present and future customer needs
Business orientation	Transaction-oriented	Relationship-oriented
Product positioning	Highlight features and advantages of product	Highlight benefits to customer
Organizational focus	Internally focused on ways to increase sales and development new products; marketing a separate function	Externally focused, based on making profits as the result of customer loyalty; sees employees as strategic resources; marketing function integrated into all departments
Performance metrics	Numbers of products; profit per product; market share by brand	Share of customer, customer satisfaction, customer loyalty, customer lifetime value, service climate
Selling philosophy	How many customers can we sell to?	How can we most appropriately satisfy each customer by providing as many produces and services to meet their individual needs?
Customer knowledge	Customer data a control mechanism	Customer knowledge a valuable asset

Service encounter / Customer contact employees

Given the fundamental premise that service is often provided in an interaction between employees and customers, it is important to be aware of some of the important issues around the 'moment of truth' in service, or what is called the service encounter. A service encounter can be defined as the interaction between a tourist and the service provider. The outcomes of service encounters thus depend on the skills, knowledge, personality, behaviour, and performance of these employees. If successful, effective service encounters can lead to many favourable outcomes, including satisfaction, loyalty, and positive word-of-mouth recommendation. It is therefore imperative that tourism firms understand how to manage these critical service encounters.

At the heart of service management is the unavoidable fact that a significant proportion of tourism experiences are delivered by people (tourism employees, managers, owners). The unfortunate irony about this fact is that many customer contact employees are the youngest and least trained of employees. Although many services have become more reliant on technology (vending machines, airline self (or 'e') check in), person-to-person interactions still predominate in most tourism businesses. The employees who deliver the service obviously have a direct influence on tourists, as of course do owners, managers, and other stakeholders who indirectly contribute to the service. Moreover, other people in the service environment at the time of service delivery, including other tourists, also play a part. The personal appearance, attitudes, and behaviour of all involved, directly or indirectly, have an influence on a tourist's perception of service.

From the tourist's perspective, the most immediate evidence of service quality is the service encounter itself. Interactions with service employees are the experiences that tourists are most likely to remember, and employees who are uncomfortable in dealing with tourists or who lack the training and expertise to meet expectations can cause tourists to retain unpleasant memories of a service experience. Service employees are thus the primary resource through which service businesses can gain a competitive advantage (Lovelock & Wirtz, 2004).

A number of management approaches have been suggested which can help tourism businesses manage or control service encounters. Examples of these include:

1   **Scripts** – where service providers follow pre-determined statements, such as, "would you like fries with that?"

2   **Role-play training** – putting employees into mock service situations to assist them in correctly dealing with a range of circumstances.

3   **Clearly defined service processes** – a more general approach than scripts, but with clear expectations of steps of service.

4   **Engrained service culture** – embedding the importance of customers into the fabric of the organization (more on this below).

5   **Effective recruitment / Human resource management** – ensuring that the right people are employed and that individual development continues throughout the term of employment.

Customer contact employees have been given many labels, including 'boundary spanners', 'gatekeepers' and 'image-makers' (Bowen and Schneider, 1985). They are a tourism organization's primary interface with customers and, as such, are often perceived by the customer as *the* product. Bowen and Schneider (1985) insist that employees not only create and deliver the service, but also are the entire image of the organization. Within tourism businesses, service is performed for a customer by a service person (e.g., a waiter, front desk receptionist, a tour guide). From the customer's point of view, service is essentially the performance of the staff who serve as the public face of the organization or in some cases, the destination. It should be noted that most services do have a tangible aspect which must also be acceptable to the customer, and it is this package of tangible and intangible aspects that define a tourist's experience.

Bowen and Ford (2002) argue that managing the service employee is different to managing employees located in positions with little or no customer contact. There are six basic differences:

1   Service employees must be both task and interactive capable, because customers are present in the service 'factory' (producing and engaging simultaneously).

2   Attitudes and behaviours are more critical than technical skills for service employees (and skills can be taught more easily than attitude).

3   Formal mechanisms for employee control cannot be used with service employees. Instead, a service culture and climate must be in evidence to fill gaps which form as the result of unexpected or unplanned customer-interactions or circumstances.

4   Emotions play a role with service employees, as observable facial and body displays create impressions, and emotional displays by service providers can have positive/negative effects on customers. Therefore, service employees, to be most effective, must be skilled to understand which emotions are appropriate in different circumstances (empathy when something has gone wrong, excited when a customer is, etc.).

5   Service employees must be trained to deal with role-related conflict. For example, if a customer is unhappy with a service standard, he might become angry with the service provider, even though the employee was doing their job as expected by the organization.

6   Service employees are expected to be 'part-time marketers' (selling future service while providing a service). This implies that service employees are expected to fully understand their firm's offerings and demonstrate enthusiasm for them. This can be enhanced through the concept known as 'internal marketing'. Here, a firm's products and service should first be marketed to its employees so that they are in the best position to 'sell' when interacting with customers.

Tourist (or Customer) Satisfaction

The term *customer satisfaction* is used often as an ideal to which tourism businesses and destinations strive (refer to the note at the beginning of this review which explains the interchangeability of the terms customer and tourist). But what *exactly* is meant by satisfaction? How can it be measured? And is 'satisfaction' sufficient? This section seeks not to provide in-depth detailed discussion as to its definition, but rather a brief overview of the construct, its importance and its implications.

Customer satisfaction is difficult to define. Oliver (1997) concluded that everyone knows what customer satisfaction is, until they are asked to define it. He defined customer satisfaction as:

> "a judgement that a product or service feature, or the product or service itself, provided (or is providing) a pleasurable level of consumption-related fulfilment..." (Oliver, 1997, p. 13).

Satisfaction is an emotional state, however, it is also likely to lead to repurchase intentions and recommendations. So understanding customer expectations and then striving to meet or exceed these expectation should be of central concern to all tourism managers.

Regardless of its definition or conceptualisation, there is general agreement that when tourists are satisfied, a range of actions and behaviours follow. Tourists who are satisfied with a destination or tourism business:

1 Are likely to become loyal and visit repeatedly;
2 Will deepen their relationships with the destination and its individual service providers;
3 Are more likely to recommend the destination to others; and
4 Demonstrate less price sensitivity.

It is therefore important for destination marketers as well as individual organizations within a destination to understand the importance of customer perceptions of their experiences and to work hard to measure and continually improve ways to satisfy tourists.

Rather than aiming only to satisfy customers, some suggest 'delight' as the more appropriate ambition (Rust & Oliver, 2000; Torres & Kline, 2006). Customer delight has been defined as a higher emotional state than satisfaction, more of a pleasant or unexpected surprise. This type of provision, however, does not come without extra effort on the part of the tourism firm. Therefore, some suggest that a policy of customer delight is not sustainable, as the expectations of customers will continue to rise, making it more and more difficult to delight customers on subsequent visits. Nonetheless, the concept is an interesting one, and one which tourism industry practitioners can learn from: We must do more than aim to merely satisfy our visitors! There is a potential for building a loyal customer base from whom the business will capitalise on in a long perspective due to the repeat visits and positive word-of-mouth.

For further information about customer satisfaction and delight, see (Giese & Cote, 2000; Rust & Oliver, 2000; Szymanski & Henard, 2001; Torres & Kline, 2006)

Service failure and recovery

No business can satisfy every customer every time. The likelihood of failure in services is significantly magnified because of the human element! When we refer to the human element, we do not only mean that service employees can make errors. Customers can at times be dissatisfied even if the service is provided correctly and appropriately! (According to the firm's definition of correct and appropriate!) This can be due to many reasons, such as customer expectations being misaligned with the businesses service offering or due to the customer being in a poor state of mind (for a review of customer misbehaviour (see Harris & Reynolds, 2004).

Regardless who is to blame for a service failure or a perceived service failure, it is vital for service firms to make every effort to retain their customers. It is often suggested that it costs five times as much to attract a new customers as it does to retain an existing one.

Adding to the challenge of service failure is the fact that many customers will simply not complain (Voorhees, Brady and Horowitz, 2006). This is because it is often too time consuming to do so, or that they do not see it as likely that the firm will take notice. In addition, complaining can be unpleasant and stressful (more so in some cultures than others). It is therefore critical for service managers to (a) encourage customers to voice their complaints and (b) take immediate action wherever possible to return aggrieved customers into satisfied ones.

Customers who do complain often do so for one of four main reasons:

1   To obtain some kind of compensation (or to have the service performed again);

2   To release anger;

3   To help improve the service organisation; and

4   Concern for others.

      (Lovelock, et al., 2009).

Top performing service firms, aware of the potential harm of service failures – but also understanding the potential benefits of rectifying service failure – take extraordinary measures to train staff in how to identify service failures and how to handle customer complaints.

In order for businesses to reassure tourists in the reliability of service, a service guarantee can be implemented. Due to the intangible nature of service and its inseparability (services are produced and consumed simultaneously), customers are not given an option to try or test 'a service' before buying it. Therefore, a service guarantee serves as a promise from the company to deliver a good-quality. In case the company does not, the customer would receive some kind of compensation.

Linking Employees, Customers and Firm Performance

Although we have been addressing the concept of service from the perspective of how to improve tourist satisfaction within a tourism firm or destination, individual organizations are generally motivated to initiate quality programs which can be directly tied to financial performance. In other words, business owners are most interested in profitability – hence any motivation to improve service must have direct implications for profitability.

Two related conceptual frameworks link internal organisational function to customers and firm performance outcome measures. These are the service-profit chain and employee-customer linkage research.

Service-profit chain

The service-profit chain conceptual framework proposes a hypothetical chain of events which link the internal functioning of an organization to employee loyalty and productivity, service value, customer satisfaction and finally to revenue growth and profitability (Figure 2) (Heskett et al., 2008).

For further information about the service-profit chain, see: http://www.serviceprofitchain.com/

Figure 2 highlights the fact that tourism firms would benefit from focusing on the left side of the chain (inside the organisation), including investment in the various elements that make up the chain, rather than directly focusing on revenues and profits. The internal functioning of the organization is defined as what goes on within an organization in terms of workplace design, and those functions which facilitate employees' ability to service customers. The key aspects of the service-profit chain are:

1 Customer satisfaction drives customer loyalty, which drives revenues and profits.

2 Customer perceived value drives customer satisfaction.

3 Employee satisfaction drives employee productivity which enhances customer value.

4 Solid internal organizational practices drive employee satisfaction.

5 Top-management leadership in the chain underlies the chain's success.

Figure 2: The Service-Profit Chain (adopted from Heskett et al., 2008)

Employee-customer linkage research

The boundaries between employees and customers in most tourism organizations are fairly permeable – a condition termed "psychological closeness" between employee and customer (Schneider & Bowen, 1993). Because of the closeness between employees and customers in services, further interest in better understanding these links has become known as *linkage* research (Pugh, Dietz, Wiley and Brooks, 2002). Linkage research is similar to the service-profit chain, in that it suggests a relationship between employees, customers and firm performance. However, linkage research focuses *explicitly* on employee perceptions of various intraorganisational practices and the corresponding relationships to customer perceptions. In other words, linkage research is interested in a more detailed picture of the left-hand side of the service-profit chain (Figure 3).

The specific dimensions of internal organisational function mirror measures of organisational climate (discussed below). Linkage research finds the specific levers, or drivers, which *link* employee perceptions to customer perceptions. By doing so, management can become acutely aware of these areas which have the greatest influence on customers, and can therefore focus on improving those areas. The main differences between linkage research and the service-profit chain approaches are:

1   The service-profit chain purports employee satisfaction to be an important part of the chain, whereas linkage research suggests it is more about employee perceptions of service-climate factors which link to customer outcomes; and

2   The service-profit chain conceptualises links directly to organizational performance criteria, whereas linkage research focuses on the direct links between employee perceptions and customer perceptions.

Both of the concepts discussed above rely on matters *inside* the organisation. The study of organisational culture and climate are critically relevant to the understanding about organisational practices.

Service culture and climate

The study of climate and culture is drawn from the discipline of organisational (or industrial) psychology, a field that seeks to better understand how individuals behave, or are likely to behave, in an organization or business setting. Organisational psychologists research and analyse how workplace practices impact employee behaviour and attitudes, and how this can be altered for the benefit of the employee and the workplace. This focus is particularly important when studying tourism service businesses because of the aforementioned 'psychological closeness' between employees and tourists in tourism-related businesses. Knowledge gleaned from the study of individuals in organisational settings can be applied in order to assist organizations function more effectively—a generally accepted precursor to hard performance measures, such as profits.

Every organization, whether intended or not, has a culture of some kind. Culture, from an organisational point of view, is often defined as the values and norms embedded into an organization. An organisational culture, particularly in a service business has the ability to fill the gaps between:

1 What the organization can anticipate and train its people to deal with; and

2 The opportunities and problems that arise in daily encounters with customers (Ford & Heaton, 2001).

Since managers cannot supervise every interaction which takes place between employees and tourists it is important for tourism service organizations to develop a predominating norm of behaviour which is focused on customers and service quality. Such an approach minimises the gaps which unforseen circumstances might cause in services and also works to motivate unsupervised employees. One such strategy is to create a *climate for service.*

Organisational climate, similar to culture, is defined as employee perceptions of the practices and procedures in the organization (Denison, 1996). It differs from culture in that it represents an assessment of how employees perceive various aspects of an organization, whereas culture represents the values and norms, often the aspirations of management. Climate represents how well these aspirations are actually perceived by employees and those who come into contact with an organization. These aspirations are often communicated through artefacts, stories and myths.

Climate is normally obtained by measuring respondent perceptions of what goes on around them, in terms of organisational events, policies, practices, expectations, and so on.

A climate *for service* represents the degree to which all of a firm's activities, policies and practices are focused on service quality and customer satisfaction. Schneider and White (2004) summarise it as follows -

> 'So, when employees perceive that they are rewarded for delivering quality service *and* when employees perceive that management devotes time, energy, and resources to service quality *and* when employees receive the training they require to effectively deal with diverse customers, *then* a positive service climate is more likely to be the theme or meaning attached to these experiences' (p. 100).

A positive climate for service is said to exist when all of the aggregate conditions are present for excellent service to be provided to customers. Climate is usually measured by using a survey methodology. Many best practice tourism organizations employ climate measures as a part of their organisational learning process. With regular measures of an organisational climate, progressive-thinking companies use the results to improve employee perceptions, and then utilise improved employee perceptions as a key part of performance measurement (see the final section on Balanced Scorecards for ways in which climate can be used strategically).

Employee Engagement

An aspect of organisational climate which has resonated very strongly in service organisations over recent years is employee engagement. In the context of a climate for service, tourism managers constantly seek ways to harness the 'discretionary effort' of often unsupervised employees (Macey, Schneider, Barbera and Young, 2009). The concept of employee 'engagement' is somewhat new to the study of the study of organisational psychology but similar to the growth of service management, this particular area has been gaining much popularity over the past 15 years of so. Kahn (1990) is regarded as the first scholar to apply the psychological concept of engagement to the workplace. His broad conceptualisation suggests that the more employees feel they are able to express their preferred selves at work, the more they invest in their work role and their organisation. Since the introduction of employee, or work, engagement concept, its popularity in the business arena has grown much faster than in academic circles.

Schneider and his colleagues (Macey, et al., 2009; Schneider, Macey, Barbera and Martin, 2009) define employee engagement as comprising two major components. The first relates more to 'feelings', and describes an elevated state of energy and enthusiasm towards the organisation and the work tasks. The second component, 'behaviours', are the actions demonstrated by employees in pursuit of achieving organisational goals.

It is important to emphasise the distinction between engagement and satisfaction. While job satisfaction is related to what a company is doing for its employees and involves employees' evaluations of such drivers as job security, benefits and opportunities for advancement, engagement is concerned with the full utilisation of an employee's skills and abilities and a link between individual and organisational objectives (Schneider et al., 2009). In this light, an employee can be satisfied with their job, in that it pays well enough, is stable and offers future opportunities, yet still not be engaged in their work as the employee feels under-utilised and personally misaligned with organisational goals and values. Similarly, scholars have emphasised that although there is a perceived overlap between engagement and established constructs such as organisational commitment and job involvement, there is sufficient evidence to support engagement as its own distinct construct.

Measures of employee engagement are seen as critically important predictors of future business performance, with many large tourism organisations adopting the strategy that enhanced employee engagement leads to improved financial outcomes (similar to the service- profit chain, but with employee engagement a key aspect of intraorganisational practices). The need to understand and measure these 'soft' (non financial, often less easy to measure) performance criteria has been given significantly increased attention via Balanced Scorecards.

Measuring Performance – Using a Balanced Scorecard

Given the service and people centric nature of tourism, how then would it be most appropriate to gauge performance? Traditionally, organisational performance has been based only on a range of *financial* measures. Kaplan and Norton (1992) devised a new way to link firm strategy (value drivers) with measuring performance. They named this system the *Balanced Scorecard*. Recognizing some of the weaknesses and vagueness of previous management approaches, the Balanced Scorecard approach provides a clear prescription as to what companies should measure in order to 'balance' the financial perspective.

The Balanced Scorecard allows managers to look at the business from many different perspectives, based on the strategic objectives of the particular organization. Its application provides answers to four basic questions:

1   How do customers see and think of us (perspective from the outside)?

2   What must we be good at inside our business in order to satisfy our internal customers or employees (internal processes)?

3   How can we ensure that we continue to improve and grow (learning and development)?

4   How do we look to our owners / shareholders (financial picture)?

The Balanced Scorecard is a management and measurement system that enables organizations to clarify their vision and strategy and translate them into action. It provides feedback around both the internal business processes and external outcomes in order to continuously improve strategic performance and results. When fully deployed, the Balanced Scorecard transforms strategic planning from an academic exercise into the nerve centre of an enterprise.

When used effectively, a Balanced Scorecard forces managers and employees to focus on key drivers of organisational success. In many ways, the Balanced Scorecard becomes a quantitative yardstick which measures various aspects of the service-profit chain or the linkage research model discussed earlier in the chapter. Whilst there are challenges in its implementation, such as costs, time, expertise and references, the Balanced Scorecard can be an effective conceptual tool or program by which service organizations can be managed and measured.

Case Example: Cactus Jacks Restaurants – Queensland, Australia

Always open-minded to new ways to improve the business, the owner of Cactus Jacks, an Australian casual theme restaurant chain, learned about the Balanced Scorecard as applied to tourism businesses via a 2006 financial review magazine article written by the author of this review. The benefits of implementing a Balanced Scorecard type of system was highlighted in this article, principally for the purposes of:

a   Identifying the important drivers of success;

b   Clarifying standards of customer experiences;

c   Measuring the performance of the business based on non-financial measures; and

d   Paying staff bonuses based on key metrics *additional to* financial performance.

Step one was to clarify the strategic drivers of the business. These were determined to be:

1 **Financial performance** – principally driven by revenue growth and profitability;

2 **Customer satisfaction and loyalty** – based on the entire customer experience including food, service, value and ambiance;

3 **Employee attitudes** – a system to identify and focus on critical issues about employee well being and workplace practices;

4 **Individual performance** – of supervisors and managers.

Over the course of the first 12 months, work was undertaken in consultation with management and staff to create a diagnostic system which would effectively measure the key strategic drivers listed above. This was designed to help the owner identify and gauge the long-term performance of the business.

The summary below provides further information about the way in which the Balanced Scorecard was set up for this particular business, and highlights some of the key issues related to each

1 **Financial performance.** A matrix was created which was modelled on the company budgets for sales and profits. Weightings were then allocated to each criteria based on the importance given to that area by the owner and the company leadership team.

2 **Customer perceptions.** A detailed and complex customised Customer Experience Evaluation Program (similar to what is often called a Mystery Shopper Program) was created. The first step in this process was a detailed mapping of the customer experience standards for the business (one of the benefits of this type of program is that it forces the business to clarify these standards in great details). Once the standards were created, and some pilot tests run on the questionnaire, a regular series of visits were undertaken during every 6-month period by highly trained evaluators. The results of each key service criteria were then tabulated and scored, with detailed reports which outline opportunities and provide scores for each aspect of each visit. Each report and the corresponding scores were emailed to the corporate office and the respective management teams for review. This information was used to (a) improve the business, (b) let the corporate office gain an in-depth perspective about satisfaction and standards adherence and (c) inform the management remuneration program (Table 4 provides a summary of the key measures used).

3   **Employee perceptions.** A customised organizational engagement survey was developed, which integrated service climate factors coupled with other related measures such as staff turnover intentions, internal service quality, employee engagement and perceptions of owner commitment to excellence. The survey was administered every six months with scores continually assessed for improvement and opportunities to improve. Managers met in teams to strategise ways to improve various aspects of the survey results to ensure continuous work was done to improve the way employees perceive their workplace.

4   **Intangibles.** Each member of staff was given a comprehensive appraisal of their performance by their respective supervisors as well as an overall effectiveness rating by the managers and company owner, and a point score allocated.

Table 4: Sample Categories and Scores for Customer Perceptions Evaluation Program

Average of 7 for ALL questions	5.74
Average of 100	81.99%
KEY CATEGORY TOTALS	of 100
Phone Service	87.98%
Reception / greeting	88.57%
Drink Service	79.37%
Food waitperson	75.32%
Following service standards	72.86%
Care and Concern shown	82.14%
Manager / Supervisor perceptions	85.71%
Food freshness, presentation, taste	85.71%
Kitchen - Food and cooktimes	90.48%
Cook / Service times	90.00%
Value for money	85.71%
Critical 'overall satisfaction' questions	85.71%
Weighted Score	**83.01%**
	6 visits
Cumulative Weighted Score	80.72%
Cumulative Kitchen - Food and Cooktimes	85.79%
Cumulative Overall Satisfaction Score	78.38%

The items in Table 4 are weighted for importance with weightings varying from one year to the next, depending upon which areas the owner believes need particular focus for that year. All full time staff and management are given specific goals whereby bonuses are paid provided certain targets where achieved.

As a result of this program, major changes have occurred in this company. The entire team began to rally around the exact performance measures which the owner identified as important drivers for success. By focusing on customers, employees, training and individual performance ("What gets measured gets managed!"), sales and profits naturally flowed. The team has been able to share in small wins, work more closely in teams trying to make their targets and feel as though they could share in the successes of the business.

Rather than driving success through financial measures only, the Balanced Scorecard measurement system has altered the focus to the important drivers of success and have helped take Cactus Jacks to a higher plane and protect its long-term viability.

Acknowledgement

This case study was derived from the author of this review in conjunction with Jon Van Grinsven, owner of the Pierre Restaurant Group and the Cactus Jacks group of Mexican restaurants and Bars based in Townsville, Queensland, Australia.

Emerging Issues and a Future Focussed Agenda for the Field

There is no doubt that increased interest, deeper understanding and the ongoing growth of service management, particularly in the context of tourism, will continue. To ensure this growth, more and more university programs are now embedding variations of service marketing and management into their core curriculum, viewing this subject on par with other business core disciplines such as accounting, finance and human resource management. With this growth at university level will come an enhanced understanding through generational changes in tourism leadership.

Similarly, the discourse about whether or not service should 'break free' from mainstream marketing and management thought, or whether this is counterproductive and a remnant of traditional goods based approaches, will continue. However, it will be the practitioners in tourism who will ultimately decide which terminologies are most appropriate, and whether or not service management should break free or not.

Listed below are a list of current 'hot' topics in service management and marketing. Some have been established in the literature for a while now, but continue to be of interest in the academic and practice communities, others are emerging.

1   **Multiculturalism and Globalisation** – Improved understanding about how service management will be affected by globalisation and multiculturalism, particularly on employee-customer interactions in service recovery, and service encounters.

2   **Era of Digital Marketing** - Online reviews and tourism websites gain more popularity nowadays and play a significant role in tourists' destinations choices and services purchase.

3   **Experience Management** – Pine and Gilmore (1998) advocate customer experiences as critical to tourism; creating and managing tourism experiences will gain further emphasis in the tourism and service management literature.

4   **Social Psychology / Social Identity** – the role of group dynamics in the provision of service (for a review, see Solnet, 2006).

5   **Service Speed / Efficiency** – Continued challenges in understanding the conflicts between staffing levels, ever-tightening margins / cost control and consumer demands for service speed.

6   **Self Service Technologies (SST / e-service)** – Ongoing study of SST in terms of customer satisfaction; comparing consumer attitudes against traditional service methods.

7   **Intraorganisational Practices (and Employee-customer-firm performance linkages)** – Continued examination into the impacts of various workplace practises on customer perceptions and financial performance.

8   **Emotional Intelligence** – The extent to which stress and emotions play a role in customer and employee interactions and their impact on service, customer satisfaction, service failure and recovery.

9   **Loyalty** – Drivers of customer loyalty and the effectiveness of loyalty programs.

10   **Generational Issues** – Gaining an improved understanding about how new generations (particularly Generation Y) will differ as customers and employees.

11   **Customer Feedback** – Improved ways to gain more accurate and timely feedback from customers which provides effective information for the business with minimal intrusion on the customer.

Summary of Review

The context for this review is that tourism is an assemblage of interrelated elements, each of which contributes to a tourist's overall experience. By understanding some of the key drivers for managing service, a more holistic understanding for managing tourism destinations and organizational performance for businesses within the destination can occur. The principle of placing tourist perceptions as the predominate and central tenet for all tourism management and planning activities was introduced. This was explained as a contrasting view to conventional management thinking, which places a more industrial or manufacturing paradigm to management, focused on organisational systems, efficiencies, waste minimisation, cost controls, distribution (and the like) as the core of management activities. A review of the evolution of management from a 'product' to a 'service' based position was provided, along with an introduction to some of the current discourse on service dominant logic.

A number of key concepts were identified as important for understanding service management in tourism. These concepts included service quality (conceptualisation and measurement), the service encounter, customer satisfaction, service failure and recovery, linking employees, customers and organisational performance, organisational culture and climate, employee engagement and a discussion and case example regarding the Balanced Scorecard. The review concluded by introducing some of the emerging research issues in service management.

Whilst this review has offered a range of concepts and frameworks for understanding why service is such an important aspect of managing tourist destinations, it must be remembered that tourism is complex and that there is no 'off the shelf' approach to tourism management or to managing the service aspect of tourism. However, this introduction is meant to provide a conceptual starting point for better understanding tourism from a service perspective.

References

Albrecht, K. (1988). *At America's Service: How Your Company Can Join the Customer Service Revolution*. New York: Warner Books.

Albrecht, K. and Zemke, R. (2002). *Service America in the New Economy* (2nd ed.). New York: McGraw-Hill.

Berry, L. and Parasuraman, A. (1993). Building a new academic field - The case of services marketing. *Journal of Retailing*, **69**(1), 13-60.

Booms, B. H. and Bitner, M. J. (1981). *Marketing Strategies and Organizational Structures for Service Firms*. Chicago: American Marketing Association.

Bowen, D. E. and Schneider, B. (1985). Boundary-spanning role employees and the service encounter: Some guidelines for management and research, in J. Czepiel, M. Solomon & C. Suprenant (Eds.), *The Service Encounter* (pp. 127-147). Lexington: Lexington Books.

Bowen, J. and Ford, R. C. (2002). Managing service organizations: Does having a 'thing' make a difference? *Journal of Management*, **28**(3), 447-469.

Cronin Jr., J. J. and Taylor, S. A. (1992). Measuring service quality: A reexamination and extension. *Journal of Marketing*, **56**(55-68).

Cronin Jr., J. J. and Taylor, S. A. (1994). SERVPERF versus SERVQUAL: Reconciling performance-based and perceptions-minus-expectations measurement of service quality. *Journal of Marketing*, **58**(1), 125-131.

Denison, D. (1996). What is the difference between organizational culture and organizational climate? A native's point of view on a decade of paradigm wars. *Academy of Management Review*, **21**(3), 619-654.

Drucker, P. F. (1954). *The Practice of Management*. New York: HarperCollins.

Fisk, R., Brown, S. and Bitner, M. J. (1993). Tracking the evolution of the services marketing literature. *Journal of Retailing*, **60**(1), 61-100.

Ford, R. C. and Heaton, C. P. (2001). Lessons from hospitality that can serve anyone. *Organizational Dynamics*, **30**(1), 30-47.

Fuchs, V. (1968). *The Service Economy*. New York: Columbia University Press.

Giese, J. L. and Cote, J. A. (2000). Defining customer satisfaction. *Academy of Marketing Science Review*, **1**, 1-24.

Gronroos, C. (1990). *Service Management and Marketing* (First ed.). Lexington: Lexington Books.

Gronroos, C. (1993). From scientific management to service management. *International Journal of Service Industry Management*, **5**(1), 5-20.

Gronroos, C. (2000). *Service Management and Marketing: A Customer Relationship Management Approach* (2nd ed.). West Sussex: John Wiley & Sons, Ltd.

Harris, L. C. and Reynolds, K. L. (2004). Jaycustomer behavior: An exploration of types and motives in the hospitality industry. *Journal of Services Marketing*, **18**(5), 339-357.

Heskett, J.L., Jones, T.O., Loveman, G.W., Sasser, W.E. and Schlesinger, L.A. (2008). Putting the service-profit chain to work. *Harvard Business Review*, **86**(7,8), 118-129.

Kahn, W. A. (1990). Psychological conditions of personal engagement and disengagement at work. *Academy of Management Journal*, **33**, 692-724.

Kandampully, J. (2002). *Services Management: The New Paradigm in Hospitality*. Frenchs Forest, NSW: Pearson Education Australia.

Kandampully, J. (2006). The new customer-centred business model for the hospitality industry. *International Journal of Contemporary Hospitality Management*, **18**(3), 173-187.

Kaplan, R. S. and Norton, D. P. (1992). The balanced scorecard - measures that drive performance. *Harvard Business Review*, **70**(1), 71-79.

Kvist, A. and Klefsjo, B. (2006). Which service quality dimensions are important in inbound tourism? *Managing Service Quality*, **16**(5), 520-537.

Lovelock, C. and Wirtz, J. (2004). *Services Marketing: People, Technology, Strategy* (5th ed.). Upper Saddle River, NJ: Pearson / Prentice Hall.

Lovelock, C., Wirtz, J. and Chew, P. (2009). *Essentials of Services Marketing*. Singapore: Prentice Hall.

Lusch, R. F., Vargo, S. L. and O'Brien, M. (2007). Competing through service: Insights from service-dominant logic. *Journal of Retailing*, **83**(1), 5-18.

Macey, W. H., Schneider, B., Barbera, K. M. and Young, S. A. (2009). *Employee Engagement: Tools for Analysis, Practice and Competitive Advantage*. West Sussex: Blackwell Publishing.

Marshall, A. (1929). *Principles of Economics* (8th ed.). London: MacMillan & Co.

McCarthy, E. J. (1960). *Basic Marketing*. Homewood, Ilinois: Irwin.

Morrison-Coulthard, L. J. (2004). Measuring service quality: A review and critique of research using SERVQUAL. *International Journal of Market Research*, **46**(4), 479-497.

Oliver, R. (1997). *Satisfaction: A Behavioral Perspective on the Consumer*. New York: McGraw-Hill.

Parasuraman, A. (1996, October 5). Understanding and leveraging the role of customer service in external, interactive and internal marketing. Paper presented at the Frontiers in Services, Nashville.

Parasuraman, A., Berry, L. and Zeithaml, V. (1988). SERVQUAL: A multiple-item scale for measuring consumer perceptions of service quality. *Journal of Retailing*, **64**(1), 12-40.

Parasuraman, A., Berry, L. and Zeithaml, V. (1991). Understanding customer expectations of service. *Sloan Management Review*(Spring), 39-48.

Parasuraman, A., Zeithaml, V. and Berry, L. (1985). A conceptual model of service quality and its implications for future research. *Journal of Marketing*, **49**(Fall), 41-50.

Pine, J. and Gilmore, J. (1998). Welcome to the experience economy. *Harvard Business Review*, July-August, 1998, 97-106.

Pugh, S. D., Dietz, J., Wiley, J. W. and Brooks, S. M. (2002). Driving service effectiveness through employee-customer linkages. *Academy of Management Executive*, **16**(4), 73-84.

Rafiq, M. and Ahmed, P. K. (1995). Using the 7Ps as a generic marketing mix: An exploratory survey of UK and European marketing academics. *Marketing Intelligence and Planning*, **13**(9), 4-15.

Rust, R. and Oliver, R. (2000). Should we delight the customer? *Journal of Academy of Marketing Science*, **28**(1), 86-94.

Schneider, B. (2004). Research briefs: Welcome to the world of services management. *Academy of Management Executive*, **18**(2), 144-150.

Schneider, B. and Bowen, D. (1993). The service organization: Human resources management is crucial. *Organizational Dynamics*, **21**(4), 39-43.

Schneider, B., Macey, W. H., Barbera, K. M. and Martin, N. (2009). Driving customer satisfaction and financial success through employee engagement. *People and Strategy*, **32**(2), 22-27.

Shah, D., Rust, R., Parasuraman, A., Staelin, R. and Day, G. (2006). The path to customer centricity. *Journal of Service Research*, **9**(2), 113-124.

Sheth, J. N., Sisodia, R. S. and Sharma, A. (2000). The antecedents and consequences of customer-centric marketing. *Academy of Marketing Science Journal*, **28**(1), 55-66.

Shostack, L. (1977). Breaking free from product marketing. *Journal of Marketing*, **41**(2), 73-81.

Solnet, D. (2006). Introducing employee social identification to customer satisfaction research: A hotel industry study. *Managing Service Quality*, **16**(6), 575-594.

Szymanski, D. M. and Henard, D. H. (2001). Customer satisfaction: A meta-analysis of the empirical evidence. *Journal of the Academy of Marketing Science*, **29**(1), 16-35.

Torres, E. and Kline, S. (2006). From satisfaction to delight: a model for the hotel industry. *International Journal of Contemporary Hospitality Management*, **18**(4), 290-301.

Vargo, S. L. and Akaka, M. A. (2009). Service-dominant logic as a foundation for service science: Clarifications. *Service Science*, **1**(1), 32-41.

Vargo, S. L. and Lusch, R. F. (2004). The four service marketing myths - Remnants of a goods-based, manufacturing model. *Journal of Service Research*, **6**(4), 324-335.

Vargo, S. L. and Lusch, R. F. (2008). Why 'service'? *Journal of the Academy of Marketing Science*, **36**, 25-38.

Voorhees, C. M., Brady, M. K. and Horowitz, D. M. (2006). A voice from the silent masses: An exploratory and comparative analysis of noncomplainers. *Journal of the Academy of Marketing Science*, **34**(4), 514-527.

Zeithaml, V., Berry, L. and Parasuraman, A. (1996). The behavioral consequences of service quality. *The Journal of Marketing*, **60**(2), 31-46.

Glossary

4 Ps of the 'Marketing Mix' : First coined by E.J. McCarthy in 1960, the four Ps stand for Product, Price, Place and Promotion. Also known as the marketing mix.

Product – Includes both tangible products such as a mass produced product or product produced on a large scale or intangible such as industries.

Price – the amount that is paid for the product

Place – where the product can be purchased

Promotion – how it is marketed for sale to the consumer

McCarthy, E. J. (1960). *Basic Marketing*. Homewood, Ilinois: Irwin.

7 Ps (or the 'extended marketing mix'): The 'extended marketing mix' includes the 4 Ps (link to 4 Ps), product, price, place and promotion, but also includes the following:

People – Those who influence the value of the product both directly and indirectly. Includes the use of staff, for example, recruiting the appropriate staff and their training both in the job and interpersonal skills in order to be able to effectively engage the customer.

Process – Systems put in place and the flow of activities in order for an company to provide the service and lead to an exchange of value

Physical evidence – Environment in which the service is delivered and in which the service provider and consumer interact.

Booms, B. H., & Bitner, M. J. (1981). *Marketing Strategies and Organizational Structures for Service Firms*. Chicago: American Marketing Association.

Balanced Scorecard: A performance management tool that enables managers to monitor the activities of their staff, both the actions and consequences of them. This form of management tool uses both economic and non-economic measures. Climate for Service: Climate represents an evaluation of employee perceptions of the organisation. It looks at how well the aspirations of the company, the developed predominating norm of behaviour, are perceived by employees and others who have contact with the company. So, in relation to service it stands for the extent that all of a firm's activities, policies and practices are focused on service quality and customer satisfaction.

Customer contact employees: The primary contact or interface with the customer. Bowen and Schneider (1985) argued that the employees that are in contact with the customer deliver not only the service but the image of the organisation.

Customer centricity: Refers to the importance of the customer within decisions made by a firm/company in relation to service management. The customer forms the focal point of decisions rather than cost saving or convenience.

Kandampully, J. (2002). Services management: The new paradigm in hospitality. Frenchs Forest, NSW: Pearson Education Australia.

Customer satisfaction: "a judgement that a product or service feature, or the product or service itself, provided (or is providing) a pleasurable level of consumption-related fulfilment…" (Oliver, 1997, p. 13)

Employee customer linkage research: Looks at understanding the links between the employee and the customer within services. It suggests a relationship between employees, customers and firm performance. However it focuses explicitly on "employee perceptions of various intraorganisational practices and the corresponding relationships to customer perceptions."

Employee engagement: A climate for service represents the degree to which all of a firm's activities, policies and practices are focused on service quality and customer satisfaction.

Heterogeneity: The idea that a system or object has a number of variations in its make-up. The link between service and people is linked, thus creating variability.

Inseparability: Services are usually produced and consumed at the same time.

Intangible service: Not a physical product, it is usually created and sold at the same time.

Logic (S-D or Service Dominant): "The foundational proposition of S-D logic is that organizations, markets, and society are fundamentally concerned with exchange of service—the applications of competences (knowledge and skills) for the benefit of a party. That is, service is exchanged for service; all firms are service firms; all markets are centered on the exchange of service, and all economies and societies are service based. Consequently, marketing thought and practice should be grounded in service logic, principles and theories." www.sdlogic.net

Manufacturing orientation: A business or organisation that concentrates primarily on the manufacture of products

Nordic Framework: Developed by Gronroos in the early 1980s, the framework looks at service experience comparing the expectation of the consumer and how it is delivered. It is based on functional and technical elements within the service encounter. Functional elements look at how the service is delivered from the perspective of the consumer. Technical elements refer to the technical quality the customer receives from the service. The consumer forms service quality perceptions based on the expectations and actual service performance. The framework highlights the importance of what companies promise to the consumer through marketing and promotion and the need to provide customers with realistic expectations of the service they are providing.

Perishability: In relation to services, once it is gone it cannot be sold again or stored, for example an airline ticket

Service/services: The act of a service (verb) is the application of skills by one person, company or organisation for the assistance or advantage of a customer. Whereas services can be defined as intangible units of output, oractivities (a noun) which in a commercial sense are offered for sale or as part of a sale (for example, restaurant service accompanies the food to form a total experience; both food and service are critical to the value perception of the customer).

Service culture: The values and norms embedded in an organisation. In terms of service this is focussed on the customer and quality of service.

Service employee: Employees within the service sector who have direct contact with the customer.

Service encounter: The interaction between the customer and service provider.

Service failure and recovery: Linked to customer satisfaction, service failure occurs when the company fails to provide the customer with their expected service. The human element is often at fault, whether this be the mistakes by the service employees or customers dissatisfied with the service even if it is provided correctly. Service recovery refers to how customers and firms attempt to rectify the failure, through complaint in the part of the customer, and then how the company the way in which a firm assigns resources to rectify and/or compensate for a service failure.

Service management: The act of managing the process of providing a service.

Service orientation: A business or organisation that concentrates primarily on providing a service

Service marketing: The marketing of services or a product, based on relationship and value.

Service quality: A measure of how well a service is delivered and whether it meets customer expectations. Andrew Lockwood, UK in J Jafari (2003). *Encyclopaedia of Tourism*. Taylor & Francis

SERVQUAL: Developed by Zeithaml, Parasuraman & Berry (1988), it is a service quality framework. "The gap model maintains that satisfaction is related tothe size and direction of disconfirmation of a person's experience vis-à-vis his/her initial expectations" (Parasuraman, A., Zeithaml, V., & Berry, L. 1985).

Also known by the acronym RATER, the framework measures 5 aspects of service quality:

> Reliability
>
> Assurance
>
> Tangibles
>
> Empathy, and
>
> Responsiveness

These five aspects were drawn from the initial ten aspects of service quality which included: reliability, responsiveness, competence, access, courtesy, communication, credibility, security, understanding or knowing the customer and tangibles.

SERVPERF: Conceived in response to SERVQUAL . SERVPERF was a performance based component of the service quality framework, SERVQUAL (link to definition).

Service Profit Chain: This conceptual framework proposes a hypothetical chain of events which link the internal functioning of an organization to employee loyalty and productivity, service value, customer satisfaction and finally to revenue growth and profitability.

Heskett, J. L., Sasser, W. E., & Schlesinger, L. A. (1997). *The Service-profit chain.* New York: Free Press. www.serviceprofitchain.com

Tangible good: Goods that can be held in your hand, a physical product, that can be created and sold or used at a later date, unlike a service or advice.

Tourism: The United Nations defines three types of tourism:

> (a) Domestic tourism, involving residents of the given country travelling only within this country;
>
> (b) Inbound tourism, involving non-residents travelling in the given country;
>
> (c) Outbound tourism, involving residents travelling in another country.

The United Nations World Tourism Organisation defines tourists as "travel to and stay in places outside their usual environment for more than twenty-four (24) hours and not more than one consecutive year for leisure, business and other purposes not related to the exercise of an activity remunerated from within the place visited"

Recommendations on Tourism Statistics, (1994) UN/WTOrganization, p.5. unstats. un.org/unsd/newsletter/unsd_workshops/tourism/st_esa_stat_ser_M_83.pdf

Technical Manual: Collection of Tourism Expenditure Statistics. World Tourism Organization. 1995. p. 14.

Tourism and Transport

Gui Lohmann
David Timothy Duval

Contents

Gui Lohmann has taught and undertaken research in several universities around the world, including Waikato (New Zealand), São Paulo (Brazil), and USA). Currently, he is a lecturer at the School of Tourism and Hospitality Management at Southern Cross University (Australia). He has authored several books and peer-reviewed journal articles on tourism transport issues both in English and Portuguese. He has also worked as a consultant on tourism transport matters for the Brazilian Ministry of Tourism, the World Tourism Organization and the Abu Dhabi Tourism Authority.

David Timothy Duval is Associate Professor in the Faculty of Business and Economics at the University of Winnipeg, and Honorary Associate Professor at the University of Otago. He has written on the economic regulation of international commercial air transport and the politics of government air access policy. Prior to entering academia, David worked in the private sector, undertaking research that included image studies, advertising evaluation and visitor studies.

A hyperlinked PDF version of this review is available for download from the CTR area of Goodfellow Pubishers' website: http://www.goodfellowpublishers.com/ctr

Introduction

The interconnectedness between transport and tourism remains perhaps one of the more important relationships within the wider tourism system. It is a fundamental fact that people travel varying distances by various means for a variety of reasons, with transport provision sitting at the heart of that movement. Transport is important for tourism because it a) facilitates the movement of tourists between their place of origin and their destinations, and b) acts as the means of movement within a destination, thus allowing for wider dispersal of visitor movement and, as a result, maximum exposure of visitor flows to areas perhaps not otherwise possible (Page 2009).

Transport, for the purposes of tourism, can be expressed as a series of modes operating across vast networks consisting of points (or nodes) and routes (or vectors). Modes of transport can include air, water and land (road and rail), with various types of transport provision possible within these modes. The networks through which modes of transport operate function as important economic conduits for many destinations (Duval 2007). Networks can, of course, be global, such that the movement of tourists (as passengers, for example, on an international airline) constitutes one of the more common means of international visitor arrivals for any given destination. Networks can also function on a regional level. For example, the European Community offers an excellent example of the removal of political and economic barriers to inter-State, regional travel. Finally, local networks, or those networks of transport which operate within a country, are critical in ensuring that the economics benefits of tourism are not simply concentrated in one particular locality. Critically, it is important that local networks are integrated into regional and international networks in order to maximise visitor flows into a destination. As a result, transport can often be the single most important factor in determining the viability of a destination's tourism sector (Lohmann and Duval, 2014).

Duval (2007) argued that a natural 'blurriness' features when examining the linkages between transport and tourism. First, it is apparent that transport can be both a mode of travel and a destination; cruise ships are perhaps the most obvious example of this. Second, the segmentation of transport use into tourism and non-tourism is difficult, but not necessarily impossible for transport planners. Airlines, for example, will only initiate (or expand) services between two points if at least one segment shows signs of robust growth. Finally, a more pertinent question becomes one akin to the classic question of the chicken and the egg: which arguably must come first – the provision for transport services to and from a destination or the quality, scale and scope of attractions and activities that appeal to certain tourist market segments? The answer to this question is elusive as there is a strong sense of co-dependence between the two sectors, which is to be expected. Transport relies on the viability and attractiveness of a destination, and a destination relies on transport for visitor access. The underlying strategic perspective of this relationship is manifested in determining whether either (or both) are responsible for ensuring tourist flows are maintained.

The two most critical facets that influence successful transport-tourism relationships are accessibility and connectivity (Duval 2007, Page 2009). Understanding the degree of accessibility and connectivity of a destination is important because it helps establish the role of both government and private firms in the movement of tourists. Accessibility is simply a geographic comparative measure of various points within a network, measuring the connections that are possible given existing transport provision. Connectivity is a similar measure, but examines the practical and technological constraints and opportunities for increased accessibility (e.g., shorter travel time or more efficient means of transport).

A critical question at this juncture is what role government plays in the provision of transport for tourism. As tourism is largely seen as a public good where the benefits can often extend deep into an economy, there are strong arguments to support the heavy involvement of national or local governments in ensuring that accessibility is maintained through efficient and attractive tourism-related transport. This involvement can range from direct subsidisation (i.e., underwriting) by governments to private providers of transport services to active ownership and control of services. On the other hand, the involvement of government can actively distort the market from operating freely and profitably. Thus, where government involvement is heavy in transport provision, the logical question to ask is whether that involvement constrains private operators who may offer cheaper and more efficient services to tourist key markets.

Our intent with this review is to highlight some of the more salient aspects of the tourism-transport relationship. Throughout, we utilise real cases and situations to demonstrate the complexity and important of transport to tourism development. Throughout the main part of the review we focus on issues directly related to transport and tourism, however, it is also acknowledged that transport provision and its terminals contribute to environmental impacts such as noise, waste, atmospheric pollution, accidents and congestion (Abeyratne, 1999; Johnson, 2002; Milan, 1999; Wheatcroft, 1991), they are also blamed by what is happening in terms of climate change (Gössling and Upham, 2009). Hence, a case study on transport greenhouse gas emissions, particularly in reference to air transport, is presented at the end of this review, with some implications for tourism discussed.

The tourism-transport interface: symbiotic relationships

The intrinsic relationship between transport and tourism can be considered from two major approaches: from the tourism perspective and from the transport perspective.

The World Tourism Organisation (WTO) defines tourists (WTO, 1995: p.1) as 'people who are travelling to and staying in places outside their usual environment for not more than one consecutive year for leisure, business and other purposes not related to the exercise of an activity remunerated from within the place visited'. From this definition it is possible to highlight that tourism will only happen when people leave their usual environment (i.e. their 'place of origin'), undertaking a displacement which is not part of their usual environment (such as work, school etc), in order to reach a 'tourist destination'.

Apart from linking the origin to the destination, various means of transport are also required in order to provide accessibility within a destination (from the airport to the hotel, from the hotel to a tourist attraction etc), and in the case of a multiple destination trip, to link the various destinations within the trip. The scheme on Figure 1 illustrates the participation of transport (1) between the origin and the destination, (2) within the various destinations visited, and (3) between the different destinations visited during a holiday trip.

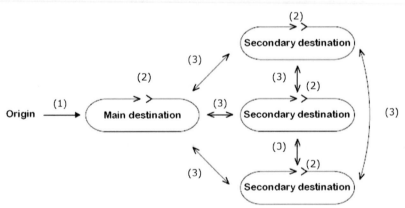

Figure 1: Transport linking to, from and within destinations.

Another way to understand the importance of transport to tourism is by analysing how the introduction of a new transport technology has impacted tourism development. There are several examples, such as the railway development in the UK in the 19th Century and the flourishing of seaside resorts; the increase of mass tourism within the USA and Europe after cars became more affordable in the 1930s; and the boom of international tourism in the 1960s with the introduction of jet planes (Boeing 707) and in the 1970s, with the arrival of wide-body jets (Boeing 747), sending tourists to all corners of the world (Lohmann, Fraga and Castro, 2013).

From the perspective of the transport activity, tourism is a vital part of many regional and long-haul transport providers. A study conducted in Canada shows that while tourists account for only 3% of urban passengers using urban transport (and nearly 30% of taxi passengers), they account for at least 80% of air, sea, rail and rental car business (see Figure 2).

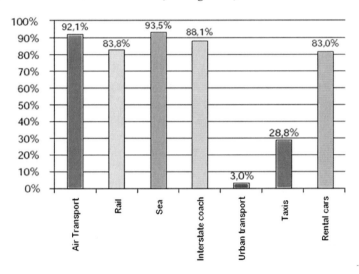

Figure 2: The participation of tourists in different modes of transport (adapted from Lapierre and Hayes, 1994)

Transport operations also provide some characteristics and attributes that are relevant to tourists and the study of tourism. Some of them are presented and briefly described on Table 1.

While it is not the purpose of this review to discuss each of the attributes described in Table 1, intermodality is a topic that deserves further development. Intermodality often brings both competition as well as integration. In recent years, improvements in transport technology have changed the way different modes of transport integrate with each other. Stubbs and Jegede (1998) suggest that, traditionally, there has been some competition between road and rail modes, with the preponderance of the latter. Cars are popular because they provide the convenience of private door-to-door transportation without the need to adhere to a timetable. In many parts of the world such as large landmass countries like Australia, Brazil and the USA it is clear that massive investment in road transport has contributed to the decline of the importance of long-haul rail passenger transportation

Table 1: Operational attributes of transport systems.

Attribute	Description
Comfort	Measured in many different ways, including the pitch of the seats, noise, quality of the waiting area etc.
Confiability	Ability to accomplish the contract (e.g. punctuality).
Domestic or international	Whether or not the trip involves more than one country. In most cases, international trips require more complicated arrangements to comply with the procedures of two different countries such as immigration issues and regulations related to the provision of transport services (bilateral agreements).
Elements	Power: defines the mode of transport and in most instances the speed travelled Terminal: place of change from one mode of transport to another Vehicle: the carrying unit where passengers and goods will be accommodated. Way: classified as natural (e.g. sea and air) or artificial (e.g. railways and highways). In some cases the vehicle is subject to traffic control.
Fare	The transportation charge that can be a flat rate for any seat available or be calculated by a variety of methods including, for example, complicated pricing strategies involving revenue management where, for example, passengers flying the same flight in the same class pay completely different prices depending on how far in advanced they have booked, restrictions imposed on cancellation, length of stay in the destination (e.g. passengers staying a Saturday night are charged less as the are more likely to be on a leisure trip rather than a business traveller) etc.
Intermodality	The ability to connect two or more different modes of transport. Intermodal connections exist in different ways: Physical: where a terminal integrates two or more modes of transport in a way to provide passengers with the best technology to access the terminal and reach their final destination. Fare: where the same fare covers two or more modes of transport (e.g. limousine offered by some airlines for passengers flying business and first classes) Operational: where, for example, the timetables of two different modes of transport are coordinated to minimize connecting times. Institutional: when the same organization operates two or more interconnected modes of transport.

Mode	Air: the fastest mode of transport, linking most parts of the world.
	Rail: dedicated ways make it a reliable and safe mode of transport, usually with a high level of comfort. High speed trains are becoming competitive with airplanes, particularly for short and medium trips (less than 1,000km)
	Road: provides the convenience of door-to-door transport
	Water: a slower mode of transport, but can provide high levels of comfort and amenities on board while carrying a large number of passengers (e.g. cruise ships).
Public or private	Public transport is a shared passenger transport system that can be operated and owned either by a private or public company. It is available to any member of the public, usually paying a fare to access it. Most public transport runs to a scheduled timetable.
	Private transport is characterised by either the driver or the hirer having control over who has access to that transport and the route and destinations travelled to by that transport.
Scheduled or charter	Scheduled transport follows a timetable and it is required to offer the service regardless of the number of passengers on board. Charters are usually arranged with a particular customer, not having to follow a given timetable or itinerary. The term charter flight has acquired a more specific meaning as it can be linked to holidaymakers who are buying a flight as part of a holiday package (in some cases flying a schedule flight, but buying the ticket from the tour operator, not the airline).
Security	Covers a few variables, including safety issues (e.g. the number of accidents or fatalities), robbery, terrorism etc.
Speed	How fast a certain transport technology travels.

A similar competition also exists between air and sea transport. While passenger ships, or cruise liners, were once the only form of transport between continents and across large expanses of water, the introduction of jet aircraft in the 1970s all but eliminated point-to-point passenger sea transport because air travel is much faster than sea transport and, in most cases, cheaper. Since then sea transport has only succeeded in the cruise and the relatively short-haul passenger ferry sectors.

Figure 3: The fast ferry catamaran, The Lynx, which used to operate across the Cook Strait in New Zealand. Above, the ship at port ready to embark cars.

Traditionally, integration has been strong between rail and water transport, as most railways serve large ports to transport goods and freight between ports and hinterlands. This link benefits passengers as well. Road and air are also heavily linked to each other, as many air passengers tend to use their own car or taxis to reach or leave an airport. In recent years, however, while the competition among road-rail and air-sea still exists, new possibilities for integration have emerged. Stubbs and Jegede (1998) give as examples the rail-air integration, particularly as a means to connect Central Business Districts to large airports in a faster and more reliable way, avoiding increasingly heavy road traffic in metropolitan areas around the world. Also, the integration between road and water transport is possible through the new fast ferry catamaran technology.

Roll-on roll-off ferries are able to transport both vehicles and passengers and are used in different parts of the world, particularly in Europe. New fast ferry catamarans have, in some cases, tripled the speed travelled by traditional ferries and created new markets for travelers willing to bring their own car on their trips (see photos on Figure 3). The traditional and contemporary views of transport integration and competition proposed by Stubbs and Jegede (1998) are presented in Figure 4.

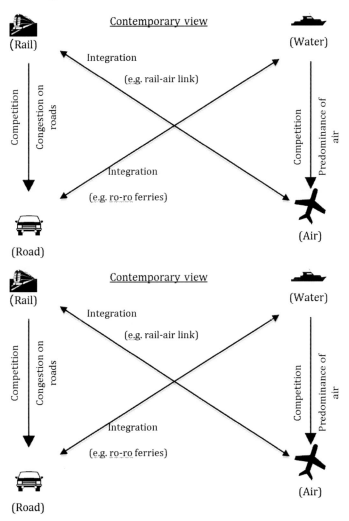

Figure 4: Stubbs and Jegede's views of traditional and contemporary transport integration and competition (adapted from Stubbs and Jegede, 1998).

Another relevant aspect of the tourism-transport relationship that deserves some attention is transport networks. While in the introduction a general overview of transport networks was presented, a more detailed explanation is required in order to better understand some of the issues presented in this review. It is particularly important to understand the role and functions of nodes in a transport network because they are the focal point of most tourist activities. Nodes can have several functions including being the origin of a trip or a tourist destination, as previously discussed at the beginning of this review. However, other nodal functions are also possible as presented by Lohmann and Pearce (2010):

- **Gateways**: in a general sense, gateways are seen as major entry/exit points into or out of a national or regional system (Pearce, 2001c). Gateways not only link other nodes within a national or regional network – see the example of nodes C and E on Figure 5 – but also serve to link one network to another (Burghardt, 1971). Several writers have considered the gateway or portal function of communities adjacent to national parks (Mules, 2005), while for others, gateway cities are synonymous with large metropolitan centres (Bowen, 2000).

- **Hubs**: traditionally used in a fairly general sense to mean a place which functions as a crossroads or any large airport or airline operating base. However, the concept of hubs has come to assume a more technical meaning as the result of changes in airline practices. An airline hub relates to transfer functions of aircraft within a wider network (Dennis, 1994). O'Kelly and Miller (1994: p.31) define a hub as 'a major sorting or switching centre in a many-to-many distribution system... the key idea is that the flow between a set of origin–destination cities passes through one or more hubs en route to the final destination'. Fleming and Hayuth (1994) use the terms 'centrality' and 'intermediacy' as spatial qualities that enhance the traffic levels of transportation hubs, and hence indicate that they are places strategically located within transportation systems (see Figure 5).

- **Stopovers**: the concept of stopovers is less developed than the other functions and derives from analyses of touring or circuit travel. As the name suggests, stopovers refer to places which serve as way points between destinations or function as secondary destinations on longer circuits (Pearce and Elliott, 1983).

- **Multiple functions**: other terms are one indication that places may have multiple functions. Caves and Gosling (1999), for instance, use the term 'gateway hubs' to refer to gateways on the periphery of Europe which provide onward services to secondary centres. In his model of urban tourism spaces, Pearce (1981) explicitly incorporated the idea that larger urban centres in particular may have multiple nodal functions due to their size, infrastructure and place in the urban hierarchy. He later developed the practical implications of multiple nodal functions with regard to tourism planning (Pearce, 1995).

Gateways and hubs in particular are in a position to attract connecting passengers to spend time visiting and discovering the destinations in which they are located. Section 3.1 provides the example of Singapore and Dubai and how a well-orchestrated strategy was implemented in order to create world-class destinations (Lohmann *et al.*, 2009). One example of the potential for gateways to improve their destination aspects is presented by Lohmann and Pearce (2010; 2012) as the result of a research undertaken with Cook Strait ferry passengers and the likelihood of those passengers to become tourists for the gateway ferry ports of Wellington (North Island) and Picton (South Island). Their major findings include the preference among international tourists to have a stopover in Wellington rather than in Picton if they were offered more information about these two locations, as well as a deal that would include the ferry ride and an accommodation in either Wellington or Picton.

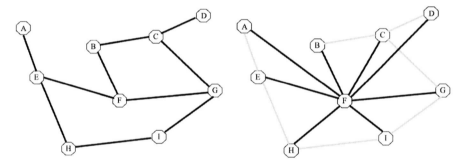

Figure 5: Theoretical examples of networks showing gateway (left) and hub (right) functions.

Modes of transport and tourism

While international and domestic tourism functions as one of the more pervasive leisure activities worldwide, it both relies and drives transport provisions at a variety levels. As the previous section has outlined, there exists a fundamental synergy between tourism and transport but quite often the ability to separate the use of transport for the purposes of tourism can be difficult and in some cases, such as cruise ship transport, virtually impossible. Not only does this inability to separate them make planning and development difficult, but it also renders a more detailed analysis of the key aspects of the relationship between the two problematic.

Nonetheless, there are some obvious (and not-so-obvious) examples that illustrate the inherent importance of transport in the provision of tourism. We have elected to dissect the broad sector of transport into the sub-sectors of air, water and ground-based transport. Each of these has particular characteristics vis-à-vis tourism from a development and impact perspective, yet each has the common purpose of serving the need of moving tourists through a variety of scales, including between origin and destination, inter-destinations (where appropriate) and intra-destination.

Air transport: shrinking the world and developing mass tourism

In terms of the individual modes of transport, aviation is probably the most studied facet of tourism transport and often reaches top of mind when one considers transport in the context of tourism. One explanation for this phenomena can be attributed to the growth of airline networks and airport infrastructure, the decrease of the real costs of air travel and the increase of capacity and speed which have all contributed to the development of the international tourism industry over the last decades (Palhares, 2003; Sypher:Mueller International Inc, 1990). In addition, the airlines' on-going contribution to tourism expansion goes far beyond providing essential transportation links.

Beginning in the 1970s and 1980s and continuing to a certain degree up to this day, vertical integration and 'bundling' packages with the accommodation and the packaged tour sectors – as well as other tourism-related activities such as restaurants and rental cars – was a reality within the aviation industry (Lafferty and Fossen, 2001; Pyle, 1985). One current example is Emirates Airlines, which is part of a larger corporate group that embraces various tourism activities including a travel management company, hotels and resorts, a tour operator and attraction providers (Lohmann *et al.*, 2009). While the wider packaging of tourist experiences is still a feature of some carriers' business plans, their own operations reflect an increasing trend for them to outsource some of these functions. In fact, it is very common for some carriers to outsource or sub-contract even core parts of their operations, including aircraft maintenance, aircraft leasing, computer reservation systems technology and in-flight catering (Debbage and Alkaabi, 2008).

In the past, airlines have also actively contributed to the promotion of destinations. One can clearly identify the destinations served by the airlines through television ads (many of which are available on YouTube) produced by them in the 1980s. Airlines have an interest in selling destinations in order to achieve profitable load factors (or, more properly, seat factors) on specific routes. In this sense, airlines and national destination marketing organisations (DMOs) have similar goals and objectives, with both exerting some influence on the activities of the other. Airlines, for instance, may exert pressure on DMOs to increase marketing efforts in a particular source market in order to drive traffic. DMOs may try to exert pressure on airlines to increase frequency of service from a particular destination in recognition of latent demand that is not being met. Importantly, the decision to fly a particular route by an airline is almost entirely an economic one, namely the ability to achieve a stream of revenue that exceed costs (although in a strict sense, there may be strategic reason to offer a particular origin-destination sector at a loss in order to secure traffic flows across a wider network – see Holloway 2003 for more on airline economics). In some cases, though, political pressures can compel an airline to open a new route, particularly when this is aligned by the desire of the national or state government to strength its international trade links. One of many examples is the recent decision of Etihad to establish a flight between Abu Dhabi (UAE) and Astana, the capital city of Kazakhstan.

As a means of driving traffic and increasing seat factors, airlines compete not only on the basis of the destinations they serve, but also on the product/service they offer. With the increase in competition and the slow but gradual emphasis on deregulation and liberalisation of access, airlines begin to differentiate themselves in terms of the product they offer, i.e. the pitch of the seats, the level of service and entertainment provided on board, the age of their fleet etc. Additionally, with the consolidation that is occurring in many parts of the world, particularly in Europe, air carriers do not operate from just their home country. A good example is the recent mergers undertaken by Lufthansa (including SWISS in 2005, Brussels Airlines in 2008, and Austrian Airlines in 2009) and British Airways with Iberia (April 2010).

It is critical to point out, then, that the tourist experience can often be very much informed by the nature of the product and service on offer by an airline. One example of this is the concept created by Singapore Airlines in the 1970s, where female air stewards, also known as Singapore Girls, embrace and introduce the country's hospitality on board their aircrafts (Chan 2000). Hence, the tourist experience can start during travel, and not necessarily only after arriving at the destination. Given that a significant proportion of international long-haul travel by tourists takes place via air, this is not an insignificant consideration in assessing the critical function of airlines.

Perhaps the most studied aspect of the relationship between aviation and tourism is deregulation (Koo and Lohmann, 2013; Shaw, 1982; Wheatcroft, 1994). As surprising as this may seem, the reality is that some countries regulate competition, accessibility and capacity of airlines to operate at certain airports. As noted above, there has been an increased push toward the removal of these barriers (see for example, IATA's Agenda for Freedom – www.agenda-for-freedom.

aero). One argument for their removal is that tourism benefits as the ability of passengers to fly to a destination increases, providing opportunities for the tourist sector to grow. This has happened in different countries and regions such as in the US in 1978 (Shaw, 1982), in the EU as a result of the EU's liberalisation process during the 1980s and 1990s (Simons, 1992; Subrémon, 2000) and within many Asia-Pacific countries in the mid-1980s (Boberg and Choy, 1988; Kissling, 1998). The importance of air access is particularly high for geographically remote destinations. In fact, many islands and isolated parts of the world rely particularly on tourism for their economic survival (Grech, 2000; Kissling, 1998; Lohmann and Nguyen, 2011) while air transport to many destinations is the predominant means of transportation (e.g. Hawaii, Australia and New Zealand).

Tourism development and low-cost carriers

Recently, growth in short-haul tourism in some instances has been amplified by the introduction of services from so-called 'low-cost carriers' (low-cost airlines), by either grabbing market share away from incumbent 'network' carriers or by growing origin-destination markets through the introduction of new services. Well-established low-cost carriers can exercise their power to negotiate access and privileges to new destinations and airports as they usually increase the traffic generated, luring passengers from other modes of transport to airplanes. Southwest Airlines (SWA), Ryanair and easyJet are excellent examples of successful and profitable airlines. In January 2014, for example, Southwest Airlines had its 41st consecutive profitable year.

Southwest Airlines is by no means is a small airline as in December 2013 it had the biggest fleet of Boeing 737 models in the world (over 610!)[1], being the fifth largest airline in the world in terms of passenger-kilometre flown (167,932 millions). Proportionally, Southwest serves fewer destinations than most other major US airlines, but once they commence a new route, they offer frequent services within that route. In addition, as some people say, "wherever Southwest goes, lower airfares follow" because competitors are forced to reduce their prices, and the size of the market increases as it becomes more affordable to travel. Hence, Southwest Airlines is a desired airline for any airport and destination in the US. The text below, extracted from the Mobile's (Alabama) airport website (http://www.mobairport.com/news_faq.html), reflects the struggles that many airports go through in order to attract SWA:

---

1 www.southwest.com/about_swa/press/factsheet.html

> ## Is there something Mobile can do to convince Southwest Airlines to serve Mobile?
>
> Southwest makes decisions as they fit into the airline's strategy, and there is little a community can do to attract short of keeping them abreast of an expansive and growing economy. […] That number of flights requires ~ 750,000 potential passengers in a new market. The Mobile market currently has 600,000 total passengers. However, we have worked closely with Southwest for 10 years and, hopefully, one day they may change their business model to fit cities Mobile's size. In fact, Southwest has been to Mobile to speak to our Air Service Task Force. Their message was clear – there are things that can be done now to help improve our business case for Southwest service – support competition (fly on all Mobile carriers) and fly from your local airport. If they ever begin serving smaller markets like Mobile, we hope to be one of the first.

Short-haul services provided by low-cost carriers might help establish or enhance visitor flows, but these services are not without controversy. Firstly, there is considerable tension over the nimble ability of low-cost carriers to almost pick and choose airports to service. This can mean airports (often government owned) may be willing to forgo particular revenues from aeronautical charges (e.g., landing fees) in order to appear attractive. As airlines effectively operate mobile capital as opposed to airports which are fixed, they can strategically position aircraft almost anywhere in a catchment area that is limited only by the range of the aircraft itself. In addition, some low-cost carriers continually come to the media's attention regarding what some consider to be insufficient efforts at providing customer service. However, given the success of low-cost carriers in some markets (particularly Europe), cost appears to be a key driver, so much so that fringe service options on short-haul flights may not always be critical in securing market share.

Finally, it is also worth mentioning that for many travellers, the lower fares offered by low-cost carriers provide them with an opportunity to escape their routines and spend leisure time somewhere else. When airlines such as Ryanair offer online airfares of £5, the destination itself often matters least for potential travellers living in the UK. Most of them just want a break, preferably to warmer weather. Thus, destinations served by low-cost carriers benefit, as passenger traffic will be enhanced with tourists spending money while visiting these destinations. In this sense, price is driving the market irrespective of the destination

Premium long haul airlines and destination development [2]

Despite the general success of the low-cost carrier business model in many countries/regions worldwide, long-haul operational models still feature and can generally be profitable (negative and uncontrollable externalities notwithstanding) – see Lohmann and Koo (2013) for a discussion of the airline business model spectrum. Long-haul operations clearly provide the fastest and most efficient way for a destination to tap into a distant source market. Two interesting examples of destination development linked to air transportation are Singapore and Dubai. Both destinations combine a well-orchestrated initiative involving airlines, airports, tourism marketing and government actions to convert transit passengers into tourists. The transport network created by both Singapore Airlines (SQ) and Emirates (EK) made Changi and Dubai airports respectively key hubs between the Western and Eastern hemispheres. With small local markets from which to attract passengers, Singapore with approximately 4.5 million inhabitants and Dubai with 1.4 million, SQ and EK market aggressively within other markets to generate the traffic they need to make their operations viable.

Singapore Airlines, which provides a premier service to long haul passengers, serves almost 100 destinations around the world. It operates over a third of all flights using Changi airport, with the carrier being the sole operator on several routes to and from its home base. Changi is a world-class airport providing a wide range of services to passengers (including special recreation zones consisting of themed gardens and a swimming pool; duty free shops; free sightseeing tours for passengers with at least a five-hour overlap connection etc) and airlines (eg maintenance hangars and catering facilities). Singapore as a destination offers many outdoor attractions such as the Botanical Gardens, Jurong Bird and Reptile Parks, Singapore Night Zoo, Bukit Timah Reserves, Orchid Gardens and Sentosa, the Island of Tranquility. It is also the number one MICE (Meeting, Incentive, Conference and Exhibition) destination in Asia and the sixth worldwide. Another developed feature to attract tourists is the promotion of Singapore as a low-cost 'shoppers' paradise', particularly in terms of high tech products, fashion, jewellery and watches.

Emirates is one of the few airlines in the world to fly to all continents, taking advantage of Dubai's well-positioned location for Europe-Asia travel (about 3.5 billion people live within an 8-hour flying radius of Dubai). It has a strong presence in Australia and New Zealand, Europe, Asia and Africa. More recently, it

---

2   Based on Lohmann, G., Albers, S., Koch, B., Pavlovich, K. 2009 From hub to tourist destination – An explorative study of Singapore and Dubai's aviation-based transformation. Journal of Air Transport Management, 15, 205-211.

has also opened up routes to North and South America. Emirates makes use of several successful operational and managerial strategies including (Lohmann *et al.*, 2009):

♦ lower labour costs due to the use of expatriate workers from low wage countries;

♦ outsourcing of accounting and IT tasks to India and Pakistan companies;

♦ bulk orders of aircraft from Airbus and Boeing to achieve volume discounts;

♦ entering a new destination market offering at least one daily flight, and through increased demand builds up the route with larger aircrafts and then higher frequencies.

It appears that the strategy created by Singapore to develop its destination, making use of a well-established air transport network, has been successfully imitated by Dubai. It is possible to argue that the integration and governance of the airlines, airports and tourism organizations has been made possible in both locations because both governments have implemented a consistent and long-term oriented investment and development strategy (Henderson, 2006; Lohmann *et al.*, 2009). Many companies operating at Changi or Dubai airports are subsidiaries of corporate groups that include their respective airlines. This is an example of vertical integration at the operational level. In addition, these airlines also have strong links with tourism organisations to develop entice-ments for stopovers; e.g. airfares that also include two or three night accommo-dation for a minor additional expenditure. Emirates has even more consolida-tion through owning hotels, adventure travel agencies and tourism attractions.

Cruise tourism and ferries: the new reality for water passenger transport

Although water transport as a means of point-to-point travel lost some of its appeal for travellers, during the 1970s when ocean liners gave way to wide-body jets as the main long-haul transport of choice, cruise ships and, to a certain degree, ferries (because of the advent of new fast ferry technologies) are now once again one of the most popular means of transport used by tourists. In fact, cruise tourism is considered to be one of the fastest growing sectors of the travel industry, with an average increase of 10% per year in the last 30 years (Tourism New South Wales).

The cruise industry is a substantial component of international tourism and operates as a unique and complex transport sector (Cartwright and Baird, 1999;

Chin 2008; Dickinson and Vladimir, 1997; Gui and Russo 2011). Not entirely unlike air access, global cruise tourism is pervasive in most regions, including Africa (Irandu, 2004), Asia (Kwag and Lee 2009; Singh, 1999, 2000), Australasia (Dwyer et al., 2004; Dwyer and Forsyth, 1996;), Oceania (Douglas and Douglas 2004) the Caribbean (Brida et al 2012; Johnson, 2006; Lester and Weeden 2004; Showalter, 1994; Wilkinson, 1999), Europe (Andriotis and Agiomirgianakis 2010; Gibson and Bentley, 2006; Marusic et al., 2009; Soriani et al 2009), Latin America (Brida and Zapata 2010; Seidl et al., 2007) and the USA (Hobson, 1993a; Hobson, 1993b; Mak, 2008; Marti, 2007). Unlike air transport, cruise tourism also extends to the polar regions (Lück, Maher and Stewart 2010). The supply side of cruise tourism (Biehn, 2006; Gibson, 2008; Testa, 2004; Thompson, 2004) incorporates concepts of cruise line management, such as route planning, capacity, operations management, sophisticated IT and communications systems and planning (Leong and Ladany 2001; Rodrigue and Notteboom 2013; Sun, Jiao and Tian 2011; Véronneau and Roy 2009), while the parameters of cruise demand focus on understanding passengers' behaviour and motivations for cruise travel (Kwortnik, 2008; Miller and Grazer, 2003; Yarnal, 2004).

Of special interest to many tourist destinations is the ability to attract new cruise ships and therefore compete with other destinations (Barron and Greenwood 2006; Gui and Russo 2011) Although well-established destinations such as the Caribbean (37.3% of all ship deployments), Europe/ the Mediterranean (30%), Australia/New Zealand (5.9%) and Alaska (4.5%) – respectively the top four in the world accounting for approximately three-quarters of industry capacity in 2013 (CLIA 2014), the European and North American destinations have a competitive advantage over other ports worldwide considering their proximity to the USA and Europe (including the UK and Ireland), the industry's two major source markets with 51.7% and 26,6%, respectively (CLIA 2014). That said, more and more destinations are positioning themselves to receive cruise ships, particularly in Australasia where the increases in cruise berths in recent years point to a robust future (ReportLinker, 2010). In fact, there was a 22% increase in ship deployments to Australasia in 2014 (CLIA 2014),

Like aircraft, and from an accounting perspective, cruise ships are mobile assets which can be relocated from one place to another, even though usually itinerary planning generally tends to be undertaken two to three years in advance (London 2010). This lead-time not only provides cruise lines with the opportunity to try to secure priority berthing (dates and position) (London 2010), but it also provides them with the opportunity to try new destinations without necessarily committing themselves in the long run. Brazil, for example, is a destination where there has been a significant grow in terms of both the supply and demand for cruise tourism (Lohmann and Trischler, 2012). Until 1995, the country's constitution prohibited cabotage – the transport of domestic passengers by a foreign transport operator – unless the ship was leased to a national company that should employ part of the crew the locals. With the change in the legislation, more and more cruise lines became interested in relocating their fleet to explore the vast Brazilian coast, predominantly during the summer season in the Southern hemisphere when ships were more available as a consequence of the off-peak season in the Northern hemisphere (Lohmann, Fraga and Castro, 2013). In 2009, over 500,000 passengers (90% of them domestic tourists) undertook a cruise in Brazil, particularly due to the air transport crises that lasted for several months when travellers become scared of flying, opting for a cruise vacation (Costa et al., 2010).

Usually ports provide different roles for cruise ship operations as described below (McCalla 1997; Thompson Clarke Shipping, 2006):

♦ **Ports of call or destination ports**: a port where passengers spend up to eight or ten hours or perhaps remaining in port for one or more nights visiting local attractions. No new passengers are brought on board although there may be limited exchanges of crewmembers. Ports of call often provide basic facilities for the cruise ship, such as a berth or anchorage and limited provisioning, maintenance and waste services, while reception, transport and activities (shore excursions) services are provided for passengers;

♦ **Ports of embarkation/disembarkation or turnaround ports**: provide the same facilities as a port of call, but also provide facilities for the complete exchange of passengers and crew and more substantial provisioning, maintenance and waste disposal services. Good accommodation and transport infrastructure is usually required for both cruise passengers and crew. The port terminal needs large areas for processing both disembarking and embarking passengers and their luggage, including space for customs, quarantine/bio-security and immigration agencies. Re-fueling (bunkering) is likely to occur at turnaround ports, but not in all cases;

♦ **Home ports**: home ports provide all the facilities of the previous two ports, but in many cases are also home to the cruise line itself and/or permanently base one or more ships at that port. Repair, maintenance and drydock facilities are often available.

Most destinations and ports would like to be either a turnaround or home port given the opportunities for add-on services to be provided either before or after the cruise. For example, passengers will often arrive in their embarkation city at least a day or two before their cruise starts, and perhaps stay in their disembarkation city for an equal or greater time. In such cases, Local businesses may also benefit from the supply of goods to the ships as they start their new voyages, although many goods (such as food) are shipped in by air. However, the reality is that very few ports will become turnaround or base ports because of the sheer need for hotel rooms, efficient connecting transportation, ability to supply the ship and the presence of sufficient regulatory officials. However, cruise ships provide many great opportunities for destination ports as well. Firstly, it is not rare to find that for small destinations, the arrival of a cruise ship with thousands of tourists in one single day can generate sales that sometimes equal or surpass the equivalent of a week's or even a month's worth of revenue. Cruise passenger spend can be significant (Dwyer and Forsyth 1996). Secondly, a day spent in a destination port can give the visitor the opportunity to experience the destination and eventually give them reasons to return for a longer visit.

The real challenge for destination marketing organizations is to market their destinations to the cruise lines for inclusion in future cruise ship itineraries. However, the decision is not solely one relating to the attractiveness of the destination, but also involves a series of navigational issues such as the distance between ports, the cost of fuel, the speed of travel, sea conditions and the weather (Marti 1990; Rodrigue and Notteboom 2013) and non-navigational issues such as port and passenger taxes and other levies (Mak 2008). When seeking new destinations, the cruise lines consider a wide range of factors including, for example, the availability of varied and interesting shore excursions, activities and attractions (London 2012); the presence of appropriate infrastructure, supplies and services (Lekakou, Pallis and Vaggelas 2009); the investment in, development, ownership and operation of cruise terminals (Gui and Russo 2011); climate (Barron and Bartolome Greenwood 2006); the attractiveness (scenically) of a destination (CITE); opportunities for shopping (CITE) ; and safety and security (CITE).

One additional factor worth further consideration is the impact of the widening of the Panama Canal. Within North America, mega cruise ships will be able to be moved more quickly and cheaply between the East and West Coasts rather than being re-positioned to more distant destinations to take advantage of seasonal cruising, and somewhat paradoxically, it will be easier for mega cruise ships to visit ports in Australasia and other distant destinations.

Although ferries serve a different purpose than cruise ships and are not as popular a means of transport worldwide, they are very common in certain parts of the world, including Europe (in the Baltic, across the English Channel between France and the UK, in the Adriatic between Italy and Croatia, in the Irish Sea, among the Spanish islands and around the Greek islands and Eastern Mediterranean), Australasia, particularly in Tasmania and across the Cook Strait and in

Southeast Asia. Roll-on/roll-off ferries are ships whose major advantage is the ability to cross large bodies of water, transporting both vehicles and passengers at the same time. Some of the more generic studies on ferries describe particular experiences of certain countries and regions such as Japan, UK, Indonesia and Europe (Baird, 1999, 2000; Dunlop, 2002; Rutz and Coull, 1996). One particular issue that deserved some attention in the literature is the impact of the construction of the Channel Tunnel on the North Sea / Channel ferry routes (Garnett, 1993; Peisley, 1992, 1997).

As water transport has always been the slowest mode of transport, Wang and McOwan (2000) consider the development of high speed craft technology as an alternative way to make sea travel more competitive. However, the new fast ferry twin hull technology has still to prove itself as a sustainable and viable option for sea transport, particularly in terms of its impact on the marine flora and fauna. Recent failures include examples from The Lynx, across the Cook Strait, New Zealand (see Figure 3) and the Superferry in Hawaii (Lohmann and Nguyen, 2011). During its tenure of operation in New Zealand, The Lynx opened up new tourism markets as its trips across the Cook Strait took only one hour and fifteen minutes, rather than the three hours required by the traditional ferries. Day trips out of Wellington to the vineyards in the Marlborough region were just one of the day-trip possibilities while The Lynx was in operation.

Ground-based transport

Ground-based transport, also known as land transport, comprises two modes of transport: rail and road. Rail tourism was one of the first forms of modern travel, particularly because of its ability to transport large number of passengers between long-haul destinations in an affordable way. Railways were built in many countries in the 19th Century and in the early decades of the 20th Century. However, because of the perceived advantages of road transport options such as the motor car (e.g. door-to-door accessibility, a lack of the need to adhere to a timetable, the ability to choose one's own itinerary and a sense of privacy), the importance of rail as a means of transport for vacationing travellers diminished after the second half of the 20th Century (Boniface and Cooper, 2001).

At present, rail tourism is restricted to a few specific regions and countries around the world, as well as to some niche markets including scenic trains (e.g. the Rocky Mountaineer in Canada, the Glacier Express, in Switzerland and the Taieri Gorge Railway in New Zealand), heritage railways (e.g. the Orient Express, Rovos Rail and the Darjeeling Himalayan Railway), overnight trains (in Europe and Australia) and high-speed trains (in France and Japan). The advent of high-speed rail is, in some instances, providing a fast (but not as fast) and viable alternative to air transport between major urban centres. Perhaps the most obvious example is the EuroStar operations in Europe, which bring the added advantage of having urban terminus points which can often be more convenient for certain travellers, particularly those travelling on business.

Unlike research about air transport which can be found in several notable dedicated academic journals, the treatment of rail transport in the academic literature has been spread out across a number of publications. For this reason, Table 3 provides a brief list of articles on rail transport published in both tourism and more general transport journals.

Despite the current importance of road transport to tourism - particularly for short and regional touring travel - there has been comparatively little research undertaken about this mode of transport. However, the existing literature demonstrates that some types of road transport (e.g., cars, buses and coaches) feature as the most common means of transport used by tourists to reach their destinations as well as to travel within a specific destination. In large part, this is a function of the size and scale of domestic tourism worldwide (Palhares, 2003). For example, in Europe, the USA, New Zealand and Brazil as well as among other countries, at least 80% of domestic tourists use cars, buses and coaches (Ward, 1987). In the case of private vehicles, the lack of a rich understanding of the use of road transport by tourists can be attributed to the absence of a formal, globally standardised method to gather and collect information in a systematic, coherent way and to the reality that access to road transport can disperse travellers over a wide geographic area, making access to them more expensive and difficult (Hensher *et al.*, 1991).

Some of the research which associates road transport with tourism tends to analyse particular forms of travel or vehicles normally associated with tourists and other visitors, such as taxis (Waryszak and King, 2000), recreational vehicles (e.g. campervans and caravans) (Fidgeon, 1983; Gnoth, 1999; Janiskee, 1990; Jobes, 1984) and coaches (Dean, 1993; Lohmann, Santos and Allis, 2011). Other road transport research focuses on the road and highway perspective, such as the studies by Tyrell and Davit (1999), Smith *et al.* (1986) and Wallis (2001). Useful studies describing drive tourism in a particular country have also been undertaken, fe.g. Australia (Carson *et al.*, 2002; Prideaux *et al.*, 2001), Taiwan (Shih, 2006) and Bermuda (Teye, 1992).

Table 3: List of articles about rail transport on tourism and transport journals (adapted from Lohmann and Oliveira, 2008).

Author(s)	Year	Title	Journal	Keywords	Region	Topics
Campos, J. (Campos, 2001)	2001	Lessons from railway reforms in Brazil and Mexico	Transport Policy	Concessions, Latin America	Brazil and Mexico	Privatizations and public-private partner-ships
Charlton, C.; Gibb, R.; Shaw, J. (Charlton et al., 1997)	1997	Regulation and continuing monopoly on Britain's railways	Journal of Transport Geography	Privatization, Competition, Regulation, Deregulation	UK	Privatizations and public-private partner-ships
Dallen, J. (Dallen, 2007b)	2007	Sustainable Transport, Market Segmentation and Tourism:	Journal of Sustainable Tourism	Market segmentation	UK	Rail tourism
Dallen, J. (Dallen, 2007a)	2007	The challenges of diverse visitor perceptions:	Journal of Transport Geography	Branch line railways; Destination transport; St Ives; Cornwall	UK	Rail tourism
Docherty, I. (Docherty, 2000)	2000	Rail transport policy-making in UK Passenger Transport Authority areas	Journal of Transport Geography	Passenger Transport Authorities and Executives; Rail policy-making; Urban regime theory	UK	Privatizations and public-private partner-ships
Everett, S. (Everett, 2006)	2006	Deregulation and reform of rail in Australia: Some emerging constraints	Transport Policy	Deregulation	Australia	Deregulation
Fearnley, N.; Bekken, J.; Norheim, B. (Fearnley et al., 2004)	2004	Optimal performance-based subsidies in Norwegian inter-city rail transport	International Journal of Transport Management	Incentive; Contract; Performance	Norway	Service quality
Gibb, R.; Lowndes; T.; Charlton, C. (Gibb et al., 1996)	1996	The privatization of British rail	Applied Geography	Deregulation, privatization, British Rail	UK	Privatizations and public-private partner-ships

Author	Year	Title	Journal	Keywords	Country	Theme
Givoni, M. (Givoni, 2006)	2006	Development and impact of the modern high-speed train: a review	Transport Reviews	High-speed train, investment, infrastructure	Europe and Japan	New technologies
Givoni, M.; Banister, D. (Givoni and Banister, 2006)	2006	Airline and railway integration	Transport Policy	Modal integration, high-speed trains, air transport	UK	Integration and competition
Givoni, M.; Banister, D. (Givoni and Banister, 2007)	2007	Role of the railways in the future of air transport	Transportation Planning and Technology	Air-rail; integration; substitution; air transport policy; airports		Integration and competition
Gutiérrez, J.; González, R.; et al. (Gutiérrez et al., 1996)	1996	The European high-speed train network	Journal of Transport Geography	Accessibility, high-speed trains	Europe	New technologies
Halsall, D. A. (Halsall, 2001)	2001	Railway heritage and the tourist gaze: Stoomtram Hoorn-Medemblik	Journal of Transport Geography	Railway heritage; Leisure; Tourist gaze	The Netherlands	Rail tourism
Haywood, R. (Haywood, 2007)	2007	Britain's National railway network: fit for purpose in the 21st century?	Journal of Transport Geography	Railway network; Planning; Regeneration	UK	The role of railways in the economy
Jahanshahi, M. F. (Jahanshahi, 1998)	1998	The US railroad industry and open access	Transport Policy	US railroad industry, bottleneck, open access	USA	Deregulation
Knowles, R. D. (Knowles, 1998)	1998	Passenger rail privatization in Great Britain and its implications, especially for urban areas	Journal of Transport Geography	Rail privatization, franchising, regulation, subsidy	UK	Privatizations and public-private partnerships
Link, H. (Link, 2004)	2004	Rail infrastructure charging and on-track competition in Germany	International Journal of Transport Management	On-track competition; Access charging; Competitive tendering	Germany	Privatizations and public-private partnerships

Milan, J. (Milan, 1996)	1996	The trans European railway network: Three levels of services for the passengers	Transport Policy	Trans European Railway Network, passenger transport, quality of services, travel speed, schedule delay	Europe	Service quality
Milan, J. (Milan, 2003)	2003	Multicriteria evaluation of high-speed rail, Transrapid Maglev and air passenger …	Transportation Planning and Technology	High-speed transport systems; Multicriteria analysis; Entropy method; Interest groups	Europe	New technologies
Park, Y.; Ha, H.-K. (Park and Ha, 2006)	2006	Analysis of the impact of high-speed railroad service on air transport …	Transportation Research Part E	Aviation demand; Stated preference; Utility function	South Korea	Integration and competition
Pearce, D. G. (Pearce, 2001b)	2001	Tourism, Trams and Local Government Policy-making in Christchurch….	Current Issues in Tourism	Trams, urban tourism, policy development	New Zealand	Rail tourism
Pearce, D. G. (Pearce, 2001a)	2001	Tourism and urban land use change: Assessing the impact of Christchurch's tourist tramway	Tourism and Hospitality Research	Urban tourism, urban re-generation, trams, impact assessment, longitudinal studies, land use	New Zealand	Rail tourism
Pang, S. (Phang, 2003)	2003	Strategic Development of airport and rail infrastructure: the case of Singapore	Transport Policy	Transport infrastructure, trains, airports	Singapore	Integration and competition
Plakhotnik, V. N.; Onyshchenko, J. V. et al. (Plakhotnik et al., 2005)	2005	The environmental impacts of railway transportation in the Ukraine	Transportation Research Part D	Railway transport; Monitoring; Air pollution; Computer analysis	Ukraine	Rail and environmental impacts
Rideau, B. (Prideaux, 1999)	1999	Tracks to tourism: Queensland rail joins the tourist industry	International Journal of Tourism Research	Long-distance passenger rail; marketing; heritage nostalgia	Australia	Rail tourism

Author	Year	Title	Journal	Keywords	Country	Theme
Stubbs, J.; Jegede, F.	1998	The integration of rail and air transport in Britain	Journal of Transport Geography	Air-rail integration	UK	Integration and competition
Thompson, I. B. (Thompson, 1995)	1995	High-speed transport hubs and Eurocity status: the case of Lyon	Journal of Transport Geography	Multimodal hubs, high speed trains	France	Integration and competition
Thompson, L. S. (Thompson, 2003)	2003	Changing railway structure and ownership: is anything working?	Transport Reviews	Multiple access to infrastructure, ownership		Privatizations and public-private partnerships
Turnock, D. (Turnock, 2001)	2001	Railways and economic development in Romania before 1918	Journal of Transport Geography	Agriculture; Economic development; Industrialisation; Urbanisation	Romania	Rail development
Wardman, M.; Shires, J.; Lythgo, W.; Tyler, J. (Wardman et al., 2004)	2004	Consumer benefits and demand impacts of regular train time tables	International Journal of Transport Management	Regular timetables; Passenger benefits; Stated preference	Europe	Supply and demand
Whelan, G.; Johnson, D. (Whelan and Johnson, 2004)	2004	Modelling the impact of alternative fare structures on train overcrowding	International Journal of Transport Management	Simulation model; Train overcrowding; Yield management	Europe	Supply and demand
Wong, W. G.; Han, B. M.; Ferreira, L. et al. (Wong et al., 2002)	2002	Evaluation of management strategies for the operation of high-speed railways in China	Transportation Research Part A	High-speed railway; Railway management; Hierarchy method	China	New technologies

Road transport can be grouped efficiently into two major types: 1) self-drive, including private and rental cars, and recreational vehicles; and 2) non-self-drive, such as taxis, bus, coaches and other specialised segments such as back-packing buses (e.g. the Kiwi Experience in New Zealand) and hotel buses (e.g. the Exploranter, in Brazil). While there has been relatively little research into self-drive tourism in general (cf., Hardy 2003), it is obvious that this sector can be important in many regions around the world. Current studies on self-drive tourism can be grouped into a few disciplines. For example, studies of self-drive tourism behaviour undertaken from a psychological perspective have focused on behaviour and choices. Punter (1999) studied tourist behaviour regarding transport choices based on travel patterns including intra-regional and inter-regional trips. He concluded that the choice of holiday transport creates distinct holiday location and activity patterns for each modal group. Eby and Molnar (2002), who analysed the factors routinely taken into account by overnight drive tourists when choosing their travel routes, found that US drive tourists are more concerned with directness, safety, congestion and distance rather than if the route is entertaining or pleasant to drive. The scenic appeal of byways did not seem to be the major issue in route choice by their sample of US drive tourists. Research by Moscardo and Pearce (2004) found that there are significant motivational differences between international and domestic drive tourists, and domestic drive tourists with and without children.

Understanding the behaviours and travel patterns of tourists using different modes of transport can be useful for destination managers. For example, in a study into visitor spending, Downward and Lumsdon (2004) identified a significant difference in expenditure patterns between drive tourists and public transport visitors, with the former spending higher amounts. In another study, Fredman (2008) found that travellers who regularly use rail or air spend more than drive or coach tourists. Lohmann *et al.*'s (2010) case study of international travellers from the countries bordering the Southern part of Brazil found that their choice of the two most visited destinations in this region, respectively Florianópolis and Balneário Camboriú, is influenced by their use of a car or coach/bus. The concentration of attractions and activities in Balneário Camboriú make it easier for coach tourists to access those attractions and activities as those coach tourists can walk from one place to another while visiting this Brazilian seaside resort. On the other hand, in comparison, Florianópolis, where the popular beaches and second home locations are a distance of several kilometres from the downtown area, the use of cars make it more convenient for visitors, particularly considering that public transportation is not efficient in most Brazilian cities. The authors also highlight that drive tourists in these destinations stay longer, are more likely to be repeat visitors and spend more than coach tourists.

The most structured segment in self-drive tourism is the rental car segment. In spite of the existence of some large international rental car companies with multi-billion dollar annual revenues such as Avis, Budget, Enterprise and Hertz, the car rental industry surprisingly not well documented in either the transport or tourism academic literatures. Outside the academic arena, there are some commercially-available industry reports describing this transportation sector in different places of the world, including Europe (Russell, 1999) and the USA (Loverseed, 1996). Within the tourism literature, Lohmann and Zahra (2010) discuss the impacts that international tourist travel patterns in New Zealand have on rental car fleet management and the mechanisms used by rental car companies to relocate their fleet. Efficient capacity utilization lowers the possibility of running short on rental cars. Efficient distribution is another factor that keeps the industry profitable. Pearce and Sahli (2007) undertook a study where they compared the distribution channel system for two rental car companies in New Zealand: a multi-national and a local value-based one. The managerial and operational differences between these two companies found in this study are summarized in Table 4.

Despite the positive relationship between fleet sizes and the level of profitability, firms are constantly growing their fleet sizes because of the competitive forces associated with this sector.

Table 4: Managerial and operational differences between types of rental car companies in New Zealand (adapted from Pearce and Sahli, 2007).

	Multi-national company	Local value-based company
Outlets	Multiple outlets a national level, especially at airports, main centres and provincial centres	Limited to the main centres and do not include offices within the international airports
Fleet management strategies	Send excess leased vehicles back to the lessor (aim to have 80% of the stock used at any given time)	Reduce the fleet by storing it
Client base	One third of corporate (predominantly domestic), one third inbound travellers and one-third 'domestic leisure'.	International, leisure travellers, especially budget travellers from Europe, Australia and North America
Distribution channels	75% of the revenue made through intermediaries (travel management companies, corporate travel agents etc)	80% of its revenue comes from direct sales to the customer

Current policy and economic issues in transport

It is interesting to note that, despite the international pervasiveness of transport, transport still remains highly regulated. It is regulated because governments worldwide hold considerable interest in transport systems for national security and the carriage of passengers and vital goods. Governments are often called upon to ensure the efficient movement of goods and services as they form the backbone of national economies. Examples of regulatory oversight of transport provision include various aspects of subsidised supply (e.g., national rail or air services underwritten by government), safety and security oversight (e.g., airport scanning) and government ownership of transport service provision. Each of these is discussed in this section, but they contain an overarching theme with respect to tourism: in one form or another, each has an impact on the mobility of tourists.

Subsidisation of transport provision

Economic activities can have severe repercussions on the provision of many forms of transport (see, for example, Banister and Berechman, 2001), particularly when that transport serves a primary purpose of moving tourists from a point of origin to their destinations. This is especially true in the air transport sector where this need is amplified in those destinations that are geographically remote or distant from key source markets (IATA, 2007). In general, however, when demand for transport services falls during periods of economic or geopolitical instability, a key question for destination managers and governments is what can be done to maintain access during these periods, ensuring that valuable tourism revenues are maintained (Forsyth, 2006).

Several scenarios can be constructed. First, if the market is relatively 'open' – such that competition is not restricted through government regulation – discussion with other types of transport providers may lead to additional services being introduced. Second, and perhaps unusually, if the market is 'closed' – where competition has previously been restricted through government regulatory policy – an obvious choice would be to liberalise that access in the hope that additional capacity is realised. Finally, an increasingly common solution is for the destination/government to directly underwrite the services of the transport provider (Nolan *et al.*, 2005; Williams, 2005; Williams and Pagliari, 2004). This serves to guarantee capacity, especially for valuable inbound tourism which is generally the main source of t overall tourism revenues. Underwriting by the destination or government can also benefit the transport provider by guaranteeing that the transport provider's costs are covered, thereby rendering variances in market demand for their services less of a critical operating issue.

Some examples from the provision of air services underscore the increasing degree to which some of these services are being underwritten by governments. In the United States, AirTran confirmed in June 2009 that its operations out of Wichita Mid-Continent Airport were profitable only because of direct subsidies in the amount of US$6.5 million granted by the city, county and state governments (KSN News, 2009). Similarly, it was reported in July 2009 that Portland, Oregon, directed a lump-sum subsidy in the amount of US$3.5 million to Delta Air Lines to maintain direct links between the city and Tokyo, a route which was reported to be worth US$61.2 million to the immediate region (Wall Street Journal, 2009). Further, more formalised programmes exist in Europe (Public Service Obligation, PSO – http://ec.europa.eu/transport/modes/air/internal_market/pso_en.htm), Australia (Remote Air Service Subsidy Scheme – http://www.infrastructure.gov.au/aviation/regional/rass.aspx), and the United States (Essential Air Service Programme – http://www.dot.gov/policy/aviation-policy/small-community-rural-air-service/essential-air-service).

Several critical policy questions emerge from the option of direct subsidies for transport services by destinations/governments. The first is the obvious question of how much should be underwritten. The transport provider would likely seek not only to recover most costs (with the further question of whether this cost recovery should apply only to traffic-related costs or to longer-term capacity costs), but also expect a reasonable return in the form of a profit. The destination, on the other hand, would likely attempt to offset pressure to direct, hypothetically public funds, to a private transport service provider that, in reality, realises a small profit because of the direct subsidy. A second and equally pertinent policy question is what effect the subsidy has on the market. In other words, a critical question is what effects can arise from a direct subsidy on market structure and competition. By underwriting one provider, the market may react negatively. For example, new firms seeking to initiate comparable transport services may not wish to compete given the existence of a public subsidy to one of their competitors (see, for example, Santana (2009), for a discussion of this issue in the context of the European PSO Programme.

Passenger security

Another key area in transport policy that has a direct impact on tourism relates to passenger security. Nowhere is this more prevalent and visible that in the context of air travel, particularly since the September 2001 events in the United States. Since then, there has been substantial pressure on governments and airlines to demonstrate their ability to manage potential and threats to commercial aircraft, both on the ground and in flight. Several policy responses designed to improve security and, by extension, passenger safety have been either implemented or mooted, including physical searches and scans, biometric technology (Haas, 2004) and profiling (Baker, 2002).

The United States has been at the forefront of policy measures designed to address concerns over air service security with the creation of a federal agency (the TSA – Transportation Security Agency) whose primary visible (but not necessarily administrative) function is passenger screening at the country's airports. In some cases, passengers may complain about such screening, arguing primarily that it is invasive and time-consuming, thus leading to poorer transit experiences even before they reach their destination (Rossiter and Dresner, 2004). One issue has been the growing practice that full passenger records (including most demographic variables) must be forwarded to the appropriate agency in the destination country before passengers board at their point of origin. Such information has been required by US authorities from airlines operating services to the United States since shortly after September 2001. This practice has been the subject of debate, focusing on whether such actions violated EU privacy laws (Asinari and Poullet, 2004). While the legality of the collection and use of such detailed data has been raised (Heilbronn and von Nessen, 2009), it remains to be seen where the obligations by governments to ensure security will come at the expense of privacy laws and regulations.

Another policy 'experiment' has been the introduction and use of full body scanners at major international airports. In January 2010, United States President Barack Obama urged foreign governments to deploy such scanners as a means of enhancing existing security arrangements. Critics have branded such measures as invasive, with some in the UK suggesting that they would break existing child protection laws that prevent indecent images of children to be created (Guardian, 2010). The full cost of such scanners always appears to be a contentious issue, and has received significant attention following the alleged attempt at igniting an incendiary device on a US-bound flight from Europe on Christmas Day 2009 (Flight Global, 2010).

Many aspects of aviation security are governed internationally by the ICAO – International Civil Aviation Organisation (a UN body). The primary document that guides international efforts is the Aviation Security Manual (see http://www.icao.int/Security/SFP/Pages/SecurityManual.aspx. The importance to tourism of having an international organisation such as ICAO oversee security matters cannot be overstated. As countries become voluntary members of ICAO, they abide by, among other things, the security-related regulatory oversight that is required by all contracting states in order to enhance cooperation on common matters of concern. Compliance is seen to facilitate commercial air travel by assuring states that foreign carriers (from states that are signatories to ICAO) abide by international standards. By extension, ICAO regularly audits contracting states' security provisions through its University Security Audit Programme. This programme serves to provide a uniform approach to key aspect of security provision and establishes an agreed-upon set of rules for countries (and their designated airlines) to follow and implement.

Supply/demand – managing externalities

Transport is invariably subject to shifts in supply and demand, with many forces that impact upon both being almost entirely out of the control of the transport provider. These 'externalities' are generally seen as those factors or agents which have either a negative or positive effect on direct or indirect production, via other agents that have direct production influence. Negative externalities reduce productivity whereas positive externalities are seen to increase productivity. For transport and its relationship with tourism, negative externalities can take many forms including shifts in regulation that result in increased costs for the transport provider, increases in the price of oil (which became problematic for airlines in late 2008 and early 2009), and shifts in demand for transport services. It is the latter that is most important here, given that demand for transport products and services can be variable and thus difficult to forecast (Fischer, 1993). Therefore, there is a need to discuss the wider impact of the relationship between supply and demand in transport in general. Understanding this relationship assists policy makers make decisions in such areas as investment (directly or indirectly in the form of infrastructure), marketing promotion (to incite interest in the use of transport for the purposes of either transporting tourists to or within a destination) and calculating the economic impact of activities that actively involve transport in the tourist experience.

In many respects, the demand for transport services in conjunction with tourism will roughly correlate to the demand for the experiences on offer at a destination for which transport is required for access (Halsall, 1992). Additionally, demand is shaped by many key demographic variables including family structure (Giuliano, 1997b) and age (Giuliano, 1997a). There is also evidence to support consider cross-price elasticity when examining demand for transport and other goods as part of a wider holiday (Njegovan, 2006). Elasticity depends on the destination in question with the overall correlation between transport demand and tourism demand dependent on the nature of the tourist experience sought (Prideaux, 2004). A family of four planning a holiday from the United States to South Africa will establish up-front transport costs as part of their overall budget, with the remaining costs for such items as accommodation, amenities and attractions budgeted to fit within the overall travel budget. In this case, the demand for transport is relatively inelastic given that South Africa is the desired destination. When the destination does not form the focal point of the planned experience, more flexible planning and budgeting for transport expenditure as part of the overall holiday budget can take place, thereby making the demand for transport more elastic. For example, a family of four in Europe looking for a week-long break may opt to travel to a destination based on the destinations available to them within a limited budget. As discussed earlier, it is here where so-called 'low cost' carriers have driven business from secondary airports in Europe to (often equally secondary) airports in other parts of the same continent.

Thus, the demand for tourism and the variables that determine such demand will have a consequential flow-on effect for the demand for that mode of transport that in turn may rely on tourist flows to be profitable. When economic conditions, such as those witnessed in 2009 (ie immediately following the Global Financial Crisis), effectively curtail demand for, in this case, international travel (which comparatively may be more expensive that domestic options), the effect on the primary mode of international travel (air) is likely to be deeply affected.

Conclusion

The importance of transport for the provision of tourism development cannot be overstated. As we have shown, transport forms a critical part of the tourist experience. It not only acts as a conduit by which tourists move from origin to destination (and even within and between destinations), but also serves to supplement the very tourist experience that is consumed. Transport is perhaps best characterised as a service experience that compliments the wider the tourism experience. Both share similar service-related parameters in that they are intangible and largely perishable.

Transport provision for tourism is prone to many external forces that affect the ability for tourism consumption to take place. Recent examples include the eruption of Eyjafjallajokull in Iceland in April 2010. That eruption brought air transport throughout Europe to a grinding halt, but at the same time drove up demand for other forms of transport such as rail and marine as substitute forms of transport. In another example, the global recession of 2008/2009 served to highlight the fragility of the commercial air transport sector, which, when combined with drops in demand, meant many traditional Western destinations received fewer international tourists on an annualised basis. Overall, with transport often acting as the lynchpin for tourism, there exists an enormous amount of interest in its viability and profitability. It is for this reason that governments are careful to ensure that transport is, to some extent, protected.

It will be difficult to change the hyper mobile society that characterises much of today's Western world. In spite of the trends to diminish the carbon footprint of travellers' displacement, particularly with the EU's efforts to cap carbon emissions, encourage the use of other greener modes of transport or simply encourage visits to closer destinations, the reality is that it will be hard to re-engineer the role transport has for the existence of tourism and other activities. Transport and tourism are very resilient, as the events of 9/11 and the closure of the European air traffic in April 2010 have shown, with people choosing other types of tourism arrangements or transport choices. Regardless, however, transport will continue to play an important role in the provision of tourism development and tourist experiences.

Future issues and agendas

Predicting future trends in transport is difficult given the numerous variables that influence both the appeal and profitability of various transport modes. Several of these variables, however, play a key role at present and will likely continue to do so in the future.

1   **Safety**. Safety measures are by and large the price of entry for transport modes in that their use and uptake by potential passengers will be possible only if those passengers are a) satisfied that the mode is generally safe, and b) that the regulatory environment within which the transport mode operates provides for adequate safety oversight. Safety continues to be paramount in ensuring the viability of transport modes. Thus, potential passengers (and tourists) who perceive unsafe operations will actively seek substitutes. Oversight of safety in some modes of transport (e.g., air) generally falls to industry associations such as the International Air Transport Association and to the relevant agencies within individual countries, but a global approach to safety management and regulatory oversight is needed;

2   **Emissions and other negative externalities**. Notwithstanding the case study below, the impact of negative externalities such as emissions, noise and other visual and environmental pollutants is fast becoming a highly contentious issue. One example is the vocal and highly-publicised opposition to a new runway at London's Heathrow airport on the basis of additional noise and other environmental hazards associated with airport operations. Another is the physical alteration (e.g. by dredging) of natural harbours to accommodate larger cruise ships or the wash produced by the fast ferry catamaran technology. The ecological footprint of most forms of transport is reasonably significant enough not to ignore, but future policy debates will hinge on whether limited transport (and thus tourism arrivals from distant points of origin) will have a stronger negative economic impact than allowing transport activities to continue;

3   **Changing travel patterns**. Without question, patterns of demand have enormous impact on the provision of transport, the networks of which are ostensibly designed to both meet that demand and translate

latent into actual demand. This requires substantial and meaningful research by transport providers so that they can understand market shifts and consequently, forecast and plan appropriately. Over the past few decades, this task has become easier with the proliferation of data sources. Many of these (for example, data solutions from the International Air Transport Association or from global distribution systems such as Sabre) are used by air transport providers for route planning. In cruise markets, online market research can be used to gauge demand for specific cruise destinations and on-board ship amenities. What these examples illustrate is a clear pattern of market knowledge on a scale not previously seen. Information and market intelligence is becoming a strong competitive asset. Therefore, we expect transport providers will continue to be at the forefront of ensuring that the market information they have is timely and accurate.

Research in transport and tourism has flourished in the past few decades, as this review has demonstrated. It is becoming more mature as a subject of enquiry in not only the tourism discipline, but also in other disciplines such as air transport economics, geography, accounting and finance, and management. Much like predicting the future flows of tourists and their use of transport, predicting the direction of scholarship that investigates the tourism/transport nexus is equally difficult to predict (an attempt has been made by Lumsdon and Page, 2004). That said, we offer two key directions that we feel could (and perhaps should) receive additional attention:

4   The relationship between tourism and transport policy. For the most part, tourism and transport policy, representing separate entities, involves two distinct but overlapping policy communities, remains the most pressing area of research. What is needed is a better sense of the process followed by governments as they assess the integration between tourism development and the necessity of transport provision for general economic growth and development;

5   An understanding of the value of transport for tourism growth and development. There exists a need to fully measure the absolute value of transport for tourism development in such a way that allows policy makers to make informed decisions on transport access, development and even subsidisation, where applicable. This speaks to the desire to hold accurate and timely information as discussed above. Such information can also assist potential transport providers (where fully private or in a public-private partnership) assess the feasibility and viability of proposed or planned opportunities. "Value" can of course be measured in several ways. Economically, it incorporates opportunity

cost and can be modelled to include the role of predictors on an outcome. Socially, however, value is less concrete and more difficult to assess. In practice, the qualitative or soft measures of value are captured longitudinally in measures of social capital, wellbeing and community. Tourism contributes to both of these measures, and by extension the provision of transport does as well.

Case study – Emissions mitigation in air transport: implications for tourism

The scope and scale of global aviation is massive, accounting for an estimated 15 million jobs and US$1.1 trillion of worldwide GDP (Oxford Economics, 2009). Against this, concerns over the contribution of aviation to global climate change continue to be raised. The purpose of this case study is to a) understand the contribution by air transport to global climate change through emissions from operations, b) evaluate policy options to mitigate air transport emissions, and c) discuss potential implications for tourism.

A. Emissions and international air transport

There is a substantial body of literature that outlines the dangerous impacts of emissions from air transport (e.g., Lee *et al.*, 2009; Sausen and Schuman, 2000; Schumann, 1997). Critically, the damage from air transport emissions is increasingly being recognised, but even though the overall impact of air transport emissions is relatively small, the concern is that the rate of growth of global international air transport, and to some extent its association with leisure activities such as tourism, render it a target for mitigation action. Consumer awareness is building. Active research on ethics, public awareness and behaviour (e.g., Becken 2007, Cohen and Higham 2011) is helping to frame the issue from multiple perspectives as industry and governments address the challenge of emissions.

The aviation sector has not ignored these realities. In September 2009, the International Air Transport Association, a trade industry organisation representing approximately 230 airlines that account for over 90% of the world's scheduled traffic, pledged to a) reduce net CO2 emissions by 50% by 2050, b) make all industry growth carbon-neutral by 2020, and c) cut CO2 emissions by 1.5% per year each year until 2019. For some, however, such pledges may do little to stem the growth in commercial air transport and, by extension, the growth in resulting emissions.

Initially, it is important to gain a broad understanding of the nature of aircraft emissions and their impact on the environment. Emissions from aircraft occur at varying stages of flight, including during activities that precede and follow a flight. Ground level emissions have been measured with some accuracy, however it is the impact of a jet aircraft at cruising altitude (between 30,000 and 40,000 feet) where a considerable amount of science is currently focused. At issue is the relative impact of emissions from jet fuel combustion at cruising altitude, with some research suggesting that the damage caused is significantly higher than emissions on the ground (Schumann, 1997). In addition, the precise impact of air transport activities at flight level on cloud formation is still not entirely known (cf. Williams and Noland, 2005), although there is strong evidence to suggest that aircraft contrails (the water vapour trails left in the sky) can contribute to some alterations in cloud formation and movement (Schumann, 2000) as well as ozone (Ponater *et al.*, 1999).

B. Policy options

Policy options with respect to mitigating or assigning responsibility for international air transport emissions remain elusive, largely because of the political nature of the problem and the fact that air travel is an international activity that some economists, industry trade groups and airlines suggest necessarily necessitates a global solution. First, it is necessary to review concepts related to mitigation policy options.

Perhaps the most visible policy instruments are emissions taxes (sometimes called Pigouvian taxes or carbon taxes) and emissions trading schemes. Both put a price on carbon as a negative externality of commercial aircraft activities, but they do so in different ways. A carbon tax rate is set by a government such that any emissions over and above a particular amount shall be taxed (usually on a per tonne basis). Thus, the firm is incentivised to streamline production – or introduce innovations in production – that will minimise its tax liability. Emissions trading, on the other hand, simply puts a price a carbon by allowing firms to buy and sell permits in an open market. For each unit of emissions produced by a firm, one permit is required to be surrendered. In such a system, firms need to either reduce emissions or acquire enough permits to cover their emissions.

How each policy option can be efficiently applied to international air transport is somewhat problematic. Implementing a carbon tax is problematic for several reasons. First, aviation fuel is not combusted solely in the jurisdiction where the tax is imposed. Thus, a flight from London to New York will have expended fuel and generated emissions across the Atlantic as well as in both United Kingdom and United States airspace. If the United States were to tax all of the fuel from that particular flight, it raises the question as to why that airline is responsible to the United States for emissions generated across the entire flight. This is one reason why aviation and maritime bunker fuels have not featured as part of any global climate accord, including the Kyoto Protocol (and thus, international aviation is not included within Kyoto, although there were recommendations made to limit emissions from aircraft). Second, there is some concern that unilateral taxation or imposing carbon costs on international carriers within a particular jurisdiction violates many trade agreements that either directly or indirectly cover air services. These agreements feature fairly common sections that outline whether additional charges or duties ('taxes' are not usually mentioned specifically) can be imposed on flights arriving or departing a particular territory, or whether one country can apply legislation that violates the sovereignty of another's carrier (see, for example, Schwarze, 2007).

Europe offers an interesting example in this regard. The European Union has attempted to incorporate aviation emissions into its emissions trading scheme. At the time of writing, only flight within the EU are currently covered by the scheme, although an attempt was made to include flights to and from non-European countries, such as those originating from Asia or North America. Under those original conditions, emissions that generated outside of EU airspace by, for example, a United States airline, would still be accountable under the trading scheme. The EU eventually (and potentially temporarily) succumbed in 2012 to substantial pressure from various governments, including the United States, with respect to sovereignty, and these requirements were suspended. While the EU has publicly stated its support for global market-based measures in accounting for aviation emissions, no such trading scheme exists that would encompass all international airlines at the time of writing. In November 2009, IATA argued that a global sector approach was necessary, rather than treating aviation within regional- or country-specific reduction efforts. There exists a possibility of a global agreement being reached at the 2016 Montreal meeting of ICAO.

As both a carbon tax and a trading scheme seek to price the externality (carbon) generated from air transport, airlines naturally seek to minimise their fuel burn in order to reduce their exposure to their associated additional costs. As fuel represents perhaps the most significant variable cost in an aircraft's operation, reducing fuel use – especially during periods of high oil prices – has always been the goal of most airlines. Aircraft manufacturers have responded over the past several decades by designing aircraft that are increasingly fuel-efficient. Technological innovations include more efficient power plants from engine manufacturers (under pressure from both airlines and aircraft manufacturers), winglets on the end of wings, and lighter composite materials to reduce weight. The purpose of these innovations has generally been to help keep airline costs low, but they also serve an important function in ensuring that emissions are as low as possible.

Airlines have also enacted operational procedures to reduce emissions, including removing weight from aircraft and reducing in-flight waste. Navigational procedures have also been enhanced recently in various regions around the world. One procedure, known as RNAV (or Area Navigation), allows for GPS-directed flight paths as opposed to ground-based systems, which result in inefficient flight paths that deviate from the shortest path (Elder, 1996-1997). In addition, RNP (Required Navigational Performance) is a guidance system for facilitating constant descent rates at airports as a way of facilitating aircraft movements as efficiently as possible, thus saving fuel and reducing emissions and noise (Clarke, 2003).

One area of operations that deserves attention is the use of biofuels (often simply called alternative fuels) as either a supplement to standard jet aviation fuels. These fuels, generally derived from an algae base as opposed to a kerosene base, appear to hold significant promise. Airbus indicated in November 2009 that alternative fuels could power up to 15 percent of global traffic by 2020. Several airlines (including, e.g., Air New Zealand, Continental, Qatar and KLM) have already undertaken demonstration flights, using a variety of blends and organic derivatives. The immediate near future of alternative fuel development seems to be focused on certification processes that will allow commercial production. Not surprisingly, many airlines are keen to see such fuels be developed and made available as they will help with cost management and any environmental operating targets.

C. Implications for tourism

The implications for tourism from consideration of air transport emissions are likely to be varied and complex. Any attempt to put a price on carbon generated from air transport may result in the increased cost being passed on to the passenger. In some instances, and depending entirely on the price elasticity of particular markets and segments, this could have devastating effects for some destinations. A good example of this is the UK Air Passenger Duty as discussed earlier. In this case, the amount of the duty is correlated positively with the distance travelled. Thus, long-haul destinations, which thus rely on the UK market as a source for tourists, are therefore concerned that the APD will render their destinations uncompetitive. Several destinations (e.g., Australia, New Zealand, various West Indian countries) expressed concern over the impact on their tourism sector when the UK has raised the level of the APD, starting in 2009 and subsequently in 2012 and 2013.

Another implication for tourism is the consequence of operational decisions made by carriers and their resulting impacts on travel flows. A fundamental principle of airline economics generally holds that a carrier's costs (calculated as a cost per available seat kilometre, or CASK) should necessarily be lower than its revenue (calculated as the revenue per available seat kilometre) (Holloway, 2003). When costs increase, the resulting impact on margins means that the airline must find a way to either increase revenue or lower costs. In many markets, active competition has resulted in operations with extremely narrow margins such that cost reduction and revenue enhancements are already in place. Requiring an airline to account for the cost of carbon to its cost may result in unprofitable operations on a particular route where the regulation of carbon is present. This is especially the case if the airline is unable to recover from passengers additional costs arising from imposed carbon or emissions charges. For example, it is reasonable to assume that a carrier may opt to cease operations to a particular country because that country has imposed a measure of accountability on the carrier for its emissions. It may do so because its assets (the aircraft it operates) can be more productive elsewhere where it may not face additional costs. In fact, this is one reason why critics of the EU ETS and its impending inclusion of aviation amounts to more or less a regional solution to a global problem (see, for example, Chen, 2009).

D. Conclusion

It is clear that air transport-related emissions and their impact on climate are a pressing global concern. It is also evident that air transport as an economic sector will not likely be completely immune from any attempt to price the negative climate-related externalities generated by its activities. Perhaps the most critical task is to determine the precise balance between aviation's negative externalities and its benefits to local, national and international economies (Chapman, 2007; Gossling *et al.*, 2008). Finding this balance is clearly a political problem. On the one hand, the connectivity and accessibility enjoyed by a territory as a result of air transport is positive for the economy as a whole, and thus in the short-term it is in the interests of a sitting government to ensure that employment and overall development potential is maintained. On the other hand, this short-term gain from connectivity and its resulting trade must be balanced against long-term damage caused by those very activities. Many suggest that this inability to identify and agree upon the precise balance between the two lays at the heart of 'failure' of attendees at the Copenhagen summit in December 2009 to arrive a new global accord relating to climate change at a more general level.

E. Questions for consideration

1   If you were to advise a national government on whether to include inbound international flights into its domestic emissions trading scheme, how would you account for the relative importance of those inbound flights to the overall economy? What scenarios would be consider *post hoc*?

2   How might a global policy on internalising aviation emissions be
     structured such that developing countries are not shouldered with more
     than what some would consider to be their 'fair share' of emissions
     reductions? What could this mean to the shape of tourist flows if
     developed countries are asked to carry more of the burden in mitigating
     commercial aviation emissions?

Acknowledgements

The authors would like to thank Wendy London for her contribution towards this chapter.

References

Abeyratne, R. I. R. (1999) Management of the environmental impact of tourism and air transport on small island developing states. *Journal of Air Transport Management,* **5,** 31-37.

Andriotis, K. and Agiomirgianakis, G. (2010) Cruise visitors' experience in a Mediterranean port of call, *International Journal of Tourism Research,* **12** (4), 390-404.

Asinari, M. V. P. and Poullet, Y. (2004) Public security versus data privacy: the airline passenger disclosure case and the EU-US debate. *Computer Law and Security Report,* **20,** 98-116.

Baird, A. (1999) A comparative study of the ferry industry in Japan and the UK. *Transport Reviews,* **19,** 33-55.

Baird, A. (2000) The Japan coastal ferry system. *Maritime Policy Management,* **27,** 3-16.

Baker, E. (2002) Flying while Arab: racial profiling and air travel security. *Journal of Air Law and Commerce,* **67,** 1375-1406.

Banister, D. and Berechman, Y. (2001) Transport investment and the promotion of economic growth. *Journal of Transport Geography,* **9,** 209-218.

Barron, P. and Bartoleme Greenwood, A. (2006) Issues determining the development of cruise itineraries: a focus on the luxury market, *Tourism in Marine environments,* **3,** 22, 89-99.

Becken, S. (2007) Tourists' perception of international air travel's impact on the global climate and potential climate change policies. *Current Issues in Tourism,* **15,** 351-368.

Biehn, N. (2006) A cruise ship is not a floating hotel. *Journal of Revenue & Pricing Management.* Palgrave Macmillan Ltd.

Boberg, K., Choy, D. J. L. (1988) Emerging trends in Trans-Pacific air routes. *Journal of Travel Research,* **26,** 15-23.

Boniface, B. and Cooper, C. (2001) *Worldwide Destinations: The Geography of Travel and Tourism*, Oxford, Butterworth Heinemann.

Bowen, J. (2000) Airline hubs in Southeast Asia: national economic development and nodal accessibility. *Journal of Transport Geography*, **8**, 25-41.

Brida, J. and Zapata, S. (2010), Economic impacts of cruise tourism : the case of Costa Richa, *Anatolia*, **21**(2), 322-338.

Brida, J., Pulinab, M., Rianoa, E. and Zapata-Aguirrea, D. (2012) Cruise passengers' experience embarking in a Caribbean home port : the case study of Cargagena de Indias, *Ocean & Coastal Management*, **55**, 135-145.

Burghardt, A. F. (1971) A hypothesis about gateway cities. *Annals of the Association of American Geographers*, **61**, 269-85.

Campos, J. (2001) Lessons from railway reforms in Brazil and Mexico. *Transport Policy*, **8**, 85-95.

Carson, D., Waller, I. and Scott, N. (Eds.) (2002) *Drive Tourism: up the wall and around the bend*, Altona, Common Ground.

Cartwright, R. and Baird, C. (1999) *The development and growth of the cruise industry*, Oxford, Butterworth-Heinemann.

Caves, R. E. and Gosling, G. D. (1999) *Strategic Airport Planning*, Oxford, Pergamon.

Chan, D. (2000) The story of Singapore Airlines and the Singapore Girl. *Journal of Management Development*, **19**(6), 456-472.

Chapman, L. (2007) Transport and climate change: a review. *Journal of Transport Geography*, **15**, 354-367.

Charlton, C., Gibb, R., Shaw, J. (1997) Regulation and continuing monopoly on Britain's railways. *Journal of Transport Geography*, **5**, 147-153.

Chen, Y. (2009) Does a regional greenhouse gas policy make sense? A case study of carbon leakage and emissions spillover. *Energy Economics*, **31**, 667-675.

Chin, C. (2008). *Cruising in the Global Economy: Profits, Pleasure and Work at Sea*, Aldershot, Ashgate.

Clarke, J.-P. (2003) The role of advanced air traffic management in reducing the impact of aircraft noise and enabling aviation growth. *Journal of Air Transport Management*, **9**, 161-165.

Cohen, S.A. and Higham, J.E.S. (2011) Eyes wide shut? UK consumer perceptions on aviation climate impacts and travel decisions to New Zealand. *Current Issues in Tourism*, **14**, 323-335.

Costa, T. F. G., Lohmann, G., Oliveira, A. V. M. (2010) A model to identify airport hubs and their importance to tourism in Brazil. *Research in Transportation Economics*, **26**, 3-11.

Cruise Lines International Association Inc (2014), The state of the cruise industry in 2014: global growth in passenger numbers and product offerings, CLIA, Ft Lauderdale, http://www.cruising.org/news/press_ releases/2014/01/state-cruise-industry-2014-global-growth-passenger-numbers-and-product-o (accessed 8 September 2014).

Dallen, J. (2007a) The challenges of diverse visitor perceptions: rail policy and sustainable transport at the resort destination. *Journal of Transport Geography Transport at Tourist Destinations,* **15,** 104-115.

Dallen, J. (2007b) Sustainable transport, market segmentation and tourism: The Looe Valley Branch Line Railway, Cornwall, UK. *Journal of Sustainable Tourism,* **15,** 180-199.

Dean, C. J. (1993) Travel by excursion coach in the United Kingdom. *Journal of Travel Research,* Spring, 59-64.

Debbage, K. G. and Alkaabi, K. (2008) Market Power and vertical (dis) integration? airline networks and destination development in the United States and Dubai. In Graham, A., Papatheodorou, A. and Forsyth, P. (Eds.) *Aviation and Tourism: Implications for Leisure Travel.* Aldershot, Ashgate.

Dennis, N. (1994) Airline hub operations in Europe. *Journal of Transport Geography,* **2,** 219-233.

Dickinson, R. H., Vladimir, A. N. (1997) *Selling the Sea: An Inside Look at the Cruise Industry,* New York, John Wiley & Sons.

Docherty, I. (2000) Rail transport policy-making in UK Passenger Transport Authority areas. *Journal of Transport Geography,* **8,** 157-170.

Douglas, N. and Douglas, N. (2001) The cruise experience. In Douglas, N., Douglas, N. and Derrett, R. (Eds.) *Special interest tourism – Context and cases.* Milton, John Wiley & Sons Australia.

Douglas, N. and Douglas, N. (2004) Cruise ship passenger spending patterns in Pacific island ports. *International Journal of Tourism Research,* **6,** 251-261.

Downward, P. and Lumsdon, L. (2004) Tourism transport and visitor spending: A study in the North York Moors National Park, UK. *Journal of Travel Research,* **42,** 415-420.

Dunlop, G. (2002) The European ferry industry – challenges and changes. *International Journal of Transport Management,* **1,** 115-116.

Duval, D. T. (2007) *Tourism and Transport: modes, networks and flows,* Clevedon, Channel View Publications.

Dwyer, L., Douglas, N. and Zelko, L. (2004) Estimating the economic contribution of a cruise ship visit. *Tourism in Marine Environments,* **1,** 5-16.

Dwyer, L. and Forsyth, P. (1996) Economic impacts of cruise tourism in Australia. *The Journal of Tourism Studies,* **7,** 36-43.www.jcu.edu.au

Eby, D. W. and Molnar, L. J. (2002) Importance of scenic byways in route choice: a survey of driving tourists in the United States. *Transportation Research Part A*, **36**, 95-106.

Elder, B. 1996-(1997) Free flight: the future of air transportation entering the twenty-first century. *Journal of Air Law and Commerce*, **62**, 871-914.

Everett, S. (2006) Deregulation and reform of rail in Australia: Some emerging constraints. *Transport Policy*, **13**, 74-84. www.sciencedirect.com

Fearnley, N., Bekken, J.-T. and Norheim, B. (2004) Optimal performance-based subsidies in Norwegian intercity rail transport. *International Journal of Transport Management*, **2**, 29-38. www.sciencedirect.com

Fidgeon, P. R. (1983) Holiday caravaning in Wales: Construction of a national site inventory. *Tourism Management*, **4**, 199-208.

Fischer, M. M. 1993 Travel demand. In Polak, J.,Heertje, A. (Eds.) *European Transport Economics*. Oxford, Blackwell.

Fleming, D. K. and Hayuth, Y. 1994 Spatial characteristics of transportation hubs: centrality and intermediacy. *Journal of Transport Geography*, **2**, 3-18. www.sciencedirect.com

Flight Global (2010) MEPs on collision course with ministers over airport security financing, 2 March, www.flightglobal.com/

Forsyth, P. (2006) Martin Kunz Memorial Lecture. Tourism benefits and aviation policy. *Journal of Air Transport Management*, **12**, 3-13.

Fredman, P. (2008) Determinants of visitor expenditures in mountain tourism. *Tourism Economics*, **14**, 297-311.

Garnett, C. (1993) Impact of the Channel Tunnel on the tourism industry – A sea of change in cross-Channel travel. *Tourism Management*, **14**, 436-439.

Gibb, R., Lowndes, T. and Charlton, C. (1996) The privatization of British Rail. *Applied Geography*, **16**, 35-51.

Gibson, P. (2006) *Cruise operations management*, Oxford, Butterworth-Heinemann.

Gibson, P. (2008) Cruising in the 21st century: Who works while others play? *International Journal of Hospitality Management*, **27**, 42-52.

Gibson, P. and Bentley, M. (2006) A study of impacts – cruise tourism and the South West of England. *Journal of Travel and Tourism Marketing*, **20**, 63-77.

Giuliano, G. (1997a) Age and trip-making. *Journal of Transport Geography*, **5**, 44-44.

Giuliano, G. (1997b) Family structure and travel demand. *Journal of Transport Geography*, **5**, 43-43.

Givoni, M. (2006) Development and impact of the modern high-speed train: A review. *Transport Reviews*, **26**, 593 – 611.

Givoni, M. and Banister, D. (2006) Airline and railway integration. *Transport Policy*, **13,** 386-397.

Givoni, M., Banister, D. (2007) Role of the Railways in the Future of Air Transport. *Transportation Planning and Technology*, **30,** 95 – 112.

Gnoth, J. (1999) Tourism expectation formation: the case of campervan tourists in New Zealand. In Pizam, A.,Mansfeld, Y. (Eds.) *Consumer Behavior in Travel and Tourism.* New York: The Haworth Hospitality Press.

Gossling, S., Peeters, P. and Scott, D. (2008) Consequences of climate policy for international tourist arrivals in developing countries. *Third World Quarterly,* **29,** 873-901.

Gössling, S. and Upham, P. (Eds.) (2009) *Climate Change and Aviation: issues, challenges and solutions,* London, Earthscan.

Guardian (2010) New scanners break child porn laws, 4 January, www. guardian.co.uk

Gui, L. and Russo, A. (2011) Cruise ports : a strategic nexus between regions and global lines – evidence from the Mediterranean, *Maritime Policy & Management*, **38,** 2, 129-150.

Gutiérrez, J., González, R. and Gómez, G. 1996 The European high-speed train network. *Journal of Transport Geography*, **4,** 227-238.

Haas, E. P. (2004) Back to the future? The use of biometrics, its impact on airport security, and how this technology should be governed. *Journal of Air Law and Commerce*, **69,** 459-489.

Halsall, D. A. (1992) Transport for tourism and recreation. In Hoyle, B. S.,Knowles, R. D. (Eds.) *Modern transport geography.* London, Belhaven.

Halsall, D. A. (2001) Railway heritage and the tourist gaze: Stoomtram Hoorn-Medemblik. *Journal of Transport Geography*, **9,** 151-160.

Haywood, R. (2007) Britain's national railway network: fit for purpose in the 21st century? *Journal of Transport Geography*, **15,** 198-216.

Heilbronn, G. and Von Nessen, P. (2009) Airline and aviation industry information retention: problems for privacy law proposals on data breach notification in Australia. *Air and Space Law*, **34,** 261-284.

Henderson, J. C. (2006) Tourism in Dubai: overcoming barriers to destination development. *International Journal of Tourism Research*, **8,** 87-99.

Hensher, D. A., Hooper, P. G. and Smith, N. C. (1991) *Developments in surface passenger transport: implications for tourism,* Sydney, NSW, University of Sydney Institute of Transport Studies.

Hobson, J. S. P. (1993a) Analysis of the US cruise line industry. *Tourism Management*, **14,** 453-462.

Hobson, J. S. P. (1993b) Increasing consolidation within the cruise line industry. *Journal of Travel and Tourism Marketing,* **2,** 91-96.

Holloway, S. (2003) *Straight and Level: Practical Airline Economics,* Aldershot, Ashgate.

IATA (2007) Aviation economics benefits: measuring the economic rate of return on investment in the aviation industry. *IATA economics briefing no. 8.* Montreal, International Air Transport Association. www.iata.org

Irandu, E. M. (2004) The Potential for Cruise Tourism in Kenya. *Anatolia: An International Journal of Tourism and Hospitality Research,* **15,** 69-86.

Jahanshahi, M. F. (1998) The US railroad industry and open access. *Transport Policy,* **5,** 73-81.

Janiskee, R. L. (1990) Resort camping in America. *Annals of Tourism Research,* **17,** 385-407.

Jobes, P. C. (1984) Old timers and new mobile lifestyles. *Annals of Tourism Research,* **11,** 181-189.

Johnson, D. (2002) Environmentally sustainable cruise tourism : a reality check. *Marine Policy,* **26,** 261-270.

Johnson, D. (2006) Providing ecotourism excursions for cruise passengers. *Journal of Sustainable Tourism.* Multilingual Matters.

Kissling, C. (1998) Liberal aviation agreements – New Zealand. *Journal of Air Transport Management,* **4,** 177-180.

Knowles, R. D. (1998) Passenger rail privatization in Great Britain and its implications, especially for urban areas. *Journal of Transport Geography,* **6,** 117-133.

Koo, T. T. R. and Lohmann, G. (2013) The spatial effects of domestic aviation deregulation: a comparative study of Australian and Brazilian seat capacity, 1986–2010. *Journal of Transport Geography,* **29,** 52-62. http://dx.doi.org/10.1016/j.jtrangeo.2012.12.011

KSN News (2009) Airtran chief calls public money crucial.

Kwag, H. and Lee, E. (2009), Analysis of the Asian cruise industry and its future implementation, In Papathanassis, A. ed, *Cruise Sector Growth : Managing Emerging Markets, Human Resources, Processes and Systems* (17-29), Gabler, Wiesbaden.

Kwortnik, R. J., Jr (2008) Shipscape influence on the leisure cruise experience. *International Journal of Culture, Tourism and Hospitality Research,* **2,** 289-311.

Lafferty, G. and Fossen, A. (2001) Integrating the tourism industry: Problems and strategies. *Tourism Management,* **22,** 11-19. www.sciencedirect.com

Lapierre, J. and Hayes, D. (1994) The Tourism Satellite Account. *National Income and Expenditure Accounts.* Ottawa, Statistics Canada.

Lee, D., Fahey, D. W., Forster, P. M., Newton, P. J., Wit, R. C. N., Lim, L. L., Owen, B. and Sausen, R. (2009) Aviation and global climate change in the 21st century. *Atmosphere Environment*, **43**, 3520-37. www.tiaca.org

Lekakou, M., Pallis, A. and Vaggelas, G. (2009) Which homeport in Europe: the cruise industry's selection criteria, *Tourismos: an International Multidisciplinary Journal of Tourism*, **4**(4), 215-238.

Leong, T-Y. and Ladany S. (2001) Optimal cruise itinerary design development, *International Journal of Services Technology and Management*, **2**(1/2), 130-141.

Lester, J-A. and Weeden, C (2004) Stakeholders, the natural environment and the future of Caribbean cruise tourism, *International Journal of Tourism Research*, **6**(1), 39-50.

Link, H. (2004) Rail infrastructure charging and on-track competition in Germany. *International Journal of Transport Management*, **2**, 17-27.

Lohmann, G., Albers, S., Koch, B. and Pavlovich, K. (2009) From hub to tourist destination – An explorative study of Singapore and Dubai's aviation-based transformation. *Journal of Air Transport Management*, **15**, 205-211.

Lohmann, G. and Duval, D. T. (2014) Destination morphology: A new framework to understand tourism–transport issues? *Journal of Destination Marketing & Management*, **3**, 133-136.

Lohmann, G., Fraga, C. and Castro, R. (2013). *Transportes e Destinos Turísticos: Planejamento e Gestão*. Rio de Janeiro, Campus/Elsevier.

Lohmann, G. and Koo, T. T. R. (2013) The airline business model spectrum. *Journal of Air Transport Management*, **31**, 7-9. http://dx.doi.org/10.1016/j.jairtraman.2012.10.005

Lohmann, G. and Nguyen, D. N. (2011) A holistic approach to sustainable tourism transportation in Hawai'i. In Carlsen, J., Butler, R. (eds.) *Island Tourism Development: Journeys Toward Sustainability*. Wallingford, CABI.

Lohmann, G. and Oliveira, M. V. O. (2008) Transporte Ferroviário de Passageiros Turísticos: o estado da arte. *Turismo em Análise*, **19**, 1-19.

Lohmann, G. and Pearce, D. G. (2010) Conceptualizing and operationalizing nodal tourism functions. *Journal of Transport Geography*, **18**, 266-275.

Lohmann, G. and Pearce, D. G. (2012) Tourism and transport relationships: the suppliers' perspective in gateway destinations in New Zealand. *Asia Pacific Journal of Tourism Research*, **17**, 14-29. http://dx.doi.org/10.1080/10941665.2011.6132

Lohmann, G., Santos, G. and Allis, T. (2010) 'Los hermanos' visiting Brazil: differences between drive and coach tourists. In Prideaux, B., Carson, D. (Eds.) *Drive Tourism – Trends and Emerging Markets*. London and New York: Routledge.

Lohmann, G. and Trischler, J. (2012) Tourism transport issues in Brazil, in Lohmann, G., Dredge, D. (Eds.), *Tourism in Brazil: Environment, Management and Segments*. London and New York: Routledge.

Lohmann, G. and Zahra, A. (2010) The influence of international tourists travel patterns on rental car fleet management in New Zealand, in Prideaux, B., Carson, D. (Eds.) *Drive Tourism – Trends and Emerging Markets*. London and New York: Routledge.

London, W (2010), *Ship to Shore: the Nexus and Optimisation of Risk*, Ministry of Tourism, Wellington.

London, W (2012), Shoreside activities, 184-195, in Vogel, M, Papathanassis, A. and Wolber, B. (2012) *The Business and Management of Ocean Cruises*, CABI, Wallingford.

Loverseed, H. (1996) Car Rental in the USA. *Travel & Tourism Analyst*, **4**, 4-19.

Lück, M., Maher, P and Stewart, E., (eds) (2010), *Cruise Tourism in Polar Regions: Promoting Environmental and Social Sustainability?* Earthscan, London.

Lumsdon, L. and Page, S. (2004) Progress in transport and tourism research: reformulating the transport-tourism interface and future research agendas. In Lumsdon, L. and Page, S. (Eds.) *Tourism and Transport: Issues and Agenda for the New Millenium*. Amsterdam, Elsevier.

McCalla, R. (1997) An investigation into site and situation: cruise ship ports *Tijdschrift voor Eeconomische en Sociale Geografie*, **9**(1), 44-55.

Mak, J. (2008) Taxing cruise tourism: Alaska's head tax on cruise ship passengers. *Tourism Economics*, **14**, 599-614.

Marti, B. 1990 Geography and the cruise ship port selection process, *Maritime Policy and Management*, **17**(3), 157-164.

Marti, B. E. (2007) Trends in Alaskan Cruising. *Tourism Analysis*, **12**, 327-334.

Marusic, Z., Horak, S. and Tomljenovic, R. (2009) The socioeconomic impacts of cruise tourism: a case study of Croatian destinations. *Tourism in Marine Environments*, **5**, 131-144.

Milan, J. (1996) The trans European railway network : Three levels of services for the passengers. *Transport Policy*, **3**, 99-104.

Milan, J. (1999) Aviation and externalities: the accomplishments and problems. *Transportation Research Part D*, **4**, 159-180.

Milan, J. (2003) Multicriteria evaluation of high-speed rail, transrapid maglev and air passenger transport in Europe. *Transportation Planning and Technology*, **26**, 491 – 512.

Miller, A. R. and Grazer, W. F. (2003) Complaint behavior as a factor in cruise line losses: an analysis of brand loyalty. *Journal of Travel and Tourism Marketing*, **15**, 77-91.

Moscardo, G. and Pearce, P. L. (2004) Life cycle, tourist motivation and transport: some consequences for the tourist experience. In Lumsdon, L.,Page, S. (Eds.) *Tourism and Transport: issues and agenda for the new millenium*. Oxford, Elsevier.

Mules, T. (2005) Economic impacts of national park tourism on gateway communities: the case of Kosciuszko National Park. *Tourism Economics,* **11,** 247-259.

Njegovan, N. (2006) Elasticities of demand for leisure air travel: A system modelling approach. *Journal of Air Transport Management,* **12,** 33-39.

Nolan, J., Ritchie, P. and Rowcroft, J. (2005) Small market air service and regional policy. *Journal of Transport Economics and Policy,* **39,** 363–378.

O'kelly, M. E. and Miller, H. J. (1994) The hub network design problem: a review and synthesis. *Journal of Transport Geography,* **2,** 31-40.

Oxford Economics (2009) *Aviation: The Real World Wide Web*. Oxford Economics.

Page, S. (2009) *Transport and Tourism: Global Perspectives,* Frenchs Forest: Pearson.

Palhares, G. L. (2003) *Transportes Turísticos,* São Paulo, Aleph.

Park, Y., Ha, H.-K. (2006) Analysis of the impact of high-speed railroad service on air transport demand. *Transportation Research Part E: Logistics and Transportation Review,* **42,** 95-104.

Pearce, D. G. (1981) L'éspace touristique de la grande ville: éléments de synthèse et application à Christchurch (Nouvelle-Zélande). *L'Espace Géographique,* **10,** 207-213.

Pearce, D. G. (1995) Planning for tourism in the nineties: an integrated, dynamic, multi-scale approach. In Butler, R. W. and Pearce, D. G. (eds.) *Change in Tourism: People, Places, Processes*. London, Routledge.

Pearce, D. G. (2001a) Tourism and urban land use change: Assessing the impact of Christchurch's tourist tramway. *Tourism and Hospitality Research,* **3,** 132-148.

Pearce, D. G. (2001b) Tourism, trams and local government policy-making in Christchurch, New Zealand. *Currents Issues in Tourism,* **4,** 331-354.

Pearce, D. G. (2001c) Towards a regional analysis of tourism in Southeast Asia. In Teo, P., Chang, T. C. and Ho, K. C. (Eds.) *Interconnected Worlds: Tourism in Southeast Asia*. Oxford, Pergamon.

Pearce, D. G. and Elliott, J. M. C. (1983) The trip index. *Journal of Travel Research,* **22,** 6-9.

Pearce, D. G. and Sahli, M. (2007) Surface transport distribution channels in New Zealand: A comparative analysis. *Journal of Travel and Tourism Marketing,* **22,** 73-87.

Peisley, T. (1992) Ferries, short sea cruises and the Channel Tunnel. *Travel & Tourism Analyst,* **4,** 5-26.

Peisley, T. (1997) The cross-channel ferry market. *Travel & Tourism Analyst,* **1,** 4-20.

Phang, S.-Y. (2003) Strategic development of airport and rail infrastructure: the case of Singapore. *Transport Policy,* **10,** 27-33. www.sciencedirect.com

Plakhotnik, V. N., Onyshchenko, J. V. and Yaryshkina, L. A. (2005) The environmental impacts of railway transportation in the Ukraine. *Transportation Research Part D: Transport and Environment,* **10,** 263-268.

Ponater, M., Sausen, R., Feneberg, B. and Roeckner, E. (1999) Climate effect of ozone changes caused by present and future air traffic. *Climate Dynamics,* **15,** 631-642.

Prideaux, B. (1999) Tracks to tourism: Queensland Rail joins the tourist industry. *International Journal of Tourism Research,* **1,** 73-86.

Prideaux, B. (2004) Transport and destination development. In Lumsdon, L. and Page, S. J. (Eds.) *Tourism and Transport: issues and agenda for the new millennium.* Amsterdam, Elsevier.

Prideaux, B., Wei, S. and Ruys, H. (2001) The senior drive tour market in Australia. *Journal of Vacation Marketing,* **7,** 209-219.

Punter, M. S. (1999) *Tourist Transport Systems with Particular Reference to the South West of England.* Exeter, University of Exeter.

Pyle, T. I. (1985) The International Air Transport Association and Tourism. *Annals of Tourism Research,* **12,** 648-650.

Reportlinker (2010) Analysis of Global Cruise Market. Lyon.

Rodrigue, J-P. and Notteboom, T. (2013), The geography of cruises : itineraries, not destinations. *Applied Geography,* **38,** 31-42.

Rossiter, A. and Dresner, M. (2004) The impact of the September 11th security fee and passenger wait time on traffic diversion and highway fatalities. *Journal of Air Transport Management,* **10,** 225-230.

Russell, P. (1999) Car rental in Europe. *Travel & Tourism Analyst,* **1,** 1-28.

Rutz, W. O. A., Coull, J. R. (1996) Inter-island passenger shipping in Indonesia: development of the system. *Journal of Transport Geography,* **4,** 275-286.

Santana, I. (2009) Do public service obligations hamper the cost competitiveness of regional airlines? *Journal of Air Transport Management,* **15,** 344-349.

Sausen, R. and Schuman, U. (2000) Estimates of the climate response to aircraft CO_2 and NOx emissions scenarios. *Climatic Change,* **44,** 27-58.

Schumann, U. (1997) The impact of nitrous oxides emissions from aircraft upon the atmosphere at flight altitudes – results from the Aeronox project.

Atmosphere Environment, **31,** 1723-1733.

Schumann, U. (2000) Effects of aircraft emissions on ozone, cirrus clouds, and global climate. *Air and Space Europe*, **2,** 29-33.

Schwarze, G. (2007) Including Aviation into the European Union's Emissions Trading Scheme. *European Environmental Law Review*, **16,** 10-22.

Seidl, A., Guiliano, F. and Pratt, L. (2007) Cruising for colones: cruise tourism economics in Costa Rica. *Tourism Economics*, **13,** 67-85.

Shaw, S. (1982) Airline deregulation and the tourist industry. *Tourism Management*, **3,** 40-51.

Shih, H-Y. (2006) Network characteristics of drive tourism destinations : an application of network analysis in tourism, *Tourism Management*, **27**(5), 1029-1039.

Showalter, G. R. (1994) Cruise ships and private islands in the Caribbean. *Journal of Travel and Tourism Marketing*, **3,** 107-118.

Simons, M. S. (1992) Competition law, air transport deregulation and the tourism industry in the European Economic Community Part I A legal perspective. *International Journal of Hospitality Management*, **11,** 33-45.

Singh, A. (1999) Growth and development of the cruise line industry in Southeast Asia. *Asia Pacific Journal of Tourism Research*, **3,** 24-31.

Singh, A. (2000) The Asia Pacific Cruise Line Industry: current trends, opportunities and future outlook. *Tourism Recreation Research*, **25,** 49-61.

Smith, V. L., Hetherington, A. and Brumbaugh, M. D. D. (1986) California's highway 89, a regional tourism model. *Annals of Tourism Research*, **13,** 415-433.

Soriani, S., Bertazzon, S., Cesare, R. & Rech, G. (2009) Cruising in the Mediterranean : structural aspects and evolutionary trends, *Maritime Policy & Management*, **36**, 3, 235-251.

Stubbs, J. and Jegede, F. (1998) The integration of rail and air transport in Britain. *Journal of Transport Geography*, **6,** 53-67.

Subrémon, A. (2000) La libéralisation du transport aérien dans l'Union européene et les perspectives pour le tourisme. Paper presented at WTO, Tourism and Air Transport conference, Funchal, Madiera, 25/26 May.

Sun, X., Jiao, Y. and Tian, P. (2011), Marketing research and revenue optimization for the cruise industry : a concise review, *International Journal of Hospitality Management*, **30,** 746-755.

Sypher:Mueller International Inc (1990) *Air Transportation and Tourism: Competing and Complementary Needs*. Tourism Canada.

Testa, M. R. (2004) Cultural similarity and service leadership: a look at the cruise industry. *Managing Service Quality*, **14,** 402 – 413.

Teye, V. B. (1992) Land transportation and tourism in Bermuda. *Tourism Management*, **13**, 395-405.

Thompson Clarke Shipping (2006) *Cruise Destinations... A How to Guide.* Brisbane, Tourism Queensland.

Thompson, E. A. (2004) An orderly mess: the use of mess areas in identity shaping of cruise ship workers. *Sociological Imagination*, **40**, 15-29.

Thompson, I. B. 1995 High-speed transport hubs and Eurocity status: the case of Lyon. *Journal of Transport Geography*, **3**, 29-37.

Thompson, L. (2003) Changing railway structure and ownership: is anything working? *Transport Reviews*, **23**, 311-355.

Tourism New South Wales (n.d) The NSW cruise market: a discussion paper. Tourism New South Wales, sg.sydney.com/Cruise_Tourism_p1478.aspx

Turnock, D. (2001) Railways and economic development in Romania before 1918. *Journal of Transport Geography*, **9**, 137-150.

Tyrrell, T. J. and Devitt, M. F. (1999) Valuing changes to scenic byways. In Pizam, A.,Mansfeld, Y. (eds) *Consumer Behavior in Travel and Tourism.* Binghamton, Haworth Hospitality Press.

Véronneau, S. and Roy, J. (2009) Global service supply chains: an empirical study of current practices and challenges of a cruise line corporation, *Tourism Management*, **30**, 128-139.

Wall Street Journal (2009) Air hubs pay to keep their spokes, 10 July, http://online.wsj.com/articles/SB124718465623720407

Wallis, M. (2001) *Route 66: the Mother Road,* New York, St Martin's Press.

Wang, J. and Mcowan, S. (2000) Fast passenger ferries and their future. *Maritime Policy and Management*, **27,** 231-251.

Ward, J. (1987) Tourism and the private car. *Tourism Management*, **8,** 164-165.

Wardman, M., Shires, J., Lythgoe and W., Tyler, J. (2004) Consumer benefits and demand impacts of regular train timetables. *International Journal of Transport Management*, **2,** 39-49.

Waryszak, R. and King, B. (2000) Tourists and taxis: an examination of the tourism transport interface. *Journal of Vacation Marketing*, **6,** 318-328.

Wheatcroft, S. (1991) Airlines, tourism and the environment. *Tourism Management*, **12,** 119-124.

Wheatcroft, S. (1994) *Aviation and Tourism Policies: Balancing the Benefits.* London, World Tourism Organization and Routledge.

Whelan, G. and Johnson, D. (2004) Modelling the impact of alternative fare structures on train overcrowding. *International Journal of Transport Management*, **2,** 51-58.

Wilkinson, P. F. (1999) Caribbean cruise tourism: delusion? illusion? *Tourism Geographies,* **1,** 261-282.

Williams, G. (2005) European experience with direct subsidization of air services. *Public Money & Management,* **25,** 155–161.

Williams, G. and Pagliari, R. (2004) A comparative analysis of the application and use of public service obligations in air transport within the EU. *Transport Policy,* **11,** 55-66.

Williams, V. and Noland, R. B. (2005) Variability of contrail formation conditions and the implications for policies to reduce the climate impacts of aviation. *Transportation Research Part D: Transport and Environment,* **10,** 269-280.

Wong, W. G., Han, B. M., Ferreira, L., Zhu, X. N. and Sun, Q. X. (2002) Evaluation of management strategies for the operation of high-speed railways in China. *Transportation Research Part A: Policy and Practice,* **36,** 277-289.

WTO (1995) *Concepts, Definitions and Classifications for Tourism Statistics.* Madrid, World Tourism Organization.

Yarnal, C. M. (2004) Missing the boat? a playfully serious look at a group cruise tour experience. *Leisure Sciences,* **26,** 349-372.

Glossary

Apart from the terms presented at Table 1, other key terms used in this review include:

ASK (available seat kilometers): in airline economics refers to the number of seats (sold or otherwise) transported between two points (thus a standard measure of output)

Cabotage: a term used to describe the carriage of passengers taken on at one point and off loaded at another point within the territory of the same sovereign country.

Freedoms of the air: the nine freedoms-of-air regulate the rights of an airline to overfly, land and transport passengers in a foreign country.

Gateway: a concept from spatial geography, refers to a stopping or intermediate point of social or economic importance within a wider, linear network.

Hub: a concept from spatial geography, a hub refers to a central point of confluence of activities that radiate bidirectionally.

International Air Transport Association (IATA): An international organisation representing and serving the airline industry worldwide.

International Civil Aviation Organization (ICAO): United Nations special-ised agency which is the global forum for civil aviation, working to achieve safe, secure and sustainable development of civil aviation through cooperation amongst its member States.

RPK (revenue passenger kilometers): in airline economics refers to the stand-ard measure of the total number of paid passengers transported over a particu-lar distance (as such, it is a distance-weighted measure of revenue).

Tourism Area Life Cycle

R.W. Butler

Contents

R.W. Butler is Emeritus Professor Strathclyde Business School, University of Strathclyde. He has published widely in tourism journals, and produced eleven books on tourism and many chapters in other books. His main fields of interest are the development process of tourist destinations and the subsequent impacts of tourism, issues of carrying capacity and sustainability, and tourism in remote areas and islands. He is currently editor Emeritus of *The Journal of Tourism and Hospitality Research.*

A hyperlinked PDF version of this review is available for download from the CTR area of Goodfellow Pubishers' website: http://www.goodfellowpublishers.com/ctr

Introduction

It is now more than three decades since the original Tourism Area Life Cycle (TALC) article first appeared (Butler 1980), and rather surprisingly the model proposed in that article is still being cited and used in tourism research. That fact alone makes the TALC somewhat extraordinary, as most models have a short life span before they are relegated to at best a passing reference in more recent text books or articles. The reason for the longevity of the TALC is not entirely clear. It is very much a classic academic model (Griere 2004), in other words "a representation, usually on a smaller scale, of a device, structure etc." (Collins:1988, 730), intended to aid in the discussion of, and research on, the development of tourist resorts. It attempts to portray a common pattern of the development of such places, a pattern which it argues is common to many resorts throughout the world. Such an argument may well be thought to be presumptuous and arrogant in the 21st century, given the variety and range of tourist destinations that have been developed, in particular over the last few decades. This range reflects the massive changes which have occurred in transportation, politics, economics and societies over that period, which have seen destinations appear in what might have been envisaged as hostile or unwelcoming environments and communities a few years earlier.

Political changes such as the disappearance of the Iron Curtain and the demise of communism, the end of Apartheid, the opening up of China, Vietnam and other countries to tourism (Butler and Suntikul 2010) combined with the development of budget airlines, the world wide web (WWW) and a generally increased affluence in the world at large, have all contributed to create a very different face of global tourism over the past three decades. Indeed, one might well argue that tourism has changed more in the last three decades than at almost any other comparable time period. The two World Wars, the Great Depression and the Oil Crisis of the 1970s have all had significant effects on tourism, mostly in terms of delaying expansion rather than fundamentally changing the geography, economics and social character of the phenomenon over the long term. Thus one may well expect that models developed in the decades before the 1980s would have become redundant and outmoded because of subsequent events. Somewhat to the contrary, the TALC model has continued to be used in attempts to describe and understand the process of the development of tourist destinations in a wide variety of settings (see for example Canavan 2013, 2014; Chapman and Speake 2011; Garay & Cànoves, 2011 and Zhong, et al, 2008).

This review briefly examines the origin of the model, its early utilisation, its criticisms and modifications, and its current relevance in tourism research. In conclusion it examines some of the basic assumptions of the model and its suitability in the present day and speculates on why the model has continued to be used in such a rapidly changing world.

Development of the Field

Research on tourist destinations, and resorts in particular, has a relatively long history, although much of the early literature published was essentially descriptive and based on specific case studies (e.g. Hobs 1913; Webster 1914). Gilbert (1939) was one of the first authors to discuss in more general and theoretical terms the development of resorts, albeit only in the context of England. It is not really until after World War Two that what might be seen as the real beginnings of research on resorts, particularly their morphology and development, emerge (see for example Barrett 1958; Christaller 1963; Plog 1972, 1973; Stansfield 1972, Stansfield and Rickert 1970). The influence of these early researchers was significant in the development of the TALC model, as noted by Butler (1980). More detailed discussion of the TALC model, including its origins, have been discussed at some length elsewhere (Butler 1990, 1997, 1998, 2000, 2006a,b,c, 2009a, b) and will be dealt with comparatively briefly here. A comprehensive review of the application of the TALC up to the early years of this century can be found in Legiewski (2006), and thus much of that literature is referenced but not cited in detail here. Many other references to the TALC can be found on the WWW, where there a search for 'Tourism Area Life Cycle' produced a surprisingly large number (1,360,000) of hits.

The TALC's origins (Butler 2006a) stem from the belief that, even if not fully appreciated in many tourist destinations, resorts are essentially products, i.e. they have normally been developed and modified to meet the needs of specific markets (holidaymakers) in a similar way to the production of other goods and services. As such, therefore, it appeared to be reasonable to make the assumption that resorts would follow a generally similar pattern of development to that of most other products, namely, to have a 'life cycle' (Catry and Chevalier 1974). This would include acceptance and rejection of the product as the market first desired the product and then eventually viewed it as outmoded and unattractive (Avlonitis 1990). While the life cycle model may have fallen out of favour in the business literature (see for example, Dhalla and Yuspeh 1976, and Tellis and Crawford 1981) and is a simplistic representation of the marketability of a product, it can still have relevance.

Examples from other fields, such as automobile production, reveal how markets in most cases slowly accept a new product, then become enthusiastic, mirrored in a rapid growth in sales, and eventually grow tired of the model and sales decline. Only in a very few cases do sales take off immediately (E type Jaguar), continue for decades (Volkswagen Beetle) or experience a rebirth (Mini), and these are normally a reflection of an element of genius and/or true innovation in the original model concerned. In most cases models experience incremental change in the form of performance improvements, structural and design change, and the addition of new features, all aimed at maintaining an existing market and/or capturing an additional market. Tourist resorts are little different, except in one fundamental element, that of control. Most commercial products are manufactured by one company which has control over the product design, production and marketing, whereas tourism resorts are rarely under a single controlling force and their component parts often display a remarkable lack of ability to co-ordinate either product offering or marketing. This is mainly because they are comprised of a large number of elements of vastly differing size, ambition and focus. Thus while modifications and improvements are relatively easy to undertake in the case of most manufactured products, such changes in tourist resorts are harder to achieve, especially when the component parts may have no common direction or goal and there may be no clear controlling force. "Destination management" in the vast majority of cases is really destination development and marketing, as few destinations (except for single-owner resorts such as the Disney theme parks) actually have an real management. As well, resorts offer an intangible experiential product to which the consumer must travel in order to enjoy and which cannot be stored until markets change.

The original TALC model also drew on ecological models in a very simplistic way. There has been criticism of the use of the term "evolution" in the context of tourism resorts (Ravenscroft and Hadjihambi 2006) from the conceptually correct standpoint that such features are not living phenomena and therefore incapable of evolution in the strict Darwinian sense. However, the term 'evolution' is commonly used to refer to a process of apparently natural change and development along a generally consistent path, and this is what was envisaged when the term was used in the context of the TALC. Clearly resorts are not living entities, although they are dynamic, and the time scale over which they change is far from that found in the natural evolutionary process of species, but one can argue that the development process which they undergo is evolutionary in that it is often gradual, and generally reflects adjustments to ensure survival in a competitive environment (Ritchie and Crouch 2003). Ravenscroft and Hadjihambi (2006: 163) concluded that changes in tourist destinations "are best viewed from an evolutionary perspective in which the external environment is understood in relation to Darwinian selection, while changes to the built environment are mediated according to Larmarckian inherited traits".

Thus it is reasonable to infer that without such changes to a resort, its extinction, or at least economic decline and perhaps 'death', is likely. Indeed, that was the basic argument in the original model, and the subtitle of the 1980 article was "Implications for management of resources" (Butler 1980). This latter phrase was meant to make it clear to readers of the article that resorts would face decline (however measured) if there was no appropriate intervention to manage the resources (in a very wide sense of the word) to keep them competitive to the tourist market. Such intervention would not come about from natural processes as in biological evolution, but rather through the deliberate actions of those with an interest in the wellbeing and continued attraction of the destination. The model was not arguing that the decline of all resorts was inevitable (as Plog (1972) had suggested), but that without appropriate interventions such decline was highly likely.

A focus on the 'Cycle of Evolution' and the figure (Figure 1) in the original article appears to have distracted many readers' attention from the argument about the need for intervention to ensure survival. The figure itself had emerged from earlier papers dealing with the process of destination location and development (see for example Brougham and Butler 1972) where the focus had been on how new development would not be located in declining resort(s) but instead would be located in nearby locations sharing similar physical features to the original resort(s). It was argued that when development and growth peaked, astute potential developers would seek new locations with lower costs, untouched resources, and greater opportunities for expansion. This is a process which is clearly still followed to this day, as shown by the pattern of resort developments in areas as disparate as southern Thailand, the Caribbean, Turkey, and North Africa. The key issue for potential developers was to identify when the peak popularity of the original resort was about to be, or had been, reached. The original model did not deal with the potential predictability of the model; this was an aspect explored some time later by other researchers (Manente and Pechlaner 2006, Berry 2006).

As has been stated elsewhere (Butler 2006a,c), the TALC was a creature of its time, and, as noted above, its origins reflected the literature which existed in the 1970s, in particular the writings of pioneering tourism researchers such as Christaller (1963), Cohen (1972), Doxey (1975), Plog (1973), Stansfield (1972) and Wolfe (1966). To many contemporary readers and researchers in tourism these references may appear now to be of limited validity, the majority not being based on empirical research of any depth, and most would almost certainly not survive the refereeing process of academic journals in the 21st century. The latter comment is perhaps more of an indictment of modern journal reviewing than it is of those particular articles, all of which displayed innovative and insightful thinking and made significant contributions to the theoretical development of tourism research. The TALC model also reflects the nature of tourism in the 1970s, when the rapid expansion of destinations was underway following the technological innovation of jet aircraft, along with increased levels of affluence in western countries (based in part on the economic innovation of credit cards), decreased restrictions on travel, and rapid increases in mobility. Travel abroad was no longer the privilege of a small elite, and mass tourism in its modern form (or perhaps nearly post-modern form) was well established. Thus fundamental changes were occurring in markets, in tastes, in destination locations, and modes of travel for large numbers of potential tourists in the western world, and not surprisingly, those changes were increasingly visible in tourist resorts, particularly those which had been established a century or so earlier, based on limited restricted markets and the railways.

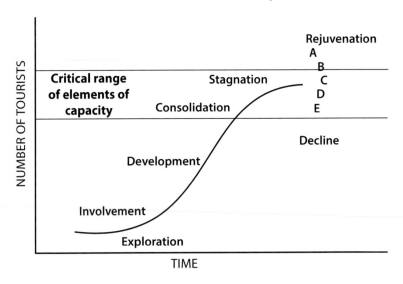

Figure 1: Hypothetical evolution of a tourist area (Butler 1980)

Framing the Field

The TALC model is just that, a model, and as such is a representation of reality rather than a complete picture of reality (Giere 2004). The purpose of the model was to draw attention to the dynamic nature of destinations and propose a generalised process of development and potential decline which might be avoided by appropriate interventions (of planning, management and development), or as suggested in the title of the article, the management of resources. It did this by proposing a common pattern of development of resorts that had multiple stages (exploration, involvement, development, consolidation, stagnation, and then a range of possibilities from rejuvenation to decline, Figure 1). Key to this was the concept of carrying capacity, in the sense that it was argued that if the carrying capacity of a resort was exceeded, the relative appeal of that resort would decline, it would become less competitive, and this would be reflected in declines in visitation, investment, and development. The appropriate interventions noted above would be the key to ensuring that the various carrying capacities (economic, social-cultural and environmental) of the resort were not exceeded, or where possible, were increased to meet growing pressures. It should perhaps be noted that in the 1970s the concept of carrying capacity in tourism was very much in vogue, although it has fallen out of favour since then (Butler 1996, 2010), in part because of the difficulty of identification and measurement of specific limits and in part because of dynamic nature of resorts and advances in technology which allow impacts to be mitigated or overcome and thus 'limits' to be exceeded and capacity levels to be adjusted upwards. The early seminal literature on carrying capacity (Lucas 1964, Wagar 1964) while being relevant and applicable to wilderness areas with a limited range of visitor motivations, was much less applicable to the widely varying and highly dynamic motivations of tourists to many resorts.

The resources on which destinations depend for their success in the tourist market vary widely. The early tourist market in the developed western countries in the northern hemisphere at least had for a long time tended to perceive tourist destinations as commonly coastal (particularly marine coasts), or at least associated with and adjoining water, having accommodation and related facilities, and being accessible, often by public transport. As these markets grew both in size and in personal mobility and affluence their expectations and demands changed. They became more sophisticated and demanding in terms of quality of infrastructure and facilities, in terms of a greater range of offerings of attractions, and in terms of cheaper, quicker and easier access from their origin regions. Resorts which did not accommodate such changes very quickly fell out of favour and were replaced in consumers' minds with new resorts being created, often in greenfield(or perhaps 'bluecoast') locations, i.e, locations undeveloped as far as tourism was concerned, generally with desired physical features such as amenable climate, water and space. Increasingly technology has become a substitute for some, or even all, of these attributes. The most apparent examples of this are Dubai, Las Vegas and Macao, and perhaps also the Disney theme parks, where technological features such as rides and 'artificial' experiences along with massive luxurious hotels sometimes imitating real world locations (e.g.the Venetian, Luxor, New York hotels in Las Vegas, pseudo movie sets in Disney parks, or artificial ski slopes in an area experiencing temperatures of 40C or more such as Dubai) substitute for conventional beaches or traditional cultural heritage.

Given such massive changes, at least at one end of the destination spectrum (Prideaux 2000), it is reasonable to query whether the TALC model still has relevance. Given that it was conceived in the context of destinations that had first appeared several decades before, often based originally on the railway for access by their restricted markets, equipped with few facilities or attractions, and with a heavy reliance on repeat visitors who were not mobile when they were staying at the destination, it would not be surprising if few modern destinations followed precisely the TALC process of development and decline. As well, the original model did not have a fixed time scale; it was accepted when the model was proposed, that some destinations might take a century or more to pass through the cycle but it appears now that destinations are going through such a cycle in a few decades at most. Such is the rate of change as a result of technological and other innovations in the global economy and society that destinations based on technology are particularly vulnerable to obsolescence. Markets now have a vast range of choice from which to choose their holiday destination, they are no longer tied by limited transportation connections to just a few or even one destination. Anyone can reach almost any destination in the world within 24 hours in relative comfort and safety, quite often at almost absurdly low cost if budget airline travel is involved. Repeat visitation is no longer a necessity because of lack of choice and limited means of access and time, but very much just one of many choices which holidaymakers have and almost inevitably destination loyalty has declined rapidly.

The TALC model has received considerable attention from other researchers. In the first quarter century after its publication it was used in a variety of ways and locations, and the relevant literature during this period is reviewed, as noted above, by Lagiewski (2006). Despite the dynamic nature of tourism and the factors affecting both it and resorts, the continued application and testing of the TALC (see for example Dodds and McElroy 2008; Cole 2009; Komppula et al 2010; Oreja Rodríguez, et al 2008; Pechlaner et al 2010) would suggest that it still has relevance even in the present dynamic situation. Kapczynski and Szromak (2008) suggest that Polish spas over the last half century have followed the basic pattern of the TALC despite the major upheavals in Poland during this period, but have managed to overcome a decline phase and enter a new expansion phase in the last few years. In most resorts, however, it is only when decline, or initially stagnation, occurs that much attention is given to proactive planning and development rather than reactive measures. Cohen–Hattab and Shoval (2004) note that failure to follow established planning policies may well be a factor in explaining resorts entering the final stages of their life cycles, as shown by their research in Israel.

In more recent years the TALC model has been used in a wide variety of situations beyond its original focus on resorts. For example Xie and Lane (2006) propose a variation on the original figure in their paper on Aboriginal Arts Performance in Tourism, substituting a 'cycle of authenticity' based on the TALC. In so doing they were following an argument presented by this author that appeared in a rather obscure publication (Butler 1997) and an illustration used then, but not published which made a similar point (Figure 2).

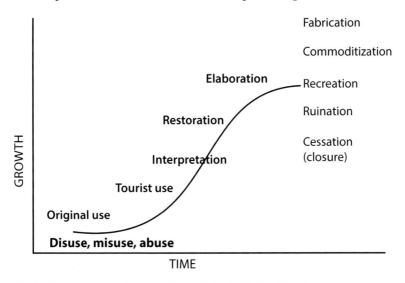

Figure 2: Heritage opportunities and the Life Cycle (Butler 1996)

It is perhaps logical to expect that the model might be adapted to examine the life cycle of specific events as these are phenomena that exist in resorts as well as other locations. It is also not unexpected, given the occurrence of such tragedies, that it might be utilised in the examination of the impact of crises and negative events on tourism places. Putra and Hitchcock(2006) applied the model in reviewing redevelopment and the life cycle in the aftermath of the Bali bombing in 2002, and Cohen (2008) examined the impact of the tsunami on Thailand, the disaster applying a catastrophic 'shock' to the destination and its pattern of development, a feature discussed more below. In a similar vein, Moss et al (2003) have used the cycle model in the context of two terrorism acts, the Twin Towers destruction in New York and the Madrid train bombings. They argued that their research is the first to model the magnitude of the episode, the duration of the effect, and the shape of the associated life cycle. They concluded that "the impact on tourist air travel from these catastrophes follow scalable and fad life cycles, respectively" (op cit p.207).

Kompulla et al (2010) used the model in a more traditional manner to examine the life cycle of a particular product, namely Christmas in Lapland, where that product is tied both to the image of the area and specific localised offerings. In contrast, it has been featured in *Surf Economics* (Nelson 2008) in the context of the life cycle of surfing sites. It has also been used in the context of wine tourism by Tomljenović and Getz (2009), who examined the life cycle concept in terms of the development of wine tourism regions in Croatia, with the innovation of incorporating winery owners' perceptions and attitudes. Whitfield (2008) applied the model to cyclical aspects of conference tourism in the UK, with a focus on the use of refurbishments as triggers for rejuvenation, an aspect which, as noted later, could usefully be applied to conventional tourist resorts, and in a somewhat similar vein, Sundt (2006) examined hotels in Switzerland from a life cycle perspective. The TALC, along with other models, was also used by Duffus and Dearden (1990) in the context of wildlife tourism to illustrate how changes in demand can affect specific 'products' (in line with Zimmermann's (1997) ideas) and assist in the management of wildlife resources, an approach also suggested by Weizenegger (2006).

Other researchers have examined tourist area life cycles using different approaches and alternative models; Toh, et al (2001) for example, in their study of the tourism life cycle of Singapore, utilized a travel balance approach. Cole (2009), in an application of logistic modeling, examined the TALC by producing a logistic tourism model which he used to explore whether the tourism industry was 'chaotic', concluding that quite different dynamics were exhibited compared to those of traditional growth models. The application of more sophisticated modeling techniques such as those above to the TALC has also been followed by Chinese researchers (see for example, Xu 2001; Xie 1995; Yi 2001; Zhong, L. Z., et al 2008), along with more conventional applications of the model (Bao 1994, 1998)in a variety of settings, both physical and cultural.

The TALC has also been used in the context of gambling, as for example when Moss et al (2003; 393) applied the model to casino winnings, and concluded that "The model supports the position that casinos conform to Butler's S-shaped product life cycle for resorts, suggesting that the rapid increases in early-period gaming revenues will not continue without intervention to rejuvenate the industry". Gambling presents an interesting topic for the application of the TALC, as the logic of the model might have suggested that by the present day a resort such as Las Vegas would be well into decline. The perhaps surprising continued success and popularity of Las Vegas no longer stems from its monopoly on legalised gambling in the United States, which had meant that it had a unique selling point that seemed impervious to overdevelopment. That privileged position disappeared with the legalisation of gambling in New Jersey (and then virtually every other state in the United States) and on Indian reserves (Stansfield 1996, 2006). The continued success of Las Vegas relies at least in part on the continued renovation, replacement and addition of its attractions, in other words, appropriate (in the context of Las Vegas) interventions by major developers and support from local and state administrations. While Las Vegas may not appear to be an ideal model to put forward in an age of supposed sustainability, energy conservation, and protection of authenticity, in fact it shows exactly how a destination can continue to attract a market, even one that is highly volatile and has many alternatives from which to choose. Las Vegas may well be unique (although Macao and Dubai may prove similar in longevity as well as reliance on similar technology) but in its possible uniqueness it is tending to prove the continued relevancy of the TALC model. It may well implode following a further economic recession, a new wave of high energy prices, or a broad rejection of gambling, but until then it is likely to continue to frustrate academics and others who support the idea of a simpler, less extravagant and less energy-consuming setting for a holiday, and in fact support the basic ideas implicit in the TALC, namely that adaptation and change are necessary to maintain a market.

Issues, Controversies and Debates

It would have been surprising if the TALC article had not provoked criticism, rejection and alternative suggestions about the development process of destinations. While the first application of the model (Hovinen 1981) appeared, only a year after the original article, criticism took a little longer to appear (Wall 1982a,b, Hayward 1986). Wall's comments were in a mostly conceptual manner to linkages between the concept of carrying capacity of tourist areas and its application to the development cycle, and perhaps related to the decline in interest in the topic of carrying capacity in a tourist context over the past few decades (Butler 2010), but his specific concerns have not been followed up. Hayward's early criticisms related to a number of specific issues (Lagiewski 2006), including measurement issues and the identification of the stages outlined in the model. In a later review of the model Hayward (2006) noted not only that many of these issues had not been resolved completely but also addressed the fact that the "within the industry, however, the TALC concept is virtually ignored" (op cit. p. 29), although its existence and applicability is acknowledged by numerous public sector agencies in tourist destinations in many locations. He suggests that the TALC "may need to be reconceptualised. Operational ambiguity must be overcome" (op cit: 30) but did accept that tourism is a living system and drew attention to the need to identify constraints (to change, to progress and to possible actions) as well as the possible relevance of the application of chaos theory to destination development.

Other researchers have argued for the abandonment or rejection of the TALC, although few as strongly as the late Neil Leiper (2004: 135) who stated that the model "should now be assigned to the archives of history – as a former theory, now discredited, shown to be false". There have been a number of other criticisms about the model's non-validity or failings and alternative approaches (Choy 1992,; Bianchi 1994; Prideaux 2000; McKercher 2006). Aguiló, et al (2005) argued that the model was essentially only theoretical, although others (e.g. Getz 1992) have supported its relevance in tourism planning. Prosser (1995) noted a number of criticisms of the model, related to doubts about there being a single model of resort development, limitations on capacity issues, limitations of the life cycle model itself, a lack of empirical evidence and limited practical utility. However, he concluded (1995: 9) " The extensive criticism leveled (sic) at the resort life cycle concept shows no sign of dissuading researchers from adopting the model as a framework for their research...the original model survives largely intact and according to some, offers the prospect of further development". Given the great variety of resorts and environments, to say nothing of the widely differing aspects of tourism, it is not surprising that the model would fail in relevance or accuracy in specific locations or types of resorts. As this author has noted elsewhere (Butler 2004: 167) "It is perhaps more appropriate to consider whether it still has validity in the twenty-first century rather than whether it totally explains all examples of destination development". The fact that researchers are still applying the model to examine resorts, as noted earlier, would suggest that its validity is at least still worth examining. Nevertheless, several researchers have made critical and enlightening comments on the model when utilizing it in their research.

Papatheodorou (2004) drew attention to the relative absence in the literature on the TALC from the beginning of the relationship between the development process and competition. He argued that in tourism there is competition between resorts at one level, and competitiveness between individual enterprises at another level, and the final pattern of tourist flows (demand) combines these elements of competition along with consumer tastes and constraints. Given that competition is dynamic and subject to individual actors, the TALC is likely to be at best limited in its ability to incorporate the array of influences resulting from competition at different scales. He argued that "the demand management policies of the TALC should be complemented by an integrated, supply-driven planning framework" (Papatheodorou 2006: 81). In essence such a call can be argued to be supporting the original idea of appropriate intervention at the resort level, but taking this a stage further to include recognition of the competitive element between resorts and the need to reconcile this with a more regional spatial outlook to maximise benefits to an area by maximising competitiveness and thus supporting their common future. This point has been addressed to some degree by Weidenfeld and Butler (2012) in their investigation of the response of tourist enterprises to competition and cooperation in tourist destinations at different stages of their life cycle.

Papatheodorou (2006) is following a somewhat similar line to Coles (2006) who placed the TALC in the context of related retailing and marketing models. He notes that many of the criticisms of the business Life Cycle model are appropriate to the TALC, namely relating to the question of products being living things, a possible lack of validity for all classes and forms, that phases are not definable and precisely placing a product on the curve at a particular time is not feasible (op cit 56). As well, he noted that price (as competition) is not considered explicitly in the model, there is no mention of individual actions (e.g. entrepreneurship) and does not deal with the presence of multiple forms of tourism in what are mostly mass tourism destinations and their impacts on demand, behaviour and promotion. In response one might note that competition is implied within the TALC in the sense that it is argued that one of the main reasons why resorts decline is because they have ceased to be attractive to customers, or in other words, uncompetitive, perhaps at both the local (regional) and global scales. The issue of price is also implicit, if not in the original model, then in the discussion in later papers about the tendency of destinations to resort to lowering prices in order to retain a market and remain competitive if and when they are experiencing a decline in visitor numbers.

The criticism of the above authors about the lack of attention to individual entrepreneurship and the role of key individuals in shaping the process of resort development is one that has been addressed in subsequent contributions to the literature by Russell in particular (Russell 2006b; Russell and Faulkner 1999). The need to pay more attention to the importance of local resident opinions and actions, particularly in the local political context has been noted by Gale and Botteril (2005), and the role of single individuals in not only establishing resorts but also in changing the face of tourism at the global scale has been addressed in recent publications (Butler and McDonnell 2011; Butler and Russell 2010). This aspect of the TALC and destinations has also been addressed by Weaver (1988, 1990), in particular, who has pointed out that in certain economies, in his example, plantation societies, it may not be local indigenes who initially become involved in tourism development, but rather local resident ex-patriots who have the capital and experience to invest in tourism development. Whether this group represents something different to the local residents noted in the original TALC paper (Butler 1980), or whether ex-patriots should be considered to be part of the 'local population' may be controversial in both semantic and political, as well as anthropological, contexts, but it is clear that there are variations in the beginning phases of development of resorts in different economies and societies and this aspect warrants further research.

Rather in contrast, there has been considerable discussion about the accuracy of the TALC in illustrating the mature stages of destination development and whether there needs to be additional stages added to the model. Agarwal (1994; 1997;1999; 2002) has explored this aspect more than others and her criticisms and contributions have justifiably found support (Priestley and Mundet 1998; Knowles and Curtis 1999; Smith 2002). Agarwal has argued for "the insertion of an additional stage in order to take into account the series of restructuring efforts that are inaugurated before decline sets in" This stage, termed as 'reorientation' should be added between the stagnation and the post-stagnation stages of the TALC model to represent continued efforts at restructuring" (Agarwal 2006 214-5). Priestley and Mundet (1998) also discussed the need for additional stages in the model, in particular post-stagnation and reconstruction stages, along very similar lines to Agarwal. One may argue as to whether additional stages such as those proposed are necessary, although there is little doubt that many resorts do go through a process, if not a stage, of re-orienting themselves, or attempt to do so. In many cases this is related to 'going up-market' and/or becoming more sustainable, in the belief that such steps will counter any decline in image or appeal and reduced visitor numbers (Rodriguez et al 2008). Whether becoming more sustainable would result in rejuvenation or not, one might argue that such an approach does represent something of an acknowledgement of the importance of maintaining the quality of the destination environment and hence visitor experience, which can be likened to the importance of constraining development within capacity limits as argued in the original model.

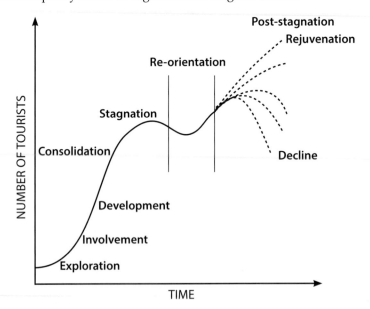

Figure 3: Modification of the Butler Tourist Cycle of Evolution model (Agarwal 2006)

While it would not be unreasonable to add such a stage, albeit possibly increasing the difficulties of determining when one stage ends and another begins, it is harder to justify the amendment to the original curve (Figure 1) as shown in Figure 3 as there is not overwhelming evidence of such a temporary decline and rise in visitation before the onset of either rejuvenation or continuous decline after a period of stagnation. One could also argue that if sustainability was achieved, perhaps as a result of re-orientation, the result would be a continuation of a relatively flat or only very slightly increasing line from stagnation over the long term future. A decline and subsequent rise would depend on the speed of success or failure of promotion and market acceptance of the re-orientation and new offerings by the resort.

If re-orientation did take place but was unsuccessful in terms of recapturing the declining market or attracting a new market, then, as Baum (1998) has suggested, there may be a need for an additional stage to be added at the 'end' of the cycle, namely, that of 'complete re-invention' whereby a resort would endeavour to make a complete change in the nature of its offerings. To date the best example of complete re-invention is probably Atlantic City (Stansfield 2006) which re-invented itself from a traditional family summer beach resort to a year-round mature market gambling destination. However, a recent report (Frean 2014) suggests that Atlantic City is now experiencing decline once again, as the innovations and rejuvenation brought about by replacing its image as a family beach resort with one of a gambling Mecca appear to have reached the decline phase rather more suddenly (27 years) than may have been anticipated. Four of the twelve casinos in the town have been closed in 2014, with the loss of over eight thousand jobs and revenues have fallen 46% over the last seven years. Local politicians are now calling for a return to the promotion of other attractions such as the beach and the boardwalk (op cit p.51). Baum (2006) also proposed an alternative final stage, namely an exit from tourism completely, which could occur when a resort acknowledged that it had no further future in tourism. In the case of Atlantic City there appears to be an exit in part from what had become its major selling point and brand characteristic.

The suggestion of re-invention proposed by Baum is not entirely new to the TALC as the case of Atlantic City was noted in the original article as one example of rejuvenation. If and when such a step occurred, it was assumed that the destination would then in effect begin a new cycle of development, which may well mirror the previous cycle over time and thus need another reinvention in due course. Where such reinvention is made on the basis of technology, one might expect the subsequent new life cycle to be relatively short, as whatever one resort can produce through the application of technology, in time a competitor will reproduce, almost certainly in a larger, more complex, challenging, less costly, and inevitably, more attractive form to the ever-changing market. The rise of Macao as a gambling destination which has now surpassed Las Vegas in terms of income generation is a case in point (McCartney 2010). The appearance of ever more bizarre and larger hotels and casinos in Las Vegas is illustrative of the technological 'fix' and the decline of Atlantic City noted above reflects in part the loss of its east coast monopoly on gambling as well as changing preferences and behaviours of its market.

Future Research Agenda

The basic focus of the TALC has been on 'What', in the sense that it is focused on what happens to tourist destinations in terms of their development process or cycle. As a descriptive model it has performed remarkably well for a considerable time, partly because many of the destinations studied have been well established ones and to some extent therefore, are remnants of an earlier stage of tourism. Thus one important area of future research should be to test the TALC on what might be defined as 'instant' or 'post-modern' resorts, particularly with respect to their patterns of investment, physical development and markets. This author has been informed (personal communication 2007) that Sharm El Sheikh in Egypt has seen declines in some national markets and is actively pursuing replacement markets already, less than two decades after its establishment as an international destination. Establishing the time scale of movement of resorts through the cycle and whether different types of destinations or those in different types of locations operate at different rates would be informative and useful, adding a considerable refinement to the original model. Di Benedetto and Bojanic (1993), almost two decades ago, suggested that the faster the speed at which a destination was developed the shorter would be its life cycle. This is an intriguing hypothesis that deserves further exploration and if true, has significant implications for many modern destinations, but unfortunately their innovative idea does not appear to have been pursued, although it is supported also by research by Bao and Zhang (2006) and perhaps also by the example of Atlantic City (above) which saw its casino development proceed at a very fast rate once approval of gambling had been obtained.

Clarification and increased differentiation of the stages of the cycle would also be valuable. The excellent work of Berry (2006) on the predictive potential of the TALC did much to broaden understanding of what indicators could be used to identify not only the stages themselves but also to predict imminent movement from one stage to another. Additional work on determining a more complete set of indicators of each stage would be useful in clarifying the degree of exclusivity of the stages themselves. In the context of the stages of the cycle, few authors have challenged the model on the question of whether there are stages or that these might be identified. The initial criticisms of Haywood (1986) are still valid and while he has revisited the topic (Haywood 2006) his original reservations, particular on the difficulty of identifying stages remain mostly unaddressed, Berry's work noted above notwithstanding. Of interest in this respect would be whether objective empirical indicators of where a resort lay on the cycle (i.e. in which stage it was), were matched by subjective perceptions of decision makers and operators of services and facilities within that resort. Whatever objective indicators demonstrate, no actions are likely to be taken unless those responsible for the development of the destination agree with the location of the destination on its 'curve' and hence its likely future pattern of development or decline.

The destinations on which the original TALC model was based were mostly existing communities which had taken on a tourist function in addition to, or as a replacement of, more traditional economic activities. It would therefore, be informative to explore more modern resorts that have not had 19th or early 20th century transport modes as their means of access in terms of their progress through the development cycle. In recent years the advent of low cost carriers has meant the rapid, almost immediate growth of tourism in places not previously viewed as tourist destinations (Papatheodorou 2002, 2010) and as yet, the growth patterns of these locations have not been examined. Whether they will follow the traditional life cycle or face a different future with a different pattern of growth, given that their initiating causes were external agencies not directly concerned with the development of the destination but rather access to it, remains to be seen.

As noted above, there have been a number of suggestions of variations from the original model, Baum (1998) suggesting an 'exit' stage; and in particular, Agarwal (1994; 1997;1999; 2002) who has argued powerfully for the examination of restructuring as a factor in the development of the cycle and possible adjustment of stages in the post-stagnation period. The need for or justification of additional stages in the cycle could be explored in much more detail than has been done to date and might better illustrate post-Fordist arguments about restructuring in the tourism context. Gale (2007: 29) has noted that a problem with unilinear models is that they do not address structural changes such as economic restructuring and cultural changes in societies which clearly influence resort relevance in the post-modern world, echoing some of the earlier arguments of Gordon and Goodall (2000).

Also in the spirit of moving from 'what' to 'why', it is of critical importance to identify triggers which affect the transition process from one stage of development to another. Keller (1987) touched on this topic when discussing instability (a topic which has experienced major interest in the form of chaos theory as noted below), particularly in relation to control of development in destinations, and movement between stages in relation to capital investment. Important questions include whether there is a consistent set of triggers that operate throughout a destination's cycle, or if different triggers are more influential at different stages; whether specific triggers only affect destinations of particular types or in specific locations; and whether such triggers can be controlled and managed or only dealt with in a reactive manner. Gale and Botteril (2005) have suggested some of the elements that are involved based on their study of Rhyl and proposed a challenging research agenda in this area, noting that decisions about aspects of development reflect choices and preferences of those in control or at least influencing development or non-development. Haywood (2006: 63) goes on to note that "TALC studies must consider, not simply the existence of choice in reaction to change, but the conditions that both underlie change and enlarge or restrict choice". Clearly destinations are not passive phenomena, and those individuals, businesses and organisations managing, planning and controlling operations within destinations need not react passively to influences, either external or internal. They can, and perhaps should, be more pro-active in determining stage shifting in a destination, as called for in the original model (Bramwell and Lane 2000). How and why such decision-makers make those decisions is partly what Gale and Botteril (2005) were concerned with and this suggests that research into the power and politics of destination development is necessary if we are to understand more about the life cycle of destinations, and tourism in general, an approach long argued for by Hall (1994) in particular.

The vulnerability of destinations to both internal and external 'shocks' is an area also warranting more detailed examination. Endogenous influences often reflect local politics and viewpoints (Martin 2006), an issue that has received attention from tourism researchers for several decades, Doxey (1975) being one of the earliest studying the changing attitudes of local residents in destinations, and this area has been the focus of many other researchers since (for example, Smith 1978; Lankford and Howard 1994; Ap and Crompton 1998). Exogenous influences (such as the introduction of low cost airlines noted above), however, have been investigated less, and yet they have the potential to create massive impacts upon destinations. Few locations have escaped the influence of events such as the energy price rises of the early 1970s, conflicts in the Middle East, terrorism, natural disasters such as tsunamis, epidemics such as SARS or ebola, global trade and political agreements, or the recent economic downturn. Increased turbulence in the global economic and political systems has seen the application of chaos theory in tourism and specifically in the context of destinations and the TALC model (McKercher 1999; Faulkner and Russell 1997; 2001). Russell and Faulkner (1999) brought some of the issues raised above together in their examination of individuals (chaos-makers) involved in tourism development and their role in the changing fortunes of destinations. The key importance of individuals in changing the face of tourism in general has been explored only briefly, and is a topic that needs further examination, both in the context of tourism broadly (Butler and Russell 2010) and specifically at the destination level, where single individuals can be both initiators of development (Butler and McDonnell 2010) and agents causing a destination to move from one stage to another (Butler and Russell op cit).

One other area which has not been investigated to any degree is that of multiple cycles at work in a destination. This author has suggested previously (Butler 2009) that it is highly likely that many destinations are not on one single curve or cycle but rather are experiencing a series of cycles at different stages of development. It is likely that some of these will be in their early stages, some at their peak and still others in decline. The TALC curve for a destination, therefore, is likely to represent the overall aggregated pattern of development based on these multiple cycles. Different market segments will be at different stages in a destination at any point in time, some markets will be growing and some declining. The same can be said of the products or attractions (facilities, activity opportunities) that a destination is offering. Zimmermann (1997) suggested there are different cycles for different forms of tourism and even for individual activities and illustrated this with a figure showing patterns of activity popularity or life cycles from 1860 to 2000 (Figure 4)

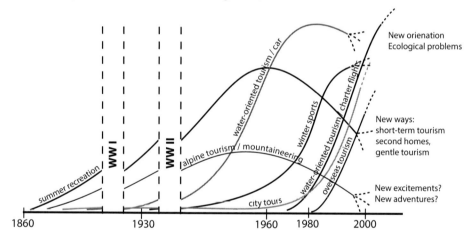

Figure 4: European tourism products – a product life cycle approach (Zimmermann 1997)

Research is needed to integrate the myriad forms of tourism, their respective markets, and their development cycles with the cycles of development of destinations. Thus Atlantic City has perhaps reached decline in its cycle as a gambling destination and may now move towards rejuvenation and a second cycle as a beach resort, with resulting changes in cycles for accommodation enterprises, retail units and market characteristics. The aggregated curve for that resort cannot capture either the detailed dynamics of the individual cycles occurring in that place or their effects on the destination. It was somewhat different in earlier times, when tourism and tourists at a destination were more homogeneous, when holidaymakers tended to come from a common origin, shared many common socio-economic characteristics and engaged in a more limited number of activities than is the case now. It was much easier to anticipate the likely pattern, scale and timing of development then, but as tourism has become more fragmented and resorts more complex in development, it is now much more difficult to predict patterns and rates of change.

In the context of the shocks to the system noted earlier, it is interesting to note that Zimmermann's diagram (Figure 4) also shows an interruption in cycles as a result of war, and such interruptions, although most likely at a smaller scale and shorter in time, might also be expected as a result of the rapid rise in energy prices in the 1970s, the Gulf and Balkan wars at the turn of this century, the economic recession of 2007-9 and even, although at a different time scale, climate change (Gossling et al 2010). As well, these interruptions can be expected not only in participation rates and the relative popularity of various forms of tourism, but also particularly in destinations, with correspondingly greater effects on some specific destinations. Rapid rises in energy prices would affect greatly those destinations dependent on long haul travel or that are high in energy consumption (e.g. Dubai); conflict in a region would have particularly negative impacts on destinations such as those in the Middle East; and the economic recession affect negatively all foreign travel. Climate change might be expected to impact on tourism cycles in more complex ways, including rises in numbers in some locations from 'last chance' tourists, and falls in other areas as attractions decline in quality or disappear, or potential tourists succumb to 'do-right' or 'do-good' inclinations and decide not to travel at all. In all cases, such effects on the TALC of specific destinations can be significant, speeding up or delaying the progress of the cycle, or even halting it in extreme cases. Corak (2006) noted the effect of conflict (wars in 1914-19, 1939-45, and 1991-5) on the TALC of resorts in Croatia, in effect causing the cycles to begin over again after each conflict ended. Thus the relationship between conflict (Butler and Suntikul 2012) and other causes of 'interruptions' in the TALC for destinations could be a fruitful area of further research.

A final area of research which could yield useful information in an applied context would be to explore the applicability of the TALC model to the prediction of the nature of change in destinations. Berry (2006) has illustrated how this might be done, and Manente and Pechlaner (2006) have also integrated the model into an "early-warning system" to predict decline in destinations. Clearly, given the number of destinations in a wide range of locations that are entering or have already entered a decline stage in their pattern of development, predictions would be useful. Predictions, however, have little benefit unless they are correct and are acted upon. Decision-makers in many destinations are well aware of the potential of decline but few seem willing to act on such knowledge, and denial or "business as usual" is frequently a more common reaction than endogenously inspired change or intervention. Attempts to quantify the TALC are beginning to appear (Coelho. and Butler (2012) but these have been limited to date. Few destinations have undertaken the depth of research and subsequent attempts to ensure sustainability and a prolonged life cycle that Hawaii has (Sheldon et al 2005) but this is a subject that many more destinations and researchers need to investigate if destinations are to avoid the need for sudden rejuvenation (Faulkner 2003) because of their failure to anticipate decline. Even where such research has been undertaken and policies framed, the effective implementation of relevant policies is rare (Dodds and Butler 2009).

Conclusions

Whether the TALC model will continue to be used in the future remains to be seen. It has already had a life much longer than could reasonably be anticipated. The reasons for this are not entirely clear; as Lundgren (1984: 22) noted some years ago " Butler put into the realistic cyclical context a reality that everyone knew about, and clearly recognised, but had never formulated into an overall theory". Perhaps the most important and fundamental future research agenda item in this field should be to explore the forces at work that provoke change in destinations (Butler 2010), as such knowledge would allow researchers to better understand the 'why' as well as the 'what' of destination development and cycles. The broad influences are clear and have been noted above, political and economic change, both internally and externally, environmental deterioration, technological (particularly transportation related) innovations and improvement, shifts in tastes and behaviours, and media influences. However, the way such forces impact on specific locations and communities, the duration and degree of permanence of their effects, and what can be done to mitigate or control such forces are still relatively unclear. Identifying the likely pattern and process of destination development is useful, but how this process might be controlled, protected, maintained and managed would be a considerable step forward and is well worthy of continued research effort.

References

Agarwal, S. (1994) The resort cycle revisited: implications for resorts, in *Progress in Tourism, Recreation and Hospitality Management*, C. P. Cooper and A. Lockwood, Wiley: Chichester, pp 194-208

Agarwal, S. (1997). The resort cycle and seaside tourism: an assessment of its applicability and validity. *Tourism Management*, **18** (2), 65-73.

Agarwal, S. (2002) Restructuring seaside tourism: The resort lifecycle. *Annals of Tourism Research* **29** (1), 25-55.

Aguiló, E. Alegre, J. and Sard, M. (2005). The persistence of the *sun and sand* tourism model. *Tourism Management,* **26** (2), 219-231

Akama, J.S. (1999). The evolution of tourism in Kenya. *Journal of Sustainable Tourism*, **7** (1), 6-25

Andereck, K. L. and Vogt, C. A. (2000) The relationship between residents' attitudes towards tourism and tourism development options, *Journal of Travel Research*, **39** (1), 27-36.

Ap, J. and Crompton, J. (1998) Developing a tourism impact scale, *Journal of Travel Research*, **37** (2), 120.

Avlonitis, G.J. (1990) Project dropstart: product elimination and the product life cycle concept. *European Journal of Marketing*, **24** (9), 55-67.

Bao, J. (1994a) Big Theme Park Distribution research. *Research of Geography,* **13** (3), 83-89.

Bao, J.(1994b) Tourism Development of Karst Cave. *Geographic Sinica,* **50** (4), 353-359

Bao.J. (1998) Tourism Planning and Tourist Area Life Cycle Model. *Architect,* **12**, 170-178

Bao, J., and Peng.H. (1995) Tourist area expanding research: case study of Danxia Mountain.*Science of Geography,* **15** (1), 63-70.

Baum, T.G. (1998) Tasking the exit route: Extending the tourism area life cycle model *Current Issues in Tourism* **1** (2) 167-175

Baum, T.G. (2006) Revisiting the TALC: Is there an off-ramp? in Butler, R.W. (ed.) *The Tourism Area Life Cycle Volume 2 Conceptual and Theoretical Issues* p.219-230 Clevedon: Channelview Publications.

Berry, T. (2006) The predictive potential of the TALC Model, in Butler, R.W. (ed.) *The Tourism Area Life Cycle, Volume 2 Conceptual and Theoretical Issues* p. 254-280 Clevedon: Channelview Publications.

Bianchi, R. (1994) Tourism development and resort dynamics: an alternative approach. *Progress in Tourism, Recreation and Hospitality Management,* **5**, 181-193

Brougham, J.E. and Butler, R.W. (1972) The Applicability of the Asymptotic Curve to the Forecasting of Tourism Development Paper presented to the Research Workshop, Travel Research Association 4th Annual Conference, Quebec, July 1972

Butler, R.W. (1973) *The Tourist Industry in the Highlands and Islands* Unpublished PhD thesis, Glasgow: University of Glasgow

Butler, R.W. (1980) The concept of the tourist area life-cycle of evolution: implications for management of resources. *Canadian Geographer* **24** (1), 5-12

Butler, R.W. (1990) The resort cycle revisited – a decade of discussion, Paper presented to Association of American Geographers Conference, Toronto, March

Butler, R.W. (1997) The destination life cycle: implications for heritage site management and attractivity, in Nuryanti, W. (ed) *Tourism and Heritage Management*, 44-53, Gadjah Mada University Press: Yogyakarta.

Butler, R. W. (1997) Modelling tourism development: evolution, growth and decline, in S. Wahab and J. Pigram (eds) *Tourism Development and Growth*, pp. 109-128 London: Routledge,

Butler, R.W. (1998) Still peddling along. The resort cycle two decades on, Paper to *Progress in Tourism and Hospitality Research*. CAUTHE Conference, Gold Coast

Butler, R.W. 1996 Concept of carrying capacity: dead or merely buried? *Progress in Tourism and Hospitality Research* **2** (3/4) 283-293

Butler, R.W. (2000) The resort cycle two decades on, in *Tourism in the 21st Century: Reflections on Experience*, B. Faulkner, E. Laws and G. Moscardo, (eds.). London: Cassell. 284-299

Butler, R.W. (2006a) The origins of the Tourism Area Life Cycle, in Butler, R.W. (ed) *The Tourism Area Life Cycle Volume 1 Applications and Modifications* p. 13-26 Clevedon: Channelview Publications.

Butler, R.W. (2006b) *The Tourism Area Life Cycle Volume 1 Applications and Modifications* Clevedon: Channelview Publications.

Butler, R.W. (2006c) *The Tourism Area Life Cycle Volume 2 Conceptual and Theoretical Issues*. 49-66 Clevedon: Channelview Publications.

Butler, R.W. (2009a) Tourism destination development: cycles and forces, myths and realities , *Tourism Recreation Research* **34** (3) 247-254

Butler, R.W. (2009b) Tourism in the future: cycles, waves or wheels? *Futures*, **41**, 352

Butler, R.W. (2010) Carrying capacity, in Pearce, D.G. and Butler, R.W. *Tourism Research A 20-20 Vision* p.53-64, Oxford: Goodfellow

Butler, R.W. and McDonnell, I. (2011) One man and his boat (and hotel and pier…) Henry Gilbert Smith and the establishment of Manly, Australia *Tourism Geographies* **13** (3) 343-359

Butler, R.W. and Russell, R. (2010) *Giants of Tourism* CABI: Wallingford

Butler, R.W. and Suntikul, W. (2010) *Tourism and Political Change,* Oxford: Goodfellow

Butler, R.W. and Suntikul, W. (2012) *Tourism and War* Abingdon: Routledge

Canavan, B. (2013) Send more tourists! Stakeholder perceptions of a tourism industry in late stage decline: the case of the Isle of Man. *International Journal of Tourism Research,* **26** 15(2): 105-121

Canavan, B. (2014) Sustainable tourism: development, decline and de-growth. Management issues from the Isle of Man. *Journal of Sustainable Tourism,* **22**(1), 127-147.

Catry, B. and Chevalier, M. (1974) Market share strategy and the product life cycle, *Journal of Marketing* **38**, 29-34

Chapman, A. and Speake, J. (2011) Regeneration in a mass-tourism resort: the changing fortunes of Bugibba, Malta. *Tourism Management* **32**(3), 482-491.

Chen, J. (2001) Disscusion on "the lifecycle of the tourist products". *Journal of Guilin Technical College.* **3**, 18-20

Choy, Dexter J. L. (1992) Life cycle models for Pacific Island destinations. *Journal of Travel Research* **30**, 26-38

Choy, D. J. L. (1991) Tourism planning: the case for market failure, *Tourism Management,* **12** (4), 313-330

Chunxiao (1997) Thoughts on " Tourist Products Lifecycle", *Tourism Tribune,* **12** (5), 44-47

Coelho, J. and Butler, R. (2012) A quantitative approach of the tourism area life cycle, *European Journal of Tourism, Hospitality and Recreation* **3** (1) 9-32

Cohen, E. (1972) Toward a sociology of international tourism. *Social Research,* **39** (1), 164–82.

Cohen, E. (1979) Rethinking the sociology of tourism. *Annals of Tourism Research,* **6** (1), 18–35.

Cole, S. (2009) A logistic tourism model – resort cycles, globalisation and chaos, *Annals of Tourism Research* **36** (4) 689-714

Cole, S. (2007) Beyond the resort life cycle: the micro-dynamics of destination tourism, *Journal of Regional Analysis and Policy* **37** (3) 254-266

Coles, T. (2006) Enigma variations? The TALC, marketing models and the descendents of the product life cycle, in Butler, R.W. (ed.) *The Tourism Area Life Cycle Volume 2 Conceptual and Theoretical Issues.* 49-66 Clevedon: Channelview Publications.

Collins (1998) *The Collins Concise Dictionary of the English Language* Glasgow: Collins

Cooper, C. (1990) Resorts in decline- the management response, *Tourism Management*, **11** (1), 63-67.

Cooper, C.P. (1992) The life cycle concept and strategic planning for coastal resorts, *Built Environment*, **18** (1), 57-66.

Cooper, C.P. (1994) The destination life cycle: an update. in *Tourism: the State of the Art*, Editors A. V. Seaton, C. L. Jenkins, R. C. Wood, P.U.C. Dieke, M. M. Bennett, L. R. MacLellan, and R. Smith. 340-346 Brisbane: Wiley.

Cooper C.P. (1997a) The environmental consequences of declining destinations, *Progress in Tourism and Hospitality Research*, **2** (3), 337-345

Cooper C.P. (1997b) Parameters and indicators of the decline of the British seaside resort, pp 79-101 in G Shaw and A Williams (eds) *The Rise and Fall of British Coastal Resorts*, Cassell, London

Cooper, C., Fletcher, J., Noble, A and Westlake, J (1996) Changing tourism demand in Central Europe: the case of Romanian tourist spas, *Journal of Tourism Studies*, **6** (2), 30-44

Cooper, C. and Jackson, S. (1989) Destination life cycle: The Isle of Man case study, *Annals of Tourism Research*, **16** (3), 377-398

da Conceiçáo Gonçalves, V. F. and Roque Águas, P. M. (1997) The concept of the life cycle: An application to the tourist product. *Journal of Travel Research* **36** (2), 12–22.

Costa, P. and M. Manente (1995), Venice and its visitors: a survey and a model of qualitative choice, *Journal of Travel and Tourism Marketing*, **4** (3), 45-69.

Debbage, K. (1990) Oligopoly and the resort cycle in the Bahamas. *Annals of Tourism Research*, **17**, 513-527

Debbage, K. (1992). Tourism oligopoly is at work. *Annals of Tourism Research* **19**(2), 355-359.

Dhalla, N.K. and Yuspeh, S. (1976) Forget the product life cycle concept, *Harvard Business Review* **54** (January/February), 102-12

Diedrich, A., & García Buades, E. (2009). Local perceptions of tourism as indicators of destination decline. *Tourism Management*, **30**, 512-521

Digance, J. (1997) Life cycle model. *Annals of Tourism Research*. **24** (2), 452-455.

Din, K.H. (1992) The involvement stage in the evolution of a tourist destination. *Tourism Recreation Research* **17** (1), 10-20.

Din, J.,and Bao.J. (2000) A study on the life cycle of special karst cave with a case of Jinashui Swallow Cave in Yunnan Provice. *Carsologica Sinica*,19 (3), 284-289.

Dodds, R and McElroy, J (2008) St Kitts at a Crossroads. *ARA Journal of Travel Research.* **1** (2) 1-10

Douglas, N. (1997) Applying the life cycle model to Melanesia. *Annals of Tourism Research* **24** (1), 1-22.

Doxey, G. V. (1975) When enough's enough: The natives are restless in Old Niagara, *Heritage Canada*, **2**, 26-27.

Duffus, D.A.,and Dearden, P., (1990). Non-consumptive wildlife-oriented recreation: a conceptual framework. *Biological Conservation*, **53**, 213-231.

Faulkner, B. (2003) Rejuvenating a maturing tourist destination: The case of the Gold Coast, in Fredline, E, Jago, L and Cooper, C (eds) *Progressing Tourism Research: Bill Faulkner*, Clevedon, Channelview

Faulkner, B. & Russell, R. (1997) Chaos and complexity in tourism: in search of a new perspective. *Pacific Tourism Review*, **1** (2), 93-102

Faulkner, B. & Russell, R. (2001) Turbulence, chaos and complexity in tourism systems: a research direction for the New Millennium, in B.Faulkner, G. Moscardo and E. Laws (eds) *Tourism in the 21st Century*. London: Continuum.

Formica, S. and Uysal, M. (1996) The revitalisation of Italy as a tourist destination. *Tourism Management*, **17** (5), 323-31

Foster, D. M. and Murphy, P. (1991) Resort cycle revisited: The retirement connection. *Annals of Tourism Research*, **18**, 553–67.

Faulkner, H. W. (1990) swings and roundabouts in Australian tourism, *Tourism Management*, **11** (1), 29-37.

France, L. (1991) An application of the tourism destination area life cycle to Barbados. *Revue de Tourisme*, **46** (3), 25-30.

Frean, A. (2014) As the wheel stops, Atlantic City's number is up *The Times*, September 6, p. 21

Gale, T. (2007) Modernism, postmodernism and the decline of British seaside resorts as long holiday destinations: a case study of Rhyl, North Wales. *Tourism Geographies* **7** (1), 86-112.

Gale, T. and Botterill, D. (2005) A realist agenda for tourist studies, or why destinations areas really rise and fall in popularity, *Tourist Studies* **5** (1) 151-174.

Garay, L. & Cànoves, G. (2011). Life cycles, stages and tourism history: The Catalonia (Spain) experience. *Annals of Tourism Research*, **38**(2), 651-671

Getz, D. (1983) Capacity to absorb tourism concepts and implications for strategic planning, *Annals of Tourism Research*, **10** (1), 245-257.

Getz, D. (1992) Tourism planning and destination life-cycle. *Annals of Tourism Research*, **19**(4), 757-770.

Getz, D. (2000). Festivals and special events: life cycle and saturation issues, in W.C. Gartner and D.W. Lime (eds.), *Trends in Outdoor Recreation, Leisure and Saturation Issues,*175-185.

Gilbert, E. W. (1939) The growth of inland and seaside health resorts in England. *Scottish Geographical Magazine* **55**, 16-35.

Godkin, E.L. (1883) Evolution of the Summer Resort, *The Nation* July 19, 47-48

Goncalves, V. F. da C. and Aguas, P. M. R. (1997). The concept of life cycle: an application to the tourist product, *Journal of Travel Research*, **36**(2), 12-22.

Gordon, I. and Goodall, B. (1992) Resort cycles and development processes. *Built Environment*, **18** (4), 41-56.

Gordon, I. and Goodall, B. (2000) Localities and tourism. *Tourism Geographies*, **2** (3), 290-311.

Gormsen, E. (1981), The spatio-temporal development of international tourism, attempt at a centre-periphery model, in *La Consommation d'Espace par le Tourisme et sa Preservation*. Centre d'etudes touristiques, Aix-en-Provence.

Gosling, S. (2000). Tourism development in Sri Lanka: The case of Ethukala and Unawatuna. *Tourism Recreation Research* **25**(3), 103-114.

Giere, R. N. (2004) How models are used to represent realit,y *Philosphy of Science* **71** (5) Supplement S742-752

Harrigan, N. (1974) The legacy of Caribbean history and tourism, *Annals of Tourism Research*, **2** (1), 13-25

Harrison, D. (1995) Development of tourism in Swazilan, *Annals of Tourism Research*, **22** (1), 135-56.

Haywood, K.M. (1986) Can the tourist area life-cycle be made operational? *Tourism Management*, **7** (3), 154-167.

Haywood, K.M. (1992) Revisiting resort cycle, *Annals of Tourism Research* **19**(2), 351-354.

Haywood, K. M. (1998) Economic business cycles and the tourism life-cycle concept, in Ioniddes, D. and Debbage, K (eds) *The Economic Geography of the Tourist Industry*, 273–84, London: Routledge

Hayward, K.M. (2006) Legitimising the TALC as a theory of development, in Butler, R.W. (ed.) *The Tourism Area Life Cycle Volume 2 Conceptual and Theoretical Issues* 29-44 Clevedon: Channelview Publications.

Hobbs, C. (1913) The ruin or the redemption of Lake Quinsigamond, *The Worcester Magazine*, February, 35-38

Hovinen, G. (1981) A tourist cycle in Lancaster County, Pennsylvania, *Canadian Geographer*, **15** (3), 283-286.

Hovinen, G. (1982) Visitor cycles: outlook in tourism in Lancaster, *Annals of Tourism Research*, **9**, 565-583.

Hovinen, G. (2002) Revisiting the destination life cycle model, *Annals of Tourism Research*, **29** (1), 209-230

Ioannides, D. (1992) Tourism development agents: the Cypriot resort cycle. *Annals of Tourism Research*, **19** (4), 711-731.

Ioannides, D. and Debbage, K. (1998a) *The Economic Geography of the Tourist Industry: a Supply-side Analysis*, London: Routledge.

Jansen-Verbeke, M. (1986) Inner-city tourism: resources, tourists and promoters, *Annals of Tourism Research*, **13** (1), 79-100.

Javiluoma, J. (1992) Alternative tourism and the evolution of tourist areas, *Tourism Management*, **13** (1), 118-120

Johnson, J and D. Snepenger (1993). Application of the tourism life cycle concept in the Greater Yellowstone region. *Society and Natural Resources*, **6**, 127-148.

Johnston, C.S. (2001) Shoring the foundations of the destination life cycle model, part 1: ontological and epistemological considerations, *Tourism Geographies*, **3** (1), 2-28

Jordon, P. (2000) Restructuring Croatia's coastal resorts: change, sustainable development and the incorporation of rural hinterlands. *Journal of Sustainable Tourism*, **8** (6), 525-539.

Juelg, F. (1993) Tourism product life cycles in the Central Eastern Alps: A case study of Heiligenblut on the Grossglockner. *Tourism Recreation Research*, **18** (1), 20–6.

Kapczynski, A. and Szromek, A.R. (2008) Hypotheses concerning the development of Polish Spas in the years 1949-2006 *Tourism Management* **29** 1035-1037

Karplus, Y. and S. Kracover (2005). Stochastic multivariable approach to modeling tourism area life cycles. *Tourism and Hospitality Research*, **5** (3), 235-253.

Keller, C. P. (1987) Stages of peripheral tourism development — Canada's Northwest Territories. *Tourism Management*, **8**, 2–32.

Kermath, B.M. and R.N. Thomas (1992). Spatial dynamics of resorts: Sousa, Dominican Republic. *Annals of Tourism Research* **19**, 173-190.

Knowles, T. and Curtis, S. (1999). The market viability of european mass tourist destinations. A post-stagnation life-cycle analysis. *Journal of Tourism Research*, **1**(2), 87-96.

Kokkranikal, J. and Morrison, A. (2002). Entrepreneurship and sustainable tourism: the houseboats of Kerala, *Tourism and Hospitality Research*, **4**(1), 7-20

Lankford, S.V. and Howard, D.R. (1994) Developing a tourism impact attitude scale, *Annals of Tourism Research*, **21**, 121-139

Legiewski, R.M. (2006) The application of the TALC model: A literature survey, in Butler, R.W. (ed.) *The Tourism Area Life Cycle Volume 1 Applications and Modifications* p. 27-50 Clevedon: Channelview Publications.

Lewis, R. and Green, S. (1998). Planning for stability and managing chaos: the case of Alpine ski resorts, in Laws, E., Faulkner, B. and Moscardo, G. (Editors), *Embracing and Managing Change in Tourism: International Case Studies*, 138-160, London: Routledge.

Liu, J.L., P.J. Sheldon, and T. Var. (1987) Resident perception of the environmental impacts of tourism, *Annals of Tourism Research*, **14**(1), 17-37.

Liu, J.L., T. Var. (1986) Resident attitudes to tourism impacts in Hawaii, *Annals of Tourism Research*. **13** (2), 193-214.

Lu, L. (1997) A study on the life cycle of mountain resorts: a case study of Huangshan Mountain and Jiuhanshan Mountain. *Scintia Geographic Sinica*, **17** (1), 63-69.

Lucas, R. (1964) The recreational carrying capacity of the Quetico-Superior area USDA *Forest Service Research Paper*, LS-15, St. Paul: USDA

Lundgren, J.O. (1984) Geographic concepts and the development of tourism research in Canada *Geojournal* **9**, 17-25

Lundtorp, S. and Wanhill, S. (2001) The resort lifecycle theory generating processes and estimation, *Annals of Tourism Research* **28**, 947-964.

Manente, M., and Pechlaner, H. (2006) How to define, identify and monitor the decline of tourist destinations: towards an early warning system, in Butler, R.W. (ed.) *The Tourism Area Life Cycle Volume 2 Conceptual and Theoretical Issues* p. 235-253 Clevedon: Channelview Publications.

Marchena Gomez, M. and Vera Rebollo, F. (1995) Coastal areas: processes, typologies, prospects, in A. Montanari and A. Williams (editors), *European Tourism: Regions, Spaces and Restructuring*, 111-126, Chichester: Wiley.

Martin, B. S., and M. Uysal (1990) An examination of the relationship between carrying capacity and the tourism lifecycle: management and policy implications, *Journal of Environmental Management*, **31**, 327-333

Massey, G. (1999) Product evolution: a Darwinian or Lamarckian phenomenon? *Journal of Product and Brand Management*, **8** (4), 301-318.

McCartney, G. (2010) Stanley Ho Hung-sun: the 'King of Gambling', in Butler, R.W. and Russell, R. (eds.) *Giants of Tourism* 170-181 Wallingford: CABI.

McElroy, J. L., deAlbuquerque, K. and Dioguardi, A. (1993) Applying the tourist destination life-cycle model to small Caribbean and Pacific Islands. *World Travel and Tourism Review*, 236–244

McKercher, B. (1999) A chaos approach to tourism. *Tourism Management*, **20**, 425-434.

McKercher, R.(2006) Are psychographics predictors of destination life cycles? *Journal of Travel & Tourism Marketing*, **19** (1), 49-55

Messerli, H.R. (1993) Tourism area life cycle models and residents' perceptions: the case of Santa Fe, New Mexico (City Planning). Unpublished Ph.D Thesis, Cornell University.

Meyer-Arendt, K. J. (1985) The Grand Isle, Louisiana Resort cycle. *Annals of Tourism Research*, **12**, 449–466.

Milne, S. (1998) Tourism and sustainable development: exploring the global-local nexus, in C.M. Hall and A. Lew (editors), *Sustainable Tourism: A Geographical Perspective*, 35-48, London, Longman.

Miossec, J.M. (1977) Un modèle de l'espace touristique, *L'Espace Géographie* **1**, 41

Morgan, N.J. and Pritchard, A. (1999) *Power and politics at the seaside. The development of Devon's resorts in the Twentieth Century*. Exeter: University of Exeter Press.

Moss, S.E., Ryan, C., and Wagoner, C.B. (2003) An empirical test of Butler's resort product life cycle: forecasting casino winnings *Journal of Travel Research*. **41** (4) 393-399

Nelson, C. (2008) Life cycle of Santosha, *Surf Economics* May 12 issue, p. 1

O'Hare, G and H. Barrett (1997) The destination life cycle – international tourism in Peru. *Scottish Geographical Magazine* **113**(2), 66-73

Oppermann, M. (1995) Travel life cycle, *Annals of Tourism Research* **22** (3), 535–552.

Opperman, M. (1998a). Destination Threshold Potential and the Law of Repeat Visitation. *Journal of Travel Research* **37** (2), 131-137.

Oppermann, M. (1998b) What is new with the resort cycle? *Tourism Management*, **19** (2), 179–80.

Orejo Rodríguez,O., J. R. Parra-López, E. and Yanes-Estévez, V. (2008). The sustainability of island destinations: Tourism area life cycle and teleological perspectives. The case of Tenerife. *Tourism Management* **29**(1), 53-65

Papatheodorou, A. (2001a) Why people travel to different places, *Annals of Tourism Research*, **28** (1), 164-179

Papatheodorou, A. (2001b) Tourism, transport geography and industrial economics: a synthesis in the context of Mediterranean Islands, *Anatolia*, **12** (1), 23-34.

Plog, S.C. (1972) Why destination areas rise and fall in popularity. Paper presented at the Southern California Chapter of the Travel Research Bureau, October 10, 1972.

Plog, S.C. (1973) Why destinations areas rise and fall in popularity, *Cornell Hotel and Restaurant Association Quarterly* **13** 6-13

Plog, S. C. (1991) Why destination areas rise and fall in popularity. pp. 75-84 in *Leisure Travel: Making It a Growth Market...Again!* New York: John Wiley & Sons, Inc.

Plog, S.C. (2001). Why destination areas rise and fall in popularity: an update of a *Cornell Quarterly* classic. *Cornell Hotel and Restaurant Administration Quarterly* **42** (3), 13-24.

Pollard, J. and Rodriguez, R. (1993) Tourism and Torremolinos. Recession or reaction to environment. *Tourism Management*, **12** (4), 247-258.

Prideaux, B. (2000). The resort development spectrum (a new approach to modeling resort development). *Tourism Management*, **21**, 225-240.

Prideaux, B. (2004), The resort development spectrum: the case of the Gold Coast, Australia, *Tourism Geographies*, **6**(1), 26-59.

Priestley, G. and Mundet, L. (1998) The post-stagnation phase of the resort life-cycle. *Annals of Tourism Research*, **25** (1), 85-111.

Prosser, G. (1995) Tourism destination life cycles: Progress, problems and prospects, paper to *National Tourism Research Conference*, Melbourne.

Ravenscroft, N., and Hadjihambi, I. (2006) The implications of Lamarckian theory for the TALC Model, in Butler, R.W. (ed.) *The Tourism Area Life Cycle Volume 2 Conceptual and Theoretical Issues* p. 150-163 Clevedon: Channelview Publications.

Richardson, S.L. (1986) A product life cycle approach to urban waterfronts: the revitalisation of Galveston. *Costal Zone Management Journal*, **14** (1/2):21-46

Putra, N.D. and Hitchock, M. (2006) The Bali bombs and the tourism development cycle *Progress in Development*, **6** (2) 157-166

Ritchie, J.R.B., and Crouch, G.I. (2003) *The Competitive Destination: A Sustainable Tourism Perspective* CABI: Wallingford

Rodriguez, J., Parra-Lopez, E. And Yanes-Estavez, V. (2008) The sustainability of island destinations: Tourism area life cycle and teleological perspectives. The case of Tenerife. *Tourism Management* **29**(1): 53-65.

Russell, R. (2006a) Chaos theory and its application to the TALC Model, in Butler, R.W. (ed.) *The Tourism Area Life Cycle Volume 2 Conceptual and Theoretical Issues* p. 164-180 Clevedon: Channelview Publications.

Russell, R. (2006b) The contribution of entrepreneurship theory to the TALC Model, in Butler, R.W. (ed.) *The Tourism Area Life Cycle Volume 2 Conceptual and Theoretical Issues* p. 105-123 Clevedon: Channelview Publications.

Russell, R., and B. Faulkner. (1998) Reliving the destination lifecycle in Coolangatta. An historical perspective on the rise, decline and rejuvenation of an Australian seaside resort, in Laws, E., Faulkner, B. and Moscardo, G. (eds) *Embracing and Managing Change in Tourism: International Case Studies.* London: Routledge, pp.95-115.

Russell, R. and B. Faulkner. (1999) Movers and shakers: chaos makers in tourism development. *Tourism Management,* **20,** 411–423.

Russo, A.P. (2002). The vicious circle of tourism development in heritage cities. *Annals of Tourism Research* **29** (1), 165-182.

Shaw, G. and Williams, A.M. (1994, 2002) *Critical Issues in Tourism: a Geographical Perspective,* Oxford, Blackwell, 1st Edition, 2nd Edition.

Sheldon, P. J., Knox, J.M. and Lowry, K. (2005) sustainability in a mature mass tourism destination: The case of Hawaii, *Tourism Review International* **9** (1) 47-60

Singh, Shalini. (1998) Probing the product life cycle further, *Tourism Recreation Research,* **23**(2), 61-63.

Smith, R.A. (1992). Beach resort evolution: implications for planning. *Annals of Tourism Research,* **19,** 304-322.

Stansfield, C. Jr. (1972) The development of modern seaside resorts. *Parks and Recreation,* **5** (10), 14 – 46

Stansfield, C.A. (1978) Atlantic City and the resort cycle. background to the legalization of gambling, *Annals of Tourism Research,* **5** (2), 238-251

Stansfield, C. Jr. (2006) The rejuvenation of Atlantic City: The resort cycle recycles, in Butler, R.W. (ed.) *The Tourism Area Life Cycle Volume 1 Applications and Modifications* p. 287-305 Clevedon: Channelview Publications.

Stansfield, C. A. and Rickert, J.E. (1970) The recreational business district, *Journal of Leisure Research* **2** (4) 213-225

Strapp, J.D. (1988) The resort cycle and second homes, *Annals of Tourism Research,* **15** (4), 504-516

Teye, V., Sonmez, S.F., Sirakaya, E. (2002) Residents' attitudes toward tourism development, *Annals of Tourism Research,* **29** (3), 668-688

Toh, R.S.; Khan, H. and Koh, A-J. (2001) A travel balance approach for examining tourism area life cycles: The case of Singapore, *Journal of Travel Research,* **39,** 426-432.

Tomas P.S. (2000) Development and sustainability of aging tourist resorts. *Future Strategies in the Balearic Islands* (Spain) 29th International Geographic Congress, Cheju, Korea

Tooman, L.A. (1997) Applications of the life-cycle model in tourism, *Annals of Tourism Research,* **24** (1), 214-234

Twinning-Ward, L. and Baum, T. (1998) Dilemmas facing mature island destinations: cases from the Baltic, *Progress in Tourism, Recreation and Hospitality Management*, **4** (3), 131-140.

Twining-Ward, L. and Twining-Ward, T. (1996) *Tourism Destination Development: the case of Bornholm and Gotland*, Nexo: Research Centre of Bornholm.

Urry, J. (1997) Cultural change and the seaside resort, in G. Shaw and A. Williams (editors) *The Rise and Fall of British Coastal Resorts*, 102-113, London: Cassell.

Voase, R. (2002). The influence of political, economic and social change in a mature tourist destination: the case of the Isle of Thanet, South-East England, in R. Voase (ed.) *Tourism in Western Europe: A Collection of Case Histories*. p. 61-84 Lincoln: The University of Lincoln.

Wagar, J. A. (1964) The carrying capacity of wildlands for recreation, *Forest Service Monograph No 7* Washington D.C.: Society of American Foresters

Wall, G. (1982a) Cycles and capacity: Incipient growth or theory, *Annals of Tourism Research*, **9** (2), 52-56.

Wall, G. (1982b) Cycles and capacity: Incipient theory or conceptual contradiction? *Tourism Management* **3** (3) 188-192

Weaver, D.B. (1988) The evolution of a 'plantation' tourism landscape on the Caribbean Island of Antigua. *Tijdschrift Voor Econ. En Soc Geografie*, **69**, 319-331.

Weaver, D.B. (1990) Grand Cayman Island and the resort cycle concept. *The Journal of Travel Research*, **29** (2), 9-15.

Weaver, D.B. (1992) Tourism and the Functional Transformation of the Antiguan Landscape. pp. 161-75, in *Spatial Implications of Tourism*, A. M. Conny (ed). Groningen, The Netherlands: Geo Pers.

Weaver, D. (1993), Model of urban tourism for small Caribbean islands, *Geographical Review*, **83**, 134-40.

Weaver, D.B. (2000a) A broad context model of destination development scenarios. *Tourism Management*, **21**, 217-224

Weaver, D.B. (2000b) The exploratory war-distorted destination life cycle *International Journal of Tourism Research*, **2** (3), 151-162

Weaver, D.B. (2001) Mass tourism and alternative tourism in the Caribbean, in: Harrison, D. (ed) *Tourism and the Less Developed World: Issues and Case Studies*, p. 161-74 CABI Publishing, Wallingford, UK,.

Weber, S. (1988). Life cycle of Croatian tourism product: What have we learned from the past. In *Europaische Tourismus und Freizeitforschung*, Band 6, 37-51.

Webster, A.G. (1914) The evolution of Mt Desert, *The Nation* **92** (256), 347-348

Weidenfeld, A. and Butler, R. W. (2012) Cooperation and competition during the resort lifecycle *Tourism Recreation Research* **37** (1): 15-26

Weizenegger, S. (2006) The TALC and protected natural areas: African Examples in Butler, R.W. (ed.) *The Tourism Area Life Cycle Volume 2 Conceptual and Theoretical Issues* p. 124-137 Clevedon: Channelview Publications.

Wilkinson, P.F. (1987) Tourism in small island nations: a fragile dependence. *Leisure Studies* **26**(2), 127-146

Wilkinson, P.F. (1996) Graphical images of the commonwealth Caribbean: The tourist area cycle of evolution. pp.16-40 in *Practicing Responsible Tourism International Case Studies in Tourism Planning, Policy and Development*, Editors L.C. Harrison, W. Husbands: John Wiley and Sons.

Williams, M. T. (1993) An expansion of the tourist site cycle model: the case of Minorca (Spain). *The Journal of Tourism Studies* **4**, 24–32.

Wolfe, R.I. (1952) Wasaga Beach – the divorce from the geographic environment, *The Canadian Geographer*, **2**, 57-66

Wolfe, R.I. (1982) Recreational Travel – the new migration revisited, *Ontario Geography* **19**, 103-122.

Wong, P.P. (1986) Tourism development and resorts on the east coast of Peninsular Malaysia, *Singapore Journal of Tropical Geography*, **7**, 152–62.

Xu. H. (2001) Study on the potential tourists and life cycle of tourism product: a system dynamic approach. *System Engineering*, **19**(3), 69-75.

Xie.Y. (1995) Control and adjustment of the tourist area life cycle. *Tourism Tribune*, **10**(2), 41-44.

Yang.S. (1996) Doubts about the life cycle of a tourist product. *Tourism Tribune* **11** (1), 45-47.

Yi, Y. (2001) An analysis of the theory of life cycle in tourist areas. *Tourism Tribune*, **16**(6), 31-33

Zh, L. (1997) On the theory of the life cycle of tourist destination, a discussion with Yang Senlin. *Tourism Tribune*, **12**(1):38-40.

Zhong, L. Z., Deng, J. and Xiang, B. (2008). Tourism development and the tourism area lifecycle model: A case study of Zhangjiajie National Forest Park, China. *Tourism Management*, **29**, 841-856.

Zimmermann, F. (1997) Future perspectives of tourism: traditional versus new destinations, in Oppermann, M. (ed) *Pacific Rim Tourism* p. 231-239 CAB International: Wallingford

Glossary

Attractions: Places or features of interest, such as sites of cultural, historical or religious significance, of natural beauty or places of amusement such as theme parks to which people travel for pleasure.

Authenticity: Something that conforms to the fact, linked to integrity and has not been created specifically for tourists.

Budget Airlines: Also known as 'low cost airlines', low cost carriers or 'no frills' airlines. These airlines generally provide low fares but charge for other services such as in-flight food, baggage, check-in, priority boarding and seat allocation. These airlines have a unique business model that is distinct from the legacy carriers.

Carrying Capacity: The maximum number of people or level of use that an environment (such as a destination) can accommodate without experiencing irreparable change.

Climate Change: Changes in the earth's climate, generally in the context of the effects of global warming caused by human population growth and development. Markets: In economics, the system by which buyers and sellers exchange goods and services.

Product: Anything that can be offered for consumption or acquisition that could satisfy a need or want of a market. This could include physical objects or services.

Resources: A resource is something that is perceived to have instrumental and sometimes monetary value in economic development.

Sustainability: The capacity to endure or continue, generally used in the context of 'sustainable development', implying living or operating within the limits of the specific environment.

Tourism Area Life Cycle (TALC): A process describing how a destination starts off slowly with visitor numbers limited by the facilities and access. As the destination attracts more visitors, amenities are improved, and visitor numbers grow rapidly towards and sometimes beyond the carrying capacity of the destination.

Tourist Destinations: A place where tourists plan to spend time away from home. This geographical area could be as small as a self-contained centre, such as a village, town or city, or be as broad as a region, island or country. It encompasses all the organizations, companies, individuals and government bodies (stakeholders) which offer products and services to people visiting the destination, as well as natural and artificial resources and attractions. More than one destination may be visited as part of a holiday, for example, on a tour or cruise.

The term is considered complex to define but it tends to refer only to the geographical unit in which products can be purchased or experienced.

Tourist Resorts: Small geographic areas with attractions and services for the tourist. The population during the high season is mainly made up of transient visitors. The economy of resorts is based on tourism and transactions by tourists.

Event Management

Michelle Whitford

Contents

Michelle Whitford is Research Member, Centre for Tourism, Sport and Services Research at the Department of Tourism, Leisure, Hotel and Sport Management of Griffith Business School, Nathan Campus, Griffith University, Australia. Her main areas of research have been event and tourism policy and planning, indigenous tourism and sustainable events. Her current teaching areas are conference and convention management and entrepreneurship in tourism, hospitality, sport and events.

Introduction

History clearly illustrates the prominent role that events have always played in peoples' lives. They have the capacity to not only generate economic benefits but importantly, social capital as they facilitate constant rejuvenation of the community experience, bind communities together and establish "...a sense of co-operation, goodwill, reciprocity, belonging and fellowship" (Arcodia and Whitford, 2006:2). According to Derrett (2004), events are like an elixir as they provide us with a vehicle to celebrate a particular date and occasion (Bowdin, Allen, O'Toole, Harris and McDonnell, 2006) which according to Wrathall and Gee, (2011:11) "...is an essential part of human nature". Thus events, such as festivals, fairs, sporting, religious, artistic, cultural and personal events (and others) not only provide us with a means of recognizing significant personal and/or public milestones but they also contribute to defining our personal lives, culture, communities, regions and nations (Bowdin and McPherson, 2006).

This review provides some introductory insights into the global phenomenon called events and event management. Given that event management is arguably, still in a nascent stage of development (compared to industries such as manufacturing, mining, agriculture), there are a multitude of issues that could undergo a detailed examination. The introductory overview in this review first, provides an historical synopsis of events and the event industry. Next, the review covers definitional issues and the categorisation of the array of events that constitute the event industry. This is followed by an overview of the broad research areas pertaining to events and event management before highlighting the future trends in the field of study of event management.

An Introduction to Events

Towards the latter part of the 20th Century due to an increase in leisure time and discretionary income (Allen et al., 2011), there was a ground swell in the number, size, scope and complexity of events being staged around the globe (Thrane, 2002). For instance, by the mid 1990s in the USA, the staging of thousands of festivals per annum were attracting millions of visitors (approximately 31 million per annum) (TIA, 2004 cited Quinn, 2013) while in Europe, the International Festival and Event Association (IFEA) maintained the 'special events industry is estimated to comprise between four and five million regularly occurring events' (Wood, 2012 cited Quinn, 2013: ix). This proliferation of festivals and events facilitated the emergence of a global event industry, which has developed into a significant economic, socio-cultural and political phenomenon. The increasing significance of the event industry in contemporary society emanated from a shift away from a strong reliance on the manufacturing industry to greater dependence on the service industry which occurred in the Western world from the 1960s onwards (Yeoman et al., 2004). According to Bourdieu (1984) and Voase (1994), there was a vacuum left by the demise of the manufacturing sector and consequently governments, industry and society at large have demonstrated an increased interest in both tourism and events in a quest to fill the void while searching for a new quality of life.

It was during the 1980s that governments globally, began to realise the potential for events to generate positive impacts including 'political kudos' and community pride. It was however, the general perception that the large major and mega international events in particular, could generate very significant economic benefits for a host city or country, that initially encouraged governments' involvement in events (Burgan and Mules, 2000). For instance, the 1984 Olympic Games in Los Angeles (www.olympic.org/los-angeles-1984-summer-olympics) demonstrated the economic capacity of a mega sporting event and set a standard for future events to aspire towards. It soon followed that 'sports mega-events have become integral to the entrepreneurial strategies of cities seeking to gain competitive advantage in the global economy' (Hall, 2006:67).

Amongst the first countries to capitalise on the apparent benefits of major and mega events, were various State governments of Australia with the establishment of specialised government event agencies (e.g., Events Queensland, www.eventsqueensland.com.au; Victoria Major Events, www.vmec.com.au; NSW Events, www.nswevents.com/NSW) (Getz, 2000). As a result of the success of these pioneer Australian government event agencies, it was not long before similar specialist event agencies were established by governments around the globe through the creation of event development corporations, sport commissions, or other event specific companies (see, e.g., Pugh and Wood, 2004; Stokes 2004; Thomas and Wood, 2004). In essence, the mandate of these agencies was and continues to be, to provide the best opportunities to successfully bid for, secure, facilitate and produce many of the world's mega and major events (Emery, 2001; Westerbeek et al., 2002). Therefore, in all corners of the world, governments have become increasingly active in their pursuit of mega and major events in particular, as they continue to demonstrate a capacity to generate positive economic, socio-cultural, environmental and political impacts (Quinn, 2013). For instance, in the United Kingdom, the level of government commitment and support for major events (e.g., Meet England, www.meetengland.com/Home.aspx; Events Scotland, www.eventsscotland.org) is evidenced by London spending an estimated 15 million pounds on bidding for (Benneworth and Dauncey, 2010) and securing the 2012 Olympic Games (www.london2012.com) and Glasgow's 2014 Commonwealth Games (www.glasgow2014.com/) (for discussions on bidding for major/mega/hallmark sporting events see Emery, 2002; Westerbeek et al., 2002; Walters, 2011; Foley et al., 2012; Shaw, 2013).

During the 1990s, cities throughout the world were celebrating with events such as the Mumbai International Film Festival, established in 1990 (miffindia.in), Exposition in Seville and Arts Week in Toronto (www.artsweek.ca). Other longer established events such as the Edinburgh Tattoo (www.edintattoo.co.uk), Munich's Oktoberfest (www.munichsoktoberfest.com) and New Orleans Mardi Gras (www.mardigrasneworleans.com) amongst many others, were flourishing. Concomitantly, governments at all levels and across the globe, were realising the vast array of benefits and positive impacts generated by events. Indeed globally, governments were increasing their capital investment in events, which were rapidly becoming '...part of their strategies for economic development, nation building and destination marketing' (Allen et al., 2002:5; Benneworth and Dauncey, 2010). According to Yeoman et al. (2004), events became increasingly important to the public sector due to place promotion, image regeneration and the economic and social multiplier effect. For example, throughout Europe in the 1990s there was an increase in applications to the European Union Structural Funds for a great range of events (Voase, 1994) while in Scotland, events were seen as an important part of the country's strategy for economic development (Lederer cited Yeoman et al., 2004).

Thus, in the first decade of the 21st Century and in all corners of the world, there has been unparalleled interest and participation in events as they continue to demonstrate a capacity to generate positive economic impacts, including increased revenues and employment (Ritchie, 1984; Dwyer et al., 2000; Van de Wagen, 2005). Additionally, events have the capacity to provide various opportunities for positive tourism and commercial outcomes for the host region (Soutar and McLeod, 1993; Alston, 1998, Van de Wagen, 2005). For instance, in 2014, Rio De Janeiro, Brazil hosted the FIFA World Cup (www.fifa.com/worldcup) and will host the Olympic Games in 2016 (www.rio2016.com/en). China was host to the Olympic Games in Beijing (www.olympic.org/beijing-2008-summer-olympics) in 2008 and World Expo in Shanghai (en.expo2010.cn) in 2010 while India hosted the 2010 Commonwealth Games in Delhi (d2010.thecgf.com). The 2018 Commonwealth Games will be held on Gold Coast, Australia (www.gc2018.com).

Events continue to play a central, socio-cultural role in different societies and cultures (Alomes, 1985) and have the capacity to generate positive socio-cultural impacts including the opportunity for communities to not only enhance their image and celebrate place identity, (Wolman and Spitzley, 1996; De Bres and Davis, 2001; Pennington-Gray and Holdnak, 2002) but to also increase community cohesion and arguably, social capital (Arcodia and Whitford, 2006). Indeed, there is increasing recognition of the role that events can play beyond entertainment, with increased focus on culture, arts, regeneration, education, tourism and other strategies (Bowdin et al, 2011). Thus, the ability of an event to not only attract visitors to a host region but also its subsequent contribution to the economic and social well being of a region (Jago and Shaw, 1998), contributes to the importance and significance afforded to events and the event industry around the globe. Therefore governments around the world are increasingly utilising events as vehicles for regional development as they continue to demonstrate a capacity to generate and array of positive outcomes for host regions (Van de Wagen, 2005; Getz, 2007; Whitford, 2009).

The Event Industry

The early years of the 21st Century have seen the event industry become recognised as an industry in its own right rather than as part of the hospitality, leisure, travel and tourism sectors (Bowdin and McPherson, 2006). While events and festivals have always played an important role in the functioning of society, it has only been since the latter half of the 1900s that this role changed as the market became more aware and demanding of a burgeoning, professional event industry (see Getz, 2010; Kim et al., 2013; Mair and Whitford, 2013, for a comprehensive review of event literature). Consequently, the industry became increasingly competitive with the emergence of both private and public event industry organisations and associations, training courses, formal education programmes and accreditation schemes. With an increase in the amount of events activity and the consequent growth in specialist event management companies and suppliers, there was a strong move to classify and standardise the event industry.

Defining and Categorising Events

There have been numerous attempts in the literature to define what constitutes an event (e.g., Shone and Parry 2004; Allen et al., 2005; Getz, 2005; Goldblatt, 2005; Bowdin et al., 2011) with limited consensus on standardised terms, definitions or categories to use (Bowdin and McPherson, 2006; Getz, 2008). According to Goldblatt (1990), in 1954 Robert F. Jani, the first director of public relations at Disneyland described the Main Street Electric Parade as 'a special event'. When Jani was asked for a definition by the media, he said 'I suppose it is that which is different from a normal day of living' (Goldblatt, 1990). In essence then, an event can be broadly defined as something of significance that occurs such as a celebration, an important occurrence or a ceremony or any mutually beneficial activity involving the local population in a shared experience. According to Bowdin and McPherson (2006:1) however, there is limited agreement on standardised terms, definitions or categories of events and they suggest terms used to describe sectors of the events industry, include 'business events, festivals/fairs/ cultural events, community events, outdoor events, entertainment/live music events/concerts/theatre/shows, sports events/spectator sports, charity events/ fundraising/voluntary sector and party planning/wedding planning/social life-cycle events/special events'. In short, events can range from small private or local community gatherings to international spectacles featuring participants and attendees from around the globe.

Many events are categorized as 'special events' which constitute 'a one-time or infrequently occurring event outside the normal program or activities of the sponsoring body' providing 'an opportunity for a leisure, social, or cultural experience outside the normal range of choices or beyond everyday experience (Getz, 1997:4). According to French et al., (cited Jago and Shaw, 1998), the necessity of defining special events is rooted in being able to measure their effects. Standardised definitions are not only important for research purposes and measuring economic activity but also in the planning and management of such events. Yet Getz (2007) maintains it will never be possible to develop an all-encompassing, standardised definition of what constitutes a special event, nor will we be able to classify what it is that makes an event special or exceptional. Rather, Getz (1997) suggests that the context is what makes an event special and attributes that might contribute to the specialness of an event include but are not limited to, uniqueness, quality, authenticity, tradition, hospitality and festive spirit. Another defining characteristic of a special event is its transience (Gilbert and Lizotte, 1998) suggesting that it is difficult to induce and sustain the same sense of occasion and excitement if such an event was to be held more frequently. In essence however, a special event recognises a unique moment in time with ceremony and ritual to satisfy specific needs (Goldblatt, 1997). Not surprisingly, 'special events have become a growth industry' (Allen et al, 2011:12) and are often categorised by their size and content and/or theme.

Event Size

From 1987 onwards, the term 'event tourism', which has become an important segment of international tourism (New Zealand Tourist and Publicity Department 1987; Backman, Backman, Uysal and Sunshine, 1995), is often used to collectively refer to the development of all planned events (Getz, 1989). The term 'event tourism' however, does not provide any means of identifying the size of an event (see Getz, 2008 for a comprehensive discussion on event tourism). Common categories used in relation to the size of events are hallmark events, mega-events, major and minor events.

Hallmark Events

Hallmark events are those events that become so identified with the spirit or ethos of a town, city or region that they become synonymous with the name of the place and gain widespread recognition and awareness (Allen et al, 2008). Hallmark events include Brazil's Rio de Janeiro Carnival (www.rio-carnival. net), Spain's La Tomatina (www.latomatina.org/) or the United Kingdom's Wimbledon (www.wimbledon.com/) all of which are considered to be tourism image makers (Burns and Mules, 1986) providing a competitive advantage for the host destination (Getz, 2005; Van de Wagen and White, 2010). According to Ritchie (1984:2), hallmark events are:

> major one-time or recurring events of limited duration, developed primarily to enhance awareness, appeal and profitability of a tourism destination in the short term and/or long term. Such events rely for their success on uniqueness, status, or timely significance to create interest and attract attention.

Mega Events

Mega-events are the largest type of events (Roche, 2000; Van de Wagen and White, 2010). They usually target an international market, are so large they affect whole economies and are widely covered in the global media. According to Getz (2005:18) mega events '…should exceed 1 million visits, their capital cost should be at least $500 million and their reputation should be that of a 'must see' event'. Moreover, Hall (1992:5) suggests that mega events '… are expressly targeted at the international tourism market …'. For instance, the Superbowl is 'televised to an audience of 800 million and adds US$300 million to the local economy' (Van de Wagen and White, 2010:7). Thus mega-events attract thousands of spectators to the host city and country and the economic impacts are measured in the tens of millions or hundreds of millions of dollars. As hosts to the 2014 FIFA World Cup, Brazil expected 3.7 million people to travel throughout Brazil generating an economic windfall in the vicinity of $3.03 billion to Brazil's economy (Forbes, 2014). Nevertheless, securing mega-events like the FIFA World Cup or the Rugby World Cup (www.rugbyworldcup.com) is both expensive and competitive because of their mass appeal, dramatic character and international significance (Roche, 2000 cited Horne, 2007). Thus mega events have an unprecedented ability to generate high exposure through media coverage that yields significant economic and tourism impacts and international prestige for host communities (Getz, 1997).

Major Events

Major events are those events that, by their scale and media interest, are capable of attracting significant visitor numbers, media coverage and economic benefits. In the competitive global marketplace, governments promote and position themselves to develop events as they have the capacity to stimulate investment, promote employment and contribute to economic development. Thus, major events are often driven by strong economic imperatives such as place promotion, investment attraction and employment generation (Getz, 2007; Jago et al., 2003; Stokes, 2008). For instance, a major event such as the Australian Formula One Grand Prix (www.grandprix.com.au/), attracts national and international media attention (albeit on a smaller scale than a mega event) and provides host cities with an opportunity to showcase their destination's unique qualities (Carlsen, 2002).

Minor Events

Minor events target local audiences in a community or region and are often staged by and/or receive support from, local government. Minor events occur in most cities, towns, villages and are 'owned' by the local community '... because they use volunteer services from the host community, employ public venues such as streets, parks and schools and are produced at the direction of local government agencies or non-government organizations such as service clubs, public safety organizations or business associations' (Janiskee, 1996:404). According to Arcodia and McKinnon (2004), community festivals have become prolific since the late 1990s. The aim of minor events is often to generate sociocultural benefits over and above commercial gain. Minor events can occur across the spectrum of Getz's (2005) typology of planned events.

Types of Events

According to Getz (2005:19-20), 'depending on the purpose and circumstances, events can fall into more than one category'. Getz (2005) identified seven categories of planned events that he maintained could be found in virtually every culture and community including cultural celebrations, business events and sporting events.

Cultural Celebrations

Cultural celebrations can manifest in different ways including festivals, religious events, art and entertainment (among others). Festivals are common forms of cultural celebration (Getz, 2005), as communities often host and/or stage festivals to enhance and preserve culture, tradition and history, promote creativity, increase tourism and rejuvenate community cohesion (Hall, 1992b cited Derrett, 2000). A key characteristic of a festival is the sense of community (Dunstan, 1994) and celebration engendered by an occasion which is a public and freely accessed social gathering (Goldblatt, 1997; Bush, 2000). In *Time Out of Time: Essays on the Festival*, Falassi (1987:2) said a festival is 'a sacred or profane time of celebration marked by special observances'. Thus a festival may occur for:

1   the annual celebration of a notable person or event,

2   the harvest of an important product,

3   performances of works in the fine arts,

4   a single artist or genre,

5   a fair and

6   generic gaiety, conviviality, cheerfulness

(Getz, 1997:8).

Furthermore, a festival may emulate cultural traditions or mark a religious or historical occasion associated with the community staging the festival and provide opportunities for:

1   community entertainment,

2   community service

3   multicultural celebrations,

4   religious celebrations and

5   seasonal and or harvest celebrations

(Arcodia and Robb, 2000).

Importantly, festivals provide unique opportunities for communities to 'showcase their skills and their capabilities and to create a sense of excitement, community pride and cohesiveness' (Lee and Taylor 2005:72). Moreover, in many countries around the globe, major cities have recognised the value of developing and staging festivals as vehicles to not only facilitate the improvement of the quality of life in their communities but also as a means for both redefining the cultural profile of a city and boosting tourism (De Bres and Davis, 2001). Key festivals that act as tourism drawcards often become hallmark events winning fame both for themselves and the relevant city, region or country (i.e., Venice Biennale www.labiennale.org:, Edinburgh International Festival, www.eif. co.uk: Salzburg Festival, www.salzburgerfestspiele.at/en, Melbourne Comedy Festival, www.comedyfestival.com.au) Edinburgh Festiva,l www.eif.co.uk; Carlsen et al., 2007). Although the development of world-class hallmark festivals takes many years and significant investment, festivals have the potential to facilitate the regeneration and/or repositioning of a city as a dynamic, livable cultural oasis with strong appeal to tourists from around the world.

Festivals often focus on cultural aspects of a community and present representations of heritage, life, traditions and ceremony. These are commonly called cultural festivals or events and they can be used by communities and individuals to communicate and practice spiritual and/or religious belief and rituals in a demonstration of cultural identity. Moreover, using cultural events as a medium, communities and individuals can also embrace their cultural purpose and find peace and sanctuary in which to share their stories and experiences amongst themselves and others. Such enriching displays are central to cultural events which can take the form of

1   multi-cultural events, e.g., Festival of World Cultures (Ireland) www. festivalofworldcultures.com/

2   artistic events, e.g., Cannes Film Festival (France) www.festival-cannes.fr

3   indigenous events, e.g., Canadian Aboriginal Festival www.canab.com; Garma Festival (Northern Territory, Australia) www.yyf.com.au; Riddu Riđđu (Sami Festival) www.riddu.no/home.21023.en.htm; Rukai Day (Taiwan) wn.com/rukia; Guelaguetza, (Mexico) www.viveoaxaca.org/p/ guelaguetza-2014.html .

The growth in cultural festivals is arguably attributed to (among other things), the desire of visitors to "do as the locals do" (Litvin and Fetter, 2006). Cultural festivals also focus on community cultural development by providing participants with an opportunity to explore different community values, aspirations and beliefs within a nurturing festival environment (Derrett, 2004). Thus cultural festivals are a manifestation of a cultural phenomenon and help diversify local economies, improve local networks and encourage cooperation and often have goals that foster and promote inclusion, celebration and community development (Gibson et al., 2010). Not only do cultural events present such benefits for the community, but they also provide an outlet for individuals to regain control of their lives, away from the pressures of society.

Cultural festivals have also proved beneficial for Indigenous communities (Ruhanen and Whitford, 2011, 2012, 2014; Whitford and Ruhanen, 2013). Phipps (2010:217) claims "cultural festivals are one of the few consistently positive spaces for indigenous communities to forge and assert a more construct view of themselves". From the perspectives of the community, cultural festivals help to share, celebrate and maintain culture which is fundamental in sustaining Indigenous worlds (Slater, 2010) by enhancing the development of a sense of place and community through connections, support, empowerment, belonging and participation (Derrett, 2003).

"People have always been interested in making sense of their lives and the world in which they live and, it is claimed, have looked to the sacred for meaning" (Blackwell, 2007:36). Consequently, people have in the past and continue to, visit sacred sites and attend religious festivals and events all over the world. One form of this type of travel is called the 'pilgrimage' where large numbers of people gather together at sacred sites (Blackwell, 2007). For instance, hundreds of thousands of people come together for the celebration of Kumbh Mela in India. Similarly, the pilgrimage to Mecca attracts approximately two million attendees from over 100 countries and is considered to be one of the world's largest events of any type (Getz, 2007).

Religious events can also be staged in various ways including parades and processions and/or meetings. For instance, in 2006 at the 5th World Meeting of Families at Valencia, a meeting was chaired by Pope Benedict XVI. There were around 1,500,000 pilgrims from more than 87 different countries with help from nearly 11,000 volunteers (Gallarza et al., 2009). Additionally, the first official World Youth Day (celebrated by the Catholic Church) was held in Rome, Italy in 1986. Since then, twelve World Youth Days have taken place including one in 2013 in Rio De Janeiro, Brazil and one planned to be held in Krakow, Poland in 2016 (worldyouthday.com/). Importantly however, not all religious events are mass gatherings. Many are small community gatherings which are 'purely local and sacred in nature, held by and for the community...' (Getz, 2005:22) and are an integral element of the lifeblood of a community.

Business Events

Similarly, business events or MICE [Meetings, Incentives, Conventions and Exhibitions] have been an integral part of society since the earliest recorded history. The Exhibition Liaison Committee (1995) claimed that merchants displayed their wares at fairs since pre-Biblical times and according to Getz (2005), barter and trade fairs have been traced back to very early times by Waters (1939). In fact, the first North American fairs were held in French Canada in the early 1700's and the present United Kingdom exhibition industry can trace its origin back to the first industrial exhibitions held in London in 1760 and 1791 (Bowdin and McPherson, 2006). The Great Exhibition of 1851 was the first international trade show and proved to be an excellent promotional tool for British industry attracting over 6 million visitors and generating profits of over £180,000 (Exhibition Liaison Committee, 1995). The final British Industries Fair took place in 1957 due to the increasing demand for more specialized events from trade associations and exhibitors (Cartwright, 1995). However in 1928, the Bureau International des Expositions [BIE] set the policies for bidding and staging World Fairs such as Expo 2012 in Yeosu Korea (www.worldexpo2012.com/) and the 2015 World Expo in Milan, Italy (www.expo2015.org/en).

Yet it was not until the early 1970s that the business events sector began to emerge as a major player of the event industry (Fenich, 2012). Events now play a significant role in business as companies have become aware of the marketing value of business events (Jago et al., 2003; Chalip and Costa, 2005), their capacity to promote the image of a host destination (among other things) and their capacity to contribute to the economic wealth of nations worldwide (Davies and Brown, 2000, cited in Allen et al, 2000).

Business events are an extremely lucrative market as the business traveler is considered to be the highest spending visitor (Davidson, 2003, Davidson and Rodgers, 2012) with a capacity to increase destination tourism and recreational activity by 1) mixing business with pleasure through participating in tourism activities whilst at the business event or extending the visit to incorporate pre/ post-tours, 2) being accompanied by guests who participate in leisure activities and 3) returning to the destination for a holiday either alone or with family or friends. For example, direct convention spending in the US in 2007, was US$34.6 billion (Fenich, 2012). Moreover, business events in the US are 'responsible for 15% of all travel related spending, create nearly US$40 billion in tax revenue .... and generate more than 1 million jobs' (Fenich, 2012:11). In short, business delegates create a high economic impact by spending more (in areas including retail, events and local attractions), staying longer and indulging in leisure activities over and above hotel and restaurant expenditure (Clark, 2004 cited McCartney, 2008). Business events therefore, are regarded as an integral component of the tourism industry with links to foreign affairs, science, trade, training, communications and education (Deery et al., 2005).

Not surprisingly then, the international growth of the business events industry is substantial. For instance China's exhibition industry has experienced considerable growth over the past decade (Wang et al., 2014). China and other countries in South East Asia including India and Singapore are investing huge sums in constructing numerous world-class convention and exhibition centres as are Middle Eastern destinations such as Dubai and Bahrain. Another contributing factor to growth in the business events sector is that it has relevance to a wide cross-section of the business community and government. In particular, the significance of business events in creating business legacies (e.g., through research collaboration, innovation, investment) and sociable legacies (e.g., through knowledge expansion, networking and friendship) is increasingly recognised (Small et al., 2011; Foley et al., 2013; Foley et al., 2014). For instance, business events not only generate high yield visitor traffic but also provide important platforms for export promotion, business networking and professional development. Moreover, business events provide employment opportunities and enhance a destination's image with the advantage of reducing the seasonality of tourism (Baum et al., 2009; Bernini, 2009) and cover all industry sectors including medical and scientific research, technology, financial services, education, health, agriculture, transport, environment and social issues. Thus corporate involvement in events has become the norm, with corporate sponsorship integral to the staging of major events (Bowdin et al., 2011) and in particular, sporting events.

Sporting Events

Sporting events have the capacity to provide a multitude of benefits to an array of stakeholders including competitors and event staff (from both outside the region and locally), tourists attracted to the event (either participants or observers) and the local community (including spectators, participants, volunteers, workers) (Ritchie and Adair, 2004; Weed, 2009). Sporting events can vary in size, style and purpose and each come with their own set of benefits and costs but generally they range through the broad categories of mega events, hallmark events, major events, festivals and smaller events (Chalip, 2006). Overall, both large and smaller sport events have demonstrated that they can generate significant economic activity within the local region, particularly if the event can create interest or attract attention as a result of its uniqueness, status or timely significance (Ritchie, 1984; Downey, 1993; Gamage and Higgs, 1996; Gratton et al., 2000; Saayman and Saayman, 2012).

Sports mega-events however, have been defined as the leisure industry 'supernovas' (Roberts, 2004 cited Horne, 2007:82) as they provide opportunities for cities to reposition themselves within the international arena, gaining world class status as a tourist destination and increasing visitor growth within the host region (Stevens and Wootton, 1997; Cushman, 2002; Green et al., 2003; Masterman, 2004; Chalip and Costa, 2005, 2006; Deery and Jago, 2005; Kim and Morrison, 2005; Miline et al., 2005; Hennessey et al., 2008; Papadimitrou and Gibson, 2008; Henderson et al., 2010; Ziakas and Costa, 2011). There is little argument that large sporting events can generate significant numbers of visitors, both in the immediate short term and over the long term as a result of increased destination awareness. For example, Olympic Games have consistently demonstrated the power of a mega sporting event to bring increased profile and economic benefits to the host city (Hede, 2006; Dansero and Puttilli, 2010). Not surprisingly then, there is fierce competition between governments around the world to bid for and secure mega sporting events (e.g., Olympic Games or FIFA World Cup, see Heijman and Jongenburger, 2011, NFL Super Bowl) as they are increasingly being employed as a means of facilitating tourism growth in the host destination and providing the host community with other things including positive socio-economic impacts (Graham et al., 1995; Andersson and

Solberg, 1999; Schulenkorf et al., 2011). Over and above the short and medium-term impacts (i.e., long-term impacts across economic, social and environmental dimensions) sports events' legacies are also frequently promoted by public policy planners and event organisers to justify the costs associated with hosting these events (Thomson et al., 2013).

While some researchers argued that strategic social planning of events is scant and too often focused on sport events (Kellett et al., 2008; Schulenkorf, 2010; Williams and Elkhashab, 2012; Ziakas and Boukas, 2012), according to McPherson Curtis and Loy (1989), large sporting events have emerged as a significant social phenomenon and contribute to community pride and well-being (Coaffee and Shaw, 2005). Similarly though, smaller sporting events also have the capacity to provide an opportunistic avenue for economic dispersion and social community engagement (Miline et al., 2005 cited Fredline et al., 2005). Consequently sports events, both large or small in size have always and will undoubtedly continue to, represent a significant element of the event industry generating both positive and negative impacts on the host community.

Research in the Field of Events

Until the 1990s, there was a paucity of literature focusing on events and event management in particular. The small cache of studies that had been undertaken up to the early 1980s predominantly focused on economic issues, affording little to no attention on the social-psychological context of events (Formica, 1998). Indeed, the main identified areas of research pertaining to events, according to Formica (1998) and Getz (2010) were economic and financial impacts, marketing, profiles of festival or events, sponsorship, management, trends and forecasts.

From the 1980s onwards, the event industry became an increasingly significant player on the global stage. Concurrently, the body of research focusing on the diverse range of issues associated with events and the event industry also began to grow exponentially (see Getz, 2009, Mair and Whitford, 2013 and Quinn, 2013 for a comprehensive review of research agendas in events), Nevertheless in the early 2000s, events as a field of study was still a nascent field of study (Getz, 2009).

Economic focus of research

According to Quinn (2013), the event research agenda has focused heavily on economic development and the economic impacts of events. Indeed, a primary driver of early research output in the field of event management can be attributed to academic interest in examining the extent to which events facilitate economic growth (e.g., see Gartner and Holecek, 1983; Lynch and Jensen, 1984; Ritchie, 1984; Centre for Applied and Business Research, 1986; Burns et al., 1986; Burns, 1987; Hall, 1987, 1992; Burgan and Mules, 1992; McCloud and Syme, 1987). From the 1990s onwards, research from around the globe emerged focusing on economic issues including forecasting, assessing and evaluating economic impacts (see Long and Perdue, 1990; Getz 1991, 1994, 1997, 2007, 2009; Faulkner, 1993; Hinch and Delamere, 1993; Soutar and McLeod, 1993; Crompton and McKay, 1994; Mules and McDonald, 1994; Uysal and Gitelson, 1994; Walo, Bull and Green, 1996; Hiller, 1998; Kim et al., 1998; Andersson et al., 1999; Dwyer et al., 1999; Burgan and Mules, 2000; Dwyer et al., 2000; Carlsen et al., 2001; Thrane, 2002; Dwyer et al., 2004, 2005; Gursoy et al., 2004; Lee and Taylor, 2005; Jago and Dwyer, 2006; Gil and de Esteban Curiel, 2008; McCartney, 2008; Felenstein and Fleischer, 2009; Flyvbjerg and Stewart, 2012; Ramchandani and Coleman, 2012; Davies et al., 2013).

Thus the economic impact of events has been and continues to be a focus of research and although some studies claim that many purported positive economic impacts are best considered as estimates only (Hiller, 1998; Davis et al., 2013), there has been little argument that events have the capacity to generate, to varying degrees, positive economic benefits for a range of stakeholders (Long and Perdue, 1990). For instance, studies found events provide opportunities for tourism and positive commercial outcomes and thus have the potential to boost the economy in local regions (Soutar and McLeod, 1993; Alston, 1998; Hanly, 2012). In turn, this may bring about increased revenue, employment, business opportunities (Ritchie, 1984; Soutar and McLeod, 1993; Alston, 1998; Dwyer et al, 2000), the development of new infrastructure and increased indirect financial inflows from, among other things, visitors' expenditure (Anderson and Solberg, 1999). Consequently, events are increasingly being utilised as vehicles for economic development and such positive economic benefits are often used to justify the economic costs of an event (Burgan and Mules, 2000). It is not only these positive economic impacts, but also the negative economic impacts of events such as inflated prices, residents' exoduses and interruption of normal business (Dwyer et al., 2000), inflated return on investment (Getz, 2007) leakages associated with imported goods and services (Faulkner, 1993), opportunity costs (Dwyer et al, 2000) and congestion and strains on local facilities that appear to have generated the greatest interest among researchers to date.

Wood, Robinson and Thomas, (2005) reiterated the argument that at the outset, applied research focusing on economic rather than socio-cultural benefits was prevalent and dominated the event management research agenda. Indeed, compared to the body of research concerned with the social impacts of tourism, Fredline and Faulkner (2000, p. 764) noted that 'relatively little progress has been made on social impacts specifically associated with events.' This could be attributed to a significant proportion of academics researching in the field of event management being located in business and/or management departments/faculties (Dredge and Whitford, 2010). If this trend continues, the economic focus of events will undoubtedly continue to receive attention from researchers (see Jago and Dwyer, 2006; Dwyer et al. 2006) however, with the launch of new event focused journals and event study programs around the globe (Getz, 2007) and an increasing focus on the sustainability of events, we are beginning to witness increasing interest in a broader array of issues pertaining to events and event management. Therefore instead of relying on assessing the direct economic contributions of an event to determine the success (or not) of the event, studies are heeding the early warnings of Dwyer et al., (2000) and are also examining the positive and negative impacts associated with the socio-cultural, physical and political environments of an event.

Socio-cultural focus of research

During the 1980s and 1990s then, there was not a large body of work relating to the socio-cultural environment of events (see DaMatta, 1984; Falassi, 1987; Hall, 1992; Earls, 1993; Hinch and Delamere, 1993; Soutar and McLeod, 1993; Baum et al, 2009). Additionally, according to Mair and Whitford (2013), studies were undertaken on sport, business and cultural events (among others), which have been underpinned by a 'variety of disciplines (sport and event management, anthropology, tourism or leisure studies, regional planning, etc.). These studies demonstrate in each case, that events are occasions for (re)affirming or contesting the social order (Handelman, 1990; Holland and Skinner, 1995), building group and place identity (Green and Chalip, 1998) and fostering social networks (Fortes, 1936; Walter, 1981; Kemp, 1999).

It was not until the early 2000s that a growing number of researchers began focusing their attention on a variety of issues relating to the social impacts of events (Burgan and Mules, 2000; Dwyer et al., 2000; Fredline and Faulkner, 2000; Roche, 2000; De Bres and Davis, 2001; Delamere, 2001; Delamere et al., 2001; Burbank et al., 2001; Deccio and Baloglu, 2002; Fredline et al., 2003; Kim and Uysal, 2003; Waitt, 2003; Xie, 2003; Gursoy et. al, 2004; Richards and Ryan, 2004; Sims and D'Mello, 2005; Bob et al., 2005; Wood, 2006; Arcodia and Whitford, 2006; Butler and Hinch, 2007; Carlsen et al., 2007; Petterson and Viken, 2007; Small, 2007; Collins et al., 2009; Baumann et al., 2009; Robertson et al., 2009; Deery and Jago, 2010; Schulenkorf, 2010; Balduck et al., 2011; Rogers and Anastasiadou, 2011). In particular, Hall, (1992), Earls (1993), Soutar and McLeod (1993) and Fredline and Faulkner (2000) found the staging of an event could impact the social life and structure of a community by either enhancing or detracting from the social environment of the region. For instance, Earls, (1993:32) found that events have the capacity to enrich community well-being by providing opportunities 'to break away from daily routines' and socialize 'with family and friends within the larger community'. Moreover, events were found to enhance community cohesiveness and cooperation and present opportunities to raise a destination's cultural profile abroad (Williams and Elkhashab, 2012; Jamieson, 2014). Importantly, such positive impacts are often used to offset the negative impacts which include disruption to resident lifestyles, traffic congestion, vandalism, overcrowding, crime (Dwyer et al., 2000) and commercialisation and commodification of culture (Butler and Hinch, 2007). Commodification occurs when 'cultural and relational expressions are transformed to commodities in a market' resulting in loss of content which in turn is 'assessed on the basis of economic values and values of actors external to the culture' (Petterson and Viken, 2007:185). Often, commodification of culture is brought about by over-enthusiastic attempts to increase economic capital over and above social capital which, according to Arcodia and Whitford (2006), Misener and Mason (2006a, 2006b) and Schulenkorf et al. (2011) is generated by events and can help develop and weave the cultural and artistic fabric of the society. Moreover, events have been found to have the capacity to influence social renewal (Essex and Chalkley, 1998; Smith and Fox, 2007; Hiller, 2006; Minnaert, 2011), facilitate community development (Carlsen and Taylor, 2003; Arcodia and Whitford, 2006; Chalip, 2006; Misener and Mason, 2006a; Picard and Robinson, 2006; Schulenkorf, 2009), build group and place identity (Green and Chalip, 1998; De Bres and Davis, 2001) and facilitate urban regeneration (Harcup, 2000; Hiller, 2000; Gratton and Henry, 2001).

Other emerging research and theoretical themes during the 2000s include (but are not limited to) a focus on the host community and in particular, motivation and perception of event participants and tourists and residents' perceptions of and attitudes towards events (Soutar and McLeod, 1993; Backman et al., 1995; Jeong and Faulkner, 1996; Mihalik and Simonetta, 1998; Fredline and Faulkner, 1998, 2000, 2002a, 2002b; Delamere 1997, 2001; Delamere et al. 2001; Fredline et al. 2003, 2005; Cegielski and Mules 2002; Xiao and Smith 2004; Ohmann et al., 2006; Gursoy and Kendall 2006; Fredline 2006; Monga, 2006; Yuan and Jang 2008; Boo, Wang, Yu, 2011; Pauline 2011; Wysong et al., 2011; Hixson et al., 2011; Son et al., 2011; Van Winkle and Woosnam, 2014; Wang et al., 2014). Thus while research has uncovered that events can be utilised as vehicles for social development and accomplish a range of effects (Moscardo, 2008; Gibson and Connell, 2011) the planning, management and evaluation of not only the social and economic aspects of events have been investigated but also the environmental aspects of events (Hede, 2008).

Environmental focus of research

Research focusing on environmental issues associated with events gained momentum at the turn of the 21st century. Sherwood (2007) maintained that in the early 2000s, May (1995) and Harris and Huyskens (2002) were the only two published papers that dealt with the environmental impacts of events. Increasingly however, there has been a growing number of studies investigating the impact of events on the physical attributes of a host destination, which may often be environmentally fragile and require specific policy to ensure protection against negative impacts including environmental damage, noise and overcrowding, especially from a local population standpoint (Rupf-Haller and Oberholzer, 2005; Dávid, 2009). Conversely, events can help bring about enhanced quality of life and urban renewal in a neighbourhood through increased tourism infrastructure and the construction or redevelopment of venues. Moreover, events can also raise public awareness of environmental issues through the participation of environmental organizations and government support. Not surprisingly then, there is a cluster of literature focusing on the greening of events (e.g., Collins and Flynn, 2008; Raj and Musgrave, 2009; Mair and Jago, 2010; Goldblatt and Goldblatt, 2011) and associated issues pertaining to the adoption of environmentally-friendly practices and the management processes necessary to accomplish waste reduction and the event's overall ecological footprint (Block, 2008; Ponsford, 2011). Endorsed by the rise in the environmental protection movement is the prevalence of sustainably responsible initiatives embedded within festivals and events, termed as 'green events' (Getz, 2009; Goldblatt, 2011; Rittichainuwat and Mair, 2012; Strick and Fenich, 2013). These actions highlight the measures event organisers are taking to preserve the environment for future generations, to promote environmental education and to facilitate increased corporate social responsibility (see *The Cape Town Declaration on Responsible Tourism in Destinations* which is a register of responsible ethics that events should adopt) (Fabricius and Goodwin, 2002). It is within this context that the notion of developing a 'sustainable' event has gained traction (Hede, 2008).

Sustainable focus of research

Given the increased interest in sustainable tourism development since the early 1980s, it is not surprising that there has been growing interest in sustainability issues within the event management literature (Sofield and Li, 1998; Getz, 2000; Bramwell and Alletorp, 2001; McKercher et al., 2006; Quinn, 2006; Sherwood, 2007; Getz and Andersson, 2008; Hede, 2008; Raj and Musgrave 2009; Mair, Jago, 2010; Mair, 2011; Tinnish and Mangal, 2012; Sox et al., 2013; and see the *Special Issue on Sustainability in the Event Management Sector* in *Event Management*, **15**(4), 2011).

There is a diverse range of literature pertaining to events and issues of sustainability. Dredge and Whitford (cited Mair and Whitford, 2013:11), have succinctly organised these issues into the following strands:

1 explanatory research that acknowledges the socio-cultural and political dimensions of sustainability, exploring dimensions such as stakeholder relationships (Dickson and Arcodia, 2010; Dredge and Whitford, 2010)

2 research that describes how planning and management of sustainable events should occur (Musgrave and Raj, 2009; Grattion et al. , 2011; Reid, 2011; Smith-Christensen, 2009)

3 procedural research that describes sustainable events planning processes, identifying its dimensions and providing directions on what needs to be considered (e.g. Getz, 2007; 2009; Ensor et al. , 2011; Lawton, 2011; Merrilees and Marles, 2011; Ziakas and Boukas, 2012; Jones 2014) and

4 implementation and evaluation research that focuses on identifying sustainable indicators and approaches for evaluating the sustainability of events (e.g. Hede, 2008).

Policy and political research focus

Getz (2009) advocated the need to institutionalise the principles of sustainability in event policy and called for a sustainable triple bottom line events policy paradigm shift. Concomitantly, Getz (2009:62) maintained 'policy research in the events field is underdeveloped and has not proceeded systematically'. Indeed, Hall and Rusher (2004, p. 229) claimed that 'there still remains relatively little analysis of the political context of events and the means by which events come to be developed and hosted within communities'.

The importance of studies examining political environments of events should not be underestimated. For instance at the local level, Jeong and Santos (2004, cited in Quinn 2013: 101) suggest that 'festivals [and events] enable invisible webs of local power networks to be made visible' while at a macro level, governments around the globe use events as a platform for industry and economic development, justifying event-related expenditure in terms of the positive economic impacts that the event brings to their host region (Burgan and Mules, 2000).

There is a small body of work that investigates issues pertaining to the power and politics of events and relationships between governments, event organisers and communities (see Gnoth and Anwar, 2000; Jeong and Santos, 2004; Shin, 2004; Getz, 2007, 2009; O'Sullivan et al., 2009; Dredge and Whitford, 2010; Clarke and Jepson, 2011; Ziakas and Costa, 2012). Moreover, there is limited research that examines governance issues and/or special legislation for events, the rationale for its use and the consequences of using such approaches (see e.g., Dredge et al., 2010; Dredge and Whitford, 2011). Rather, research has tended to focus on other areas including management issues (Ritchie and Beliveau, 1974; Walle, 1994; Getz, 1997; 2005; Goldblatt, 1997; Getz and Frisby, 1988; Jago et al., 2003; Green and Chalip, 2004; Hemingway and Maclagan, 2004; Hede, 2008; Swart and Bob, 2007; Stokes, 2008; Xing and Chalip, 2009; Gibson et al., 2010; Ziakas and Costa, 2011) and more specifically, festival management (Frisby and Getz, 1989; Janiskee, 1994; Janiskee, 1996; Getz, 2002; Andersson and Getz, 2009; Jaeger and Mykletun, 2009; Getz et al., 2010), destination management (Prentice and Anderson, 2003; Hede and Jago, 2005; Kim and Morrison 2005; Monga, 2006), stakeholders (Getz et al., 2007; Getz and Andersson, 2008; Andersson and Getz, 2009; Karlsen and Nordström, 2009) and marketing (Formica and Uysal, 1996, 1998; Faulkner et al., 1999; Nicholson and Pearce, 2001; Green et al., 2003; Jago et al., 2003; Pavicic et al., 2007; Crowther, 2011; Drengner et al., 2011) of festivals and events.

There is however, a body of research exploring the roles of government, state institutions, agencies and policy networks (e.g., see Weed 2003; 2006; Pugh and Wood 2004; Thomas and Wood 2004; Whitford, 2004a, 2004b; Getz and Andersson, 2008; Whitford, 2009). Additionally, there are studies examining policy and public sector involvement in events including Ali-Knight and Robertson (2004), Whitford (2005) and Stokes and Jago (2007) while other studies examine the politics of place marketing and/or event policy and regional development (O'Sullivan and Jackson, 2002; Shin, 2004; Reid, 2006; Whitford, 2009; Foley et al., 2012; Khodr, 2012). More recently, Dredge et al. (2010) examined the complicated issues characterising the hosting of an international car rally, which involved not only the host community and private sector but also many government levels. In general, this research builds understandings about the way that event policy is made and implemented, the characteristics, interests and values of stakeholders within the policy making process. Arguably however, studies relating to the political dimensions of events generally do not focus on addressing how to frame, prepare and implement event policy. Dredge and Whitford (2010) claim that event policy research should incorporate socio-political interpretations of event policy problems as well as research that focuses on what should or could be done.

According to this argument then, the political environment of events remains under researched, despite increasing criticism of governments' approach to and development of events (Gamage and Higgs, 1996; Dredge et al, 2010). Much of this criticism is derived from governments' zealous pursuit of and emphasis on, economic development objectives in contrast to socio-cultural and environmental objectives and the increased use of statutory corporations and private companies which increasingly blur lines between public and private interests and serve to distance government from direct responsibility for negative impacts and failures (Stokes and Jago, 2007; Dredge and Whitford, 2011; Foley et al., 2012). Despite these criticisms, governments continue to promote the benefits of events and in the process, often become embroiled in highly politicised battles, which arguably, are predominantly driven by ideology (see e.g., Phi, Dredge and Whitford, 2014). In the future, Getz (2007:391) suggests to 'watch for more ideological interest being taken in planned events' as governments continue to debate public sector involvement in the event industry.

Future Trends and Issues in Event Management

Investigating the drivers and inhibitors relating to why governments do, or do not continue to support events and the event industry is undoubtedly, one of the many areas that researchers will examine in the ensuing years as event management research matures and becomes increasingly broader (Getz, 2008). Indeed, it is imperative that event research is extended well beyond the prevailing concentration on relatively confined economic and business dominated perspectives that focus on management and marketing concerns, economic impacts assessment and the planning and design of festivals and events (Carlsen et al., 2008; Getz, 2009). Arguably though, there is a shift towards the investigation and incorporation of alternative perspectives that will provide the event industry with the knowledge and tools to continue successful development of the events industry by avoiding mistakes made in the past and confidently embracing the future with a greater and more nuanced understanding of the phenomenon known as events (Getz, 2012; Baum, Lockstone-Binney and Robertson, 2013). Key economic, socio-cultural, environmental, political and management trends and issues that could shape the future environment of events and the event industry include:

Economic Issues

The ongoing global competitiveness of tourism destinations is likely to lead to continued use of large events to enhance the image and positioning of cities and regions. As a result of increasing competition for large (i.e. mega/major) events and despite many international federations and associations significantly raising hosting fees, there appears to be no shortage of cities bidding for mega/major events. This trend is likely to continue as more countries seek the economic and media profiling benefits that mega/major events can bring (e.g., increased media coverage and involvement in events with increased opportunities for event television product due to the expansion of technologies). Importantly however, increasing competition and increasing costs coupled with the repercussions from the Global Financial Crisis undoubtedly endorses the need for more justifiable economic impact assessments of events than have been seen in the past (Lee and Goldblatt, 2012)

Socio-cultural Trends and Issues

Increased value is being placed on maintaining a host destination's social, cultural, natural and built resources. Determining the value or worth of events from a multi-stakeholder perspective should be a priority (Getz, 2010) therefore progress can be made in gaining a deeper and more comprehensive understanding of the conditions necessary for generating desired social and cultural impacts.

Environmental Trends and Issues

The impact of climate change on events will require the event industry to underpin proactive development of event policy and planning with a 'green' approach in order to find new ways of reducing the environmental impacts of events (Mair, 2011; Merrilees and Marles, 2011). Consequently, there is increased interest in the sustainability of events (Raj and Musgrave, 2009) and hence there is a growing trend to adopt a more balanced, triple bottom line approach for the evaluation of events. Increasingly, events are being examined in the context of sustainability and corporate social responsibility (Whitfield and Dioko, 2011). According to Getz (2010), a top priority should be to make advances in the triple bottom line approach to valuing events and assessing their outcomes.

Political Trends and Issues

There is an increased need for greater national/local leadership in event policy and strategic planning. Significant investment from government will continue to be important to maintain and grow event portfolios. Thus, there is a need for sustainable and responsible event policy frameworks and within the event literature, the absence of critical debate about governance, its influence on how the role of government is constituted and its impacts on public interest, democracy and transparency, are blind spots in the theoretical landscape (e.g., Dredge and Pforr 2008; Dredge and Whitford 2012; Ziakas and Boukas, 2012). Therefore Dredge and Whitford (2010) called for the liberation of event policy narrative from what they perceive to be a normative orientation that has tended to discard more nuanced understandings about the role of government, politics and power in events policy. Similarly, Getz (2012) advocated for interdisciplinary theory building which situated event impacts in the public and political discourse.

Management Trends and Issues

The recognition of the value of business events as an effective means of communication has bought about significant international growth in both the number of business events held and the number of delegates attending business events worldwide. The exhibition industry in particular, is a highly competitive sector of the event industry and satisfying, attracting and retaining the customers have become major challenges (Fenich, 2012). Therefore there is a need for future studies to investigate the drivers and constraints on consumer behaviour (Getz, 2010) and arguably, a stronger understanding of the role that Customer Relationship Marketing plays in the management and marketing of events (see Wang et al, 2013).

Events in Developing Economies

Quinn (2013, p. 23) has drawn our attention to the Western bias in event research, despite the fact that the bidding and hosting of major and mega-events is no longer only the privilege of developed countries (i.e., Rio De Janeiro won the bid for staging the Rugby World Cup in 2014 and the Olympic Games in 2016). Future studies then, should include investigations focusing on the different utilisation of events in the developed and developing world. For instance, while events are used as vehicles to enhance economic development and social integration in the developed world, they are also regarded as an important means of overcoming poverty and consolidating democratic rule in developing countries (Torche and Valenzuela, 2011; Quinn, 2013). Additionally, research exploring the role and impacts of events in developing economies (Jones, 2012; Weber and Ali-Knight, 2012) and indigenous communities (Whitford, 2009; Whitford and Ruhanen, 2013; Ruhanen and Whitford, 2011, 2012, 2014) is also gaining momentum.

It is important to note here that the latter is not an exhaustive list of trends and issues that may impinge upon event management in future years (Mair and Whitford, 2013). Other issues for consideration include but are not limited to:

- The impact of the Global Financial Crisis, globalization and cost pressures on the event industry (see e.g. Devine and Devine, 2012; Lee and Goldblatt, 2012).
- Increased concern throughout the event industry for safety and security (see e.g. Leopkey and Parent, 2009; Reid and Ritchie, 2011).
- Effects on events from natural and manmade disasters (e.g. Mair, 2011).
- The implications and impacts of 'green' standards (e.g. Green certifications and ecolabels) and occupational standards (e.g. the Meeting

and Business Event Competency Standards) specifically developed for the meeting and business events industry (Cecil, Fenich and Krugman and Hashimoto 2013; Strick and Fenich, 2013; Fenich, 2014).

♦ The consequence of increased use of and reliance upon, technology in event planning and management (e.g., Davidson, 2011; Hudson and Hudson, 2013; Severt, Fjelstul and Breiter, 2013).

Conclusion

Events have been a fundamental feature of society from the beginning of mankind, yet the worldwide boom of the event industry occurred more recently, towards the end of the 20th century. The escalation of events and the growth of the event industry across the globe has been driven, to a large extent, by neoliberal political agendas, influenced largely by expectations of positive economic impacts. More specifically, it was during the late 1980s and early 2000s that events became a popular vehicle for regional development, seemingly providing destinations and regions with a plethora of benefits including increased economic receipts and opportunities for destination branding and image enhancement (among others). While they are regularly mooted to generate significant economic benefits, there has been increasing attention given to identifying the negative impacts of events and designing strategies to mitigate them. For instance, researchers including Dwyer et al (2000) and Getz (2009) have warned against the inaccuracies of various types of economic impact assessments and suggest the need to take a more balanced assessment of the economic benefits of events.

Importantly, events should not be seen as quick fix economic development tools. Nor should they be regarded as a panacea to societies' socio-cultural and/ or environmental quandaries or as vehicles for political grandstanding. Ideally, events should be developed as sustainable options for the facilitation of economic benefits and concomitantly, the generation of an array of socio-cultural and environmental benefits.

As event industry continues to develop and we continue to witness increasing interest in and awareness of, the eclectic utility of events, we should keep in mind that the event industry does not exist in a vacuum removed from exogenous challenges emanating from, but not limited to, economic conditions (e.g., global economic crisis), the physical environment (e.g., climate change) and technology (e.g., marketing and social media). Arguably, a driver of a growing range of comprehensive and more critical event research (which is being undertaken and which is utilising multidisciplinary approaches to understand much broader foci), can be attribute to interest in better understanding the volatility of the environment events operate in, the complexity of the industry and the multifarious challenges the event industry must overcome in order to flourish in the ensuing years.

In 2000, Goldblatt (2000:2) warned that the event field had become '...a rudderless ship subject to the winds of change but unable to correct its course to reach a safe harbor' due to a lack of proactive and strategic planning. Arguably, a decade later, 'event management has shifted from being a field of dedicated and resourceful amateurs to being one of trained and skilled professionals' (Allen et al, 2011: xvii), largely as a result of a maturing event industry which is recognising the need for a proactive, strategic approach to the growth and development of events. The increased awareness in industry has been fuelled, not only by global competition but also by a growing body of research that continually identifies, explores and addresses a multitude of issues and challenges facing the competitive and dynamic global event industry and is facilitating greater knowledge and understanding of event management in the first quarter of the 21st Century.

References

Ali-Knight, J. and Robertson, M. (2004). Introduction to arts, culture and leisure in Festival and events management: an international arts and culture perspective. In I. Yeoman, M. Robertson, J. Ali-Knight, U. McMahon-Beattie and S. Drummond (eds), *Festival and Events Management: An international arts and culture perspective*. Oxford: Butterworth Heinemann.

Allen, J., O'Toole, W., McDonnell, I. and Harris, R. (2002). *Festival and Special Event Management*. Milton, Australia: John Wiley and Sons Australia.

Allen, J., O'Toole, W., McDonnell, I., Harris, R., (2005). *Festival and Special Event Management*. Brisbane: John Wiley and Sons.

Allen, J., O'Toole, W., McDonnell, I. and Harris, R. (2008). *Festival and Special Event Management* (4th edn). Brisbane: John Wiley and Sons Australia.

Allen, J., O'Toole, W., Harris, R. and McDonnell, I. (2011). *Festival and Special Event Management* (5th edn). Brisbane: John Wiley and Sons Australia.

Alomes, S. (2001). The political uses of international sport: Tunisian soccer and Olympic and pre-Olympic Australia. Sporting Traditions: *Journal of the Australian Society for Sports History*, **2**(May), 33-47.

Alston, R. (1998). Playing, visions, festivals: Remarks by Senator Richard Alston. Retrieved from www.search.aph.gov.au/search/Parlinfo. ASP?action=viewand item=0and resultsID=66JKJ

Anderson, T. D. and Solberg, H. A. (1999). Leisure events and regional economic impact. *World Leisure and Recreation*, **41**(1), 20-28.

Andersson, A., Persson, C., Sahlberg, B. and Strom, L. (1999). *The Impact of mega events*. Ostersund, Sweden: European Tourism Research Institute.

Andersson, T. and Getz, D. (2008). Stakeholder management strategies of festivals. *Journal of Convention and Event Tourism*, **9**(3), 199 – 220.

Andersson, T. and Getz, D. (2009). Tourism as a mixed industry: Differences between private, public and not-for-profit festivals. *Tourism Management*, **30**, 847-856.

Arcodia, C. and McKinnon, S. (2005). Public liability insurance: Its impact on Australian rural festivals. *Journal of Convention & Event Tourism*, **6**(3), 101-110

Arcodia, C. and Robb, A. (2000). *A taxonomy of event management terms*. Paper presented at Events Beyond 2000: Setting the Agenda. Proceedings of Conference on Event Evaluation, Research and Education. Sydney: Australian Centre for Event Management.

Arcodia, C.,and Whitford, M. (2006). Festival attendance and the development of social capital. *Journal of Convention and Event Tourism*, **8**(2), 1-18.

Backman, K. F., Backman, S. J., Uysal, M. and Sunshine, K. M. (1995). Event tourism: An examination of motivations and activities. *Festival Management and Event Tourism*, **3**(1), 15–24.

Balduck, A., Maes, M. and Buelens, M. (2011). The social impact of the Tour de France: Comparisons of residents' pre- and post-event perceptions. *European Sport Management Quarterly*, **11**, 91-113.

Barker, M., Page, S. and Meyer, D. (2003). Urban visitor perceptions of safety during a special event. *Journal of Travel Research*, **41**(4), 355–361.

Baum, T., Deery, M., Hanlon, C., Lockstone, L. and Smith, K. (Eds.). (2009). *People and Work in Events and Conventions*. Wallingford: CABI.

Baum, T., Lockstone-Binney, L. and Robertson, M. (2013). Event studies: finding fool's gold at the rainbow's end? *International Journal of Event and Festival Management*, **4**(3), 179-185.

Baumann, R. W., Matheson, V. A. and Muroi, C. (2009). Bowling in Hawaii: Examining the effectiveness of sports-based tourism strategies. *Journal of Sports Economics*, **10**(1), 107-123.

Benneworth, P. and Dauncey, H. (2010). International urban festivals as a catalyst for governance capacity building. *Environment and planning. C, Government and policy*, **28**(6), 1083.

Bernini, C. (2009). Convention industry and destination clusters: Evidence from Italy. *Tourism Management*, **30**, 879–889.

Blackwell, R. (2007). Motivations for religious tourism, pilgrimage, festivals and events (35-47). In R. Raj and N.D. Morpeth (Eds) *Religious Tourism and Pilgrimage Festivals Management: An International Perspective*. Wallingford: CABI.

Block, D. (2008). The Green Continent. *Successful Meetings, 57*(12), 52-58.

Bob, U., Swart, K. and Moodley, V. (2005). *Evaluating socio-economic impacts of sport tourism events: Case studies from Durban, South Africa.* Paper presented at The Impacts of Events Conference 2005, UTS Australian Centre for Event Management.

Boo, S., Wang, Q. and Yu, L. (2011). Residents' support of mega-events: A re-examination. *Event Management, 15*(3), 215-232.

Bourdieu, P. (1984). *Distinction: A social critique of the judgement of taste.* London: Routledge.

Bowdin, G. and McPherson, G. (2006). *Identifying and analysing existing research undertaken in the events industry: A literature review for People 1ˢᵗ.* Leeds, UK: Association for Events Management Education (AEME).

Bowdin, G., Allen, J., O'Toole, W., Harris, R. and McDonnell, I. (2011). *Events Management.* Oxford: Butterworth-Heineman.

Bramwell, B. and Alletorp, L. (2001). Attitudes in the Danish tourism industry to the roles of business and government in sustainable tourism. *International Journal of Tourism Research, 3*, 91-103.

Burbank, M.J. andranovich, G. and Heying, C.H. (2001). *Olympic dreams: The impact of mega-events on local politics.* Boulder, CO: Lynne Rienner.

Burgan, B. and Mules, T. (1992). Economic impact of sporting events. *Annals of Tourism Research, 19*(4), 700–710.

Burgan, B. and Mules, T. (2000). *Event analysis: Understanding the divide between cost benefit and economic impact assessment.* In Events Beyond 2000: Setting the Agenda. Proceedings of Conference on Event Evaluation, Research and Education. Sydney. July, pp. 46-51.

Burns, J. P. A. (1987). Analysing special events with illustrations from the 1985 Adelaide Grand Prix. Papers of the Australian Travel Research Workshop: The impact and marketing of Special Events, Australian Standing Committee on Tourism, Mt Buffalo, pp. 1-14.

Burns, J. and Mules, T. (1986). An economic evaluation of the Adelaide Grand Prix. in Syme, G. (ed.) *The Planning and Evaluation of Hallmark Events,* 172-185.

Burns, J., Hatch, J. and Mules, T. (1986). *The Adelaide Grand Prix: The impact of a special event.* Adelaide: The Centre for South Australian Economic Studies.

Bush, J. (2000). *The Granite State Consumer, Strengthening the Sense of Community.* University of New Hampshire.

Butler, R. and Hinch, T. (Eds.). (2007). *Tourism and Indigenous peoples: Issues and implications.* Oxford: Butterworth-Heinemann.

Carlsen, J. (2000). Events industry accreditation in Australia. *Event Management, 6*(2), 117–121.

Carlsen, J. and Taylor, A. (2003). Mega-events and urban renewal: The case of the Manchester 2002 Commonwealth Games. *Event Management*, **8**, 15-22.

Carlsen, J., Ali-Knight, J. and Robertson, M. (2008). Access – A research agenda for Edinburgh festivals. *Event Management*, **11**, 3-11.

Carlsen, J., Getz, D and Soutar, G. (2001). Event evaluation research. *Event Management*, **6**, 247–257.

Cartwright, G. (1995). *Making the most of trade exhibitions*. Oxford: Butterworth-Heinemann.

Cecil, A., Fenich, G.G., Krugman, C. and Hashimoto, K. (2013). Review and analysis of the new international meeting and business events competency standards. *Journal of Convention and Event Tourism*, **14**(1), 65-74.

Cegielski, M. and Mules, T. (2002). Aspects of residents' perceptions of the GMC 400 – Canberra's V8 Supercar Race. *Current Issues in Tourism*, **5**(1), 54-70.

Centre for Applied and Business Research, (1986). *America's Cup: Economic Impact*. Perth: CABR.

Chalip, L. (2006). Towards social leverage of sport events. *Journal of Sport and Tourism*, **11**, 109-127.

Chalip, L. and Costa, C. A. (2005). Sport event tourism and the destination brand: Towards a general theory. *Sport in Society*, **8**, 218 -237.

Clarke, A. and Jepson, A. (2011). Power and hegemony within a community festival. *International Journal of Event and Festival Management,* **2**(1), 7-19.

Coaffee, J. and Shaw, T. (2005). The liveability agenda: New regionalism, liveabilty and the untapped potential of sport and recreation. *Town Planning Review*, **76**(2), 1-5.

Collins, A. and Flynn, A. (2008). Measuring the environmental sustainability of a major sporting event: A case study of the FA Cup final. *Tourism Economics*, **14** (4), 751-768.

Collins, A., Jones, C. and Munday, M. (2009). Assessing the environmental impacts of mega sporting events: Two options? *Tourism Management*, **30**, 828–837.

Crompton, J. L. and McKay, S. L. (1994). Measuring the economic impacts of festivals and events: Some myths, misapplications and ethical dilemmas. *Festival Management and Event Tourism*, **2**(1), 33–43.

Crowther, P. (2011). Marketing event outcomes: from tactical to strategic. *International Journal of Event and Festival Management*, **2**(1), 68-82.

Cushman, R. (2002). *Impact of the games on Olympic host cities*. Barcelona: Cenre D'Estudios Olympics (UAB).

DaMatta, R. (1984). Carnival in multiple planes. In J. J. MacAloon (ed.), *Rite, drama, festival, spectacle: Rehearsals toward a theory of cultural performance* pp. 208-240. Philadelphia, PA: Institute for the Study of Human Issues, Inc.

Dansero, E. and Puttilli, M. (2010). Mega-events tourism legacies: The case of the Torino 2006 Winter Olympic Games – a territorialisation approach. *Leisure Studies,* **29**(3), 321-341.

Dávid, L. (2009). Environmental impacts of events. In R. Raj and J. Musgrave (Eds.), *Event Management and Sustainability*. UK: CABI International.

Davidson, R. and Rogers, T. (2012). *Marketing Destinations and Venues for Conferences, Conventions and Business Events*. Event Management Series, London: Routledge,

Davidson, R. (2003). Adding pleasure to business: Conventions and tourism. *Journal of Convention and Exhibition Management,* **5**(1), 29–39.

Davidson, R. (2011). Web 2.0 as a marketing tool for conference centres. *International Journal of Event and Festival Management,* **2**(2), 117-138.

Davies, J. and Brown, L. (2000). Tourism: Food, wine and festivals: A delectable mix. In Allen, J, Harris, R, JagoL. and Veal, A. J. (eds), (2000). *Events beyond 2000: Setting the agenda*. Proceedings of Conference on Event Evaluation, Research and Education, Australian Centre for Event Management, School of Leisure, Sport and Tourism, University of Technology, Sydney.

Davies, L., Coleman, R. and Ramchandani, G. (2013). Evaluating event economic impact: rigour versus reality? *International Journal of Event and Festival Management,* **4**(1), 31-42.

De Bres, K. and Davis, J. (2001). Celebrating group and place identity: A case study of a new regional festival. *Tourism Geographies,* **3**, 326-337.

Deccio, C. and Baloglu, S. (2002). Non-host community resident reactions to the 2002 Winter Olympics: The spillover impacts. *Journal of Travel Research,* **41**, 45-56.

Deery, M. and Jago, L. (2010). Social impacts of events and the role of anti-social behaviour. *International Journal of Event and Festival Management,* **1**, 8–28.

Deery, M., Jago, L., Fredline, L. and Dwyer, L. (2005). *National Business Events Study* (NBES). Altona, VIC: Common Ground.

Delamere, T. A. (1997). Development of scale items to measure the social impact of community festivals. *Journal of Applied Recreation Research,* **22**(4), 293-315.

Delamere, T. A. (2001). Development of a scale to measure resident attitudes toward the social impacts of community festivals, Part II: Verification of the scale. *Event Management,* **7**, 25-38.

Delamere, T. A., Wankel, L. M. and Hinch, T. D. (2001). Development of a scale to measure resident attitudes toward the social impacts of community festivals, Part I: Item generation and purification of the measure. *Event Management,* **7**, 11-24.

Derrett, R. (2000). Can festivals brand community cultural development and cultural tourism simultaneously. In Allen, J, Harris, R, Jago LK and Veal, AJ (eds), (2000). *Events Beyond 2000: Setting the Agenda*, Proceedings of Conference on Event Evaluation, Research and Education, Australian Centre for Event Management, University of Technology, Sydney.

Derrett, R. (2003). Making sense of how festivals demonstrate a community sense of place. *Event Management*, **8**, 49–58.

Derrett, R. (2004). Festivals, events and the destination (33-50). In I. Yeoman, M. Robertson, J. Ali-Knight, U. McMahon-Beattie and S. Drummond (eds), *Festival and events management: An international arts and culture perspective*. Oxford: Butterworth Heinemann.

Devine, A. and Devine, F. (2012). The challenge and opportunities for an event organiser during an economic recession. *International Journal of Event and Festival Management*, **3**(2), 122-136.

Dickson, C. and Arcodia, C. (2010). Promoting sustainable event practice: The role of professional associations. *International Journal of Hospitality Management*, **29**(2), 236-244.

Downey, B. (1993). Major sports events in Victoria: The economic impact and related tourism opportunities. *Leisure Options*, July, 28-32.

Dredge, D. and Pforr, C. (2008). Policy networks and tourism governance. In N. Scott, R. Baggio and C. Cooper (eds), *Network Analysis and Tourism: from Theory to Practice*. Clevedon, UK: Channel View Publications.

Dredge, D. and Whitford, M. (2010). Policy for sustainable and responsible festivals and events: institutionalisation of a new paradigm - a response. *Journal of Policy Research in Tourism, Leisure and Events*, **2**(1), 1-13.

Dredge, D. and Whitford, M. (2011). Event tourism governance and the public sphere. *Journal of Sustainable Tourism*, **19** (4/5), 479-499.

Dredge, D. and Whitford, M. (2011, February). *The Use of Special Legislation for Events in Australia: If You Only Have a Hammer, Is Every Event a Nail?* Paper presented at the CAUTHE 2011 National Conference: Tourism: Creating a Brilliant Blend, Adelaide, S.A.

Dredge, D. and Whitford, M. (2012). Event tourism governance and the public sphere. In B. Bramwell, B. and B. Lane, B. (eds). *Tourism Governance: Critical perspectives on governance and sustainability*, Routledge: United Kingdom.

Dredge, D., Ford, E.J., Lamont, M., Phi, T. and Whitford, M. (2010). *Event Governance: Background to the World Rally Championship, Northern Rivers, NSW*. Gold Coast, Southern Cross University.

Dredge, D., Lamont, M, Ford., E.J., Phi., G, Whitford., M and Wynn-Moylan, P. (2010, February 8-11). *Event governance: The rhetoric and reality of the World Rally Championship, Northern Rivers, NSW*. Proceedings of CAUTHE 2010:

Challenge the Limits, Hobart, Tasmania: University of Tasmania.

Drengner, J., Jahn, S. and Zanger, C. (2011). Measuring event-brand congruence. *Event Management*, **15**(1), 25-36.

Dunstan, G. (1994) Becoming coastwise: The path of festivals and cultural tourism. *Landscape and Lifestyle Choices for the Northern Rivers of New South Wales*. Lismore: Southern Cross University.

Dwyer, L., Forsyth, P. and Spurr, R. (2004). Evaluating tourism's economic effects: new and old approaches. *Tourism Management*, **25**(3), 307-317.

Dwyer, L., Forsyth, P. and Spurr, R. (2005). Estimating the impacts of special events on an economy. *Journal of Travel Research*, **43**(4), 351-359.

Dwyer, L., Forsyth, P. and Spurr, R. (2006). Assessing the economic impacts of events: A computable general equilibrium approach. *Journal of Travel Research*, **45**(1), 59-66.

Dwyer, L., Mastilis, N., Mellor, R. and Mules, T. (1999). *A framework for forecasting the economic impacts of events by type and by location: A study for Tourism New South Wales*. Sydney: Centre for Tourism Research, University of Western Sydney, Macarthur.

Dwyer, L., Mellor, R., Mistilis, N. and Mules, T. (2000). A framework for assessing 'tangible' and 'intangible' impacts of events and conventions. *Event Management*, **6**, 175-189.

Dwyer, L.M., Forsyth, P. and Spurr, R. (2004). Evaluating tourism's economic effects: new and old approaches. *Tourism Management*, **25**(3), 307-317.

Earls, Z. (1993). First night celebration: Building community through the arts. *Festival and Event Tourism*, **1**, 32-33.

Emery, P. (2001). Bidding to host a major sports event (91-108). In C. Gratton and I. Henry (eds), *Sport in the City: The Role of Sport in Economic and Social Regeneration of London*: Routledge.

Emery, P.R. (2002). Bidding to host a major sports event: The local organising committee perspective. *International Journal of Public Sector Management*, **15**(4), 316-335.

Ensor, J., Robertson, M. and Ali-Knight, J., (2007). The dynamics of successful events – the experts' perspective. *Managing Leisure*, **12**(3), 223-235.

Essex, S. and Chalkley, B. (1998). Olympic Games: Catalyst of urban change. *Leisure Studies*, **17**, 187-206.

EventsCorp, (1992). *EventsCorp strategy document*. Perth: Western Australian Government.

Fabricius, M. and Goodwin, H. (2002). The Cape Town declaration on responsible tourism in destinations. Retrieved June 10, 2014 from icrtourism.org/Capetown.shtml

Falassi, A. (Ed.) (1987). *Time out of time: Essays on the festival.* Albuquerque, NM: University of New Mexico Press.

Faulkner B., Fredline E., Larson M. and Tomljenovic R. (1999) A marketing analysis of Sweden's Storsjöyran Festival. *Tourism Analysis,* **4**, 157-171.

Faulkner, B. (1993). Evaluating the Tourism Impacts of Hallmark Events. Occasional Paper No 16, Canberra: Bureau of Tourism Research.

Fenich, G.G. (2012). *Meetings, Expositions, Events and Conventions: An introduction to the industry* (3rd ed.). New Jersey: Pearson.

Fenich, G.G. (2014). The Dawning of a New Age, Editorial, *Journal of Convention and Event Tourism,* **15**, 111-113.

Flyvbjerg, B. and Stewart, A. (2012). *Olympic Proportions: Cost and Cost Overrun at the Olympics 1960-2012.* Oxford: Saïd Business School, University of Oxford

Foley, C., Edwards, D. and Schlenker, K. (2014). Business events and friendship: leveraging the sociable legacies. *Event Management,* **18**(1), 53-64.

Foley, C., Schlenker, K., Edwards, D. and Lewis-Smith, L. (2013). Determining business event legacies beyond the tourism spend: an Australian case study approach. *Event Management,* **17**(3), 311-322.

Foley, M., McGillivray, D. and McPherson, G. (2012). Policy pragmatism: Qatar and the global events circuit. *International Journal of Event and Festival Management,* **3**(1), 101-115.

Forbes, (2014). 2014 FIFA World Cup expected to add $3.03 billion to Brazil's economy. Retrieved August 14 from www.forbes.com/sites/darrenheitner/2014/05/14/2014-fifa-world-cup-expected-to-add-3-03-billion-to-brazils-economy/

Formica, S. and Uysal, M. (1996). A market segmentation of festival visitors: Umbria jazz festival in Italy. *Festival Management and Event Tourism,* **3**(4), 175–182.

Formica, S., (1998). The development of festivals and special events studies. *Festival Management and Event Tourism: An International Journal,* **5**(3),131-137.

Fortes, M. (1936). Ritual festivals and social cohesion in the Hinterland of the Gold Coast. *American Anthropologist,* **38**, 590-604.

Fredline, E. and Faulkner, B. (2002a). Residents' reactions to the staging of major motorsport events within their communities: A cluster analysis. *Annals of Tourism Research,* **7**(2), 103-114.

Fredline, E. and Faulkner, B. (2002b). Variations in residents' reactions to major motorsports events: Why residents perceive the impacts of events differently. *Event Management,* **7**(2), 115-125.

Fredline, E. (2006). Host and guest relations and sport tourism (131-147). In H. Gibson (ed), *Sport tourism: Concepts and theories.* London: Routledge.

Fredline, E. and Faulkner, B. (1998). Resident reactions to a major tourism event: The Gold Coast Indy Car Race. *Festival Management and Event Tourism* **5**, 185–205.

Fredline, E. and Faulkner, B. (2000). *Community perceptions of the impacts of events*. Paper presented at the Events Beyond 2000: Setting the Agenda, Sydney

Fredline, E., Deery, M. and Jago, L. (2005). *Testing of a compressed generic instrument to assess host community perceptions of events: A case study of the Australian Open Tennis Tournament*. Gold Coast, Australia: Sustainable Tourism Cooperative Research Centre.

Fredline, E., Deery, M. and Jago, L. (2006). *Development of a scale to assess the social impact of tourism within communities*. Technical Report. Queensland: Cooperative Research Centre for Sustainable Tourism.

Fredline, L., Jago, L. and Deery, M. (2003). Developing a generic scale to measure the social impacts of events. *Event Management,* **8**, 23-37.

French, C., Craig-Smith, S. and Collier, A. (2000). *Principles of tourism*. Sydney: Longman Australia.

Frisby, W. and Getz, D. (1989). Festival management: A case study perspective. *Journal of Travel Research,* **28**(1), 7–11.

Gallarza, M G; Arteaga, F; Floristan, E; Gil, I. (2009). Consumer behaviour in a religious event experience: an empirical assessment of value dimensionality among volunteers. *International Journal of Culture, Tourism and Hospitality Research,* **3**(2), 165-180.

Gamage, A. and Higgs, B. (1996). *Economics of venue selection for special sporting events, with special reference to the 1996 Melbourne Grand Prix*. Paper presented to the Asia Pacific Tourism Association '96 Conference, Townsville, Queensland, pp, 1-18.

Gartner, W. C. and Holecek, D. F. (1983). Economic impact of an annual tourism industry exposition. *Annals of Tourism Research,* **10**(2), 199–212.

Getz, D. (1989). Special events: Defining the product. *Tourism Management,* **10** (2), 125-137.

Getz, D. (1991). *Festivals, special events and tourism*. New York, NY: Van Nostrand Reinhold.

Getz, D. (1994). Residents' attitudes toward tourism: A longitudinal study in Spey Valley, Scotland. *Tourism Management,* **15**(4), 247–258.

Getz, D. (1997). *Event Management and event tourism*. New York: Cognisant.

Getz, D. (2000). *Developing a research agenda for the events management field*. In Events Beyond 2000: Setting the Agenda: Proceedings of conference on event evaluation, research and education, Sydney : Australian Centre for Event Management.

Getz, D. (2002). Editorial: on the nature and significance of events studies. *Event Management* **7**(3): 141-142.

Getz, D. (2005). *Event Management and Event Tourism* 2nd Edition. New York: Cognizant Communication Corporation.

Getz, D. (2007). *Event Studies: Theory, Research and Policy for Planned Events.* Oxford: Polity Press.

Getz, D. (2008). Event tourism: Definition, evolution and research. *Tourism Management,* **29**, 403-428.

Getz, D. (2009). Policy for sustainable and responsible festivals and events: institutionalization of a new paradigm. *Journal of Policy Research in Tourism, Leisure and Events,* **1**(1), 61-78.

Getz, D. (2010). The nature and scope of festival studies. *International Journal of Event Management Research,* **5**(1), 1-47.

Getz, D. (2012). Event studies: discourses and future directions. *Event Management,* **16**(2), 171-187.

Getz, D. and Andersson, T. (2008). Sustainable festivals: On becoming an institution. *Event Management,* **12** (1), 1-17.

Getz, D. and Frisby, W. (1988). Evaluating management effectiveness in community-run festivals. *Journal of Travel Research,* **27** (1), 22-27.

Getz, D., Andersson, T. and Larson, M. (2007). Festival stakeholder roles: Concepts and case studies. *Event Management,* **10** (2/3), 103-122.

Getz, D. andersson, T.D., Carlsen, J. (2010). Festival management studies: Developing a framework and priorities for comparative and cross-cultural research. *International Journal of Event and Festival Management.* **1**(1), 29-60.

Gibson, C. and Connell, J. (2005). *Music and tourism: On the road again.* Clevedon: Channel View Publications.

Gibson, C., Waitt, G., Walmsley, J. and Connell, J. (2010). Cultural festivals and economic development in nonmetropolitan Australia. *Journal of Planning Education and Research,* 29(3), 280-293.

Gil, A. R. and de Esteban Curiel, J. (2008). Religious events as special interest tourism. A Spanish experience. *Revista de Turismo y Patrimonio Cultural,* **6**(3), 419 – 433.

Gilbert, D. and Lizotte, M. (1998). Occasional studies: Tourism and the performing Arts. *Travel and Tourism Analyst, 1.* London, Travel and Tourism Intelligence.

Gnoth, J. and Anwar, S. A. (2000). New Zealand bets on event tourism. *Cornell Hotel and Restaurant Administration Quarterly,* **41** (4), 72-83.

Goldblatt, J. (1997). *Special Events: Best Practices in Event Management,* 2nd edn. New York: Van Nostrand Reinhold.

Goldblatt, J. (1990). *Special Events: The Art and Science of Celebration*. New York: Van Nostrand Reinhold.

Goldblatt, J. (2000). *A future for event management: The analysis of major trends impacting the emerging profession* (1–9). In J. Allen, R. Harris, L. Jago and A. J. Veal, (eds.) Events beyond 2000. Proceedings of Conference on Event Evaluation, Research and Education, Australian Centre for Event Management, Sydney.

Goldblatt, J. (2005). *Special Events: Event Leadership for a New World* 4th edn. Hoboken: John Wiley and Sons.

Goldblatt, J. (2011). *Special Events: A New Generation and the Next Frontier* (6th ed.). New York: John Wiley and Sons.

Goldblatt, S. and Goldblatt, J. (2011). *The Complete Guide to Greener Meetings and Events*. New York: John Wiley and Sons.

Graham, S., Goldblatt, J. and Deply, L. (1995). *The Ultimate Guide to Sport Event Management and Marketing*. New York: McGraw-Hill.

Gration, D., Arcodia, C., Raciti, M., Stokes, R. (2011). The blended festivalscape and its sustainability at non urban festivals. *Event Management*, **15**(4), 343-359.

Gratton, C. and Henry, I.P., (eds.) (2001). *Sport in the City: The role of sport in economic and social regeneration*. London: Routledge.

Gratton, C., Dobson, N. and Shibli, S. (2000). The economic importance of major sports events: A case-study of six events. *Managing Leisure*, **5**(1), 17-28

Green, B. C., Costa, C. and Fitzgerald, M., (2003). Marketing the host city: Analyzing exposure generated by a sport event. *International Journal of Sports Marketing and Sponsorship*, **4**(4), 335–353.

Green, C. and Chalip. L. (1998). Sport tourism as the celebration of subculture. *Annals of Tourism Research*, **25**(2), 275 – 291.

Gursoy, D. and Kendall , K. (2006). Hosting mega events: Modeling locals' support. *Annals of Tourism Research* **33**, 603–623.

Gursoy, D., Kim, K. and Uysal, M. (2004). Perceived impacts of festivals and special events by organizers: an extension and validation. *Tourism Management*, **25**, 171-181.

Hall, C. M. (1987). The effects of hallmark events on cities. *Journal of Travel Research*, **26**(2), 44-45.

Hall, C. M. (1992). *Hallmark Tourist Events: Impacts, Management and Planning*. London: John Wiley.

Hall, C. and Rusher, K. (2004). Risky lifestyles? Entrepreneurial characteristics of the New Zealand bed and breakfast sector (83-98). In R. Thomas (Ed.) *Small Firms in Tourism: International Perspectives*, London, Elsevier.

Hall, C.M. (2006). Urban entrepreneurship, corporate interests and sports mega-events: the thin policies of competitiveness within the hard outcomes of neoliberalism. *The Sociological Review*, **54**(s2), 59-70.

Handelman, D. (1990). *Models and Mirrors: Towards an Anthropology of Public Events*. Cambridge, England: Cambridge University Press.

Hanly, P. (2012). Examining Economic linkages between the irish convention market and the rest of the economy: a close-knit relationship. *Journal of Convention and Event Tourism*, **13**(3), 159-180.

Harcup, T. (2000). Re-imaging a post-industrial city: The Leeds St Valentine's Fair as a civic spectacle. *City*, **4**, 215-231.

Harris, R. and Huyskens, M. (2002). *Public events: Can they make a contribution to ecological sustainability*. Paper presented to Annual Council of Australian Tourism and Hospitality Educators' Conference, Fremantle.

Hede, A. (2006). Mega-events and the 'showcase' effect: investigating the moderating influence of exposure to the 2004 Olympic Games telecast and interest in the Olympic movement: An Australian perspective. *Tourism Review International*, **10**(4), 241-255.

Hede, A. (2008). Managing special events in the new era of the triple bottom line. *Tourism Management*, **11**(1/2), 13-22.

Hede, A. and Jago, L. (2005). Perceptions of the host destination as a result of attendance at a special event: a post-consumption analysis. *International Journal of Event Management Research*, **1** (1), 1-11.

Heijman, W. and Jongenburger, B. (2011). FIFA World Cup 2018: An ex ante input output analysis for the Netherlands. *International Journal of Event Management Research*, **6**(2), 15-29.

Hemingway, C. A. and P.W. Maclagan, P. W. (2004). Managers' personal values as drivers of corporate social responsibility. *Journal of Business Ethics*, **50** (1), 33-44.

Henderson, J., Foo, K., Lim, H. and Yip, S. (2010). Sports events and tourism: the Singapore Formula One Grand Prix. *International Journal of Event and Festival Management*, **1**(1), 60-73.

Hennessey, S., Macdonal, R. and MacEachern, M. (2008). A framework for understanding golfing visitors to a destination. *Journal of Sport and Tourism*, **13**(1), 5-35

Hiller, H. H. (1998). Assessing the impact of mega-events: A linkage model. *Current Issues in Tourism*, **1**, 47-57.

Hiller, H. H. (2000). Mega-events, urban boosterism and growth strategies: An analysis of the objectives and legitimations of the Cape Town 2004 Olympic bid. *International Journal of Urban and Regional Research*, **24**, 429-458.

Hiller, H. H. (2006). Post-event outcomes and the post-modern turn: The

Olympics and urban transformations. *European Sport Management Quarterly*, **6**, 317-332.

Hinch, T. and Delamere, T. (1993). Native festivals as tourism attractions: A community challenge. *Journal of Applied Recreation Research*, **18**(2), 131-142.

Hixson, E., McCabe and V., Brown, G. (2011). Event attendance motivation and place attachment: An exploratory study of young residents in Adelaide, South Australia. *Event Management*, **15**(3), 233-243(11).

Holland, D. and Skinner, D. (1995). Contested ritual, contested femininities: (Re)forming self and society in a Nepali women's festival. *American Ethnologist*, **22**, 279-305.

Horne, J. (2007). The four 'knowns' of sports mega-events. *Leisure Studies*, **26**(1), 81-96.

Hudson, S. and Hudson, R. (2013). Engaging with consumers using social media: a case study of music festivals. *International Journal of Event and Festival Management*, **4**(3), 206-223.

Jaeger, K. and Mykletun, R. J. (2009). The festivalscape of Finnmark. *Scandinavian Journal of Hospitality and Tourism*, **9**(2/3), 327-348.

Jago, L. and Dwyer, L. (2006). *Economic Evaluation of Special Events: A Practitioner's Guide*. Gold Coast: Sustainable Tourism CRC and Common Ground Publishers.

Jago, L. and Shaw, R. (1998). Special events: A conceptual and definitional framework. *Festival Management and Event Tourism*, **5**, 21-32.

Jago, L., Chalip, L., Brown, G., Mules, T. and Ali, S. (2003). Building events into destination branding: insights from experts. *Event Management*, **8**(1), 3-14.

Jamieson, N. (2014). Sport tourism events as community builders—how social capital helps the 'locals' cope. *Journal of Convention and Event Tourism*, **15**(1), 57-68.

Janiskee, R. (1994). Some macroscale growth trends in America's community festival industry. *Festival Management and Event Tourism*, **2** (1), 10-14.

Janiskee, R. (1996). The temporal distribution of America's community festivals. *Festival Management and Event Tourism*, **3** (3), 129-137.

Jeong, G. H. and Faulkner, B. (1996). Resident perceptions of mega-event impacts: The Taejon international exposition case. *Festival Management and Event Tourism*, **4**(1), 3–11.

Jeong, S. and Santos, C.A. (2004). Cultural politics and contested place identity. *Annals of Tourism Research*, **31**(3), 640-656.

Jones, C. (2012). Festivals and events in emergent economies. *International Journal of Event and Festival Management*, **3**(1), 9-11.

Jones, M.L. (2014). *Sustainable event management: A practical guide* (2nd ed.). New York: Routledge.

Karlsen, S. and Nordström, C. (2009). Festivals in the Barents Region. Scandinavian *Journal of Hospitality and Tourism,* **9**(2-3), 130-145.

Kellett, P., Hede, A. M. and Chalip, L. (2008). Social policy for sport events: Leveraging (relationships with) teams from other nations for community benefit. *European Sport Management Quarterly,* **8**, 101-121.

Kemp, S. F. (1999). Sled dog racing: The celebration of cooperation in a competitive sport. *Ethnology,* **38**, 81-95.

Khodr, H. (2012). Exploring the driving factors behind the event strategy in Qatar. *International Journal of Event and Festival Management,* **3**(1), 81-100.

Kim, C., Scott, D., Thigpen, J. F. and Kim, S. S. (1998). Economic impacts of a birding festival. *Journal of Festival Management and Event Tourism,* **5**(1/2), 51–58.

Kim, J., Boo, S. and Kim, Y. (2013). Patterns and trends in event tourism study topics over 30 years. *International Journal of Event and Festival Management,* **4**(1), 66-83.

Kim, K. and Uysal, M. (2003). Perceived socio-economic impacts of festivals and events among organizers. *Journal of Hospitality Leisure Marketing,* **10**(3-4), 159-171.

Kim, S. S. and Morrison, A. M. (2005). Changes of images of South Korea among foreign tourists after the 2002 FIFA World Cup. *Tourism Management,* **26**(2), 233-247.

Lawton, L. (2011). Introduction: Special issue on sustainability in the event management sector. *Event Management,* **15**(4), 313-314.

Lee, C. K. and Taylor, T. (2005). Critical reflections on the economic impact assessment of a mega event: The case of 2002 FIFA World Cup. *Tourism Management,* **26**(4), 595-603.

Lee, S.S. and Goldblatt, J. (2012). The current and future impacts of the 2007-2009 economic recession on the festival and event industry. *International Journal of Event and Festival Management,* **3**(2), 137-148.

Leopkey, B. and Parent, M.M. (2009). Risk management strategies by stakehold-ers in Canadian major sporting events. *Event Management,* **13**(3), 153-170.

Litvin, S.W. and Fetter, E. (2006). Can a festival be too successful? A review of Spoleto, USA. *International Journal of Contemporary Hospitality Management,* **18**(1), 41-49.

Long, P. T. and Perdue, R. (1990). The economic impact of rural festivals and special events: Assessing the spatial distribution of expenditure. *Journal of Travel Research,* **28** (4), 10-14.

Lynch P. G. and Jensen R. C. (1984). The economic impact of the X11 Commonwealth Games on the Brisbane region. *Urban Policy and Research,* **2**(3), 11-14.

Mair, J. (2011). Events and climate change: an Australian perspective. *International Journal of Event and Festival Management,* **2**(3), 245-253.

Mair, J. (2011). Exploring air travellers' voluntary carbon-offsetting behavior. *Journal of Sustainable Tourism,* **19**(2), 215-230.

Mair, J. and Jago, L. (2010). The development of a conceptual model of greening in the business events tourism sector. *Journal of Sustainable Tourism,* **18**(1), 77-94.

Mair, J. and Whitford, M. (2013). An exploration of events research: event topics, themes and emerging trends. *International Journal of Event and Festival Management,* **4**(1), 6-30.

Masterman, G. (2004). *Strategic Sports Event Management: An International Approach.* Oxford: Elsevier.

May, V. (1995). Environmental implications of the 1992 Winter Olympic Games. *Tourism Management,* **16**(4), 269-75.

McCartney, G. (2008). The CAT (Casino Tourism) and the MICE (Meetings, Incentives, Conventions, Exhibitions): Key development considerations for the convention and exhibition industry in Macao. *Journal of Convention and Event Tourism,* **9**(4), 293–308.

McCloud, P. and Syme, J. (1987). Forecasting the economic impact of the America's Cup (44-74). In Australian Standing Committee on Tourism. *The Impact of marketing of special event*: Papers of the Australian Travel Research Workshop, Mt Buffalo.

McKercher, B., Mei, W. *and* Tse, T. (2006*).* Are short duration festivals tourist attractions*? Journal of Sustainable Tourism,* **14**, 55-66.

McPherson B., Curtis J., Loy J. (1989). *The Social Significance of Sport: An Introduction to the Sociology of Sport.* Champaign: Human Kinetics Books.

Merrilees, B. and Marles, K. (2011). Green business events: Profiling through a case study. *Event Management,* **15**(4)**,** 361-372.

Mihalik, B. J. and Simonetta, L. (1998). Resident perceptions of the 1996 Summer Olympic Games - Year II. *Festival Management and Event Tourism,* **5**(1/2), 9-20.

Miline, S., Dickson, G., McElrea, A. and Clark, V. (2005). *Micro sporting event impacts in Regional New Zealand: The TRACE Sports Project.* Paper presented at The Impacts of Events Conference 2005, UTS Australian Centre for Event Management.

Minnaert, L. (2011). An Olympic legacy for all? The non-infrastructural outcomes of the Olympic Games for socially excluded groups (Atlanta 1996–Beijing 2008). *Tourism Management,* **33**, 361-370.

Misener, L. and Mason, D. S. (2006). Creating community networks: Can sporting events offer meaningful sources of social capital? *Managing Leisure,* **11**, 39-56.

Monga, M. (2006). Measuring motivation to volunteer for special events. *Event Management,* **10**(1), 47-61.

Moscardo, G. (2008). Analyzing the role of festivals and events in regional development. *Event Management,* **11**, 23-32.

Mules, T. and McDonald, S. (1994). The economic impact of special events: The use of forecasts. *Festival Management and Event Tourism,* **2** (1), 45-53.

Musgrave, J. and R. Raj (2009). Introduction to a conceptual framework for sustainable events. In R. Raj and J. Musgrave (eds), *Event Management and Sustainability.* Wallingford: CABI: 1-12.

New Zealand Tourist and Publicity Department, (1987). *The New Zealand domestic travel study 1986-1987: General report.* Wellington: New Zealand Travel and Publicity Department.

Nicholson, R. and Pearce, D. (2001). Why do people attend events: A comparative analysis of visitor motivations at four South Island events. *Journal of Travel Research,* **39** (4), 449-460.

O'Sullivan, D. and Jackson, M. (2002). Festival tourism: A contributor to sustainable local economic development? *Journal of Sustainable Tourism,* **10** (4), 325-342.

O'Sullivan, D., Pickernell, D. and Senyard, J., (2009). Public Sector Evaluation of Festivals and Special Events. *Journal of Policy Research in Tourism, Leisure and Events,* **1**(1), 19-36.

Ohmann S., Jones, I. and Wilkes, K. (2006). The perceived social impacts of the 2006 Football World Cup on Munich Residents. *Journal of Sport and Tourism,* **11***(2),* 129–152.

Papadimitriou, D. and Gibson, H. (2008). Active mountain sport tourists in Epirus Greece: Pre and post trip analysis. *Journal of Sport and Tourism,* **13** (1), 1-24.

Pauline, G. (2011). Volunteer satisfaction and intent to remain: An analysis of contributing factors among professional golf event volunteers. *International Journal of Event Management Research,* **6**(1), 1-32.

Pavicic, J., Alfirevic, N. and Batarelo, V. J. (2007). The management and marketing of religious sites, pilgrimage and religious events: challenges for Roman Catholic pilgrimages in Croatia (48-63). In R. Raj and N. Morpeth (eds.) *Religious Tourism and Pilgrimage Management: An International Perspective.* Wallingford: CABI International.

Pennington-Gray, L. and Holdnak, A. (2002). Out of the stands and into the community: using sports events to promote a destination. *Event Management,* **7**(3), 177-186.

Pettersson, R. and Viken, A. (2007). Sami perspectives on indigenous tourism in northern Europe: Commerce or cultural development? (pp. 177–187).

In R. Butler and T. Hinch (Eds.), *Tourism and Indigenous Peoples: Issues and Implications*. London: Elsevier.

Phi, G., Dredge, D. and Whitford, M. (2014). Understanding conflicting perspectives in event planning and management using Q method. *Tourism Management*, **40**, 406-415.

Phipps, P. (2010). Performances of power: Indigenous cultural festivals as globally engaged cultural strategy. *Alternatives: Global, Local, Political*, **35**, 217-240.

Picard, D. and Robinson, M. (Eds.). (2006). *Festivals, Tourism and Social Change: Remaking Worlds*, Multilingual Matters.

Ponsford, I.F. (2011). Actualizing environmental sustainability at Vancouver 2010 venues. *International Journal of Event and Festival Management*, **2**(2), 184-196.

Prentice, R. and Andersen, V. (2003). Festival as creative destination. *Annals of Tourism Research*, **30**(1), 7-30.

Pugh, C. and Wood, E. H. (2004). The strategic use of events within local government: A study of London Borough Councils. *Event Management*, **9**(1), 61-71.

Quinn, B. (2006). Problematising 'festival tourism': Arts festivals and sustainable development in Ireland. *Journal of Sustainable Tourism*, **14** (3), 288-306.

Quinn, B. (2013). *Key Concepts in Event Management*. London: Sage

Raj, R. and J. Musgrave (2009). *Event Management and Sustainability*. Wallingford: CABI.

Ramchandani, G.M. and Coleman, R.J. (2012). Testing the accuracy of event economic impact forecasts. *International Journal of Event and Festival Management*, **3**(2), 188-200.

Reid, G. (2006). The politics of city imaging: A case study of the MTV Europe Music Awards Edinburgh 03. *Event Management*, **10** (1), 35-46.

Reid, S. (2011) Event stakeholder management: developing sustainable rural event practices. *International Journal of Event & Festival Management*, **2**(1), 20-36

Reid, S. and Ritchie, B. (2011). Risk management: event managers' attitudes, beliefs and perceived constraints. *Event Management*, **15**(4), 329-341.

Richards, P. and Ryan, C. (2004). The Aotearoa traditional Maori Performing Arts Festival 1972-2000: A case study of cultural event maturation. *Journal of Tourism and Cultural Change*, **2** (2), 94-117.

Ritchie J. R. B. (1984). Assessing the impact of hallmark events: Conceptual and research issues. *Journal of Travel Research*, **23**(1): 2-11.

Ritchie, B. W. and Adair, D., (eds.) (2004). *Sport Tourism: Interrelationships, Impacts and Issues*. Clevedon: Channel View Publications.

Ritchie, B. and Beliveau, D. (1974). Hallmark events: An evaluation of a strategic response to seasonality in the travel market. *Journal of Travel Research,* **14** (2), 14-20.

Ritchie, B.W. and Adair, D. (2004). Sport Tourism: An Introduction and Overview *Sports Tourism: Interrelationships, Impacts and Issues.* Clevedon: Channel View Publications.

Rittichainuwat, B. and Mair, J. (2012). An exploratory study of attendee perceptions of green meetings. *Journal of Convention and Event Tourism,* **13**(3), 147-158.

Robertson, M., Rogers, P. and Leask, A (2009). Progressing socio-cultural impact evaluation for festivals: literature synthesis and measuring perceptions. *Journal of Policy Research in Tourism, Leisure and Events* **1**(2), 156-169.

Roche, M., (2000). *Mega-events and Modernity: Olympics and Expos in the Growth of Global Culture.* London: Routledge.

Rogers, P. and Anastasiadou, C. (2011). Community involvement in festivals: Exploring ways of increasing local participation. *Event Management. Special Issue: Sustainability in the Event Management Sector,* **15**(4).

Rothschild, P.C. (2011). Social media use in sports and entertainment venues. *International Journal of Event and Festival Management,* **2**(2), 139-150.

Ruhanen, L. and Whitford, M. (2011). Indigenous sporting events: More than just a game. *International Journal of Event Management Research,* **6**(1), 33-51

Ruhanen, L. and Whitford. M. (2012). Brisbane's Annual Sports and Cultural Festival: Connecting with community and culture through festivals (pp.101-117). In S. Klein and G Koch (eds) *Urban Representations: Cultural expression, identity and politics,* Australian Institute of Aboriginal and Torres Strait Islander Studies Research.

Ruhanen, L. and Whitford, M. (2014). Indigenous Tourism and Events for Community Development in Australia. In C. Cooper, C (ed) *Bridging Tourism Theory and Practice* (vol 5): *Tourism as an Instrument for Development.* UNWTO Emerald Publishing Group: United Kingdom

Rupf-Haller, R. and Oberholzer, N.L. (2005). Environmental Planning for Significant Sport Events - A Case Study of the World Ski Championships 2003. *Tourism Review,* **60**(2), 21-26.

Saayman, M. and Saayman, A. (2012). The economic impact of the Comrades Marathon. *International Journal of Event and Festival Management,* **3**(3), 220-235.

Schulenkorf, N. (2009). An ex ante framework for the strategic study of social utility of sport events. *Tourism and Hospitality Research,* **9**(2), 120-131.

Schulenkorf, N. (2010). Sport events and ethnic reconciliation: Attempting to create social change between Sinhalese, Tamil and Muslim sportspeople in war-torn Sri Lanka. *International Review for the Sociology of Sport*, **45**(3), 273-294.

Schulenkorf, N., Thomson, A. and Schlenker, K. (2011). Intercommunity sport events: Vehicles and catalysts for social capital in divided societies. *Event Management*, **15**(2), 105-119.

Severt, K., Fjelstul, J. and Breiter, D. (2013). Information communication technologies: usages and preferences of generation Y students and meeting professionals. *Journal of Convention and Event Tourism*, **14**(2), 124-143.

Shaw, C.A. (2013). *Five Ring Circus: Myths and Realities of the Olympic Games* (2nd ed.). Canada: New Society Publishers.

Sherwood, P. (2007). *A triple bottom line evaluation of the impact of special events: The development of indicators.* Unpublished Doctoral Dissertation, Victoria University, Melbourne.

Shin, H. (2004). Cultural festivals and regional identities in South Korea. *Environment and planning D: Society and Space* **22**(4), 619-632.

Shone, A. and Parry, B. (2004). *Successful Event Management: A Practical Handbook*, 2nd edn, Thomson, United Kingdom.

Sims, W. and D'Mello, L. (2005). Event denizens and the sports tourist, in Allen J. (Ed.), *Proceedings of International Event Research Conference July 2005*, Australian Centre for Event Management, University of Technology, Sydney, Lindfield.

Slater, L. (2010). Calling our spirits home: Indigenous cultural festivals and the making of a good life. *Cultural Studies Review*, **16**(1), 1-12.

Small, J., Harris, C., Wilson, E. and Ateljevic, I. (2011). Voices of women: A memory-work reflection on work-life dis/harmony in tourism academia. *Journal of Hospitality, Leisure, Sport and Tourism Education*, **10**(1), 23-36.

Small, K. (2007). *Social dimensions of community festivals: An application of factor analysis in the development of the social impact perception (SIP) scale. Event Management*, **11** (1), 45–55.

Smith, A. and Fox, T. (2007). From 'event-led' to event-themed' regeneration: The 2002 Commonwealth Games Legacy Programme. *Urban Studies*, **44** (5/6), 1125- 1143.

Smith-Christensen, C. (2009). Sustainability as a concept within events. In R. Raj and J. Musgrave (Eds.), *Event Management and Sustainability* (pp. 22-31). Wallingford: CABI.

Sofield, T. and Li, F. (1998). Historical methodology and sustainability: An 800-year-old festival from China. *Journal of Sustainable Tourism*, **6** (4), 267-292.

Son, S. M., Lee, K. M. (2011). Assessing the influences of festival quality and satisfaction on visitor behavioral intentions. *Event Management*, **15**(3), 293-303

Soutar, G. N. and McLeod, P. B. (1993). Residents' perceptions of impact of the America's Cup. *Annals of Tourism Research*, **20**, 571-582.

Sox, C.B., Benjamin, S., Carpenter, J. and Strick, S. (2013). An exploratory study of meeting planners and conference attendees' perceptions of sustainable issues in convention centers. *Journal of Convention and Event Tourism*, **14**(2), 144-161.

Stevens, T. and Wootton, G. (1997). Sports stadia and arena: Realising their full potential. *Tourism Recreation Research*, **22**(2), 49-56.

Stokes, R. (2004). A framework for the analysis of events-tourism knowledge networks. *Journal of Hospitality and Tourism Management*, **11** (2), 108-123.

Stokes, R. (2008). Tourism strategy making: Insights to the events tourism domain. *Tourism Management*, **29** (2), 252–262.

Stokes, R. and Jago, L. (2007). Australia's public sector environment for shaping event tourism strategy. *International Journal of Event Management Research*, **3** (1), 42-53.

Strick, S. and Fenich, G.G. (2013). Green Certifications and Ecolabels in the MEEC Industry: Which Are Really Worth It? *Journal of Convention and Event Tourism*, **14**(2), 162-172.

Swart, K. and Bob, U. (2004). The seductive discourse of development: The Cape Town Olympic bid. *Third World Quarterly*, **25** (7), 1311-1324.

Taylor, P. and Gratton, C. (1988). The Olympic Games: An economic analysis. *Leisure Management*, **8**(3), 32-34.

The Exhibition Liaison Committee (1995). *The Exhibition Industry Explained.* London: Exhibition Liaison Committee.

Thomas, R. and Wood, E. H. (2004). Event-based tourism: A survey of local authority strategies in the UK. *Local Governance*, **29**(2), 127-136.

Thomson, A., Schlenker, K. and Schulenkorf, N. (2013). Conceptualizing sport event legacy. *Event Management*, **17**(2), 111-122.

Thrane, C. (2002). Music quality, satisfaction and behavioural intentions within a jazz festival context. *Event Management*, **7**(3), 143-150.

TIA (Travel Industry Association of America). (2004). Domestic trip activity by US travellers. Retrieved from www.tia.org/resources/images/charts/domestic_tip_activity_2004.gif

Tinnish, S.M. and Mangal, S.M. (2012). Sustainable Event Marketing in the MICE Industry: A Theoretical Framework. *Journal of Convention and Event Tourism*, **13**(4), 227-249.

Torche, F. and Valenzuela, E. (2011). Trust and reciprocity: A theoretical distinction of the sources of social capital. *European Journal of Social Theory*, **14**(2), 181-198.

Uysal, M. and Gitelson, R. (1994). Assessment of economic impacts: Festivals and special events. *Festival Management and Event Tourism*, **2**(1), 3–10.

Van de Wagen, L. and White, L. (2010). *Event Management: For Tourism, Cultural, Business and Sporting Events*. Frenchs Forest, N.S.W: Pearson Education.

Van Winkle, C.M. and Woosnam, K.M. (2014). Sense of community and perceptions of festival social impacts. *International Journal of Event and Festival Management*, **5**(1), 22-38.

Voase, R. N. (1994). Strategy or chance? A perspective on the cultural regeneration of our cities. *Regional Review*, **4**(4) Leeds: Yorkshire and Humberside Regional Research Observatory.

Waitt, G. (2003). Social impacts of the Sydney Olympics. *Annals of Tourism Research*, **30**(1), 194–215.

Walle, A. (1994). The festival life cycle and tourism strategies: The case of the Cowboy Poetry Gathering. *Festival Management and Event Tourism*, **2**, 85-94.

Walo, M., Bull, A. and Green, H. (1996). Achieving economic benefits at local events: A case study of a local sport event. *Festival Management and Event Tourism*, **3** (3/4), 96–106.

Walter, L. (1981). Social strategies and the fiesta complex in an Otavaleno community. *American Ethnologist*, **8**, 172-185.

Wang, C., Yang, J., Zhu, H. and Yu, L. (2014). Research on Foreign Tourists' Satisfaction with the 2010 Shanghai World Expo: Based on the Blogs at a Travel Website. *Journal of Convention and Event Tourism*, **15**(2), 114-134.

Wang, Y., Moyle, B., Whitford, M. and Wynn-Moylan, P. (2014). Customer Relationship Management in the Exhibition Industry in China: An Exploration into the Critical Success Factors and Inhibitors. *Journal of China Tourism Research*, **10**(3), 1-31.

Weber, K. and Ali-Knight, J. (2012). Events and festivals in Asia and the Middle East/North Africa (MENA) region. *International Journal of Event and Festival Management*, **3**(1), 4-8.

Weed, M. (2003). Why the two won't tango! Explaining the lack of integrated policies for sport and tourism in the UK. *Journal of Sport Management*, **17**(3), 258-283.

Weed, M. (2009). Sports tourism researh? A meta-review and exploration of futures. *Tourism Management*, **30**(5), 615-628.

Westerbeek, H., Turner, P. and Ingerson, L. (2002). Key success factors in bidding for hallmark sporting events. *International Marketing Review*, **19**(3), 303–322.

Whitfield, J. and Leonardo, A.N.D. (2011). Discretionary corporate social responsibility: introducing the greener venue. *International Journal of Event and Festival Management*, **2**(2), 170-183.

Whitford, M. (2004a). Event public policy development in the Northern Sub-Regional Organisation of Councils, Queensland Australia: Rhetoric or realisation? *Journal of Convention and Event Tourism,* **6** (3), 81- 99.

Whitford, M. (2004b). Regional development through domestic and tourist event policies: Gold Coast and Brisbane, 1974-2003. UNLV Journal of Hospitality, *Tourism and Leisure Science,* **1**,1-24.

Whitford, M. (2005). *Event Public Policy and Regional Development in South East Queensland.* In J Allen (ed.), Paper presented to Third International Event Management Research Conference, Sydney.

Whitford, M. (2009). Oaxaca's indigenous Guelaguetza festival: Not all that glistens is gold. *Event Management,* **12**(3–4), 143–161.

Whitford, M. and Ruhanen, L. (2013). Indigenous festivals and community development: A socio-cultural analysis of an Australian Indigenous festival. *Event Management,* **17**(1).

Whitford, M. and Ruhanen, L. (2014). Indigenous tourism businesses: an exploratory study of business owners' perceptions of drivers and inhibitors. *Tourism Recreation Research,* **39**(2), 149-168.

Williams, P.W. and Elkhashab, A. (2012). Leveraging tourism social capital: the case of the 2010 Olympic tourism consortium. *International Journal of Event and Festival Management,* **3**(3), 317-334.

Wolman, H. and Spitzley, D. (1996). The politics of local economic development. *Economic Development Quarterly,* **10**(2), 115-151.

Wood, E. (2005). Measuring the economic and social impacts of local authority events. *International Journal of Public Sector Management,* **18** (1), 37-53.

Wood, E., Robinson, L. and Thomas, R. (2005). *The contribution of community festivals to tourism: An assessment of the impacts of rural events in Wales. Assessing the impact of tourist events.* University Nice: TMP Research Group, Juan Les Pins, France Dec 8-9.

Wood, S. (2012). The power of celebration. Retrieved from www.ifea.com/joomla2_5/index.php?option=com_contentandview=articleandid=180abdIt emid=306

Wrathall, J. and Gee, A. (2011). *Event Management : Theory and Practice.* North Ryde, N.S.W: McGraw-Hill.

Wysong, S., Rothschild, P. and Beldona, S. (2011). Receiving a standing ovation for the event: A comprehensive model for measuring fan satisfaction with sports and entertainment events. *International Journal of Event Management Research,* **6**(1), 1-9.

Xiao, H. and Smith, S. (2004). Residents' perceptions of Kitchener-Waterloo Oktoberfest: An inductive analysis. *Event Management,* **8** (3), 161-175.

Xie, P. (2003). The bamboo-beating dance in Hainan, China. Authenticity and commodification. *Journal of Sustainable Tourism*, **11** (1), 5-16.

Xing, X. and Chalip, L. (2006). Effects of Hosting a Sport Event on Destination Brand: A Test of Co-branding and Match-up Models. *Sport Management Review*, *9(1)*, 49-78.

Yeoman, I., Robertson, M., Ali-Knight, J., McMahon-Beattie, U. and Drummond S. (eds) (2004). *Festival and Events Management: An International Arts and Culture Perspective*, Butterworth Heinemann: Oxford.

Yuan, J. and Jang, S. (2008). The effects of quality and satisfaction on awareness and behavioral intentions: Exploring the role of a wine festival. *Journal of Travel Research*, **46** (3), 279-288.

Ziakas, V. and Boukas, N. (2012). A neglected legacy. *International Journal of Event and Festival Management*, **3**(3), 292-316

Ziakas, V. and Costa, C. A. (2011). Event portfolio and multi-purpose development: Establishing the conceptual grounds. *Sport Management Review*, **14**(4), 409-423.

Ziakas, V. and Costa, C.A. (2012). 'The show must go on': event dramaturgy as consolidation of community. *Journal of Policy Research in Tourism, Leisure and Events*, **4**(1), 28-47.

Hospitality and Tourism Management Accounting

Helen Atkinson
Tracy Jones

Contents

Helen Atkinson is a principal lecturer at the University of Brighton, teaching and researching in management accounting and strategy applied to hospitality, tourism, events and retail. She has long record of publishing in academic journals and textbooks in this area.

Tracy Jones (Dr) is principal lecturer in the School Accounting & Law at University of Gloucestershire. Tracy coordinates PhD student supervision within accounting & finance and has many years experience of teaching managerial accounting applied to hospitality, tourism and events sectors. Her own published research is in this applied area.

A hyperlinked PDF version of this review is available for download from the CTR area of Goodfellow Pubishers' website: http://www.goodfellowpublishers.com/ctr

Themes and Developments in Hospitality and Tourism Applied Management Accounting Research

Approach

This review seeks to explore the key themes in hospitality and tourism applied management (managerial) accounting research. This work focuses on research published through key peer reviewed journals in the field and seeks to critically review the developments in the field of research. It goes on to identify developing research themes over time and proposes potential future research developments.

Harris and Brander Brown (1998) conducted a survey of activity in this field, applied to hospitality, during the 1980s and 1990s. Further work by Atkinson and Jones (2008) provided an update on this by considering the themes and issues in the broader area of financial management and management accounting up until 2006 related to hospitality. This current study builds on these earlier works, providing a critical review of the literature in key journals since 1998 related to management accounting research applied in hospitality and tourism organisations. It is important to point out that academic research in such applied management/managerial accounting has dominantly focused on the hotel sector as opposed to other aspects of hospitality and tourism, This is also reflected in the long tradition of textbooks applied to hotel-based accounting since the 1970s.

Given that the review is meant to be synoptic and cover the development of the field it would be useful to summarise the narrative from the papers mentioned above and show how this review builds upon those previous reviews.

A systematic approach was used to identify and audit key applied journals. The inclusion of specific journals was based on the published consensus view of key journals (including Law and van der Veen 2008; McKercher *et al.* 2006; Mason and Cameron 2004; Loosekoot *et al.* 2001; Baloglu and Assante 1999), qualified with respect to where the publications in the field of accounting most frequently occur. Generally the journals selected for this review appear in some or all of the journal review articles, being the most respected in the field, and importantly because they publish articles in the area of applied management accounting. It is noteworthy that *Annals of Tourism* and the *Journal of Travel Research* (two of the top applied journals according to many ranking systems) are not included, because of the paucity, or absence, of subject specific research publications.

The key journals used in this study are therefore:

- *Cornell Hospitality Quarterly* (formally known as *Cornell Hotel and Restaurant Quarterly*);

- *International Journal of Hospitality Management* (HosMan);

- *International Journal of Contemporary Hospitality Management* (IJCHM);

- *Journal of Hospitality and Tourism Research* (ICHRIE journal)

A further database search was conducted online specific to tourism, using the terms, 'management accounting' and 'tourism' – this revealed just a handful of articles, of these the vast majority came from IJCHM and HosMan. Whilst this search also identified some in 'Tourism Management' further research identified management accounting was not the main focus of any of those studies identified.

It is interesting to bear in mind that in relation to the body of published research in hospitality, only 7.8% (out of 1073) of articles published focused on finance (including accounting) related research. Based on research by Baloglu and Assante (1999) who reviewed five top hospitality journals over a seven year period, contributions relating to finance (including accounting) were lower than marketing (18.9%), operations (20.2%), human resources (29.4%), administration/strategy (18.9%), with only articles focussing on R&D (Research and development) being lower (4.8%) than the finance area.

As an additional measure, to ensure the major research work in the field was captured, an author search was conducted of the most prolific authors in the field to identify further research outputs published outside the key four applied journals. Applied research was also identified in generic journals through subject searches in major generic management accounting journals (e.g. *Management Accounting Research*) and with the use of computer based/online journal database search. This search process yielded a database of research papers of which 100+ are included in this review and which the authors believe captures the significant work in the area.

It is also worth noting a chapter in the generic *Handbook of Management Accounting Research* (Chapman, Hopwood & Shields, 2008) which included a chapter concerning managerial accounting research in the hospitality industry by Dittman, Hesford and Potter. This review does identify a few research papers, both in generic accounting journals and industry applied journals however it is nowhere near exhaustive of research published in the field, but provides an interesting view by these American academics. It is also interesting to note that their definition of the hospitality industry did include recreation, travel related, convention and meeting services alongside the food and accommodation hospitality focus. Despite this broad definition of hospitality all their identified applied journal studies focused on hotels and in generic journals either hotels or restaurant, with the exception of four examples applied to performance measurement in airlines (Dittman *et al.* 2008). A more recent research review by Jang and Park (2011) is very specific only to hospitality applied finance, so does not address management accounting in either hospitality or tourism, thus does not overlap with this research.

Definitions

It is important that a working definition of 'management or managerial accounting' is established in the context of this review. The finance and accounting discipline is generally broken into three aspects: financial management; financial accounting; and management accounting.

Financial management focuses on the corporate finance of the business, e.g. equity versus share capital, the cost of capital and management of the capital portfolio of the business and an organisations position on the financial markets.

Financial accounting is the external focus of accounting record keeping – this is the recording of historic financial data for reporting routinely to external stakeholders, such as shareholders and government organisations for the purposes of taxation and meeting legal requirements.

Management (managerial) accounting is focused on the internal use of accounting information to support the management functions within the organisation. As such, management accounting should meet the internal needs of managers at various levels within an organisation. Management accounting grew out of 'cost accounting' and more recently strategic management accounting has provided a greater link between accounting information and strategic decision making within organisations. Strategic management accounting incorporates both financial and non-financial tools, with a view to assisting strategic decision making in competitive markets.

This review focuses on management (managerial) accounting, including strategic management accounting, so the use of accounting tools and information primarily used internally by managers in order to aid them in fulfilling their managerial roles and responsibilities. As an example, whilst Lamminmaki 2007 and 2008 are included, Lamminmaki 2005 is not included in the review as it has a financial management (asset specificity) focus.

Core Research Themes

The research findings were grouped into a number of key sub-themes, namely; performance measurement, planning and control (including costing), budgeting, price determination and revenue management, and the role of financial management/controllers. It is interesting to note that whilst the subject of costing was covered by Harris and Brander Brown (1998), limited work in this area was found by Atkinson and Jones from 1998 – 2006 (2008), however more recently further research has been conducted in this area.

The themes and sub-themes used have been drawn from those identified in the literature reviewed. By its nature management accounting, as a function, should support management decision making, therefore it is often difficult to 'pigeon hole' research under one specific heading or to avoid management accounting research being intrinsically linked with other management functions. This inter-relationship to other management areas and functions makes drawing 'hard boundaries' difficult in such a review as this. One example of this is the subject of revenue (yield) management - is this management accounting research, or operational research? A significant amount of research into revenue and yield management takes an operational management or marketing perspective (Burgess and Bryant 2001), therefore in this review revenue management research is only included where it has a specific financial, as opposed operational, focus. On the methodological side, data envelopment analysis (DEA) is another example where we have only included examples with a management accounting focus, within our working definition. This leads to some studies discussed in Dittman et al.'s 2008 review being excluded here. An example of this is Sigala et al. (2005) which focuses on operational management, both in its specific study, the authors and literature it builds upon, so would not be included in a review with our strict definitions. Equally some papers cover more than one of the sub-themes identified; where this is the case the specific aspects of the research are discussed in each sub-theme. Tables 1 and 2 included later (section 4) provide a broad overview of management accounting research reviewed in this review. By far the most published area of research is performance measurement, which has been further subdivided into three categories; a summary of these is presented in Table 1 (performance measurement = 32, alternative performance ratios and CSF = 18, standardised approaches to accounting = 8). The remaining articles are organised under four broad subheadings: planning and control including costing = 13; budgeting = 16; price determination and revenue management = 24 and the role of the financial manager/controllers (20) these are presented in Table 2. Please note these totals add to more than the total number of articles reviewed as some appear in more than one sub-topic. These groupings provide the structure for the following review of applied management accounting research.

Review of Hospitality and Tourism Applied Management Accounting Research

This review is conducted using the five sub-headings already identified in Section 3. Overall conclusions on the 'state of the art' of research are then provided, drawing the five sub-areas together alongside discussion of methodological and philosophical approaches.

Review of performance measurement research

Research in the area of performance measurement (PM) is both prolific and practical, demonstrated in the generic literature and the applied hospitality and tourism literature, and the topic covers a wide range of disciplines and subjects (Neely; 1999, 2002). Atkinson and Brander Brown identify "a new emerging competitive order" (2001:128), which has resulted in companies finding new ways to monitor and manage performance. Applied research has responded and there have been a significant number publications looking at performance measurement in hospitality and tourism settings since 1998. The use of scorecards, performance ratios, in particular, the use and effectiveness of industry statistics such as REVPAR and the development and use of standard approaches to accounting has been key.

Since the last major review up to 2006 (Atkinson and Jones 2008) there have been continued developments along these lines with several studies focusing on drivers of good financial performance and efficiency. O'Neill and Matilla (2006) and later O'Neill et al. (2008) looked at net operating income (NOI) and its drivers. These large scale quantitative studies using publically available information, found NOI was closely linked to occupancy, average daily rate (ADR), property age and location (2006) and found that increased marketing spend lead to increased revenue and NOI (2008). Interestingly, O'Neill and Matilla confirmed that it is having customers which is important and proposed that in times of recession it is preferable to sacrifice ADR for occupancy (O'Neill and Matilla 2006).

Other researchers have used quantitative techniques to identify performance drivers, Barros and Santos (2006) used data envelopment analysis (DEA) to identify 50% efficiency factor in Portuguese hotels. Gursoy and Swanger (2007) identified key internal strategic factors such as sales and human resources could lead to improved performance and enhanced performance has also been linked with e-marketing (Soo Cheong et al. 2006). Banker et al. (2000) looked at the use of non-financial performance measures (NFPM) in incentive schemes in 4 star hotels and the link to financial performance, finding that customer satisfaction significantly linked to future financial performance in terms of revenues and profitability, in addition they found that changes in the managerial incentive programmes lead to changes in financial performance.

Table 1: Performance Measurement Research

Performance measurement	Alternative performance ratios (RP) and CSF	Standardised Approaches to Accounting
Anderson, Rl Fish M Xia Y and Michello F (1999)	Atkinson and Jones 2008	Anderson & Guilding 2006
Ahrens & Chapman 2002	Banker, Potter & Srinivasan 2005	Atkinson and Jones 2008
Atkinson & Brander Brown 2001	Brotherton 2004a & 2004b	Chin & Toye 1999
Atkinson 2006	Brown & Dev 1999	Enz & Canina 2002
Atkinson and Jones 2008	Douglas 2000	Enz, Canina & Walsh 2001
Banker, Potter & Srinivasan 2000	Gursoy & Swanger 2007	Field 2007
Barros & Santos 2006	Jung 2008	Kwansa & Schimidgall 1999
Beals & Denton 2005	Kimes 2001	Rompf 1998
Behn & Riley 1999	Krakhmal 2006	
Brander Brown & Atkinson 2001	Morey & Dittman 2003a & 2003b	Total = 8
Bergin-Seers, S & Jago, L 2007	O'Neill & Mattila 2006	
Campbell 2008	O'Neill, Hansen & Mattila 2008	
Chan & Wong 2007	Sanjeev 2007	
Cruz 2007	Sin, Tse, Heung & Yim 2005	
Davila & Venkatachalam 2004	Slattery 2002	
Denton & White 2000	SooCheong, Jang & Bai 2006	
Evans 2005	Yilmaz & Bititci 2006	
Haktanir & Harris 2005	Youres & Kett 2003	
Harris & Brander Brown 1998		
Harris & Mongiello 2001	Total = 18	
Harris & Mongiello 2006		
Huckstein & Duboff 1999		
Ismail, Dalbor & Mills 2002		
Karadag & Kim 2006		
Kim, Oh & Gregoire 2006		
Liedtka 2002		
Louvieris, Philips, Warr & Bowen 2003		
Mia & Patiar 2001		
Mongiello & Harris 2006		
Patiar & Mia 2008		
Philips & Louvieris 2005		
Philips 1999a & 1999b		
Riley *et al.* 2003		
Sangster 2003		
Sharma and Upjena (2005)		
Southern G (199()		
Wilson 2001		
Youres & Kett 2004		
Total = 35		

Campbell (2008) revealed the use of financial and non-financial performance measures in promotion and demotion decisions in quick service restaurants, in a very detailed quantitative study of 852 managers over 3year period, he found non-financial measures such as service quality and employee retention were implicated in promotion and demotion decisions. Davila and Venkatachalam (2004) found NFPM, specifically passenger load factor, was linked to compensation for senior executives. This quantitative study in the airline business raised interesting questions about the impact of financial distress in the relative influence of financial and non-financial performance measures.

There has been a developing body of research looking at the link between NFPM and financial performance, Behn and Riley (1999) found predictive ability of NFPM in US Airlines, but Riley *et al.* (2003) found conflicting results when investigating the value of non-financial performance variables in the context of financial reporting, explaining the difference was due to a capital market approach. This study is arguably outside the remit of this study, but along with Leidtka's study (2002), helps demonstrate a picture of a continuing search for legitimisation of NFPM. Chan and Wong (2007) argued for a change in financial reporting linked to performance drivers. Sanjev (2007) ranked a series of causal factors using DEA to understand efficiency in hotels and restaurants in India, whilst Sharma and Upneja (2005) looked at financial performance in small hotels in Tanzania.

Studies looking more broadly at PMS and the use of management accounting information (MAI) include Cruz (2007) whose findings (in the context of joint ventures) concurred with Brander Brown and Atkinson (2001) identifying the use of budgets and rolling forecasts and Mongiello and Harris (2006) who found the choice of performance indicators used were shaped by the application of work-related values in multinational (network) hotel organisations. Patiar and Mia (2008) found the intensity of competition affected the reliance on MAI, whilst Bergin-Seers and Jago (2007) studied small motels in Australia concurring with Hakinar and Harris's (2005) earlier findings that owners and managers focus on different information. Research is both critical of (Slattery, 2002) and dependent on (Enz and Canina 2002, Sin *et al.* 2005,) RevPAR as a measure of performance. Ahrens and Chapman (2002) adopted a qualitative approach to understanding the use of performance measures in the wider context of control multi unit restaurant chain, finding contests of accountability around food costs percentages and labour costs.

Several studies have looked at multidimensional performance measurement frameworks, with some in-depth research. Many of these studies have explored how measures are used for decision-making (e.g. Harris and Mongiello 2001) and some have been conceptual papers proposing new or adapted models

(Phillips 1999, Southern 1999, Yilmaz and Bititci 2006). Since 1998 a range of methods have been applied, with a predominance of interview and survey techniques, - with these often being combined in multi-method research. Like other topic areas in this review there were few large-scale quantitative studies, where these methods are adopted, they often lack generalisability due to a pragmatic regional or industry focus (Barros and Santos 2007, Bergin-Seers and Jago 2007, Campbell 2008, Davila and Venkatachalam 2004, Sanjeev 2007). However, in common with other areas of research, and with a few notable exceptions e.g. Ahrens and Chapmen (2002) and Louvieris *et al.* (2003), most research takes place in the lodging (hotel) sector. Good use is made of publicly available information particularly evident with work emanating from Cornell e.g. O'Neill *et al.* (2008) and Kimes (2001) arguably facilitated by the widespread use of a standardised approach to accounting namely USALI (Uniform System of Accounting for the Lodging Industry). The provision of standardised data facilitates the widespread practice of external benchmarking (Enz *et al.* 2001, Rompf 1998), although not universally employed (Anderson and Guilding 2006). Field (2007) advises caution when using ratios and statistics generated from this data and alludes to USALI's legacy as a departmental rather than customer focussed reporting system.

Many of these research studies are descriptive; capturing the state of play (Atkinson and Brander Brown, 2001) and identifying benefits (Denton and White, 2000). Others are evaluative providing useful practitioner orientated outcomes (Harris and Mongiello 2001, Mongiello and Harris 2006, Phillips and Louvieris 2005) and as such are applied and problem solving. Although all these are valuable, there is little evidence of new Performance Measurement theories or ideas being generated, this is a common theme which will be discussed later in this review.

Review of planning and control, costing based research

A summary of research in this theme is included in Table 2. The late 1990s/ early 2000s saw little research specifically focused on 'costing', greater emphasis was placed on measuring and managing performance, alongside the price of products and customers' perceptions of price. Whilst such research may view product/customer costs this is as a bi-product of such research and not its key research purpose. Ahrens and Chapman (2004) research did consider control systems within restaurant chains, using an in depth case study, distinguishing between traditional top-down control systems and enabling controls, this study can be linked to their earlier work (2002), discussed in the preceding section on performance measurement. More recently a number of studies have taken place in this subject area. Assaf and Matawie (2008) considered cost efficiency modelling in health care foodservice operations, whilst Kim *et al.* (2007) under-took an examination of cost management behaviour in small restaurant firms. Sandino's 2007 study was applied to the retail sector, but 58.7% of the sample was restaurants. Sandino (2007) looked specifically at the investment in man-agement control systems and how this links specifically to their strategy at that time. The work of Lamminmaki (2007) considered outsourcing in Australian hotels from a transaction cost economics perspective. As the world continues in recession control, cost control seems to be a key concern for many organisations and the likelihood of growth in this research area over the next few years seems likely.

Whilst budgeting has a planning and control phase it is broader in scope than just planning and control, and given the number of papers purely related to budgeting, the work on budgeting has been reviewed under its own sub-theme. Research in planning and control lends itself to quantitative research methods, as shown by the modelling work of Crange (2003) in the Italian restaurant sector who tested the value of time series analysis to support effective sales forecasting. Much work has been undertaken looking at the profitability of specific market segments and how such information can be used in business planning (see Enz *et al.* 1999, Guilding *et al.* 2001, Noone and Griffin 1999). Enz *et al.* (1999), focused on the costs associated with customer mix and products offered, whilst they saw financial benefits in offering more products and service to existing custom-ers, they found widening the customer mix did not have the same impact. They therefore concluded that increasing the customer market base did not always lead to greater financial returns.

A number of researchers in this area (see Guilding *et al.* 2001, Noone and Griffin 1999) have used customer profitability analysis (CPA) in order to track prof-itability by customer group. By using CPA and activity based costing (ABC) Noone and Griffin (1999) came to similar conclusions to those of Enz *et al.* (1999) that customer diversity does not always lead to greater profitability. Whilst Guilding *et al.* (2001) also used CPA in their research, this was extended with the use of customer asset accounting (CAA) and linked to marketing based decision making. They however concluded such an approach was rather radical given the current nature of management accounting in the hospitality sector, which, in their view did not have a marketing focus – despite this view a number of the papers related to price determination and revenue management link to both marketing and accounting disciplines (see section 3.4). It should be remem-bered here that the hospitality industry, and in particular the hotel sector, has a market/customer orientation rather than a product orientation (Harris and Brander Brown 1998). The 'profit planning framework' research by Graham and Harris (1999) uses an understanding of the nature of costs and cost volume profit (CVP) analysis alongside flexible budgets to aid decision making to max-imise profit returns. Again, though a different approach, this research addressed similar issues to those researchers mentioned above and emphasised a market-orientated approach to decision making.

Table 2: Applied Research

Planning and control (incl costing)	Budgeting	Price determination and revenue mgt	Role of financial managers / controllers
Ahrens & Chapman 2004	Atkinson & Jones 2008	Atkinson & Jones 2008	Atkinson & Brander Brown 2001
Anderson & Guilding 2006	Brander Brown & Atkinson 2001	Burgess & Bryant 2001	Atkinson & Jones 2008
Assaf, & Matawie 2008	Graham & Harris 1999	Cassidy & Guilding 2007	Beals & Denton 2005
Atkinson & Jones 2008	Guilding 2003	Chan & Au 1998	Burgess & Bryant 2001
Brown & Dev 1999	Guilding & Lamminmaki 2007	Chan & Chan 2008	Burgess 2000a, 200b
Crange 2003	Harris & Brander Brown 1998	Chen & Schwartz 2008	Burgess 2003
Enz, Potter & Sigaw 1999	Jones 1998	Choi & Mattia 2006	Burgess 2004
Graham & Harris 1999	Jones 2006	Choi 2006	Burgess 2006
Guilding, Kennedy, McManus 2001	Jones 2008a	Collins & Parsa 2006	Burgess 2007a
Kim, Dalbour & Feinstein 2007	Jones 2008b	Danziger, Israeli, & Bekerman (2006)	Burgess 2007b
Lamminmaki 2007	Mia & Patiar 2002	DeRoos 1999	Countryman, DeFranco & Venegas 2005
Harris & Brander Brown 1998	Schimidgal & DeFranco 1998	Harris & Brander Brown 1998	Denton & White 2000
Noone & Griffin 1999	Sharma 2002	Hu, Parsa & Zhao 2006	Gibson 1998
Sandino 2007	Subramaniam, McManus & Mia 2002	Kimes 2008	Gibson 2002
Total = 14	Yuen 2004	Madanoglu & Brezina 2008	Gibson 2004
	Yuen 2006	Miao & Mattila 2007	Graham 2003
		Pellinen (2003)	Harris & Brander Brown 1998
	Total = 16	Quan 2002	Lamminmaki D 2008
		Quain, Sansbury & LeBruto (1998a)	Potter & Schmidgall 1999
		Quain, Sansbury & LeBruto (1998b)	Sangster 2003
		Quain, Sansbury & LeBruto (1999)	Total = 20
		Schwartz 2006	
		Tso & Law 2005	
		van der Rest & Harris 2008	
		Total = 24	

The complex nature of the 'product' (or service) being offered in the hospitality sector, with inter-product / service dependence and the complexity of tracking costs at a customer, as opposed department level is evident. Being able to do this is central to evaluating the profits generated across the multitude of products and services consumed by an individual customer. What is clear from the published research is that it is not working solely within management accounting boundaries and recognises the need to work in a wider organisational management and market-orientated decision-making context; such inter-disciplinary research can only be to the good of the industry and its future development. This research also shows a link to strategic planning and this relates well to the increase in strategic management accounting in the generic literature. Otley (2001) makes the link between management accounting and strategic research in the generic literature; this is clearly true in the hospitality applied research as demonstrated by the work of Atkinson (2006b) whose ideas derived from research in hospitality studies.

Review of budgeting research

Hospitality applied budgeting research has taken place for over 30 years. Whilst research in the 1980s and 1990s was predominantly USA based (see Harris and Brander Brown 1998) in the last decade we have seen studies that look more widely around the world to include USA (Brander Brown and Atkinson 2001, Schimidgal and DeFranco 1998,), UK (Jones 1998, 2008a, 2008b), Australia (Mia and Patiar 2002, Sharma 2002, Subramaniam *et al.* 2002,) and the Far East (Yuen 2004, 2006). In line with Baloglu and Assante's (1999) findings, the main focus of this research is still the hotel sector.

In 1998 Harris and Brander Brown described research into budgeting as being diverse in nature, this appears this has continued since that time. Research has considered operational budgeting and forecasting (Jones 1998, 2008a, 2008b, Schimidgal and DeFranco 1998,), to specific aspects of budgeting such as; 'better budgeting (Brander Brown and Atkinson 2001), participation in budgeting (Mia and Patiar 2002, Subramaniam *et al.* 2002), and the impact of environmental uncertainty (Sharma 2002). Whilst the aspects of budgeting research varies, so too does the theoretical stand point – this is in line with a study by Covaleski *et al.* (2003) of generic research into budgeting that showed a contribution from economic, psychological and sociological perspectives in such research. It is clear from the conclusions in a number of these papers that whilst the research already undertaken addresses some questions there is still much work that could be undertaken to fully understand budgeting in the hospitality industry. Whilst the above has focused generally on operational or short-term budgeting, the work of Guilding (Guilding 2003, Guilding and Lamminmaki 2007) has focused specifically on capital budgeting in an applied context, but this is outside the remit of a management (or managerial) accounting review and is considered by the authors to fall within financial management.

Review of research into price determination and revenue management

Research by Burgess and Bryant (2001), as already mentioned highlights that research into revenue management has tended to focus on operational and marketing perspectives. The need for a financial perspective to ensure revenue maximisation leads to profit maximisation is also important (Krakhmal 2006; Krakhmal and Harris 2008). So this research area seems ideal for interdisciplinary research to take place. Pricing more generally is an area where accounting meets other disciplines in research, more directly marketing and operations management. DeRoos (1999) discusses natural occupancy rates (NORs) and believes this area warrants further research into the impact this has on pricing decisions.

Another area in relation to pricing research links finance with Information Technology (IT) (Chan and Au 1998, Kimes 2008, Tso and Law 2005). The application of revenue management in specific situations is also given some attention - Choi (2006) takes an interesting look at group reservations and how their profitability can be tracked, whilst Madanoglu and Brezina (2008) look specifically at resort spas. Choi, along with Mattlia (2006) also looked at issues around hotel variable pricing policies and the cross-cultural issues of such policies. Whilst there are a number of isolated and interesting studies in this area there is still an opportunity for further research, specifically interdisciplinary research that draws on operational, marketing and financial disciplines together in relation to pricing and revenue management development.

Review of the role of financial managers/controllers research

Whilst not directly 'management accounting research' the research into this subject does look at the role of financial managers and controllers who engage in management accounting functions. Of particular interest to researchers here is their inter-relationship with managers and indeed where such functions become divorced from managers, the needs for managers to enhance their own financial management skills. Work in this area is carried out in an ever changing environment where globalisation, separation of hotel ownership and management, and outsourcing (Lamminmaki 2008) has an impact on the financial control function. This links to the financial skills required by managers, particularly as unit level financial control may be at a distance. In a UK context much research in this area has been carried out by Burgess (see Burgess 2000a, 2000b, 2003, 2004, 2006, 2007a and 2007b) – this work has particularly focused on the role of financial controllers and provides longitudinal evidence. Gibson's work (1998, 2002, 2004) focused on Hong Kong, looking at the role of the financial controller, but also their attitudes and perceptions in the decision making process. How the separation of ownership and management within the industry can lead to stakeholder tensions in demands is explored by Denton and White (2000), Sangster (2003), and Beals and Denton (2005). What is clear is that these are changing times, Burgess (2000a), Gibson (2002) and Graham (2003) all concur that the role and nature of the financial control function is changing in the 21st century. Generic accounting research trends also show accounting as a function and the accountants' role are shifting (Hopper *et al.* 2001), so this is not something that is peculiar to the hospitality industry and is likely to be any area to continue to be researched in the future.

Discussion of Research Design

For the purpose of describing and evaluating the current state of the field of research in applied management accounting research, publications in this review have been analysed in terms of whether they are empirical or conceptual/review papers. It should be noted that our definition differs from other studies (Baloglu & Assante 1999; Rivera and Upchurch 2008), who differentiate based upon employment of statistical technique; for us empirical means generating new data from primary sources, or through the analysis of secondary sources, and drawing conclusions and new insights from this, regardless of the nature of the data or the analytical approach to that data, thus we appear to have a broader definition.

Of the articles reviewed in this study, 72% (n=83) were based on empirical findings, these were grounded in data collected specifically for the purposes of the research project (e.g. Anderson and Guilding 2006) or data that was already in existence (e.g. Enz *et al.* 2001). Non-empirical pieces, which encompassed straightforward literature reviews (e.g. Burgess 2006); discussion of recent changes in the law or industry practice (Beals & Denton 2005; Wilson 2001), and more innovative conceptual pieces (Choi 2006; van der Rest & Harris 2008) collectively accounted for 28% (n=33) of output. Interestingly, these findings appear to contradict findings from Baloglu and Assante (1999) and are more inline with Rivera and Upchurch (2008) who found 82% empirical. This can be explained partially through definitional factors, the journals in question in each study and the fact that here we are focussing solely on management (managerial) accounting outputs.

Within the limitations of this broader review, we have considered the research methods employed and drawn some conclusions, which can be compared to other analysis such as that by Baloglu & Assante (1999) and Rivera & Upchurch (2008). In this analysis a variety of methods, were revealed (see Table 3).

Table 3: Research Methods in empirical studies

Method	n	%
Questionnaire	28	33.73%
Interviews	17	20.48%
Focus Group	2	2.41%
Combination of methods	12	14.46%
Analysis of Secondary Data / archival	21	25.30%
Other *	3	3.61%
	83	100.00%

It can be seen that questionnaires are still utilised the most in studies (34%), but these are often combined with other methods (14%); interviews or focus groups are used in 25% of studies. Analysis of the 83 empirical articles revealed a continued, if not increased, emphasis on the lodging sector with 65 (78%) articles based in this sector and only 14 (17%) focussing on restaurants, food service operations, broad service sector organisations, with 4 studies (5%) applied to airlines. This concurs with Rivera and Upchurch (2008) that the lodging sector is the most examined and could suggest that other sectors should be considered for more attention by researchers in the future.

We have also looked at the nature of the analysis whether this is quantitative or qualitative and whether there is some indication, be it implicit or explicit, as to the philosophy underpinning. We have separated studies into *quantitative*, where statistical techniques were used to reveal new insights and the data is predominantly numerical in nature, and *qualitative*, where data is mainly qualitative and is analysed through coding and categorisation to draw out meaning, which can confirm or develop theory. Amongst the 83 empirical studies, 41 (49%) were predominantly qualitative in nature with 33 (40%) considered quantitative and 8 studies (approx10%) employed mixed method (one was methodologically unclear) this appears to contradict conventional wisdom that there is a "preoccupation with quantitative methodology" (Losekoot *et al.* 2001:241). It is interesting to note that many of the examples of quantitative research identified in this review were in generic management accounting / accounting journals. In our analysis we have not classified research as quantitative just because descriptive statistics are used. The key for this review is where textual and interpretive analysis is employed, rather than numerical, to generate knowledge, the research is categorised as qualitative. Although philosophy is rarely mentioned, the analysis suggests a continued disposition towards positivistic research approaches (Losekoot *et al.* 2001; Taylor and Edgar 1996, 1999), even where qualitative methods and case studies are adopted, there is evidence of using a contingency approach and controlling for different factors, implying a leaning towards positivistic rather than interpretivist phenomenological philosophies. The embedding in a clear theoretical framework is not always evident, particularly with older research. Again, there seems to be a difference related to industry applied research that appears in generic journals in accounting / management accounting. In reviewing these specific examples they tend to be high rating journals, higher than the hospitality / tourism specific journals- it may be this factor, as opposed to the journal orientation, that leads to a stronger theoretical underpinning of such research. This is a noteworthy finding from this review.

Conclusions – Overview and Progress in Hospitality Applied Management Accounting Research

The review by Harris and Brander Brown (1998) traced hospitality and tourism applied management accounting research back to the 1970s, but generic research and development has a far longer history (Ryan *et al.* 2002). This difference is seen in the maturity, scope and volume of research in the generic area compared with the hospitality and tourism applied literature, including the methodological approaches used. The 2003 mapping of generic management accounting research by Luft and Shields (2003) took the six leading management accounting journals and mapped publications into sub-sections, completing a detailed review of methodological approaches applied to these studies. What is clear from this, at a broad level, is that hospitality management accounting research draws many similarities in terms of issues addressed to that undertaken in the generic literature i.e. the same topics are being investigated, but in an applied way. Differences arise when research is considered in more depth – an example of this is performance measurement; this is equally popular in generic research as in the hospitality applied domain, but the hospitality industry may use different performance measures, such as RevPAR and GOPPAR which are industry specific. Hence it can be seen certain generic management accounting techniques such as the balanced scorecard, ABC and CPA in generic literature have been taken and applied in a hospitality context, whilst in other areas industry specific tools are also developed.

It is recognised that much generic management accounting research up until the 1970s (see Ryan *et al.* 2002, Scapens 2006) was based on neoclassical economics. However since that time generic research has diversified into the wider area of social sciences and with a greater emphasis towards empirical industry based research (Scapens 2006). Whilst some hospitality applied management accounting research could be classified as 'traditional' economics based research – with empirical research being positivistic in approach this is not the case for all hospitality applied research reviewed. There is also evidence that more inter-disciplinary and interpretative work is starting to take place in the hospitality applied, as well the generic, field of management accounting research, e,g, Ahrens and Chapman 2002. There are demonstrable connections in the direction of research in both the applied and generic field.

It is clear that much of the hospitality applied research does not generate new theory development, but rather takes (and adapts) generic theory into the field of hospitality management to provide new insights and development. In terms of research methods there is still evidence of 'desk based' research, using postal surveys to describe practice, or the analysis of secondary sources to theorise concerning its application to the hospitality industry (Evans 2005, Jones 2008a). However qualitative research, using interviews, case studies, etc is on the increase and provides the opportunity to gain greater insights into industry practice (Brander Brown and Atkinson 2001, Jones 2008b, Mia and Patiar 2002, Mongellio and Harris 2006). This reflects Scapens' (2006) view that research has gone beyond 'describing' practice to research that is working alongside industry to develop practice.

With the exception of a few key individuals that publish multiple outputs in a specific subject area (see Tables 1 and 2, for example; Atkinson, Burgess, Enz, Gibson, Guilding, Harris, Jones) there is an issue with some case study and empirical based research that lacks follow through or development of an initial case study. Often research implications highlight limitations and areas for further study, but these are not addressed through further research – in some incidences this leaves an isolated case study un-generalised, reports of pilot studies, with no 'main study'. As a result the subject area does not move forward as quickly as it could, in fact it could be argued that collectively research has not moved on from 1998 and is still often 'isolated' (Sainaghi 2010) and fragmented "with preliminary findings left where they fall rather than providing a basis for further investigation" (Harris and Brander Brown 1998:174). In addition, there is no significant coordination within the academic communities and as such work is not developed or replicated in this respect Hospitality research suffers from the same frailties as wider generic management accounting research (Otley, 2001).

Another area that can be noted is the lack of hospitality/tourism management accounting researchers who also publish in the generic field. Whilst there are a number that successfully do this (examples from this review include, Atkinson 2006b, Chin and Toye 1999, Guilding 2003, Sharma 2002) this is not commonly the case. This would imply whilst many hospitality/tourism management accounting researchers draw on generic research there is limited movement outwardly to the wider generic academic journals for publication of such applied research. The criticism of hospitality applied research as being often 'inward looking' and relying heavily on theory developed in the generic field is not an issue peculiar to management accounting researchers, as this was raised by Olsen (2001) more generally related to hospitality applied research and is reflected in the UK Research Assessment Exercise (RAE) panels of 2001 and 2008, that hospitality research borrows from and lags behind mainstream research (Litteljohn, 2004; Otley 2009). Equally, though there are examples of generic management accounting researchers undertaking work applied to hospitality and tourism, often this ignores or uses on limited industry applied research in literature review sections. What also needs to be noted is the lack of substantial research material in this subject area specifically applied to tourism.

Can hospitality/tourism research offer more than a different context in which to apply generic theory? Hospitality applied research has developed since the early work of the 1970s and methodological approaches and methods are now better explored and detailed by researchers, showing a robustness in the applied research being undertaken. Hospitality applied research can offer considerable value, with the complex nature of the product/services delivered in the hospitality sector it offers a valuable, possible unique setting in which to conduct management accounting research. Such research is providing new insights and often questions generic research findings, particularly their direct application in this unique context. There are however still many opportunities for improving research applied to tourism based management accounting.

Therefore by focusing research around aspects where the hospitality/tourism industry offers a distinctive area for research due to its specific characteristics, whether this is the cost structure, the complex nature of the product/service offered, the socio-cultural context or industry specific performance measurement tools, there is a fertile ground for continued research into hospitality applied management accounting. Scapens' (2006) discusses the need for generic management accounting researchers to focus on understanding industry practice in order to aid managers – this is equally applicable in an industry applied context. If such rich opportunities for research are to be exploited there is a need for such researchers to collaborate through larger collaborative projects – this would create a greater ability to complete larger scale and truly international projects and the ability to attract more substantial research funding. Mason and Cameron (2006) suggest that a critical mass of activity can be achieved when clusters of academics interested in similar areas work together – such clusters aid the development of methodologies, philosophical debate and maturity. This review has shown how research in this applied field has grown and developed over time, demonstrating methodological and philosophical engagement, but there is much work still to be tackled and research output shows a growing number of researchers in the field willing to develop the discipline further.

References

Anderson, R. I., Fish M., Xia, Y. and Michello, F., (1999), Measuring efficiency in the hotel industry: a schocastic frontier approach, *International Journal of Contemporary Hospitality Management*, **18** (1), 45-57.
www.sciencedirect.com/science/article/pii/S0278431998000462

Anderson, S. and Guilding, C., (2006) Competitor-focused accounting applied to a hotel context, *International Journal of Contemporary Hospitality Management*, **18** (3) 206-218.
www.emeraldinsight.com/journals.htm?articleid=1554203&show=abstract

Ahrens, T. and Chapman, C., (2002), The structuration of legitimate performance measures and management: day to day contests of accountability in a UK restaurant chain, *Journal of Management Accounting Research*, **13**, 151–171
www.sciencedirect.com/science/article/pii/S1044500501901878

Ahrens, T. and Chapman, C., (2004) Accounting for flexibility and efficiency: afield study of management control systems in a restaurant chain, *Contemporary Accounting Research*, **21** (2) 271-301.

Assaf, A and Matawie, K., (2008) Cost efficiency modelling in health care food-service operations, *International Journal of Hospitality Management*, **27**(4), 604-613. www.sciencedirect.com/science/article/pii/S027843190700059X

Assaf, A., Matawie, K. and Blackman, D., (2008) Operational performance of health care foodservice systems, *International Journal of Contemporary Hospitality Management*, **20** (2) 215-227.
www.emeraldinsight.com/journals.htm?articleid=1718192&show=pdf

Atkinson, H., (2006a) Performance measurement in the international hotel industry, Ch. 3 in Harris P and Mongiello M (Eds.), *Accounting and Financial Management: Developments in the International Hospitality Industry*, Butterworth-Heinemann

Atkinson, H., (2006b) Implementing strategy: A role for the balance scorecard. *Management Decision*, **44** (10), 1441–1460
www.emeraldinsight.com/journals.htm?articleid=1580792&show=pdf

Atkinson, H. and Brander Brown ,J., (2001), Rethinking performance measures: assessing progress in UK hotels, *International Journal of Contemporary Hospitality Management*, **13** (3), 129-136.
www.emeraldinsight.com/journals.htm?articleid=867376&show=abstract

Atkinson, H. and Jones, T., (2008) Financial management in the hospitality industry: themes and issues, pp. 228-256 in Brotherton, B and Woods, R (Eds) *The SAGE Handbook of Hospitality Management*, London:Sage.

Baloglu, S. and Assante, L.M., (1999), A content analysis of subject areas and research methods used in five hospitality management journals, *Journal of Hospitality and Tourism Research*, **23** (1), 53-70.
jht.sagepub.com/content/23/1/53.short

Banker, R., Potter, G. and Srinivasan, D., (2000), An empirical investigation of an incentive plan that includes nonfinancial performance measures, *The Accounting Review*, **75** (1), 65-92.
astro.temple.edu/~banker/Accounting/10%20An%20Empirical%20
    Investigation%20of%20an%20Incentive%20Plan.pdf

Banker, R., Potter, G. and Srinivasan, D., (2005), Association of Nonfinancial Performance Measures with the Financial Performance of a Lodging Chain, *Cornell Hotel and Restaurant Administration Quarterly*, **46**(4), 394-412.
cqx.sagepub.com/content/46/4/394.short

Barros, C. and Santos, C., (2006), The measurement of efficiency in Portuguese hotels using Data Envelopment Analysis, *Journal of Hospitality &Tourism Research*, **30** (3), 378-400.
jht.sagepub.com/content/30/3/378.short

Baxter, J. and Chua, W.F., (2003) Alternative management accounting research – whence and whither, *Accounting, Organizations and Society*, **28**, 97-126.
www.sciencedirect.com/science/article/pii/S0361368202000223

Beals, P. and Denton, G., (2005) The current balance of power in North American hotel management contracts, *Journal of Retail and Leisure Property*, **4**(2) 129-145
www.palgrave-journals.com/rlp/journal/v4/n2/abs/5090204a.html

Behn, B. and Riley, R., (1999) Using nonfinancial information to predict financial performance: the case of the U.S. airline industry, *Journal of Accounting, Auditing and Finance*, **14** (1), 29-56.

Bergin-Seers, S. and Jago, I., (2007), Performance measurement in small motels in Australia, *Tourism & Hospitality Research*, **7** (2), 144-155.
http://vuir.vu.edu.au/2003/

Brander Brown, J. and Atkinson. H., (2001), Budgeting in the information age: a fresh approach, International *Journal of Contemporary Hospitality Management*, **13** (3), 137-143.
www.emeraldinsight.com/journals.htm?articleid=867377&show=pdf

Brotherton, B., (2004a), Critical success factors in UK Corporate hotels, *Service Industries Journal*, 24 (3), 19-42.

Brotherton, B., (2004b), Critical success factors in UK budget hotel operations, *International Journal of Operations and Production Management*, **24**(9), 944-969. www.emeraldinsight.com/journals.htm?articleid=849564&show=html

Brown, J. and Dev, C., (1999), Looking beyond RevPAR, *Cornell Hotel and Restaurant Administration Quarterly*, **40**(2), 23-33. cqx.sagepub.com/content/40/2/23.abstract

Burgess, C., (2000a), The hotel financial controller-challenges for the future, *International Journal of Contemporary Hospitality Management*, **12**(1), 6-12. www.emeraldinsight.com/journals.htm?articleid=867309&show=html

Burgess, C., (2000b), Hotel Accounts-do men get the best jobs?, *International Journal of Hospitality Management*, **19** (4), 345-352.

Burgess, C., (2003), Gender and salaries in hotel financial management: it's still a man's world, *Women in Management Review*, **18** (1/2), 50-59. www.emeraldinsight.com/journals.htm?articleid=1412254&show=abstract

Burgess, C., (2004), Planning for the centralization of accounting in chain hotels, *Tourism and Hospitality: Planning & Development*, **1** (2), 145-156. www.tandfonline.com/doi/abs/10.1080/1479053042000251098

Burgess, C., (2006) Hotel unit financial management: does it have a future?, Ch. 14 in Harris P and Mongiello M (Eds.), *Accounting and Financial Management: Developments in the International Hospitality Industry*, Butterworth-Heinemann.

Burgess, C., (2007a), Do hotel managers have sufficient financial skills to help them manage their areas?, *International Journal of Contemporary Hospitality Management*, **19** (3), 188-200. www.emeraldinsight.com/journals.htm?articleid=1602638

Burgess, C., (2007b), Is there a future for hotel financial controllers?, *International Journal of Hospitality Management*, **26** (1), 161-174.

Burgess, C. and Bryantt, K., (2001), Revenue management-the contribution of the financial function to profitability, *International Journal of Contemporary Hospitality Management*, **13** (3), 144-150. www.emeraldinsight.com/journals.htm?articleid=867378&show=abstract

Campbell, D., (2008), Nonfinancial performance measures and promotion-based incentives, *Journal of Accounting Research*, **46** (2), 297-332. www.chicagobooth.edu/jar/conference/docs/campbell-incentives.pdf

Cassidy, K. and Guilding, C., (2007) Tourist accommodation price setting in Australian strata titled properties, *International Journal of Hospitality Management*, **26** (2), 277-292.

Chan, W. and Au, N., (1998), Profit measurement of menu items: in Hong Kong's Chinese restaurants, *Cornell Hotel and Restaurant Administration Quarterly*, **39**(2), 70-75.

Chan, W. and Chan, L., (2008) Revenue management strategies under the lunar-solar calendar:evidence of Chinese restaurant operations, *International Journal of Hospitality Management*, **27** (3), 381-390. www.sciencedirect.com/science/article/pii/S027843190700103X

Chang, W. and Wong, K., (2007) Towards a more comprehensive accounting framework for hotels in China, *International Journal of Contemporary Hospitality Management*, **19** (7), 546-559. www.emeraldinsight.com/journals.htm?articleid=1630408&show=html

Chapman, C., Hopwood, A. and Shields, M. (2008) *Handbook of Management Accounting Research, Vol. 3*, Elsevier, Oxford.

Chen, C. and Schwartz, Z., (2008), Room rate patterns and customers' propensity to book a hotel room, *Journal of Hospitality & Tourism Research*, **32** (3), 287-306. jht.sagepub.com/content/32/3/287.abstract

Chin, J. and Toye, P., (1999), A five star accounting system for the hotel industry, *Accounting and Business*, Feb-99, 24 -27.

Choi, S. and Mattlia, A., (2006), The role of disclosure in variable hotel pricing: a cross-cultural comparison of customers' fairness perceptions, *Cornel Hotel and restaurant Quarterly*, **47** (1), 27-35. cqx.sagepub.com/content/47/1/27.full.pdf

Choi, S., (2006), Group revenue management: a model for evaluating group profitability, *Cornell Hotel and restaurant Quarterly*, **47** (3), 260-271. cqx.sagepub.com/content/47/3/260.abstract

Collins, M. and Parsa, H. (2006) Pricing strategies to maximise revenues in the lodging industry, *International Journal of Hospitality Management*, **25**(1), 91-107 www.sciencedirect.com/science/article/pii/S0278431904001288

Countryman, C.C., DeFranco, A. and Venegas, T., (2005), Controller: a viable career for hospitality students, *International Journal of Contemporary Hospitality Management*, **17** (7), 577-589. www.emeraldinsight.com/journals.htm?articleid=1524016&show=html

Covaleski, M., Evans, J., Luft, J. and Shields, M., (2003), Budgeting research: three theoretical perspectives and criteria for selective integration, *Management Accounting Research* (USA), **15**, 3-49. www.sciencedirect.com/science/article/pii/S1751324306020062

Cranage, D., (2003), Practical time series forecasting for the hospitality manager, *International Journal of Contemporary Hospitality Management*, **15**(3), 86-93. www.emeraldinsight.com/journals.htm?articleid=867462

Cruz, I., (2007) How might hospitality organisations performance measurement system, *International Journal of Contemporary Hospitality*

Management, **19** (7), 574-588.
www.emeraldinsight.com/journals.htm?articleid=1630410&show=html

Danziger, S., Israeli, A. and Bekerman, M., (2006) The relative role of strategic assests in determining customer perceptions of hotel room price, *Journal of Hospitality Management,* **25** (1), 129-145.
www.sciencedirect.com/science/article/pii/S0278431904001215

Davila, A. and Venkatachalam, M., (2004), The relevance of non-financial performance measures for CEO compensation: evidence from the airline industry, *Review of Accounting Studies,* **9,** 443-464.
faculty.fuqua.duke.edu/~vmohan/bio/files/published%20papers/DV_ RAST2004.pdf

Denton, P. and White, B., (2000), Implementing a balanced-scorecard approach to managing hotel operations, *Cornell Hotel and Restaurant Administration Quarterly,* **41**(1), 94-107.
www.sciencedirect.com/science/article/pii/S0010880400888898

DeRoos, J., (1999), Natural occupancy rates and development gaps: a look at the U.S. lodging industry, *Cornell Hotel and Restaurant Administration Quarterly,* **40**(2), 14-22.
www.hotelschool.cornell.edu/research/chr/pubs/quarterly/featured/ execsummary-14784.html

Dittman,D., Hesford, J. and Potter, G. (2008) Managerial accounting in the hospitality industry, Ch. 8 in Chapman, C., Hopwood, A. and Shields, M. (2008) *Handbook of Management Accounting Research,* Vol. 3 Elsevier, Oxford.

Douglas, P.C., (2000), Measuring productivity and performance in the hospitality industry, *The National Public Accountant,* **45** (5), 15.

Enz, C. and Canina, L., (2002), The best of times, the worst of times: differences in hotel performance following 9/11, *Cornell Hotel and Restaurant Administration Quarterly,* **43**(5), 41-52.
cqx.sagepub.com/content/43/5/41.full.pdf+html

Enz, C., Canina, L. and Walsh, K., (2001), Hotel industry averages: an inaccurate tool for measuring performance, *Cornell Hotel and Restaurant Administration Quarterly,* **42**(6), 22-32.

Enz, C., Potter, G. and Siguaw, J., (1999), Serving more segments and offering more products: what are the costs and where are the profits?, *Cornell Hotel and Restaurant Administration Quarterly,* **40**(6), 54-62.
cqx.sagepub.com/content/40/6/54.abstract

Evans, N., (2005), Assessing the balanced scorecard as a management tool for hotels, *International Journal of Contemporary Hospitality Management,* **17**(5), 376-390.
www.emeraldinsight.com/journals.htm?articleid=1509790&show=abstract

Gibson, D., (1998), A qualitative research study on perceptions held by Hong Kong financial controllers in decision-making roles., *International Journal of Hospitality Management*, **17** (1), 65-81.

Gibson, DA., (2002), On-property hotel financial controllers: a discourse analysis approach to characterising behavioural roles, *International Journal of Hospitality Management*, **21** (1), 5-23.

Gibson, D.A., (2004), Hotel controllers in the 21st Century-a Hong Kong perspective on desired attributes, *International Journal of Hospitality Management*, **23** (5), 485-503.
www.sciencedirect.com/science/article/pii/S0278431904000210

Graham, I., (2003), Hotel controllership (a speech given at the Finance/Sales and Marketing Conference of Kempinski Hotels & Resorts July (2003), *BAHA Times*, Sept, pp.5–9.

Graham, I.C. and Harris, P.J., (1999), Development of a profit planning framework in an international hotel chain: a case study, *International Journal of Contemporary Hospitality Management*, **11** (5), 198-208.
www.emeraldinsight.com/journals.htm?articleid=867293

Guilding, C., (2003), Hotel owner/operator structures: implications for capital budgeting process, *Management Accounting Research*, **14**, 179-199.
www.sciencedirect.com/science/article/pii/S1044500503000490

Guilding, C., Kennedy, D. and McManus, L., (2001), Extending the boundaries of customer accounting: applications in the hotel industry, *Journal of Hospitality & Tourism Research*, **25** (2), 173-194.
jht.sagepub.com/content/25/2/173.abstract

Guilding, C. and Lamminmaki, D., (2007), Benchmarking hotel capital budgeting practices to practices applied in non-hotel companies, *Journal of Hospitality & Tourism Research*, **31** (4), 486-503.
jht.sagepub.com/content/31/4/486.abstract

Gursoy, D. and Swanger, N., (2007) Performance-enhancing internal straeegic factors and competencies: impacts on financial success, *International Journal of Hospitality Management*, **26** (1), 213-227.
www.sciencedirect.com/science/article/pii/S0278431906000181

Haktanir, M. and Harris, P., (2005), Performance measurement practice in an independent hotel context: A case study approach, *International Journal of Contemporary Hospitality Management*, **17**(1), 39-50.
www.emeraldinsight.com/journals.htm?articleid=1463573

Harris, P. and Brander Brown, J., (1998), Research and development in hospitality accounting and financial management., *International Journal of Hospitality Management*, **17**(2), 161-182.
www.sciencedirect.com/science/article/pii/S0278431998000139

Harris, P. and Mongiello, M., (2001), Key performance indicators in European hotel properties: general manager's choices and company profiles, *International Journal of Contemporary Hospitality Management*, **13**(3), 120-128. www.emeraldinsight.com/journals.htm?articleid=867375

Harris, P. and Mongiello, M., (Eds.) (2006), *Accounting and Financial Management: Developments in the International Hospitality Industry*, Butterworth-Heinemann.

Hopper, T., Otley, D. and Scapens, B., (2001), British management accounting research: whence and whither: opinions and recollections, *The British Accounting Review*, **33**, 263 – 291. www.sciencedirect.com/science/article/pii/S0890838901901696

Hu, H., Parsa, H.M. and Zhao, J., (2006) The magic of price-ending choices in European restaurants: a comparative study, *International Journal of Contemporary Hospitality Management*, **18** (2), 110-122. www.emeraldinsight.com/journals.htm?articleid=1550265&show=html

Huckstein, D. and Duboff, R., (1999), Hilton Hotels: A comprehensive approach to delivering value for all stakeholders, *Cornell Hotel and Restaurant Administration Quarterly*, **40** (4), 28-38.

Ismail, J., Dalbor, M. and Mills, J., (2002), Using RevPAR to Analyze lodging-segment Variability, *Cornell Hotel and Restaurant Administration Quarterly*, **43**(6), 73-80.

Jang, S. and Park, K., (2011) Hospitality finance research during the last two decades: subjects, methodologies, citations, *International Journal of Contemporary Hospitality Management*, **23** (4),479–497. www.emeraldinsight.com/journals.htm?articleid=1926036

Jones, T. A., (1998), UK hotel operators use of budgetary procedures, *International Journal of Contemporary Hospitality Management*, **10**(3), 96-100. www.emeraldinsight.com/journals.htm?articleid=867237

Jones, T. A., (2006) Budgetary practice within hospitality, Ch. 4 in Harris P and Mongiello M (Eds.) *Accounting and Financial Management: Developments in the International Hospitality Industry*, Butterworth-Heinemann.

Jones, T. A., (2008a) Changes in hotel industry budgetary practice, *International Journal of Contemporary Hospitality Management*, **20** (4), 428-444. www.emeraldinsight.com/journals.htm?articleid=1728367

Jones, T. A., (2008b) Improving hotel budgetary practice – A positive theory model, *International Journal of Hospitality Management*, **27** (4), 529-540.

Jung, H., (2008) WACC as the touchstone performance indicator: the use of financial ratios as performance indicator – from operations to capital investment, *International Journal of Contemporary Hospitality Management*, **20** (6), 700-710. www.emeraldinsight.com/journals.htm?articleid=1742463

Karadag, I. and Kim, W., (2006) Comparing market-segment-profitability analysis with department-profitability analysis as hotel marketing-decision tools, *Cornell Hotel and Restaurant Quarterly*, **47** (2), pp. 155-173. cqx.sagepub.com/content/47/2/155.abstract

Kim, A., Dalbour, M. and Feinstein, A., (2007) An examination of cost management behaviour in small restaurant firms, *International Journal of Hospitality Management*, **26** (2), 435-452. www.sciencedirect.com/science/article/pii/S0278431906001046

Kim, B., Oh, H. and Gregoire, M., (2006), Effects of firms' relationship-orientated behaviours on financial performance: a case of restaurant industry, *Journal of Hospitality & Tourism Research*, **30** (1), 50-75. jht.sagepub.com/content/30/1/50.abstract

Kimes, S., (2001) How product quality drives profitability: the experience at Holiday Inn, *Cornell Hospitality Quarterly*, **42** (3), 25-28. cqx.sagepub.com/content/42/3/25.extract

Kimes, S., (2008) The role of technology in restaurant revenue management, *Cornell Hospitality Quarterly*, **49** (3), 297-309. cqx.sagepub.com/content/49/3/297.short?rss=1&ssource=mfc

Krakhmal, V., (2006) Customer profitability accounting in the context of hotels, Ch 10 in Harris P and Mongiello M (Eds.) *Accounting and Financial Management: Developments in the International Hospitality Industry*, Butterworth-Heinemann.

Krakhmal, V. and Harris, P., (2008) *BAHA Recommended practice guide: Developing customer profitability analysis for hotels*. Wimbourne: British Association of Hospitality Accountants.

Kwansa, F. and Schmidgall, R., (1999), The Uniform System of Accounts for the Lodging Industry, *Cornell Hotel and Restaurant Administration Quarterly*, **40**(6), 88-94.

Law, R. and van der Veen, R., (2008) The popularity of prestigious hospitality journals: a Google Scholar approach, *International Journal of Contemporary Hospitality Management*, **20** (2), 113-125. www.emeraldinsight.com/journals.htm?articleid=1718185&show=pdf&

Lamminmaki, D., (2005), Why do hotels outsource? An investigation using asset specificity, *International Journal of Contemporary Hospitality Management*, **17** (6), 516-528. www.emeraldinsight.com/journals.htm?articleid=1515233&show=html

Lamminmaki, D., (2008), Accounting and the management of outsourcing: an empirical study of the hotel industry, *Management Accounting Research*, **19**(2), 163-181. www.sciencedirect.com/science/article/pii/S1044500508000061

Lamminmaki, D., (2007), Outsourcing in Australian Hotels: a transaction cost economics perspective, *Journal of Hospitality & Tourism Research*, **31**(1), 73-110 jht.sagepub.com/content/31/1/73.short

Leidtka, S., (2002), The information content of nonfinancial performance measures in the airline industry, *Journal of Business Finance & Accounting*, **29** (7-8), 1105-1121.
onlinelibrary.wiley.com/doi/10.1111/1468-5957.00463/abstract?

Losekoot,E., Verginis, CS and Wood, RC. (2001) Out for the count: some methodological questions in 'publications counting' literature. *Hospitality Management* **20** (3) 233–244\
www.sciencedirect.com/science/article/pii/S027843190100007X

Louvieris, P., Phillips, D., Warr, D. and Bowen, A., (2003), Balanced scorecards for performance measurement in SMEs, *The Hospitality Review*, **5**(3), 49-57.

McKercher, B., Law, R. and Lam, T., (2006) Rating tourism and hospitality journals, *Tourism Management*, **27** (6), 1235-1252.
www.sciencedirect.com/science/article/pii/S0261517705000841

Madanoglu, M. and Brezina, S., (2008) Resort spas: how are they massaging hotel revenues?, *International Journal of Contemporary Hospitality Management*, **20** (1), 60-66.
www.emeraldinsight.com/journals.htm?articleid=1662895

Mason, D.D.M. and Cameron, A., (2006), An analysis of refereed articles in hospitality and the role of editorial board members, *Journal of Hospitality and Tourism Education*, **18** (1), 11-18.

Mia, L. and Patiar, A., (2001), The use of management accounting systems in hotels: an exploratory study, *International Journal of Hospitality Management*, **20** (2), 111-128 .

Mia, L. and Patiar, A., (2002), The interactive effect of superior-subordinate relationship and budget participation on managerial performance in the hotel industry: an exploratory study, *Journal of Hospitality and Tourism Research*, **26** (3), 235-257.
jht.sagepub.com/content/26/3/235.short

Miao, L. and Mattila, A., (2007), How and how much to reveal? The effects of price transparency on consumers' price perceptions, *Journal of Hospitality & Tourism Research*, **31** (4), 530-545.
jht.sagepub.com/content/31/4/530.abstract

Mongiello, M. and Harris, P., (2006) Management accounting and corporate management: insights into multinational hotel companies, *International Journal of Contemporary Hospitality Management*, **18** (5), 364-379.
www.emeraldinsight.com/journals.htm?articleid=1563104&show=html

Morey, R. and Dittman, D., (2003a), Update and extension to evaluating a hotel GM's performance, *Cornell Hotel and Restaurant Administration Quarterly*, **44**(5/6), 60-68.

Morey, R. and Dittman, D., (2003b), Evaluating a hotel GM's performance: A case study on benchmarking, *Cornell Hotel and Restaurant Administration Quarterly*, **44**(5/6), 53-59. cqx.sagepub.com/content/44/5-6/53.full.pdf+html

Noone, B. and Griffin, P., (1999), Managing the longterm profit yield from market segments in a hotel environment: a case study on the implementation of customer profitability analysis, *International Journal of Hospitality Management*, **18** (2), 111 -128.

Olsen, M., (2001), Hospitality research and theories: a review, in Lockwood A and Medlik T (Eds.) *Tourism and Hospitality in the 21st Century*, Oxford Butterworth Heinemann

O,Neill, J. and Mattila, A., (2006) Strategic hotel development and positioning: the effects of revenue drivers on profitability, *Cornell Hotel and Restaurant Quarterly*, **47** (2), 146-154. cqx.sagepub.com/content/47/2/146.abstract

O,Neill, J., Hanson, B. and Mattila, A., (2008) The relationship of sales and marketing expenses to hotel performance in the United States, *Cornell Hotel and Restaurant Quarterly*, **49** (4), 355-363 www.hotelschool.cornell.edu/research/chr/pubs/quarterly/featured/ execsummary-14945.html

Otley, D., (2009) RAE2008 UOA 36 subject overview report. RAE2008 Main Panel I overview report, Research Assessments Exercise. www.rae.ac.uk/pubs/2009/ov/

Otley, D., (2001), Extending the boundaries of management accounting research: developing systems for performance management, *The British Accounting Review*, **33**, 243 – 261 www.sciencedirect.com/science/article/pii/S0890838901901684

Patiar, A. and Mia, L., (2008), The interactive effect of market competition and use of MAS information on performance: evidence from upscale hotels, *Journal of Hospitality & Tourism Research*, **32** (2), 209-234. jht.sagepub.com/content/32/2/209.short

Pellinen, J., (2003), Making price decisions in tourism enterprises, *International Journal of Hospitality Management*, **22** (2), 217 -235.

Philips, P., (1999a), Hotel performance and competitive advantage: a contingency approach, *International Journal of Contemporary Hospitality Management*, **11** (7), 359-365. www.emeraldinsight.com/journals.htm?articleid=867307

Philips, P., (1999b), Performance measurement systems and hotels: a new conceptual framework, *International Journal of Hospitality Management*, **18** (2), 171-182.

Phillips, P. and Louvieris, P., (2005), Performance measurement systems in tourism, hospitality and leisure small medium sized enterprises: A Balanced Scorecard perspective, *Journal of Travel Research*, **44** (2), 201–211 jtr.sagepub.com/content/44/2/201.short

Potter, G. and Schmidgall, R.S., (1999), Hospitality management accounting: current problems and future opportunities, *International Journal of Hospitality Management*, **18** (4), 387-400.

Quain, B., Sansbury, M. and LeBruto, S., (1998a), Revenue enhancement, part 1: a straightforward approach for making more money, *Cornell Hotel and Restaurant Administration Quarterly*, **39**(5), 41-48.
www.hotelschool.cornell.edu/research/chr/pubs/quarterly/featured/execsummary-14780.html

Quain, B., Sansbury, M. and LeBruto, S., (1998b), Revenue enhancement, part 2: making more money at your hotel, *Cornell Hotel and Restaurant Administration Quarterly*, **39**(6), 71-79.

Quain, B., Sansbury, M. and LeBruto, S., (1999), Revenue enhancement, part 4, *Cornell Hotel and Restaurant Administration Quarterly*, **40**(3), 38-47.

Quan, D., (2002), The Price of a Reservation, *Cornell Hotel and Restaurant Administration Quarterly*, 43(3), 77-86.

Riley, R., Pearson, T. and Trompeter, G., (2003), *Journal of Accounting & Public Policy*, **22** (3), 231-254.

Rivera MA, and UpchurchR, (2008) The role of research in the hospitality industry: A content analysis of the IJHM between (2000) and (2005). *International Journal of Hospitality Management* **27**, 632–640

Rompf, P., (1998), Industry Operating Indices: time for a greater diversity?, *Cornell Hotel and Restaurant Administration Quarterly*, **39**(4), 20-27.

Ryan, B., Scapens, R. and Theobald, M., (2002), *Research Method and Methodology and Accounting*, 2nd Ed., London, Thomson

Sainaghi, R., (2010), Hotel performance: state of the art. *International Journal of Contemporary Hospitality Management*, **22** (7), 920-952.
www.emeraldinsight.com/journals.htm?articleid=1886750&show=html

Sandino, T., (2007) Introducing the first management control systems: evidence from the retail sector, *The Accounting Review*, **82** (1), 265-293.

Sangster, A., (2003), Splitting the bricks from the brains under fire. *BAHA Times British Association of Hospitality Accountants* (2003) Nov 1 – 2.

Sanjeev, G., (2007), Measuring efficiency of the hotel and restaurant sector: the case of India, *International Journal of Contemporary Hospitality Management*, **19** (5), 378-387. www.emeraldinsight.com/journals.htm?articleid=1615775

Scapens, R., (2006), Understanding management accounting practices: A personal journey, *The British Accounting Review*, **38**, 1-30. www.sciencedirect.com/science/article/pii/S0890838905000673

Schmidgall, R., DeFranco, A., (1998), Budgeting and forecasting: current practice in the lodging industry, *Cornell Hotel and Restaurant Administration Quarterly*, **39**(6), 45-51.

Schwartz, Z., (2006) Advanced booking and revenue management: room rates and the consumers' strategic zones, *International Journal of Hospitality Management*, **25** (3), 447-462.

Sharma, D.S., (2002), The differential effect of environmental dimensionality, size and structure on budget systems characteristics in hotels., *Management Accounting Research*, **13**, 101-103. www.sciencedirect.com/science/article/pii/S1044500502901836

Sigala, M., Jones, P., Lockwood, A. and Airey, D (2005), Productivity in hotels: a stepwise data envelopment analysis of hotels' rooms division processes, *The Services Industry Journal*, **25** (1), 61-81. www.tandfonline.com/doi/abs/10.1080/0264206042000302414

Sin, L.Y.M., Tse, A.C.B., Heung, V.C.S. and Yim, F.H.K., (2005), An analysis of the relationship between market orientation and business performance in the hotel industry, *International Journal of Hospitality Management*, **24** (4), 611-633.

Slattery, P. (2002), Reported REVPAR: unreliable measures, flawed interpretations and the remedy, *International Journal of Hospitality Management*, **21** (2), 135-149.

SooCheong, J., Hu, C. and Bai, B., (2006), A canonical correlation analysis of e-relationships marketing and hotel financial performance, *Tourism & Hospitality Research*, **6** (4), 241-250. thr.sagepub.com/content/6/4/241.abstract

Subramaniam, N., McManus, L. and Mia, L., (2002), Enhancing hotel manager's organisational commitment: an investigation of the impact of structure, need for achievement and participative budgeting, *International Journal of Hospitality Management*, **21** (4), 301 – 471.

Tso, A. and Law, R., (2005), Analysing online pricing practices of hotels in Hong Kong, *International Journal of Hospitality Management*, **24** (2), 301-307. www.sciencedirect.com/science/article/pii/S0278431904000878

van der Rest, J P & Harris P (2008) Optimal imperfect pricing decision-making: modifying and applying Nash's rule in a service sector, *International Journal of Hospitality Management*, **27** (2), 170-178. www.sciencedirect.com/science/article/pii/S0278431907000709

Wilson, R.H., (2001), Agency law, fiduciary duties and hotel management contracts, *Journal of Hospitality and Tourism Research*, **25** (2), 147-158. jht.sagepub.com/content/25/2/147

Yilmaz, Y. and Bititci, U., (2006) Performance measurement in tourism: a value chain model, *International Journal of Contemporary Hospitality Management*, **18** (4), 341-349. www.emeraldinsight.com/journals.htm?articleid=1558150

Younes, E. and Kett, R., (2004), Investment driven break-even analysis for hotels, *The Hospitality Review*, **6** (1), 10-16.

Yuen, D.C.Y., (2004), Goal characteristics, communication and reward systems and managerial propensity to create budgetary slack, *Managerial Auditing Journal*, **19** (4), 517-532. www.emeraldinsight.com/journals.htm?articleid=868697&show=html

Yuen, D.C.Y., (2006), The impact of budgetary design system: direct and indirect models, *Managerial Auditing Journal*, **21** (2), 148-165. www.emeraldinsight.com/journals.htm?articleid=1537387

Glossary

Activity Based Costing (ABC): an approach to costing that links costs to activities or tasks in an organisation. It is different to the traditional absorption based approach to costing and is seen to be more accurate in costing products and services that the traditional approach.

Budgeting: A budget is a financial plan for a future period of time. It is taking the plan for the organisation and showing it in a numerical format. Once the plan is written it can then be used for a number of purposes including control and performance measurement (Budget v Actual data).

Cost Volume Profit (CVP): This is a decision support technique, usually associated with short-term decision making. It looks at the nature of costs, how they change with volume of activity (sales) and the impact (relationship) between these aspects and profits.

Customer Profitability Analysis (CPA): Traditionally costing focuses on products or service offered. CPA changes the focus to looking at the profitability related to customer group. In service sectors where a customer can purchase multiple products and services this is a valuable technique.

Performance measurement: Is a collection of techniques and metrics for monitoring organisational performance. It is grounded in a range of disciplines from Operations Management to Human Resource Management where the emphasis and measures are different. In managerial accounting it is concerned with the utilising a range of financial and non-financial measures to monitor and control performance.

Planning and control: These are two key management functions – planning in advance of events taking place and enacting control during and post-events to evaluate performance. Financial planning & control is simply the numerical / monetary tools we can use to assist in these two key aspects of business.

Price determination: Relates to the various approaches available to determine the price of products and services. There are economic, accounting, and market based approaches and various methods available within each of those approaches to aid organisations in setting prices, some focusing on internal factors and others focusing on external factors.

Revenue management (yield management): Pioneered in the airline industry it uses predictions of past customer buyer behaviour patterns to aid in the setting of prices. Put simply, it aims to maximise revenues by selling to 'the right customer, at the right price, at the right time'.

RevPAR, GOPPAR, & TRevPAR: These are hotel specific performance ratios: Revenue Per Available Room; Gross Operating Profit Per Available room; and Total Revenue Per Available Room. They are often used in industry reports and by larger hotels to make comparison between hotels of different sizes, as they are all expressed 'per available room'.

USALI (Uniform System of Accounting for the Lodging Industry): First published in 1926 in America it is the industry standard for internal 'chart of accounts' and structures a reporting format used hotels and resorts across the world. It is commonly used in commercial software, by industry consultants, within management contracts and aids inter-company comparisons due to its standardised format (so you are comparing 'like-with-like).

Judgmental Forecasting
in Tourism

Vera Shanshan Lin
Haiyan Song

Contents

Vera Shanshan Lin, Department of Tourism Management, School of Management, Zhejiang University, Hangzhou, People's Republic of China

Haiyan Song, School of Hotel and Tourism Management, The Hong Kong Polytechnic University, Hong Kong SAR, People's Republic of China

Introduction

The unprecedented growth in tourism across the world over the past five decades has generated considerable research interest from industry practitioners, tourism analysts, and academic researchers. As an important area of tourism research, tourism forecasting has attracted much attention from both practitioners and academics, with impressive increases in publications since the 1960s. An overwhelming portion of these publications have been oriented toward quantitative approaches, with several reviews seeking to gain a better understanding of methodological developments and empirical evidence for quantitative forecasting methods (Li, Song, & Witt, 2005; Song & Hyndman, 2011; Song & Li, 2008).

Some consensus has been reached on the fact that no single model or method outperforms others on all occasions (Song & Li, 2008; Witt & Witt, 1995). Rather, the most appropriate model for a forecasting task should be determined by environment-specific conditions. Careful decisions must be made when a number of alternatives exist so that an appropriate forecasting method can be selected and adopted for the specific situation considered.

Despite the overwhelming dominance of quantitative methods, it is of great importance to pay attention to the judgmental (or qualitative) methods. The term "judgmental forecasting" is more often associated with forecasts that are made entirely on the basis of judgment or with judgmental adjustments to statistical forecasts (Wright & Goodwin, 1998). Without a doubt, human judgment is never isolated from the forecasting process (Clemen, 1989; Makridakis et al., 1982). Even for those forecasts generated by sophisticated statistical models, judgment has to be relied on in the selection of a particular forecasting method, functional form, dependent variables and regressors, and data sets (Goodwin, 2002). Judgmental forecasting methods depend on the accumulated experience of individual experts or groups of experts to make projections about the event concerned. Under certain circumstances, such as (1) insufficient historical data, (2) the unreliability or invalidity of the available time series, (3) rapid changes in the macro-environment, (4) expectations of major disturbances, and (5) a desire for long-term forecasts, judgmental forecasting methods are likely to generate more accurate forecasts than simple statistical methods (Frechtling, 2001).

The contribution of academic research to understanding and assessing the role of experts' judgment in tourism forecast accuracy, however, remains limited. Witt and Witt (1995) explained that qualitative forecasting methods lack popularity because "they are just standard applications" (p. 460) from a methodological perspective. Some review articles reported in Tisdell (2000), such as Archer (1980), Calantone, Benedetto, and Bojanic (1987), Witt and Witt (1995), and van

Doorn (1982, 1984, 1986), briefly summarised the empirical applications of judgmental forecasting techniques in tourism, but mainly focused on Delphi and scenario projections. But to date, little effort has been put into systematically examining judgmental forecasting research in tourism. This study is intended to fill this gap by providing an updated review of empirical studies. The selection of the published studies for review were made mainly by undertaking a search in the electronic databases of ScienceDirect, Scopus, Sage journals, and EBSCOhost. The initial search was carried out within six top tourism and hospitality journals: *Annals of Tourism Research, Tourism Management, Journal of Travel Research, International Journal of Tourism Management, International Journal of Contemporary Hospitality Management,* and *Journal of Travel and Tourism Marketing*. This search identified 37 relevant studies, which helped to identify another 60 entries yielding a sample of 97 studies. This study focused mainly on the academic journals as well as book chapters. The journals included in the study all have excellent track records in publishing high quality research in tourism, which provides useful information on the advances of judgmental tourism forecasting research.

Empirical findings

In the general forecasting literature, forecasts that are based on pure judgment or with judgmental adjustments to the statistical forecasts are commonly known as judgmental forecasts (Wright & Goodwin, 1998). In the tourism literature, terms such as qualitative, intuitive and speculative have been adopted in addition to judgmental. For their forecasts to be of any practical value, tourism planners and decision-makers must adjust their forecasting techniques to deal with a bundle of qualitative factors denoting "expected turning points in a policy framework along a timescale as a result and extension of quantitative data processing" (van Doorn, 1982, p. 161). The judgmental approach is thus designed to incorporate the managerial knowledge of experts into tourism forecasts in order to make more meaningful forecasts that are relevant to managerial decision-making. van Doorn (1982) described judgmental forecasting techniques as being "based on a blend of intuition, expertise, and generally accepted assumptions" (p. 156), which offers the advantage of incorporating expectations about future policy decisions by means of method-implicit procedures.

A deeper understanding of the methodological competence of the different judgmental forecasting techniques will assist tourism analysts and forecasters to make better decisions when choosing an appropriate tool for a forecasting task. This section summarises various judgmental forecasting techniques applied in tourism since the 1970s. Experimentation is often avoided in tourism studies because of the perception of the unnaturalness of the behaviour under analysis (Pizam, 1994). Therefore, this review includes only empirical applications of judgmental forecasting methods in tourism. Depending on the type of participants involved in forecasting techniques, judgmental methods in tourism can be classified into four categories: asking the stakeholders, asking the experts, asking the public, and judgment-aided methods (see Figure 1). Among the 97 studies under review, Delphi method and scenario writing have been two of the most popular judgmental forecasting techniques in tourism studies (see Figure 2).

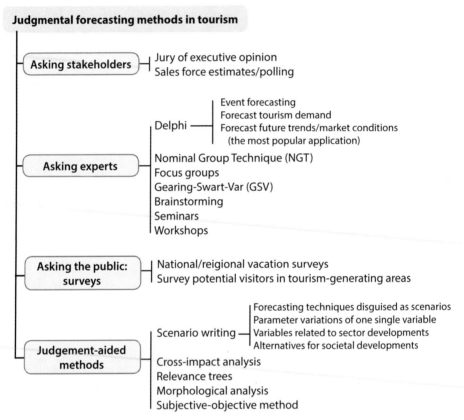

Figure 1: Sub-themes of judgmental forecasting methods in tourism

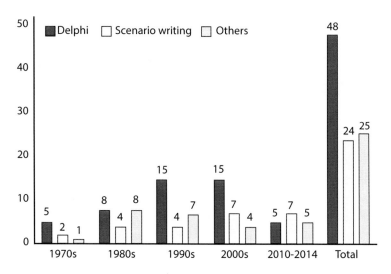

Figure 2: Summary of empirical judgmental forecasting studies in tourism

Asking the stakeholders

One of the simplest but most widely used judgmental approaches is the *jury of executive opinion*, which requires little skill or training to participate in and little historical data. It also serves to pool the experience and judgment of those most familiar with the variables to be forecast. Indeed, it is very common for chief executives to seek the opinions of other members of their organizations in order to broaden the base of forecasts and reduce subjectivity. At the micro level, for example, when deciding whether to construct a new restaurant at a particular location, entrepreneurs can sometimes predict demand as accurately as, or even more accurately than, the most rigorous econometric forecasting techniques (Archer, 2000). Given its celerity and simplicity, this method will remain a popular forecasting technique for private enterprises such as individual facilities, attractions, and destinations (Frechtling, 2001). One variant of this method is to obtain group estimates by participants via paper-and-pencil work and then combine them to produce an average estimate. This can be regarded as an informal variant of the Delphi method, the key difference being the lack of a mechanism to prevent interaction among participants. Examples of this executive judgment method include UNWTO's invitation in 1998 to its 211 member countries and territories and 50 international industry practitioners and academic researchers to contribute their views in order to develop forecasts of tourist arrivals between 44 pairs of subregional country groupings up to 2020 (Frechtling, 2001) and the UNWTO panel of tourism experts, where more than 250 experts contribute information on tourism trends (Goeldner & Ritchie, 2005).

Fernández-Güell and Collado (2014) invited 53 local stakeholders who were involved in the development of tourism products and services in the coastal areas of Andalucía to comment on the business and territorial implications of future trends and scenarios for the global tourism demand up to 2025.

One of the most damaging limitations of this technique, however, is that often the most forceful executive's opinion will dominate the group discussion, which probably reduces the forecasting ability of the whole group. Archer (2000) indicated that unless such discussions are structured, this process could deteriorate into "a guessing game" (p. 63). With this problem in mind, Moutinho and Witt (1995) applied the jury of executive opinion over the Delphi method to rank the importance and probability of the occurrence of 25 possible future developments affecting the world tourism industry and to predict the most likely years of occurrence up to 2030. They argued that it was important to permit a thorough group discussion to facilitate the interchange of ideas and clarifications of reasoning before making forecasts owing to "the radical nature of some of the proposed developments" (Moutinho & Witt, 1995, p. 49).

Another drawback of this method is that it usually provides point estimates of future variables as the most likely forecasts (Frechtling, 2001). It is often easier for a judge to suggest a probability distribution than to give a single future value. This method is called *subjective probability assessment*, but it has very few applications in the tourism field. Unlike the jury of executive opinion approach, the sales force estimates method does not analyse or amalgamate the predictions of stakeholders (e.g. travel agents or tour operators) from the tourism industry in order to examine their intentions or assess their practical forecasts of future demand (Archer, 1980). Instead, such forecasts benefit from the specialized knowledge and experience of sales representatives and sales managers and may provide meaningful forecasts for the short term, which in turn may help to reinforce self-fulfilling prophecies by means of imposing travel-capacity constraints (Archer, 1980, 2000).

Asking the experts

In a more common approach, a panel of experts is brought together to reach a consensus on a particular event or question. One basic technique, which should be combined with other advanced methods (e.g. scenario writing), is *brainstorming*. The use of this collective inspiration stimulates creative thinking and considers unconventional alternatives that may be unrestrained by present norms and values (Whyte, 1992). Although the brainstorming method considers many alternatives, it might be difficult to apply or relate to the real world. Instead, seminars are frequently used in tourism. For instance, after obtaining forecasts from its member countries and territories in the aforementioned example, UNWTO conducted follow-up regional seminars to present all of the forecasts with the aim of arriving at a consensus on the growth rates of inbound flows expected among the subregions to 2020. Workshops are another method of collecting experts' forecasts. Fernández-Güell and Collado (2014) conducted a full day workshop with 25 experts with a view to identifying and assessing any trend changes that may affect the global tourism demand with different scenarios.

Expert opinion may also prove useful for discovering themes and issues and is often correct about likely results in inexact areas of study; its forecasts can also be accurate (Whyte, 1992). Manning and Fraysier (1989) found that responses on the same questionnaire evaluating recreation issues between state experts on recreation and a representative sample of state residents differed on half of the items. They concluded that experts and other leaders tend to take a more coordinated, institutional view of community services, while the public tends to have a greater exchange or production/consumption orientation, both of which are valid and necessary to achieve viable recreation planning. The choice between using individual versus group techniques thus really comes down to the particular situation. In tourism studies, three such group techniques are commonly used, namely, the nominal group technique (NGT), the Delphi technique, and the Gearing-Swart-Var (GSV) method.

The Delphi technique

Originally developed by the RAND Corporation, the Delphi technique is a valuable working tool for both the long-term planning and the long-term forecasting of tourism development (Cunliffe, 2002; Dalkey & Helmer, 1963). Ng (1984) described it as "the systematic utilisation of the judgment of experts [that] aims to obtain consensus among judges on informed predictions of future events" (p. 48). This technique is perhaps the most formalized and studied of the structured group approaches (Wright & Goodwin, 1998). It is also well known for the following: its anonymity of response, iteration, and controlled feedback; convergence in the distribution of opinions as a consequence of the feedback of information; and statistical group response (e.g. median, mean).

There have been many reviews on the Delphi technique concerning its definition, methodology, procedure and application in tourism. For example, Donohoe and Needham (2009) critically examined the Delphi procedures for the purpose of demystifying the Delphi technique and advancing its understanding, contributing to the evolution of methodological guidelines, and providing further guidance for adapting the Delphi technique to tourism researchers. They introduced a generic Delphi procedure, discussed the advantages and disadvantages of applying a Delphi procedure specific to the tourism context, provided guidance on how to construct a Delphi panel, and identified critical design decisions (with particular attention on expert panel design) in the adaption process. However, relatively limited research efforts have been made in reviewing the Delphi technique as a judgmental forecasting or decision-aiding tool. Even fewer studies in the tourism forecasting literature have evaluated the validity of Delphi forecasts or assessed their accuracy. Lin and Song (2014) filled this gap by reporting the research progress of the Delphi forecasting method in tourism and hospitality over the past four decades in terms of topical areas, empirical applications, issues of accuracy, reliability and validity, as well a set of Delphi-specific characteristics (e.g. panel size, panel selection, consensus measures, and analysis of results).

The Delphi technique can provide information about the future that other conventional extrapolative techniques cannot reliably forecast. Based on 46 empirical studies published post-1970, Lin and Song (2014) summarised that the Delphi forecasting technique had been mainly applied in three areas: *event forecasting, forecasting tourism demand*, and *forecasting future trends/market conditions* (the most popular application).

Studies on event forecasting usually aim to predict the likelihood and/or timing of the occurrence of specific events and their impacts on tourism. The first Delphi study on event forecasting was carried out by Dyck and Emery (1970), who forecast the likelihood and probable dates of the occurrence of events in Alberta, Canada associated with leisure and recreation using six panels over the period 1970–2005. The event forecasting applications often use the Likert scale to rate the likelihood of an event's occurrence; for instance, Hawkins, Shafer, and Rovelstad (1980) used a scale ranging from 0 ('*Never*') to 10 ('*100% likelihood of occurrence*') to rate the likelihood of an event, and a scale ranging from 0 ('*Not at all important*') to 10 ('*Critically important*') to rank the importance of the event. Lin and Song (2014) found that this type of study became less popular after the 1990s, and it now often appears as a component task in forecasting the tourism market potential. For example, Kaynak and Marandu (2006) and Kaynak and Pathak (2006) used the Delphi technique to forecast tourism market potential in Botswana and the Fiji Islands, respectively.

The majority of the published studies on tourism forecasting focus mainly on projecting future trend/patterns (Müller, 1998; Weber & Ladkin, 2003; Sadi & Henderson, 2005; Austin, Lee, & Getzb, 2008), evaluating the potential impacts of certain events on tourism (Lloyd, La Lopa, & Braunlich, 2000; Pan et al., 1995), and assessing the impacts of the value changes in society and the structural changes the tourism markets on tourism (Kaynak & Cavlek, 2007; Kaynak & Marandu, 2006; Kaynak & Pathak, 2006; von Bergner & Lohmann, 2014).

Delphi is not only used for qualitative forecasting; it has also been applied to forecast tourism demand. Edgell, Seely, and Iglarsh's (1980) study was one of the very early application of this kind, in which Delphi experts were invited to adjust the statistical forecasts of tourist arrivals and tourist receipts in the USA over the period 1980–2000. Liu (1988) applied the Delphi technique to predict visitor arrivals to Hawaii, the share of domestic arrivals and Oahu's share of visitors, the visitor-resident ratio, and visitor accommodation supply. Lee, Song, and Mjelde (2008) utilised the Delphi technique in forecasting the number of domestic and international tourists to an international Expo in South Korea in 2012. Song, Gao, and Lin (2013) and Lin, Goodwin, and Song (2014) applied the Delphi technique to forecasting quarterly visitor arrivals from six source markets (i.e. China, Taiwan, Japan, Australia, the UK, and the USA) to Hong Kong over the period 2011–2015.

An apparent indicator for demonstrating Delphi's value as a forecasting tool is its accuracy. Only a few tourism studies have investigated the accuracy of Delphi forecasts. For example, McCubbrey and Taylor (2005) compared a panel's predictions for 2002 with actual results and found that the expert forecasts were very close to what actually occurred by the end of that year. Song, Gao, and Lin (2013) concluded that group performance significantly improved with the use of the Delphi technique as the mean absolute percentage error (MAPE) of group forecasts decreased from 8.02% in the first round to 7.99% in the second round. Likewise, Lin, Goodwin, and Song (2014) also found that, on average, the judgmentally adjusted forecasts via Delphi technique made on the basis of statistical forecasts significantly improved the forecast accuracy. The mean MAPE over 2011Q2–2012Q2 reduced from 8.6% to 7.5% in the first round and to 6.5% in the second round. In addition to accuracy improvement, two other important properties of forecasting performance (i.e. bias and efficiency) should also be examined (Lin & Song, 2014). Lin, Goodwin, and Song (2014) made the first attempt to evaluate both the accuracy and bias of Delphi forecasts in tourism forecasting, but they were unable to evaluate the efficiency of their forecasts as the Delphi experts did not have the information about their past forecast errors when they made their forecasts.

The quality of the Delphi findings should also be evaluated according to whether the positivist (quantitative) or the interpretative (qualitative) element is included in the forecasting exercise. The issues of reliability and validity have been subject to much discussion (Lin & Song, 2014). Several tourism studies suggested that pretesting is a vital way to ensure reliability for the Delphi technique. Lin and Song (2014) reported 14 of 46 studies used pre-tests before executing their Delphi surveys. Archer (1976) stated that the reliability of the Delphi results depends to a large extent on the expertise of the panellists. However, in practice, this has not always been the case as panel members can only have expertise in limited areas. Eschenbach, Geistauts, and Beardsley (1985) stated that a basic level of validity is inherent in Delphi. Hill and Fowles (1975) suggested two ways to interpret the validity of the Delphi survey: the data validity and method validity. The former is to check the accuracy of resultant forecasts and the latter is to check the reliability of the Delphi technique itself.

Despite its widespread application in tourism, some of Delphi's methodological issues remain unresolved. One of the persistent issues is the identification of an appropriate panel of experts to best reflect the knowledge scope and expertise of the experts in the Delphi surveys. Lin and Song (2014) found that no agreement on what is an 'expert' and how to recruit an expert had been reached. Tourism researchers have recognised the importance of selecting experts from diverse backgrounds, but very few have attempted to investigate the influence of the panel composition and size on the Delphi results (Lin & Song, 2014). The other two issues include: feedback presentation and consensus realization. Most of the Delphi forecasting studies in tourism achieved consensus through two means: descriptive statistics (prevalent application) and statistical tests. However, there are no clear-cut rules to decide when the sufficient convergence can be achieved. Different Delphi studies adopted different criteria to determine when the consensus can be reached. For example, Frechtling (2001) clearly set two rules on how to decide the number of rounds in the Delphi technique – the most restrictive rule is to continue the process until there is no significant change in the median or in the interquartile range from the previous round, while the less severe rule is to continue the process until the interquartile range becomes relatively narrow around the median. Garrod and Fyall (2005) asserted that the number of rounds should be determined by time or budgetary limitations. Lin and Song (2014) found that the number of iterations varies from one to four, and it is most commonly restricted to two or three.

Nominal group technique (NGT)

Unlike Delphi, NGT requires the assembly of participants in one location so that members are not anonymous and communication occurs directly between them (Liu, 1988). Developed by Andre Delbecq and Andrew Van de Ven in 1968 (Delbecq, Van de Ven, & Gustafson, 1975), NGT is a special-purpose technique used in behavioural science to tap the ideas and judgments of individuals while simultaneously reaching a group consensus. Ritchie (1994) presented modern applications and forecasting situations where NGT was applied as a useful forecasting tool for tourism analysts. In 1984, Travel Alberta and the Tourism Industry Association of Alberta applied NGT to identify priority issues and problems facing tourism in Alberta. As part of a three-phase study, NGT was designed to determine the views of the private sector concerning provincial tourism development and promotion (Ritchie, 1985). Another practical application of NGT is provided by the US Federal Aviation Administration (FAA), which sponsors an international Forecast Assumptions Workshop that periodically invites some 120–140 industry planners and forecasters representing airlines, aircraft manufacturers, engine manufacturers, trade associations, academic institutions, and other industry groups to critically evaluate the techniques and practices used by the FAA and other aviation forecasters and to examine the outlook for the aviation industry and its growth prospects (FAA, 2004). Workshop participants are divided into several subgroups and are then instructed to critique FAA aviation forecasts for their specific areas. Each subgroup is asked to identify specific assumptions about the short- and long-term future trends of the economic and aviation variables important to their segments of the industry, to indicate why these trends are considered important, and to explain why specific trends are anticipated. At the end of each group discussion, attempts are made to reach a consensus and the most likely future course of these variables.

Gearing-Swart-Var (GSV)

Like Delphi and NGT, the GSV technique also relies on expert opinions. This technique is particularly useful when it is hard and expensive to collect primary data and desirable to use expert judgment as a proxy (Calantone, Benedetto, & Bojanic, 1987). It has also been found to have high validity in real-life applications (Var, 1984). Liu and Auyong (1987, cited in Liu, 1988) offered such a successful application in Turkey, British Columbia, and Hawaii, where they used this method to determine the relative attractiveness of various tourist attractions in each location and to recommend optimum resource allocations in the tourism sector. One major limitation of this technique, however, is that experts are interviewed individually and there is no feedback or consensus (Kaynak & Macaulay, 1984). Furthermore, this technique is too specialized for "general trend and issue determination"; it is also "less powerful than the Delphi technique" (Whyte, 1992, p. 202).

Selecting the most suitable forecasting method using experts in tourism depends on evaluating the level of uncertainty involved, the level of forecast accuracy required, the availability of resources, and the time needed to obtain the forecasts. For example, NGT would probably be the favoured method when accuracy is critically important and cost is not a major concern, but it may also be both difficult and expensive to bring groups of experts together for a face-to-face meeting. Alternatively, it may be more appropriate to use a postal Delphi. However, if a trade-off with slight accuracy reduction is allowed, statistical group techniques, which are often much simpler and less costly, can be used. Moreover, when the potential exists for major or discrete changes, scenarios can be incorporated into either the NGT or Delphi process, providing a convenient framework for assessing the potential impact of the subjects being investigated.

Asking the public: Surveys

The judgmental forecasting methods discussed so far rely on experts, but an alternative is to ask actual purchasers to provide opinions on their future demand—in other words, to survey consumers as to whether they anticipate taking a trip over the short to medium term (Frechtling, 2001). Two traditional approaches frequently used to seek consumer opinions are the "analysis of national or regional vacation surveys" and "survey inquiries of potential visitors in tourism-generating areas" (Uysal & Crompton, 1985, p. 8). The first type of survey, usually less expensive, may provide valuable information about emerging trends, while the second type may offer useful insights into the attitudes or prevailing images of the potential market toward a tourist-receiving destination (Uysal & Crompton, 1985).

Buying intention surveys, which assume that consumers can predict their purchases in the case of consumer durable goods because they tend to get involved in long-term planning for durable purchases, have been widely used to produce sales forecasts (Huth, Eppright, & Taube, 1994). Lee, Elango, and Schnaars (1997) concluded that the successful usage of buying plans as a valuable forecasting tool had only been found when the analysis was jointly done with economic data. They also empirically tested the efficacy of the Conference Board (CB) survey as a useful forecasting tool. Since 1967, the CB of New York, in its Consumer Confidence Survey of Buying Plans, has asked a question about intentions to take a vacation trip within the next six months (CB, 2011). Since 1977, the CB has interviewed a number of respondents typically 2,500 to 3,500 from among about 5,000 households. The CB recognized the problem from using such a non-probability sample and started to use a probability-design random sample with post-stratification weights and the US Census X-12 seasonal adjustment from February 2011 (CB, 2011). This type of survey might still serve as a good guide to trends or turning points in future vacation travel activity.

Similar national surveys conducted in Australia since the early 1990s have asked about the leisure activities respondents would have liked to participate in during the survey period but had not been able to. Another example is the quarterly national online survey (or the *Travelhorizons*™) using a sample of nearly 2,300 respondents from a database of over 32,000 US adults and travellers conducted by the US Travel Association (USTA, 2011) since 2007. This survey claims itself to be the first and only tracking survey designed to measure the effects of current economic, social, and natural developments on both the leisure and business travel intentions of US residents over the next six months (USTA, 2011). Questions such as intentions to travel for leisure purposes, reasons for not taking a leisure trip (e.g. time constraints), intentions to travel by census region, and leading leisure travel indicators (e.g. intention to take a leisure trip in the next six months) are included in the survey. Veal (2010) showed that the results from such surveys are useful for market intelligence and in some circumstances could be an indicator of possible future trends in behaviour but could not necessarily be regarded as actual values.

Dwyer, Forsyth, and Dwyer (2010) concluded that forecasts derived from surveys are generally more reliable in the short to medium term than in the longer term. However, they also indicated that the accuracy and reliability of forecasts based on surveys depend on the quality of the survey instruments, the quantity and quality of the responses, and the interpretation of those responses. Drawing on the forecasting performance of two consumer intention surveys, Frechtling (2001) concluded that surveying consumers about their future travel plans may appear to be a reasonable source of valid information about future tourism demand but does not always predict that demand accurately. For example, the vacation intentions model based on the CB's bimonthly survey did not perform well on any of the three accuracy criteria (i.e. error magnitude, directional change, and trend change). The MAPE of the forecasts produced by CB was 2.4%, higher than the forecasts produced by a seasonal Naive model. Lee, Elango, and Schnaars (1997) used the longer time span of 1978 to 1992 to compare the CB's forecasts with those generated from the Naive model and the simple six-month moving average model. They found that the overall MAPE for the intention-to-buy forecasts was nearly double that of the Naive model, and even more than one-third higher than that of the moving average. The comparison showed that the performance of the judgmental forecasts obtained from the CB approach lagged badly relative to that of two very simple extrapolation methods. Frechtling (2001) noted two types of errors that could render intentions invalid as indicators of future tourism-related behaviour: sampling errors (resolved by achieving high response rates) and response errors (resolved by encouraging respondents to answer carefully constructed, practicable questions honestly and objectively). Lee, Elango, and Schnaars (1997) showed that the judgmental approach may be better used to predict "the direction of change rather than the magnitude of the change" and may have less ties to past patterns, whereas extrapolation methods "simply project past trends" (p. 130). Frechtling (2001) also suggested that "a consumer intentions survey that focuses on activities of value to tourism planners and marketers that can be accompanied by a sound time series of actual behaviour will prove a fruitful source of tourism demand forecasts in the future" (p. 233).

Judgment-Aided Models (JAMs)

The two most popular judgment-aided approaches used in tourism forecasting are *scenario writing* (also called scenario planning or scenario design) and *morphological analysis*. Examples of their applications are elaborated below.

Scenario writing

The most quoted definition of a scenario is given by Kahn and Weiner (1967) as "[a] hypothetical sequence of events constructed for the purpose of focusing attention on causal processes and decision points" (p. 6). A scenario is also defined as "an account of what could happen, given the known facts and trends" (Vanhove, 2011, p. 200) or as "a series of events intertwined to form a concept of the future" (Moeller & Shafer, 1994, p. 474). van Doorn (1986) described the scenario technique as follows: "a scenario gives a description of the present situation, of one or more possible and/or desired situation(s) and of one or more sequences(s) of events which can connect the present and future situations" (p. 36). It is evident that a complete scenario under such definition contains at least three central components: a dynamic description and analysis of an existing situation (*baseline analysis*), potential future situations (*future images*), and development lines into the future (*future paths*) (Calantone, Benedetto, & Bojanic, 1987; Dwyer, Forsyth, & Dwyer, 2010; van Doorn, 1986). The underlying assumption of scenario writing is that the "future is not merely some mathematical manipulation of the past, but the confluence of many forces, past, present and future, that can best be understood by simply thinking about the problem" (Schnaars, 1987, p. 106). This approach seeks to generate new information through discussions of an issue by a panel of experts supported by previously produced quantitative evidence. For instance, in demand forecasting, a hypothetical sequence of events is described showing how demand is likely to be affected by a particular causal process. The intent is to indicate what actions can be taken to influence the level of demand at each stage and what the repercussions of such actions might be (Uysal & Crompton, 1985).

Scenario writing usually provides a more qualitative and contextual description of how the present will evolve into the future and identifies a set of possible futures (Schnaars, 1987). Table 1, which summarises a select number of scenario writing studies, shows that scenarios built in tourism research have been used to depict different assumptions or expectations of future growth. The number of scenarios in these studies ranges between two and five, although Schnaars (1987) suggested that the optimal number of scenarios to generate is three. van Doorn (1986) summarised four forms of scenarios that have been frequently mentioned 'forecasting techniques disguised as scenarios', 'parameter variations of one single variable', 'variables related to sector developments', and 'alternatives for societal developments' (p. 39). One example of the first category is found in a study by Tesar, Edgell, and Seely (1979), who applied a modified scenario research method to develop a slightly optimistic scenario of the impact of Western German tourists on the economy of the USA. The scenario used in their study was not the same as that defined by van Doorn (1986) because it did not contain any single element of the three-component scenario concept.

Table 10.1: Studies of scenario writing in tourism research

Study	No.	Description of scenarios
Tesar, Edgell, & Seely (1979)	5	Five scenarios (optimistic, slightly optimistic, neutral, slightly pessimistic, and pessimistic) built on three sets of factors influencing tourism: institutional, functional, and product or service.
van Doorn (1986)	4	Conventional success: no change in the economic growth and value system.
		Transformed growth: selective economic growth and transformation of social values.
		Frustration: stagnated economy and conventional values.
		Self-restraint: economic decline and transformation of social values related to quality of life spheres.
Martin & Mason (1990, cited in Vanhove, 2011)	4	Four scenarios based on the dimensions of economic growth (high/low) and social attitudes (conventional/transformed) to forecast leisure trends in the UK.
Yeoman & Lederer (2005)	4	Dynamic Scotland: high disposable income, favourable exchange rates, leading international tourism destination, 7% growth in tourism expenditure, etc.
		Weekend Getaway: Strong competition for disposable income, favourable exchange rates that attract European visitors, lots of competition from other destinations, attractive leisure destination, 4% growth per year, etc.
		Yesterday's Destination: unfavourable exchange rates and outbound tourism, decline in international tourism, uncompetitive and expensive destination, substantial decline in the short-break market, second-division destination, 1% growth per year, etc.
		Exclusive Scotland: no disposable income, favourable exchange rates, weak domestic tourism, international luxury and exclusive resorts, 4% decline per year, etc.
Song, Lin, Zhang, & Gao (2010)	4	Scenario A (most pessimistic): GDP declines 3% over 2009–2010 and grows at 1% over 2011–2012; no change in prices.
		Scenario B: GDP declines 1% over 2009–2010 and grows at 3% over 2011–2012; no change in prices.
		Scenario C: GDP declines 3% over 2009–2010 and grows at 1% over 2011–2012; prices decline 1% over 2011–2012.
		Scenario D (most optimistic): GDP declines 1% over 2009–2010 and grows at 3% over 2011–2012; prices decline 1% over 2011–2012.
Varum, Melo, Alvarenga and de Carvalho (2011)	4	Depending on the four uncertainties of client dynamics and loyalty, territorial planning and sectoral regulation, industrial structure, and Portugal's attractiveness as a tourist attraction, four scenarios are built: Portugal – southern experience; Portugal – global emotions; Portugal – "sin surprise"; and non-charming Portugal.

Study	No.	Description of scenarios
Smeral, Witt, & Witt (1992)	3	Baseline scenario: no change in the external environment.
		European Community (EC) completion scenario: completion of a single internal market of the EC taking place at the end of 1992.
		Growth scenario: increased world growth likely to result from the liberalization of Eastern Europe.
Rossetto (1999)	3	Rapid return to growth (baseline forecasts): assuming Japan gradually opens its economy, while Thailand, Indonesia, Malaysia, and South Korea experience a period of contraction and stabilization.
		Steady return to growth (most optimistic).
		Slow return to growth (most pessimistic).
Patterson and McDonald (2004)	3	Scenario A: no technical change over the period 1997–2007.
		Scenario B: mid-range technical change over 1997–2007 based on the exception of some slowdown in historical rates of technical change.
		Scenario C: continuation of historical levels of technical change over 1997–2007.
Tsui et al. (2014)	3	Scenario A: the baseline forecast used the parameters from Table 4.
		Scenario B: the parameters from Table 4 (p. 70) and the future GDP per capita of Hong Kong will decrease by 5% per year between September 2011 and December 2015.
		Scenario C: the parameters from Table 4 and the future fuel prices will remain below USD 80 per barrel over the period September 2011–December 2015.
Smeral & Weber (2000)	2	The "business-as-usual" case: assuming limited progress in trade and investment liberalization.
		The "high-performance" case: assuming more progress and a higher pace of structural reform.
Yeoman, Lennon, & Black (2005)	2	Two scenarios representing the stages, events, and communications that would occur in the event of a suspected outbreak and a confirmed outbreak of foot-and-mouth disease in Scotland.
Tolley, Lumsdon, & Bickerstaff (2010)	2	A "business-as-usual" scenario (cheap, private motorized mobility; reliance on techno-efficiency, etc.).
		Sharp increase in the price of motorized transportation (peak oil, carbon taxes, generalized road pricing, etc.).
FAA (2010, 2011)	2	Optimistic forecast: lower inflation and faster growth in the labour force and capital stock than in the baseline forecast.
		Pessimistic forecast: higher inflation and slower growth in the labour force and capital stock than in the baseline forecast.

Note: The figures in the column "No." indicate the number of scenarios in each study examined.

The second category of scenarios, which takes parameter variation as a scenario, also has little to do with the three-component scenario definition as it provides neither a baseline analysis nor future images. van Doorn (1986) stated that the term "future paths" embodied considerably more than just fluctuations of the parameter value of a tourism variable; rather, it aimed at a very complex system of intended and unintended actions. However, parameter fluctuations can still be used as inputs for tourism scenarios, in particular for elaborating the approximated course of future paths. In addition, scenarios can be incorporated into the results of quantitative models. For example, Smeral, Witt, and Witt (1992) generated multiple forecasts of tourism imports and exports over the period 1991–2000 for a complete system of demand equations using three different scenarios (see Table 1). Such procedures are essentially quantitative and mechanistic in nature, but are still taken as "scenario analysis" since more than one forecast is produced (Schnaars, 1987). Similarly, Smeral and Weber (2000) incorporated two scenarios of the EU's growth path into a model as forecasting assumptions. Smeral and Weber (2000), however, claimed that caution should be exercised in using the forecasts since they captured only the indirect effects of the monetary union, such as those of stable exchange rates and growth. Also, to examine the impact of the global financial and economic crisis on Hong Kong tourism demand from the top 10 source markets over 2009–2012, Song et al. (2010) constructed four scenarios, from the most pessimistic to the most optimistic, according to different assumptions of income levels and tourism prices in those top source markets (see Table 1). To incorporate the uncertainty surrounding the global financial crisis and the resulting recession, Tsui et al. (2014) built three scenarios based on three different assumptions on Hong Kong's future GDP per capital and fuel prices in order to forecast International Airport's passenger traffic in Hong Kong up to December 2015. This technique may provide important stimuli in raising stakeholders' awareness of different tourism scenarios which might affect policymaking and acceptance (van Doorn, 1986).

The scenarios sketched in the third category are well considered variations of tourism developments based on trend extrapolations of historical tourism developments. A good demonstration of such work is conducted by the Hudson Institute, which applies a two-component scenario model: a baseline analysis component reviewing the development of tourism in the past and a future image component outlining the possibilities for tourism in the future. van Doorn (1986) criticized the use of such a scenario as it takes tourism as a system in itself and ignores the impact of societal developments on tourism.

The last category of scenarios concentrates on alternatives for societal developments in which tourism is considered as one of the subsystems of society.

van Doorn (1986) observed that there was a lack of consensus in the use of the three-component scenario definition and suggested using it to judge existing tourism-related scenarios. It is found that not all scenario applications in tourism studies incorporate all three constituent components: at least one or, more often, two are not included. One example is the work of Schwaninger (1989) who constructed scenarios about likely future trends in leisure time and tourism between the years 2000 and 2010. In particular, his study dealt with a base scenario that portrayed the most likely trends by analysing the interactions between economic, political, socio-cultural, ecological, and technological factors. van Doorn (1986) classified his work as a one-dominant-component scenario because Schwaninger (1989) solely emphasized one component of future image, although he also provided information on the component of future paths, but in much less detail. The one-component scenario discussed above deals with only one future image along with a vaguely described future path. BarOn (1975, cited in van Doorn, 1986) extended the use of scenarios by adding alternative future images based on alternative assumptions. His study on forecasting tourism in Thailand, however, still lacked a visible link from the past to the present or the component of future paths. Bearing this in mind, tourism researchers have been more cautious about the construction of scenarios using all of these three components together. Scenarios have been built upon a number of general socioeconomic factors, such as economic growth, income level, and inflation. Koster (1979, cited in van Doorn, 1982), for example, provided forecasts about seven tourism-related fields (i.e. economy, leisure time, population, nature, space, technology and science, and politics) and then correlated these forecasts in a systematic framework to generate a weighted prediction regarding the consequences of the correlations for tourism development in the Netherlands.

Drawing on alternative assumptions regarding the environment for international tourism, BarOn (1984, cited in van Doorn, 1986) produced three scenarios (optimistic, intermediate, and pessimistic) for tourism in Thailand from 1975 to 1980. The fields of interest to these scenarios were focused mainly on political factors, economic tourism development and promotion, and air transportation. van Doorn (1982), however, pointed out that the scenario writing technique needs to be "supported by more elaborate techniques that will enable the forecaster to improve his assumptions, to strengthen their predictive power, and to widen their scope to range over qualitative data" (p. 163). One of the most recent publications utilising scenario writing is from futurist Ian Yeoman, co-produced with three other authors, based largely in the Asia Pacific region. Yeoman, Yu, Mars, and Wouters (2012) identified three core drivers of change (i.e. wealth, technology and resources) up to 2050 and critically analysed the implications of these changes: (1) wealth is regarded as one of the key determinants of tourism and scenarios are constructed with a host of supporting evidence such as statistics and trends that will shape the future of tourism demand, markets, and consumption; (2) technological changes that affect tourism are contextualized in four specific locations – Edinburgh, Singapore, Amsterdam, and New Zealand – in order to present differing dimensions of the interaction between technology and tourism from social and supply-side perspectives; (3) the future of resources (food, water, oil, and the environment) are presented focusing on four aspects of tourism supply and three-city level case studies: climate change for urban metropolis Los Angeles, future consumption of food in Seoul, the shape of future hotels in Shanghai, and the future of transport. According to Yeoman et al. (2012), effective scenarios "must have meaning and relevance to the key players ... [and] be plausible to stakeholders ... [while] at the same time ... challenge the minds of these same members" (pp. 7–8).

Scenario writing methods can be qualitative or quantitative as well as some mixture of both. The strongest proponent of the qualitative approach to scenarios has been Kahn (1979), who developed scenarios for the future of the USA and the world based on narratives, and who predicted that in 2000 tourism would be the largest industry and the most important export sector in the world (Witt & Moutinho, 1989). van Doorn (1986) used quadrants and two languages (English and French) to describe the typology of scenarios and established their relationships: (1) projective and prospective scenarios, (2) normative and descriptive scenarios, (3) dominant and "limits-identifying" scenarios, and (4) preferential and aprioristic scenarios. He clarified that prospective scenarios are always normative whereas projective scenarios could either be descriptive or normative. van Doorn (1982) further showed there are no great differences between the projective and prospective scenario writing. The desired state described in the normative scenario might cause considerable difficulties, and even if such problems can be solved through an acceptable solution, it is likely to still have certain methodological problems (e.g. treatment of consistency, plausibility, and level of aggregation as a challenge). van Doorn (1982) also observed that there were only a few noteworthy applications of exploratory scenario writing in the tourism field owing to "the novelty of the technique (relatively speaking) and the difficulty in handling qualitative data with tools developed for quantitative data processing" (p. 161).

Scenario writing is not a real forecasting technique in itself but can be used to develop medium- to long-term scenarios whose likely eventualities can then be analysed for their potential effects upon tourism demand (van Doorn, 1984). Thus, it can create valuable input for group forecasting, such as with the Delphi technique. It may also be applied to a future determined by the Delphi approach, examples being Henderson and Bialeschki's (1984) study of organized camping and the future and Tolley, Lumsdon, and Bickerstaff's (2010) study of future walking.

Scenario writing is particularly useful for examining the likely impact of changes of greater magnitude, such as crises or large-scale policy changes (Dwyer, Forsyth, & Dwyer, 2010). On the basis of a scale of severity, probability, type of event, and level of certainty, Prideaux, Laws, and Faulkner (2003) developed a framework to classify group shocks into four categories (S4: "not anticipated"; S3: "unlikely but just possible"; S2: "the possible based on a worst-case scenario of past trading conditions"; and S1: "the expected based on recent past trading conditions"). It was recommended that scenarios be applied under the assumptions of S3 and S4. Yeoman, Lennon, and Black (2005) examined how a future outbreak of foot-and-mouth disease in Scotland would be treated and considered the potential reaction by government agencies with particular reference to communication and the management of crises within the tourism sector. Delphi forecasting may thus be useful in developing estimates of post-shock travel demand and supply conditions. The value of using scenarios is that by considering potential developments and responses in advance, an organization will not be forced to make quick, ill-considered decisions when such unexpected conditions occur (Faulkner & Valerio, 1995). In some other cases, forecasts produced by scenario writing have been so vague or trivial that one might wonder whether they could benefit future planning. One such example is Kahn's (1979) study, which predicted that in 1989, the tourism growth rate would be double the economic growth rate; this result was not surprising, since it had already been recognized in the literature (van Doorn, 1982).

The use of scenario projections is not only attractive to academics but has also been widely applied in real-world forecasting by tourism organizations and industry stakeholders to construct powerful policy visions. Adopting a scenario approach, the Tourism Forecasting Council postulated three scenarios (rapid/ steady/slow return to growth) representing possible future conditions in the global economy to predict future tourist arrivals (Rossetto, 1999). To describe the environmental implications of national tourism forecasts in New Zealand, Patterson and McDonald (2004) developed scenarios to construct projections of future resource use and pollution by the tourism sector from the base year of 1997 to 2007. Their study produced three scenarios highlighting the difference between three levels of technological improvement. Patterson and McDonald (2004) also explained their reasons for using scenarios rather than forecasts, namely their consideration of unpredictable events, which would have made any forecasts highly prone to errors, and their inclusion of environmental (resources and pollutants) variables, which would have made predictive forecasting very difficult and problematic. Lennon and Yeoman (2007) examined how the National Tourism Organization of Scotland (VisitScotland) utilised the scenario planning approach to capture expert opinions. "What if" thinking was applied to paint the future, and conclusions were drawn from two potential future scenarios. They found that the future of Scottish tourism to 2015 would be affected by macrotrends and drivers (e.g. globalization, sustainability, technology/communication, politics, etc.) in UK society. To reflect uncertainties in projecting economic growth, the FAA Aerospace forecasts built three scenarios to produce base forecasts of aviation demand and activity levels as well as high and low economic growth cases (FAA, 2010, 2011). The base forecasts were generated from econometric models, while the high and low economic growth rates were based on optimistic and pessimistic scenarios from *Global Insight's 30-Year Focus*.

To conclude, the basic purpose of scenario writing is to provide multiple forecasts; therefore, it makes more sense to establish a number of plausible assumptions rather than rely on a single one that may later turn out to be incorrect (Schnaars, 1987). van Doorn (1986) stressed the need to seek consensus on a common scenario methodology. Although scenario writing has been adopted primarily for medium- and long-term forecasting, there is no empirical evidence to indicate that it would not be suitable for shorter term forecasts (Schnaars, 1987). To date, very few tourism studies have examined the relative accuracy of scenario forecasts or made direct or indirect comparisons with other judgment or quantitative methods. Combining scenario analysis with other forecasting techniques, such as time-series analysis, Delphi, and cross-impact analysis, is recommended by van Doorn (1986).

Other judgmental forecasting techniques

Alternative judgmental approaches, such as morphological analysis, cross-impact analysis, relevance tree analysis, and the subjective-objective method, have also been proposed and used in tourism forecasting. The first three methods share a similar way of presenting their outputs but with different structures and content, in the form of a matrix. The matrix produced from the morphological analysis (or a *morphological box*) explores all possible solutions to a multidimensional, nonquantified, and complex problem (Uysal & Crompton, 1985), the results of which are qualitative in nature. Management looks closely at potential combinations and assesses the various attainable levels of demand under different assumptions about the performance of each variable (Uysal & Crompton, 1985). Although it has been argued that this technique lacks rigour unless supported by numerical analysis, it can provide valuable input for group forecasting discussions (Archer, 2000).

An extension of the Delphi technique, cross-impact analysis involves identifying and evaluating the impact of trends or events upon one another using a matrix format, thereby enabling tourism managers to gain deeper insight into the sensitivities and interrelationships among a number of policy options (Archer, 2000).

Data are collected by asking participants to attach probabilities to events occurring in the future and to consider how each probability is affected by each event (Archer, 2000). In much the same way as the Delphi technique, this method also depends on the ability of experts to provide meaningful estimates of the probability that an event will occur. Some strengths of such a technique are that it (1) provides "form and structure to quantitative predictive models", (2) integrates the "interests of a wide array of public" through distilling "conventional wisdom and collective judgment" in order to arrive at a consensus, and (3) can handle "complex issues where no clear consensus or interaction is available" (Whyte, 1992, pp. 201–202). Similar to Delphi, this technique also suffers from the problem of direct expert influence. Becker et al. (1985, cited in Whyte, 1992) provided one example by applying this technique to identifying possible trends and events affecting the southeast region of the US National Parks Service in the 1990s. Additionally, this technique may be time-consuming if several iterations are required; also, if the matrix is very large, it may not reflect reality and so yield insufficiently consistent responses. Unlike these two methods, the output matrix in the relevance tree approach is in the form of a visually hierarchical structure exhausting all possible ways of achieving objectives. Although these three methods have been used in other areas of forecasting, they have not yet been widely applied in tourism.

The subjective-objective method was initially proposed and developed by Ng and Knott (1979, cited in Ng, 1984) to ascertain future manpower needs for leisure services. Ng (1984) presented a forecasting framework consisting of three components (multiple regression submodels, the subjective–objective forecasting model, and the Delphi technique), to forecast the demand for leisure services manpower. From a methodological perspective, this method does not rely on historical relationships among variables of interest or on the assumptions that these relationships will continue into the future. Instead, it distils both the practical and the professional knowledge of each chief administrator regarding an organization's or company's unique situation and future plans. However, as revealed by Ng (1984), one serious limitation of this technique is that "it is quite impossible for an individual administrator to estimate correctly the effects of changing society needs on manpower situations" (p. 48); also, its outlook on the future is likely to be biased toward the optimistic or pessimistic extremes. Despite these limitations, Ng (1984) suggested that this method could be supplemented by other forecasting approaches as a short-term forecasting tool.

Integrative forecasting in tourism

It is quite difficult to capture such a diverse, dynamic, and changeable phenomenon as tourism in a limited number of variables. Sociological and psychological factors are difficult to express quantitatively, and unexpected crises and disasters are impossible to forecast. A big challenge in achieving accurate forecasts is how to utilise the best aspects of statistical predictions while also exploiting and capitalizing on the value of knowledge and judgmental information. It would therefore be natural to bring these two methods together. The general forecasting literature suggests that combining methods improves forecast accuracy, a finding that holds true for quantitative forecasting, judgmental forecasting, and the averaging of these two forecasts.

Although combined forecasting has attracted broad attention in the general forecasting literature, it has yet to receive serious attention in tourism forecasting. Tourism researchers have focused mostly on objectively combining two or more quantitative models using a weighting scheme, where the combination occurs within time-series methods or econometric methods or both (Shen, Li, & Song, 2008; Shen, Li, & Song, 2011; Song, Witt, Wong, & Wu, 2009; Wong, Song, Witt, & Wu, 2007). However, the empirical results are not yet as satisfactory as one would expect. Combined forecasts only outperform the least accurate individual forecasts; they are not as accurate as the best individual forecasts. In Wong et al.'s (2007) study, forecasting integration within the statistical category was shown to exhibit limited accuracy improvement. One common observation from the aforementioned combined studies in tourism is that none of them has incorporated contextual information into their final forecasts, which is probably the reason why the combined results are less satisfactory than expected.

A second type of combined approach is to integrate quantitative forecasts with qualitative methods; this not only forecasts tourism demand on the basis of historical data but also considers the impact of future events on tourism demand. Archer (1980) identified the need to integrate judgment and rigorous quantitative analysis. Frechtling (2001) stated that such a combination was an especially effective way of achieving convergent validity. This integrative approach has also been recommended for long-term forecasting conditions (Archer, 1980; Uysal & Crompton, 1985). Based on different forecasting horizons, Ng (1984) introduced a three-component model (multiple regression models for long-term forecasting, the subjective-objective qualitative forecasting method for short-term forecasting, and the Delphi technique for medium- and long-term forecasting) to predict the demand for leisure service manpower. However, Ng did not describe how to integrate any of the three components. Faulkner and Valerio (1995) illustrated an integrative approach developed by the Australian Tourist Commission and recommended that a combination of different forecasting techniques should be applied to facilitate a more meaningful dialogue between tourism analysts and decision-makers.

In the tourism integrative studies, forecasts from extrapolation methods or regression analysis have often been combined with Delphi estimates. Tideswell, Mules, and Faulkner (2001) adopted an integrative forecasting model combining quantitative methods (e.g. a Naïve model and a single exponential smoothing method) and Delphi techniques to predict the future tourism industry potential of South Australia. Goeldner and Ritchie (2005) asserted that a combination of various quantitative methods and a Delphi method could generate the most reliable tourism demand forecasts in any given situation. For example, Edgell, Seely, and Iglarsh (1980) conducted a two-stage study to combine time-series forecasts with a Delphi-type interview to forecast tourist arrivals and tourist receipts to the USA over the period 1980–2000. Similarly, Lee and Kim (1998) employed a two-stage integrative forecasting framework that integrated a combined time series model from the first stage with the Delphi estimates from the second stage to forecast the number of international tourists for the 2002 World Cup in South Korea. Song, Gao, and Lin (2013) and Lin, Goodwin, and Song (2014) both utilised a two-round Delphi survey via the Hong Kong Tourism Demand Forecasting System (HKTDFS) to integrate econometric and judgmental forecasts.

In addition, tourism researchers have also attempted to combine quantitative forecasts with other judgmental methods. For example, to predict leisure patterns in the UK and recreation trends in the USA, Martin and Mason (1998) adopted a combination of time series, cross-sectional, and scenario-writing techniques. Kelly and Warnick (1999) used cross-sectional cohort methods, time-series models, and consideration of trends to predict lifestyles and leisure styles, while Faulkner and Valerio (1995) offered an example of combining forecasts from econometric models with a consultative workshop.

Combined forecasting is not limited to integrating different types of forecasts obtained from different forecasting techniques. It is also used for forecasts collected from multiple sources (e.g. surveys or interviews). To predict the number of visitors to Greenwich, UK, in the pre-millennial event phase, data were collected from various sources, including visitor surveys and counts and visitor interviews at key nodal points and observations, and then combined to produce the final forecasts (Evans, 1995). International tourists and local tourist arrivals forecasts were made for paying attractions in the town of Greenwich and Greenwich Park in 1994. Lee, Song, and Mjelde (2008) used the historical data and willingness-to-visit (WTV) survey data to predict the number of domestic and international tourists to an international expo to be held in Korea in 2012. However, the lack of tests on accuracy limited the authors' findings to an appreciation that the Delphi panel predicted lower demand for the expo than the combined quantitative techniques.

Relatively little research, however, has examined the effectiveness of integrating judgmental and statistical forecasting methods in the tourism context. One notably successful application of integrative forecasting techniques has been implemented by the FAA (2010, 2011). Forecasts of aviation demand and activity measures are first made by econometric and time-series models; these are then adjusted on the basis of "expert industry opinion" to arrive at subsequent forecasts for use in making decisions. The FAA periodically reviews and adjusts its projections on the basis of forecasts and discussions with analysts outside the FAA (2004); for example, it frequently organizes workshops to improve the reliability and utility of forecasting results. Between 1995 and 2005, the average errors and the mean absolute errors for all of the forecasts provided by the FAA were less than 2.5%, suggesting significantly high forecast accuracy. Even with the negative impact of unanticipated external events (e.g. the 9/11 attacks in 2001, the outbreak of the SARS epidemic in 2003, the rapid rise of oil prices in 2004–2005), the mean absolute errors for all forecasts over the period 2002–2005, which were published a year in advance, ranged from 1.3% to 3.3%, which still suggests excellent forecasting performance using the combined forecasting approach.

Forecasting support system with judgmental forecasting

With advances in information technology, research using a forecasting decision support system (FDSS) or forecasting support system (FSS), stimulated by the rapid development of a decision support system (DSS), is becoming increasingly popular. A DSS effectively makes use of decision-making efficiency in the forecasting process achieved by combining raw data, personal knowledge, or quantitative models and identifying and solving problems in a human-machine interactive manner. Croce and Wöber (2011) emphasized that the use of an FSS is particularly meaningful in the following four situations: (1) facilitating access to data relevant for forecasts; (2) enabling selection among a set of quantitative techniques suitable for forecasting variables of interest; (3) allowing for the storage of judgmental forecasts or the adjustment of the outcome of quantitative forecasting models; and (4) providing feedback on forecasting performance (accuracy).

Implementing an FSS specific to the tourism industry would certainly provide the scope needed to gain deeper knowledge across several disciplines. This system takes advantage of statistical forecasts and the unique ability of human judgment to deal with systematic changes in patterns or relationships. One example is provided by Song, Witt, and Zhang (2008), who designed and developed a Web-based tourism demand forecasting system (TDFS). The TDFS not only utilised advanced econometric forecasting techniques for tourism demand but also incorporated the real-time judgmental contribution of experts. Further-more, this system allowed users to perform scenario analysis or to make their own 'what-if' forecasts, which incorporated uncertainty by including alterna-tive future values of the influencing factors. Song, Gao, and Lin (2013) further developed the HKTDFS and showed that the integration of quantitative and judgmental forecasts improve the overall forecast accuracy. Lin, Goodwin, and Song (2014) used the same forecasting support system to predict the interna-tional visitor arrivals to Hong Kong and recommended a mechanical combina-tion of two independent forecasts (i.e. statistical and judgmental forecasts) to utilise the best of both methods while at the same time reducing bias.

Different from the above three studies, Croce and Wöber (2011) described a group forecasting system in which base forecasts are produced by simple extrapolation forecasting methods. The system is embedded in TourMIS (a marketing-information system for the tourism industry), which supports col-laborative short-term forecasting tasks among tourism managers. Estimates in TourMIS can be made either through pure judgment, one of the two established quantitative methods (i.e. Naive 2 and Winters' exponential smoothing), or a combination of the two approaches. One of the strengths of TourMIS over other tourism forecasting systems is that it can evaluate users' forecasting perfor-mance on the basis of accuracy (measured by MAPE) and reliability (defined as the capability of the user to provide accurate forecasts in the past). Croce and Wöber (2011) concluded that users' past forecasting performance can be used as a consistent indicator of expertise and utilised to qualify a system's users as reliable experts.

The studies reviewed earlier provided only one direct approach to adjusting demand forecasts. Ghalia and Wang's (2000) study enriched the existing litera-ture by proposing an intelligent system (IS-JFK) that supports two approaches to aid hotel managers in making their forecast adjustments—a direct approach and an approach via fuzzy intervention analysis. IS-JFK was designed to sup-port the judgmental forecasting and knowledge of hotel managers. The system allows managers to adjust demand forecasts for future arrival days when there are discontinuous changes in the business environment whose impact statistical forecasting methods fail to capture. Ghalia and Wang (2000) used problem sce-narios and simulation results based on actual hotel data to illustrate the effec-tiveness of IS-JFK. They also addressed the importance of the cooperation of hotel managers in all aspects of conceptualizing and developing the intelligent system since their input was important in defining and characterizing the fuzzy sets used in the system.

Concluding remarks

There is little doubt about the critical role that judgment plays in a successful tourism forecasting process, either through a quantitative or judgmental forecasting approach. Judgment can be integrated into every stage of quantitative forecasting including selecting variables, deciding the functional form, building models, estimating parameters, and conducting data analysis. When applying a judgmental forecasting technique, judgment plays an even more important role, from selecting judges to deciding how to analyse and report final judgments.

A number of judgmental forecasting methods are available in tourism, but whichever technique is used, it is essential to recognize both its merits and limitations since this will affect the quality of the forecasts obtained. Choosing an appropriate forecasting method depends on multiple considerations, including the level of uncertainty involved, the level of forecast accuracy required, the availability of resources, and the time needed to obtain the forecasts. However, unlike quantitative forecasting models, it is difficult to evaluate the performance of judgmental forecasts. Several issues remain regarding the final evaluation of judgmental forecasting, such as the utility, accuracy, and reliability of judgmental forecasts and the need for validation. Many studies have also been carried out primarily for practical purposes, which adds to the difficulty in ascertaining the true utility of these forecasts. In addition, researchers have not paid much attention to revisiting their forecasts, thus missing the chance to evaluate the utility of judgmental forecasts. Reports on forecasting studies have thus required that more thorough comparisons be made among the various judgmental forecasting methods.

The findings suggest that the Delphi technique and scenario writing are the two most popular judgmental forecasting methods used in tourism studies. Delphi has been widely applied in projecting potential market trends or conditions, predicting the likelihood or the time of the occurrence of specified events and their impact on tourism and forecasting tourism demand variables. Most applications of the Delphi technique have been in the area of long-range forecasting, particularly for qualitative forecasting purposes. However, there has been limited use of statistical techniques in exploring and analysing the results of the Delphi forecasts. Researchers have used Delphi mainly to produce quantitative forecasts and integrated it as a major component of integrative forecasting. More attention should be given to evaluate the performance of the Delphi forecasts, especially where quantitative estimates are generated from a panel. Not performance should include accuracy, but also other properties such as bias, efficiency, reliability, and validity. Future research efforts can also be made in investigating the Delphi technique from a Bayesian viewpoint, particularly under conditions in which data are vague. Another aspect which could be covered by future research concerns the effects of situational variables (such as time horizon, data variability, contextual knowledge, and technical knowledge). Such factors as feedback, data presentation and task structure could also be examined to evaluate the relative forecasting performance of judgmental forecasts (or Delphi forecasts).

To date, the combination of multiple methods is still not widely accepted as a viable research strategy in tourism demand forecasting. Tourism demand forecasters and practitioners, however, have indicated that such a research strategy is necessary to develop and strengthen our understanding of tourism forecasting theories and practices Therefore, it is thus recommended that more effort be made to exploit the use of a combination of rigorous quantitative analysis with judgmental approaches in tourism studies.

References

Archer, B. (1976). *Demand Forecasting in Tourism.* Bangor: University of Wales Press.

Archer, B. (1980). Forecasting demand: Quantitative and intuitive techniques. *International Journal of Tourism Management, 1*(1), 5–12.

Archer, B. (2000). Demand forecasting and estimation. In C. Tisdell, *The economics of tourism* (Vol. 1, pp. 61–68). Cheltenham: Edward Elgar Pub.

Austin, D., Lee, Y. and Getzb, D. (2008). A Delphi study of trends in special and inclusive recreation. *Leisure/Loisir, 32*(1), 163–182.

Calantone, R. J., Benedetto, C. A. and Bojanic, D. (1987). A comprehensive review of the tourism forecasting literature. *Journal of Travel Research, 26*(2), 28–39.

CB. (2011). *Consumer confidence survey technical note – February 2011.* Retrieved November 20, 2011, from The Conference Board (CB): http://www. conference-board.org/data/consumerconfidence.cfm.

Clemen, R. (1989). Combining forecasts: A review and annotated bibliography. *International Journal of Forecasting, 5*(4), 559–583.

Croce, V. and Wöber, K. (2011). Judgemental forecasting support systems in tourism. *Tourism Economics, 17*(4), 709–724.

Dalkey, N. C. and Helmer, O. (1963). An experimental application of the Delphi method to the use of experts. *Management Science, 9*(3), 458–467.

Delbecq, A., Van de Ven, A. and Gustafson, D. (1975). *Group techniques for program planning: A guide to nominal group and Delphi processes.* Glenview IL: Scott, Foresman.

Donohoe, H. and Needham, R. D. (2009). Moving best practice forward: Delphi characteristics, advantages, potential problems, and solutions. *International Journal of Tourism Research*, **11**(5), 415–437.

Dwyer, L., Forsyth, P. and Dwyer, W. (2010). *Tourism Economics and Policy*. Bristol: Channel View Publications.

Dyck, H. J. and Emery, G. J. (1970). *Social Futures: Alberta, 1970–2005*. Edmonton: Human Resources Research Council of Alberta.

Edgell, D. L., Seely, R. L. and Iglarsh, H. J. (1980). Forecasts of international tourism to the USA. *International Journal of Tourism Management*, **1**(2), 109–113.

Eschenbach, T. G., Geistauts, G. A. and Beardsley, W. H. (1985). A Delphi forecast for Alaska. *Interfaces*, **15**, 100–109.

Evans, G. (1995). Planning for the British millennium festival: Establishing the visitor baseline and a framework for forecasting. *Festival Management and Event Tourism*, **3**(4), 183–196.

FAA. (2004). *FAA Aerospace forecast fiscal years 2004–2015*. Washington, DC: Federal Aviation Administration.

FAA. (2010). *FAA Aerospace forecast fiscal years 2010-2030*. Washington, DC: Federal Aviation Administration.

FAA. (2011). *FAA Aerospace forecast fiscal years 2011-2031*. Washington, DC: Federal Aviation Administration.

Faulkner, B. and Valerio, P. (1995). An integrative approach to tourism demand forecasting. *Tourism Management*, **16**(1), 29–37.

Fernández-Güell, J. M. and Collado, M. (2014). Foresight in designing sun-beach destinations. *Tourism Management*, **41**, 83–95.

Frechtling, D. C. (2001). *Forecasting tourism demand: Methods and strategies*. Oxford: Butterworth-Heinemann.

Garrod, B. and Fyall, A. (2005). Revisiting Delphi: The Delphi technique in tourism research. In B. Ritchie and C. Palmer (Eds.), *Tourism Research Methods: Integrating Theory with Practice* (pp. 85–98). Cambridge: CABI.

Ghalia, M. B. and Wang, P. P. (2000). Intelligent system to support judgmental business forecasting: The case of estimating hotel room demand. *IEEE Transactions on Fuzzy Systems*, **8**(4), 380-397.

Goeldner, C. R. and Ritchie, J. R. (2005). *Tourism: Principles, Practices, Philosophies*. Hoboken: Wiley.

Goodwin, P. (2002). Integrating management judgment and statistical methods to improve short-term forecasts. *Omega*, **30**(2), 127–135.

Hawkins, D., Shafer, E. and Rovelstad, J. (1980). *Summary and recommendations: International symposium on tourism and the next decade*. Washington, D.C.: George Washington University.

Henderson, K. and Bialeschki, M. (1984). Organized camping and the future: Research on major trends. *Camping Magazine,* **56**(3), 20–26.

Hill, K. Q. and Fowles, J. (1975). The methodological worth of the Delphi forecasting technique. *Technological Forecasting and Social Change,* **7**(2), 179–192.

Huth, W. L., Eppright, D. R. and Taube, P. M. (1994). The indexes of consumer sentiment and confidence: Leading or misleading guides to future buyer behavior. *Journal of Business Research,* **29**(3), 199–206.

Kahn, H. (1979). *World Economic Development 1979 and Beyond.* London: Croom Helm.

Kahn, H. and Weiner, A. (1967). *The Year 2000.* London: Macmillan.

Kaynak, E. and Cavlek, N. (2007). Measurement of tourism market potential of Croatia by use of Delphi qualitative research technique. *Journal of East-West Business,* **12**(4), 105–123.

Kaynak, E. and Macaulay, J. A. (1984). The Delphi technique in the measurement of tourism market potential: The case of Nova Scotia. *Tourism Management,* **5**(2), 87–101.

Kaynak, E. and Marandu, E. E. (2006). Tourism market potential analysis in Botswana: A Delphi study. *Journal of Travel Research,* **45**(2), 227–237.

Kaynak, E. and Pathak, R. (2006). Tourism market potential of small resource-based economics: The case of Fiji Islands, in M. Adams and A. Alkhafaji, *Business research Yearbook: Global Business Perspectives* (pp. 123–128). Beltsville, MD, USA: The International Academy of Business Disciplines.

Kelly, J. and Warnick, R. (1999). *Recreation Trends and Markets: The 21St Century.* Champaign, Illinois: Sagamore.

Lee, C. and Kim, J. (1998). International tourism demand for the 2002 world cup Korea: A combined forecasting technique. *Pacific Tourism Review,* **2**, 157–166.

Lee, C.-K., Song, H.-J. and Mjelde, J. W. (2008). The forecasting of international Expo tourism using quantitative and qualitative techniques. *Tourism Management,* **29**(6), 1084–1098.

Lee, M. S., Elango, B. and Schnaars, S. P. (1997). The accuracy of the Conference Boards buying plans index: A comparison of judgmental vs. extrapolation forecasting methods. *International Journal of Forecasting,* **13**(1), 127–135.

Lennon, J. and Yeoman, I. (2007). Drivers and scenarios of Scottish tourism – Shaping the future to 2015. *Tourism Recreation Research,* **32**(1), 345–367.

Li, G., Song, H. and Witt, S. (2005). Recent development in econometric modelling and forecasting. *Journal of Travel Research,* **44**(1), 82–99.

Lin, V. S. and Song, H. (2014). A review of Delphi forecasting research in tourism. [doi: 10.1080/13683500.2014.967187]. *Current Issues in Tourism*, 1–33.

Lin, V. S., Goodwin, P. and Song, H. (2014). Accuracy and bias of experts' adjusted forecasts. *Annals of Tourism Research*, **48**, 156–174.

Liu, J. C. (1988). Hawaii tourism to the year 2000: A Delphi forecast. *Tourism Management*, **9**, 279–290.

Lloyd, J., La Lopa, J. M. and Braunlich, C. G. (2000). Predicting changes in Hong Kong's hotel industry given the change in sovereignty from Britain to China in 1997. *Journal of Travel Research*, **38**(4), 405–410.

Makridakis, S., Andersen, A., Carbone, R., Fildes, R., Hibon, M., Lewandowski, R., Newton, J., Parzen, E., Winkler, R. L. (1982). The accuracy of extrapolation (time series) methods: Results of a forecasting competition. *Journal of Forecasting*, **1**(2), 111–153.

Manning, R. and Fraysier, M. (1989). Expert and public opinion: Conflicting or complementary views? *Journal of Park and Recreation Administration*, **7**(3), 44–59.

Martin, W. and Mason, S. (1998). *Transforming the future: Rethinking free time and work.* Sudbury: Leisure Consultants.

McCubbrey, D. J. and Taylor, R. G. (2005). Disintermediation and reintermediation in the U.S. air travel distribution industry: A Delphi reprise. *Communications of the Association for Information Systems*, 464–477.

Moeller, G. H. and Shafer, E. L. (1994). The Delphi technique: A tool for long-range travel and tourism planning. In J. R. Ritchie and C. R. Goeldner, *Travel, Tourism, and Hospitality Research: A Handbook for Managers and Researchers* (2nd ed., pp. 473–480). New York: Wiley.

Moutinho, L. and Witt, S. F. (1995). Forecasting the tourism environment using a consensus approach. *Journal of Travel Research*, **33**(4), 46–50.

Müller, H. (1998). Long-haul tourism 2005 – Delphi study. *Journal of Vacation Marketing*, **4**(2), 193–201.

Ng, D. (1984). A model estimating the demand for leisure services manpower. *World Leisure and Recreation*, **26**(5), 45–49.

Pan, S. Q., Vega, M., Vella, A. J., Archer, B. H. and Parlett, G. R. (1995). A mini-Delphi approach: An improvement on single round techniques. *Progress in Tourism and Hospitality Research*, **2**, 27–39.

Patterson, M. and McDonald, G. (2004). *How Clean and Green is New Zealand tourism? Lifecyle and Future Environmental Impacts.* Lincoln, Canterbury, New Zealand: Manaaki Whenua Press, Landcare Research. Retrieved August 2011, from http://www.mwpress.co.nz/store/downloads/ LCRSciSeries24_Tourism_4web.pdf

Pizam, A. (1994). Planning a tourism research investigation, in J. R. Ritchie and C. Goeldner, *Travel, Tourism, and Hospitality Research* (pp. 91–104). New York: Wiley.

Prideaux, B., Laws, E. and Faulkner, B. (2003). Events in Indonesia: Exploring the limits to formal tourism trends forecasting methods in complex crisis situations. *Tourism Management,* **24**(4), 475–487.

Ritchie, J. B. (1985). The nominal group technique: An approach to consensus policy formulation in tourism. *Tourism Management,* **6**(2), 82–94.

Ritchie, J. B. (1994). The nominal group technique: Applications to tourism research. In J. Ritchie, *Travel, Tourism, Hospitality Research* (pp. 439–448). New York: Wiley.

Rossetto, A. (1999). Using scenarios in forecasting. *The Council for Australian University Tourism and Hospitality Education (CAUTHE).* Adelaide: BTR Conference Paper 99.3.

Sadi, M. A. and Henderson, J. C. (2005). Tourism in Saudi Arabia and its future development. *Journal of Business and Economics,* **11**, 94–111.

Schnaars, S. (1987). How to develop and use scenarios. *Long Range Planning,* **20**(1), 105–114.

Schwaninger, M. (1989). Trends in leisure and tourism for 2000–2010: Scenario with consequences for planners. In S. F. Witt and L. Mouthinho, *Tourism Marketing and Management Handbook* (599–605). Cambridge: Prentice Hall.

Shen, S., Li, G. and Song, H. (2008). An assessment of combining tourism demand forecasts over different time horizons. *Journal of Travel Research,* **47**(2), 197–207.

Shen, S., Li, G. and Song, H. (2011). Combination forecasts of international tourism demand. *Annals of Tourism Research,* **38**(1), 72–89.

Smeral, E. and Weber, A. (2000). Forecasting international tourism trends to 2010. *Annals of Tourism Research,* **27**(4), 982–1006.

Smeral, E., Witt, S. F. and Witt, C. A. (1992). Econometric forecasts: Tourism trends to 2000. *Annals of Tourism Research,* **19**(3), 450–466.

Song, H. and Hyndman, R. J. (2011). Tourism forecasting: An introduction. *International Journal of Forecasting,* **27**(3), 817–821.

Song, H. and Li, G. (2008). Tourism demand modelling and forecasting—A review of recent research. *Tourism Management,* **29**(2), 203–220.

Song, H., Gao, B. Z. and Lin, V. S. (2013). Combining statistical and judgmental forecasts via a Web-based tourism demand forecasting system. *International Journal of Forecasting,* **29**(2), 295–310.

Song, H., Lin, S., Zhang, X. and Gao, Z. (2010). Global financial/economic crisis and tourist arrival forecasts for Hong Kong. *Asia Pacific Journal of Tourism Research,* **15**(2), 223–242.

Song, H., Witt, S. F., Wong, K. and Wu, D. (2009). An empirical study of forecast combination in tourism. *Journal of Hospitality & Tourism Research,* **33**, 3–29.

Song, H., Witt, S. F. and Zhang, X. (2008). Developing a Web-based tourism demand forecasting system. *Tourism Economics,* **14**(3), 445–468.

Tesar, G., Edgell, D. and Seely, R. (1979). Use of modified scenario research in forecasting of tourism in the United States. *Travel Research Journal,* **1**, 49–57.

Tideswell, C., Mules, T. and Faulkner, B. (2001). An integrative approach to tourism forecasting: A glance in the rearview mirror. *Journal of Travel Research,* **40**(2), 162–171.

Tisdell, C. (2000). *The Economics of Tourism. (Vol. 1).* Cheltenham: Edward Elga.

Tolley, R., Lumsdon, L. and Bickerstaff, K. (2010). The future of walking in Europe: Revisiting expert opinion ten years later. *PQN Final Report – Part B3: Documentation – The future of walking.* (D. Sauter et al., Eds.) Office, COST. Retrieved September 15, 2011, from Pedestrians Quality Needs (PQN): http://www.walkeurope.org/final_report/default.asp

Tsui, W. H., Ozer Balli, H., Gilbey, A. and Gow, H. (2014). Forecasting of Hong Kong airport's passenger throughput. *Tourism Management,* **42**, 62–76.

USTA. (2011). *The 2010 travelhorizons™ research program.* Retrieved November 21, 2011, from US Travel Association (USTA): http://www.ustravel.org/research/domestic-research/travelhorizons.

Uysal, M. and Crompton, J. L. (1985). An overview of approaches used to forecast tourism demand. *Journal of Travel Research,* **23**(4), 7–15.

van Doorn, J. W. (1982). Can futures research contribute to tourism policy? *Tourism Management,* **3**(3), 149–166.

van Doorn, J. W. (1984). Tourism forecasting and the policymaker: Criteria of usefulness. *Tourism Management,* **5**(2), 24–39.

van Doorn, J. W. (1986). Scenario writing: A method for long-term tourism forecasting? *Tourism Management,* **7**(1), 33–49.

Vanhove, N. (2011). *The Economics of Tourism Destinations.* Elsevier.

Var, T. (1984). Delphi and GSV techniques in tourism forecasting and policy design. *Problems of Tourism,* **3**, 41–52.

Varum, C. A., Melo, C., Alvarenga, A. and de Carvalho, P. (2011). Scenarios and possible futures for hospitality and tourism. *Foresight,* **13**(1), 19–35.

Veal, A. (2010). *Leisure, Sport and Tourism: Politics, Policy and Planning.* Wallingford, Oxfordshire: CAB International.

von Bergner, N. M. and Lohmann, M. (2014). Future challenges for global tourism: A Delphi survey. *Journal of Travel Research,* **53**(4), 420–432.

Weber, K. and Ladkin, A. (2003). The convention industry in Australia and the United Kingdom: Key issues and competitive forces. *Journal of Travel Research*, **42**(2), 125–132.

Whyte, D. N. (1992). Key trends and issues impacting local government recreation and park administration in the 1990s. *Thesis (PhD.)*. Indiana University.

Witt, S. F. and Moutinho, L. (1989). *Tourism marketing and management handbook*. Hertfordshire: Prentice Hall.

Witt, S. F. and Witt, C. A. (1995). Forecasting tourism demand: A review of empirical research. *International Journal of Forecasting*, **11**(3), 447–475.

Wong, K., Song, H., Witt, S. and Wu, D. C. (2007). Tourism forecasting: To combine or not to combine? *Tourism Management*, **28**(4), 1068–1078.

Wright, G. and Goodwin, P. (1998). *Forecasting with Judgment*. Chichester: Wiley.

Yeoman, I. and Lederer, P. (2005). Scottish tourism: Scenarios and vision. *Journal of Vacation Marketing*, **11**, 71–87.

Yeoman, I., Lennon, J. J. and Black, L. (2005). Foot-and-mouth disease: A scenario of reoccurrence for Scotland's tourism industry. *Journal of Vacation Marketing*, **11**, 179–190.

Yeoman, I., Yu, T. L., Mars, M. and Wouters, M. (2012). *2050 – Tomorrow's Tourism*. Bristol: Channel View.

Glossary

Delphi method: Originally developed by the RAND Corporation for qualitative forecasting, this is a valuable working tool for long-term planning and forecasting of tourism development. It is a special type of survey used to predict the occurrence of specified long-term and short-term events and to generate forecasts of the probability of specified conditions prevailing in future. The forecast is developed by a panel of experts who anonymously answer a series of questions. The responses are fed back to panel members who then may change their original responses. The cycle may be repeated several times.

Forecasting: Making statements estimating the outcome of events before they, often using techniques such as qualitative research and quantitative methods. A process designed to predict future events with a specific time and outcome. Typically all forecasting exercises assume that if we can predict the future, we can modify our behaviour to be in a better position than we otherwise would have been, when it arrives.

Gearing Swart-Var (GSV): A group technique, which also relies on expert opinions. This is particularly useful when it is difficult and expensive to collect primary data and desirable to use expert judgment as a proxy. It is often used to determine the attractiveness of a resource and the optimum resource allocation. It consists of four steps: determine criteria for attractiveness, weight criteria by importance, use expert judgment to evaluate each attraction using the criteria, and obtain composite scores.

Jury of executive opinion : The incorporation of expert opinions of likely outcomes and possible alternative scenarios used in the absence of reliable historical data. It compromises corporate executives or government officials meeting together and reaching consensus estimates of key variables in the future.

Nominal Group Technique (NGT): A technique developed by Andre Delbecq and Andrew Van de Ven in 1968, and used in behavioural science to tap the ideas and judgments of individuals while simultaneously reaching a group consensus. It involves a structured group meeting with many similarities to Delphi except in NGT the group actually meets so members are not anonymous and communication occurs directly between members.

Qualitative forecasting: Also called 'qualitative', 'intuitive', 'speculative' or 'subjective' forecasting. Historical information about the forecast variables are organized by analysts and forecasters using their management judgment, expertise and opinion, rather than mathematical rules. It is used generally when historical data is not available or no longer relevant to future needs, or when the planning horizon is very long.

Qualitative forecasting methods: Those are based on judgment, opinion, past experience and best guesses. Common types in tourism include: asking the stakeholders, asking the experts, asking the public, and judgment-aided methods. Delphi method and scenario writing are the two most popular qualitative forecasting techniques used in tourism studies.

Scenario writing: A qualitative forecasting method that forms a hypothetical future history or sequence of events based on current trends or consensus of expert opinions. It usually provides a more qualitative and contextual description of how the present will evolve into the future, and identifies a set of possible futures.

City Branding:
Is it really a good idea?

Dr John Heeley

Contents

John Heeley is the Director of Best Destination Marketing and Visiting Fellow, at Sheffield Hallam University.

A hyperlinked PDF version of this review is available for download from the CTR area of Goodfellow Pubishers' website: http://www.goodfellowpublishers.com/ctr

"Branding, to be crass, is a means of selling a place – a building, a district or a city. Capitalising on image demands metrics, and metrics imply control – of the image, the message and, ultimately, the men and women who flesh out the image: us. In the end, the most important metrics in city branding are increases in property values and tourist spending. Yet these are not necessarily good for city dwellers, especially rental tenants and people who depend on public services that may be underfunded while municipal budgets are diverted to creating and maintaining tourist attractions".

Sharon Zuckin (2014), extract from *Post-card-perfect: the big business of city branding*

Introduction

Brand as a term originated as a mark of identity; notoriously, it served in the medieval period as a vicious form of punishment. As a business discipline, its origins go back to the Industrial Revolution and the rise of national and then global consumer markets. By the early 1880's, Procter and Gamble in the USA was branding its products in recognisably modern ways, starting with Ivory soap with 'it floats' slogan. In Britain, Lyle's Golden Syrup with its green and gold packaging is reckoned to be one of the country's oldest brands, boasting a continuous history stretching back to 1885. By the late 1950's, product branding had emerged as an advertising-led business activity, with logos encapsulating the offer and with 'above the line' advertising being utilised to create customer awareness and generate sales. Audiences were targeted crudely, but often effectively, by reference to broad socio-economic groupings. By the end of the 20th century – and conditioned by the Internet, the World Wide Web, and the emergent reality of Marshall McLuhan's 'global village' – branding came to occupy centre stage. As the late Wally Olins (2008, p.6) succinctly put it – branding migrated "from the periphery to the centre of corporate concern". More than anyone else, his work and writings convey how branding can permeate contemporary business organisations in what he refers to as their four 'vectors':

♦   What they make and sell

♦   The environment within which they operate

♦   - How they communicate

♦   - How they deal with their employees and multiple outside stakeholders

Across these vectors, the brand – be it Orange, Nike, Waitrose, Heinz, Microsoft or Google – is reducible to 'the business', dominating its balance sheet and forming the greater part of its market value.

From a historical perspective, the branding of places – be they nations, regions, cities or other geographical entities – is in one sense a relatively recent affair. Anholt (2007, p.xi) is quite right when he states that place branding only became a discrete and professionalised domain of activity and study in the 1990's, complete "with its commercial and academic communities, consulting firms, publications, conferences, research, and a rising number of full-time professionals in national, city and regional administration". In other respects, however, the origins of place branding go back much further, and in an urban context emphasise two separate, but sometimes interlinked strands of development, both of which merit consideration here.

A first strand of historical development is evident as a part of the nineteenth century evolution of spa towns and seaside resorts, the larger ones of which became cities (e.g. Nice, Baden-Baden, Bath, Brighton and Las Palmas). In Europe, the first such urban resort to promote itself in the recognisably modern manner we would refer to nowadays as **destination marketing** was Blackpool. From 1879 onwards, it began professionally to market itself as a tourist destination courtesy of an oversight on the part of national government which permitted the municipal authority – Blackpool Corporation – to levy a two penny rate specifically for the purpose of mounting advertising campaigns "stating (i.e. marketing) the attractions and amusements of the town" (Walton, 1983: 150). Armed with these unique powers, the Corporation established the Blackpool Advertising Committee under whose auspices an annual budget of £4,000 (£400,000 in today's currency) was being expended by the outbreak of the Great War. Working with railway companies, the principal medium employed by the Committee was the picture poster, supported by visiting exhibitions and other publicity stunts. Slogans and logos were eventually employed, and with it destination branding was born.

Similar fiduciary arrangements with which to fund urban destination marketing only became available to other British spas and seaside towns following legislation in 1921 and 1936. These long-awaited powers were eagerly lapped up outside of Blackpool, so that in Britain virtually every urban seaside resort and spa town began to churn out posters and guidebooks bearing slogans and logos, some of them becoming more or less household names (notably Skegness is so bracing and Torbay as the so-called English Riviera). In this way, the **destination brand** became an integral part of destination marketing, forming the design framework for a wide range of promotional and infrastructural activities. For instance, the slogan, typeface and colour palette of the English Riviera became the 'look and feel' of the publicity and (to an extent) the place as the destination brand expressed itself in street furniture and other 'city dressing' aspects.

The second strand is the subject matter of this review and is central to what is nowadays commonly referred to as **city marketing** where, in contrast to the evolution of destination branding, marketing activity from the onset centred on the **city brand**. History here takes us to New York, where in 1977 the New York State Department of Commerce hired an advertising agency to implement a $4.3 marketing campaign which would accentuate the positives of the area, as an antidote to the negative images then prevalent about the city, especially those of financial and economic failure and of urban crime and squalor (Bendel, 2011: 179-183). On a pro bono basis, a graphic designer called Milton Glaser came up with a logo for a slogan whose author is to this day unknown. The result-ant 'civic boosterism' campaign was executed by the Wells, Rich and Greene advertising agency over the summer and autumn of 1977. *I love NY* went on to inspire several more campaigns and all manner of merchandising. It is a much copied logo and slogan which doggedly endures, passing a longevity test which defeats nearly all other city branding projects.

I love NY influenced Europe in the sense that two Atlantic-facing cities were minded to do something similar. In1983, Amsterdam and Glasgow introduced the *Amsterdam has it* and *Glasgow's miles better* city brands. They did so indepen-dently of each other, but in both cases *I love NY* served as the role model. In turn, other European cities followed the leads provided by Glasgow and Amsterdam, so that by the beginning of the twenty first century slogans and logos were increasingly finding their way into urban settings other than spas and seaside resorts. In particular, they were becoming an item in the regeneration toolkits of provincial cities anxious to carve out post-industrial futures for themselves. In Britain, in his pioneering turn-of-the-century text on urban tourism, Chris-topher Laws (2002, pp. 68-69) could refer to the use of slogans and logos as "another way of selling cities", instancing Birmingham (*Europe's meeting place*), Liverpool (*Maritime city*), and Stoke (*Do china in a day*). He noted the difficulty of devising branding approaches acceptable to all, instancing the "disaster" of Manchester's *We're up and going*.

With the benefit of hindsight, these and other early attempts at city branding (e.g. *Bradford's bouncing back*) are now readily dismissed as rather futile and simplistic exercises in sloganeering, premised on 'hyped-up' New York and Glasgow role-models which appeared on the surface to be panaceas, but whose impact in reality was slight. To be sure, city marketing (and the city branding of which it was a part) was at the commencement of the new Millennium still on the periphery of urban policymaking and planning agendas. Tellingly, the above-mentioned text by Laws devoted just one page to city branding. Having said that, the pioneering efforts at sloganeering referred to above did lay a foun-dation of knowledge and experience on which more sophisticated city marketing and associated branding platforms were to emerge from 2003 onwards, beginning in Bilbao and Birmingham with the respective launches in that year of the *Bilbao B* and the *Birmingham b* – refer Table 1. Over the ensuing years, the theory and practice of city branding effectively 'moved on', to the point where nowadays mayors and city managers view it with more than passing interest, while the branding platforms and projects themselves involve much more than simply promoting a slogan and logo. However, the effectiveness and ultimate value of city branding remains to this day deeply problematic. Indeed, some would say it is a suitable case for de-marketing.

Against such a backdrop, this review presents a state-of-the-art review of how the business discipline of branding has been applied to cities in Western Europe, taking as its empirical basis experience in the first decade of the twenty first century. Its focus is the city brands central to city marketing as opposed to the more or less routine and otherwise unproblematic destination branding undertaken by destination marketing organisations (DMOs) in both urban and rural contexts and at the national, regional and local levels. The qualification (the "less" in the "more or less") is where the destination brand is a sub-brand of the city brand, a matter taken up in the next section.

The approach taken in the review and some of its content is shaped by the author's practitioner experience over a 19 year period (1990-2009) during which time he set up and directed DMOs in four provincial British cities – Sheffield, Coventry, Birmingham, and Nottingham. In all four cities, he found himself in the position of introducing and championing a city brand project, viz. *Sheffield shines*, *Coventry inspires*, the *Birmingham b*, and the *Nottingham N*. In each case the author experienced first-hand the problematic nature of city branding, which in a nutshell is the tremendous challenges attendant upon creating and sustaining a city brand concept so that it really does take hold and 'make a difference'. In particular, the author recounts his own direct and largely unsuccessful efforts to implement city brands for Birmingham and Nottingham.

The wider, European outlook in this review derives largely from the author's close association (2002-2012) with the European Cities Marketing network, during which time he served successively as board member, Treasurer, Internal Management Advisor, and Interim Chief Executive Officer. During these years, the author became conversant with several of the more successful exemplars of city branding to be found on the continent, all of whom feature in this review, especially *Iamsterdam*.

When is a destination brand a city brand?

Across Britain and European, it is crucial from the onset that the reader under-stands that the destination branding carried out by DMOs at the national, regional and local levels, and then portrayed and otherwise commented on in the academic text books (e.g. Crouch, Morgan, Morrison, and Pike), must for the most part be differentiated from city branding. As mentioned above, des-tination brands are the more or less ubiquitous and relatively unproblematic design frameworks within which DMOs undertake their marketing operations designed to create visitors and enhance profile. Historically, as we have shown, such brands were part and parcel of the pioneering destination marketing conducted at a local scale by spa towns and seaside resorts. Eventually, they were to feature in the marketing operations of DMOs established at national and regional scales. In North America, for instance, Brand USA currently pro-motes the States as an international tourism destination through its *Discover America* brand framework, while at a state level the Virginia Tourism Corpora-tion, for example, discharges its media relations, promotions and advertising work utilising a *Virginia for lovers* destination brand introduced back in 1969. In Canada, the equivalent destination brand frameworks for Ontario and Quebec are *Ontario - yours to discover* and *Quebec - providing emotions*. In Europe, to cite just one example, the brand framework for the Vienna Tourist Board's destina-tion marketing activities is provided by *Vienna: now or never* (Heeley, 2011, pp. 71-72).

As we shall demonstrate in this review, city brands transcend destination ones in that they target audiences wider than those of the tourist (typically it is resi-dents, potential inward investors and occupiers of residential properties, pro-spective students and film producers, as well as the main tourism markets - holi-daymakers, city breakers, conference delegates and event-goers). Crucially, city brands supply an overarching set of imagery and messages within which the targeted marketing of various urban agencies (typically DMOs, inward invest-ment agencies, chambers, transport authorities and universities) may more efficaciously take place. Indeed, **the overarching or 'umbrella' nature of city branding is its hallmark**, serving to differentiate it from the destination brand-ing to which it is nearly always linked and to emphasise its multi-dimensional nature. As the editor of a recently published collection of articles on city brand-ing opines: "Part of the complexity of city brands derives from their obligation to address the needs of a spectrum of fundamentally different target audiences" (Dinnie, 2011: 4).

We can now make two simple, but important observations. First, while destina-tion brands are more or less ubiquitous in an urban context, city brands are much less common. Indeed, **the norm in an urban context is for there to be a**

destination brand, but no city brand. This is the case, for instance, in Vienna. In the Austrian capital, *Vienna: now or never* serves as the destination brand, but one searches in vain for an 'official' city brand. Indeed, London, Rome, Paris – virtually all of Europe's traditionally 'great' cities – do not work to a formal city brand in promoting themselves as places to visit and centres in which to live, work, study and invest. Indeed, in the light of their so-called "accumulated advantage" (Hospers, 2011: 31), why would Europe's 'great' cities be minded to undertake city branding projects whose outcomes are so problematic? There is a widespread absence of city branding in Europe's 'lesser' cities, too, explicable in such places by the problematic nature of the outcomes allied to the "complexity" to which Dinnie refers to above. From Reykjavik and Oulu in the far north of Europe to Zagreb and Sofia in its deep south, **city brands are conspicuous by their absence**. In my home county of Yorkshire, for instance, there are six principal cities (Bradford, Leeds, Hull, Sheffield, Wakefield and York), only one of whom currently has a city brand, viz. Leeds with its *Leeds: live it, love it* brand platform – refer Table 1. The perhaps surprising empirical reality with which we are therefore confronted is that while nearly everywhere city branding is a 'hot' and debated topic, city brands themselves are a rather scarce commodity – less rather than more likely to be present.

Secondly, where city brands do exist, the destination brand is nearly always acts as a sub-brand of the city brand. In other words, the city brand is utilised for various strands of 'official' city marketing activity, including the destination marketing undertaken by DMOs to penetrate city break and convention markets, while also embracing various of the other key audiences referred to above (Heeley, ibid, chapters 7&8). Examples of a city brand currently being used *inter alia* as a 'tourism' (i.e. urban destination marketing) sub-brand are *be Berlin*; *Edinburgh Inspiring Capital*; *Iamsterdam*; *People Make Glasgow*; and *Stockholm: the capital of Scandinavia*. Take, for instance, Berlin, whose city brand is known as *be Berlin* (Grupp, 2010). The latter campaign is implemented on a truly herculean scale by a bespoke public-private partnership called the Berlin Partner (BP) organisation. Bringing together city government and over 200 private sector companies, BP undertakes a comprehensive programme of 'civic boosterism'; every Berliner is communicated with personally, there are promotional toolkits called 'Berlin boxes', and an army of 'Berlin ambassadors' busily fashion their own online 'Berlin stories'. At the national and international scales, BP employs a flexible 'the place to be' slogan which enables specific themes to be highlighted: viz. Berlin as the place to be for conventions, for creative industries, for fashion and so forth. High profile 'Berlin Days' are organised in the world's most important capital cities, targeting VIPs and potential inward investor audiences. It is worth noting that BP has an annual budget of circa €20 million, over half of which is derived from private sector donations, and the organisation employs no less than 125 staff (Steden and Holtgrewe, 2013). As an organisational entity, however, BP is entirely separate from the city's DMO, Visit Berlin, whose independent history goes back to 1993. In terms of brand framework, however, Visit Berlin acts as a fully-fledged sub-brand of the overarching *be Berlin* city brand. In effect, the same logo, typeface, and colours are employed by both organisations.

As far as city branding is concerned, therefore, there is a preponderance of situations in which such a brand does not exist in the urban context. Where there is a city brand, however, the destination brand is invariably a sub-brand of that city brand; Madrid, the capital of Spain, and Gratz, the second city of Austria, are the only exceptions to this rule known to the author.

Having set the above context, the remainder of this review further defines and delineates city branding, and against its inherent promise will be set the constraints which limit its practical application to only a handful of Western European cities. Even here – as we shall see in subsequent sections of the review – the value of city branding exercises remains problematic, though the *IAmsterdam* city brand is arguably emerging as an exemplar of best practice.

City brand versus city image, profile, identity and reputation

City branding may be seen from both producer and consumer perspectives. As an example of the former, Kavaratzis and Ashworth (2005) define city branding as "the self-conscious application of branding to places as an instrument of urban planning and management" (p. 507). From this perspective, city branding is a process; an applied business discipline, centred upon marketing and communications activities. Its end-product is a city brand; several leading examples are identified in Table 1.

These deliberately 'engineered' city brands may be contrasted with what are often referred to as 'natural' or 'organic' city brands. Here the city brand is viewed from the consumer/audience/market perspective. As such, it may be defined as "the totality of perceptions, thoughts, and feelings that customers hold about a place" (Baker, 2007, p. 26). In a similar vein, Moilanen and Rainistro (2008, p. 6) choose to define city brand as:

> "an impression perceived in a client's mind of a product or a service.
> It is the sum of all tangible and intangible elements, which makes the
> selection unique".

'Natural'/'organic' conceptualisations of city brand are commonplace. When, for example, on the official Barcelona Metropolis web site a travel journalist Nick Rider describes *Brand Barcelona* as "a global trademark of refined urban life, advanced design and Mediterranean hedonism", he is referring to a natural/organic city brand as opposed to one of the engineered variety. Similarly, the annual City Brands Index measuring the relative brand strengths of major cities throughout the world is an assessment derived from the consumer as opposed to producer perspective (Anholt, 2007, pp. 59-62). It is based on a survey in which people's perceptions are assessed. Respondents are asked to rank the world's major cities in terms of status, physical attributes, quality of basic infrastructure, economic and social potential, lifestyle, and the local residents. On this basis, the current year results show London as the world's leading city brand, followed by Sydney, Paris, New York, Rome, Washington, Los Angeles, Toronto and Vienna.

In the slowly developing academic literature on city branding, 'engineered' and 'natural'/ 'organic' notions are haplessly intermixed, occasioning a degree of terminological confusion and related misunderstandings on the part of the readers. For instance, the case-studies of city branding in Dinnie's text are drawn in almost equal measure from the two differing perspectives (Dinnie, Op cit). Of course, the link between 'engineered' as opposed to 'natural'/'organic' brands is that the former are premised on changing (for the better) the perceptions which underpin the latter. For the sum total of 'natural'/ 'organic' perceptions make up a city's 'image', 'profile', 'reputation' or 'identity'. The challenge for those cities electing to brand themselves invariably lies in the fact that the 'natural'/ 'organic' brands do not communicate the desired messages; in other words, they do not resonate positively with residents and with prospective visitors, investors and students..

Defining city branding

To avoid the confusion and misunderstanding referred to above, the organic/ natural concept of brand mentioned above is in the view of the author best referred to as 'image', 'profile', 'identity', and 'reputation', so that the term city branding becomes confined to the consciously 'engineered' exercises of the type referred to by Kavaratzis and Ashworth. In this way, an *I love NY* city brand-type construct may be distinguished from the reputation, profile, identity and image of New York, albeit that this brand is ultimately seeking to modify that city's reputation, profile, identity and image. In this light, the author defines city branding as follows:

> the application of branding as a management discipline to the marketing of towns and cities, so as to provide an overarching framework of urban imagery and messages within which specific residential and external audiences may be more effectively addressed

through targeted marketing and sales activities; the external audiences in question are typically those of tourism, inward investment,
potential occupiers of property, and prospective students.

Defined as such, the leading city brands developed in Europe in the first decade
of the twenty first century are set out in Table 1.

The rationale for city branding – protagonists, promise, potential and problematics

The rationale for introducing city branding programmes of the kind featured
in Table 1 is that in an increasingly globalised world urban areas are competing against each other for scarce resources in marketplaces which are critical
to their prosperity and survival. These marketplaces and audiences may be
external to the city - students, tourists, migrants, investors, and events - but
they may also be internal, notably local residents, companies and other institutions. Place branding is seen by its proponents as a means of differentiating a
place from competitors, and of systematically communicating and distributing
its advantages to the key audiences. It is "an organising principle that involves
orchestrating the messages and experiences associated with a place to ensure
that they are as distinctive, compelling, memorable, and rewarding as possible"
(Baker, 2007, p.26). The potential and promise of such branding is viewed by
its proponents as huge; get it right and "the results can be far more comprehensive, economically significant and socially important than for virtually any
other branding exercise" (Whitfield, 2005). A "co-ordinated approach can significantly increase the competitive advantage" (Moilanen and Rainistro, 2008,
p1). Morgan and Pritchard (2004, p60) assert that branding is "perhaps the most
powerful weapon" in the armoury available to place marketers. The ultimate
promise of city branding is to create enhanced awareness in key marketplaces
which in turn increases customers, generating business, employment and prosperity.

So say the protagonists. The actual practice of city branding in early twenty
first century Europe to a large extent belies its promise and potential. While city
branding is topical and its utilisation has gathered some momentum in Western Europe over the 2000-2010 period, it would be a mistake to exaggerate the
extent of its application. As we have already established, and contrary to the
impression conveyed by its topicality, city branding is not a mainstream tool of
urban policy. Surveying the cities of Western Europe, the practice of city branding remains the exception rather than the rule. The vast majority do not have an
explicit city branding strategy in place. Unsurprisingly therefore, it is also the
case – as Pike (2008), Govers and Go (2009) and others have pointed out – that

place branding is characterised by a lack of published research and case materials. Scarcity is an especially marked feature of the literature on city branding, and this is especially so in respect of contributions of an applied/practitioner kind – a deficiency which this review and Dinnie's text begin to address.

As well as being ill-documented, the practice of city branding is the source of considerable misunderstanding as to its purpose, structure and modus operandi. This is as true of the principal players – the politicians, business people and other leaders – as it is of the community at large and the local media that reports on its affairs. Baker is right when he says city leaders "don't understand the benefits and concepts involved in place branding" (Baker, 2007, p.27). Amidst such misunderstanding, the delivery of city branding projects is nearly always difficult, controversial and problematic. There is keen debate, bordering on the philosophical/ideological, on the nature and extent of the local socio-economic benefits attendant upon city branding programmes. Some commentators see it as an irrelevance, arguing that city branding precludes urban renewal rather than stimulates it (Monclus et al, 2006).Indeed, the editors of a book of readings entitled "City Tourism: national capital perspectives" state flatly that urban fragmentation "inhibits developing a cohesive and unique brand" (Maitland and Ritchie, 2009, p.268). Case studies in this volume of Brussels and Budapest amply demonstrate the point being made (ibid: 142-158, 201-12). Even-handedly, Ashworth opines as follows about the effectiveness or otherwise of city branding:

> "Although commercial products have long been branded, there is just not a long enough experience of the transfer of the concepts and techniques to places to appraise the consequences of doing this" (Ashworth, 2012, p.253).

He cites supposedly "well-known" UK and Irish best practice as Glasgow, Manchester and Dublin (ibid, p.251), though the latter two cities have never successfully introduced city brands, while even in Glasgow the contribution made by city branding is questionable. The *Glasgow's Miles Better* logo and slogan (Figure 1) has been afforded an almost mythical, panacea-like status, with greatly exaggerated claims having been made on its behalf (Heeley_1987, pp.49-54).In fact, the launch of *Glasgow's Miles Better* was low key, and it never attracted significant levels of resourcing. To be sure, the clever use of the Mr. Happy children's character as the logo, together with the double meaning in the bold 'cocking a snoot at Edinburgh' slogan, did engage many ordinary Glaswegians. Over time, the brand did become effective as a rallying point for the local public and private sectors. However, while the city brand may have symbolised Glasgow's post-industrial renaissance, much more fundamental factors brought about the city's regeneration – from sustained environmental improvements to townscape through to high profile festivals (notably the 1988 Glasgow Garden Festival and the 1990 European Capital of Culture) as well as the opening of major new facilities such as the Burrell Collection (1983), the Scottish Conference and Exhibition Centre (1985), and the Glasgow Royal Concert Hall (1990). As a campaign, *Glasgow's Miles Better* was deemed to have run its course in 1989, and was briefly replaced by *Glasgow's alive*. As we shall see later, this gave way to *Glasgow: Scotland with style* which from 2013 was replaced by *People make Glasgow*.

Figure 1

In reality, the application of branding principles and techniques to the selling and repositioning of cities has so far met with only limited success The truth is that no urban destination in Europe has so far transformed itself through a city branding programme so as to deliver fully on all the promise and potential alluded to earlier. Nowhere has the rhetoric of the protagonists been justified. The author reaches these conclusions from the vantage point of someone who has been close to how cities market themselves for over forty years; first as an academic and then as a practitioner. While in appropriate circumstances city branding is capable of delivering important benefits, and as we shall see the *IAmsterdam* city brand is emerging as something of a role model, **the starting point for any city branding exercise should be an awareness of its limitations when as a business discipline it is applied to cities.**

Broadly speaking, there are four main factors constraining what in practice can be achieved by city branding projects:

1   The complexity of cities and the branding authority's lack of influence and control

2   A weak relationship between city branding and other aspects of city marketing

3   The difficulty in evaluating city branding

4   The reluctance to fund city branding

5   We shall now briefly explore each factor in turn

The complexity of cities and the branding authority's lack of influence and control

To understand the issues of complexity and lack of influence and control, it is instructive to turn to Olins's slim and elegantly written seminal work on branding entitled 'Corporate Identity' published in 1994. In this, he contrasted "explicitly engineered identity or brand" with "socially constructed image and reputation":

> "Every organisation carries out thousands of transactions every day: it buys, it sells, it hires and fires, it makes, it paints, it cleans, it promotes, it informs through advertising, the web and other media - and so on. The totality of the way the organisation presents itself can be called its identity. What the different audiences perceive is often called its image" (Olins, 1994, p1).

According to Olins, the goal of every corporate branding or identity programme, is to arrive at a situation in which 'everything the organisation does, everything it owns, and everything it produces should project a clear idea of what it is and what its aims are' (ibid, 1994, p1).The organisational settings for Olins distinguishing between 'image/reputation', on the one hand, and 'identity'/brand' on the other, are the product-based marketing communications campaigns routinely being undertaken by large, private sector concerns. Corporations such as Asda and BT and products such as Ibuprofen, Nivea and BMW.

Unlike the corporate context, however, city branding projects are faced with a larger and more complex, multi-dimensional set of products. By their very nature cities are large, heterogeneous, and pluralistic. As a consequence, what cities do and how they are perceived is a vast and ever changing landscape, anarchic and fragmented. Whichever part of the urban bureaucracy is charged with planning, co-ordinating and managing a city branding programme (i.e. the city branding authority), it will inevitably struggle to:

- Influence and control the countless things that a city does, owns, produces and markets – the very same factors which are integral to shaping a city's image and reputation

- Reduce the inherent complexity of cities to a handful of brand messages and advantages

Because of this complexity and associated lack of influence and control, there is much substance to the argument that cities cannot really brand themselves with anything like the same level of impact and effectiveness as a corporation can with respect to, say, a chocolate bar or a packet of cornflakes (Matson 1994, pp35-41).

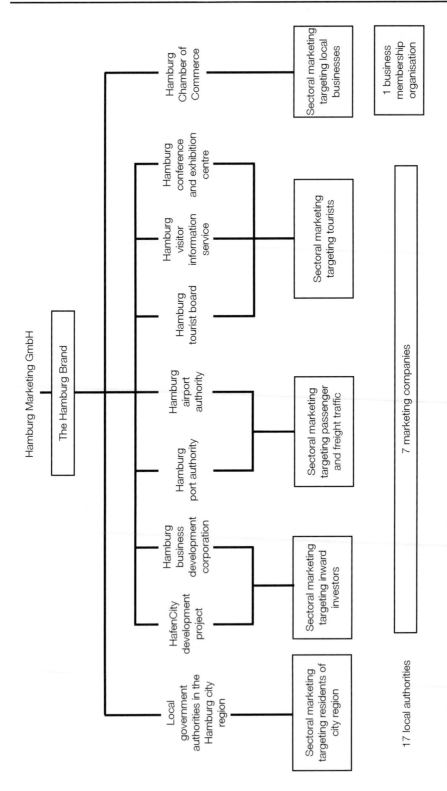

Figure 2: City marketing and city branding in Hamburg

The weak relationship of city branding to other aspects of city marketing

City branding is only one part of city marketing as a whole. As well as branding activities, city marketing embraces all those sectoral marketing activities where the 'generic' place alongside the products themselves are important in shaping perceptions and/or generating leads and/or determining sales. Typically, citywide sectoral marketing activities target students, visitors, investors, and resident audiences. The city branding executed by whosoever is the branding authority therefore supplements the sectoral marketing activities undertaken by the local authorities, universities, tourist organisations, inward investment agencies, and others. City branding is in effect a generic, promotional 'umbrella' under which these targeted sectoral activities can as it were 'take shelter' and be made more cost-effective. The argument runs as follows: city branding creates heightened awareness of places as favourable destinations in which to live, visit, invest and study, so that sectoral marketing is facilitated and/or can be concentrated on generating leads and their subsequent fulfilment. In a nutshell, **city branding aims to create a 'warm glow' about the place in the minds of resident and external audiences, 'softening up' those marketplaces for subsequent targeted, sectoral marketing activities.**

It is critical to appreciate the distinction between city branding, on the one hand, and sectoral marketing, on the other. We can exemplify it by reference to city marketing in the German city of Hamburg where a brand authority - Marketing Hamburg - was set up in 2004 specifically to provide an umbrella city brand for sectoral city marketing programmes relating to inward investment, transport, business development, and tourism. Figure 2 illustrates the city brand 'umbrella' in Hamburg, showing how the Hamburg city brand provided a framework within which no less than 25 other agencies undertook sectoral marketing activities aimed at a variety of resident, investor/business, and visitor audiences.

 The reason why city brands tend only weakly to be reflected in sectoral marketing activities lies in the fact that few of the agencies concerned will elect to become fully-fledged **sub-brands**. For instance, place brands for Nottingham and Leeds (which we shall be considering later on in this review) engendered just one and two sub-brands respectively. The reason for this is that most (if not all) of the agencies conducting sectoral marketing activities wish to retain their own carefully constructed bands and identities. In such a situation, the only way these agencies can demonstrate commitment to the official city brand is by the much looser and weaker process of **alignment** in which the logo, straplines and other aspects of brand platform are incorporated on literature, websites, letterheads and the like. Sub-branding and alignment are discussed further in section 14 below.

The difficulty in evaluating city branding

City branding projects prove resistant to evaluation and the establishment of precise rates of return on investment (ROI). It is easy to demonstrate activity, but difficult to quantify outputs and gauge success. Although claims of high and palpable ROI are made by city branding authorities, and even some academics, these should be treated with caution. Hankinson's review of city branding in 12 English cities concluded that it was little understood and rarely applied effectively, and one of the principal reasons for this was the inability to measure success (Hankinson 2001, pp127-142).

The reluctance to fund city branding

The **development** (i.e. pre-launch) costs of an engineered city brand vary widely. Budgets for the brandings of Toronto and Melbourne, for example, were £2.4 million and £121,000 respectively. The European examples in Table 1 had development and launch budgets ranging from £115,000 to nearly £1million. Grant funding from national government and the ECC has figured extensively in the development of these brands. In the author's experience, the ongoing **revenue** resourcing to implement city branding projects post-launch requires base-level funding of approximately £150,000 per annum in order to achieve a minimal level of visibility and impact. Revenue funding for city branding is especially difficult to secure on an ongoing basis. As far as the local public sector is concerned, it may decide to take on such a commitment, but more often than not there is caution and hesitancy about funding it wholly or in part: other statutory obligations may take a higher priority; the benefits are difficult to quantify; and, crucially, there may politically be a desire to avoid supporting an activity seen as irrelevant and wasteful by the media and sections of the local, voting population. For companies and other private sector institutions, city branding is clearly not their core business and - again in the author's experience - it is difficult (though not impossible) to persuade them to invest in it.

Where these funding obstacles have been overcome, as with the cities in Table 1, then two broad approaches are discernible. Some of the city branding projects listed have been financed wholly by the public purse (e.g. the Edinburgh and Belfast city brands). In the majority of cases, however, a mixture of public and private sources is evident. To raise monies from the private sector, recourse has been made to membership or corporate donor schemes. The Berlin Partner organisation, for instance, has over 200 companies in membership, while in the UK corporate donor schemes have been used by Experience Nottinghamshire, Marketing Birmingham and Marketing Leeds to help fund brand applications. Amsterdam Partners, the branding authority for the *IAmsterdam* city brand, is noteworthy for an effective blending of public and private sector support. Its annual budget for the 2010 year was approximately £2 million, split more or less equally between the city government and over forty private sector companies and institutions, each of whom provided an annual donation in excess of £20,000. The donors include Heineken, Philips, KLM, and Schiphol airport, while others were drawn from the ranks of companies in sectors such as banking, insurance, real estate and and energy.

The principal European city brands, 2000-2010

The factors and constraints discussed and exemplified above meant that during the first decade of the twenty first century 'engineered' city branding exercises were to be found in only a handful of Europe's major cities. As table 1 shows, amongst the leading examples on the continent were Amsterdam, Berlin, Bilbao, Copenhagen, Dresden, Gothenburg, Hamburg, Lyon, Maastricht, Madrid, Riga, Rotterdam, Stockholm, and The Hague. Completing the set, city brands were developed in Britain over the 2000-2010 period for Belfast, Birmingham, Cardiff, Glasgow, Edinburgh, Leeds, Liverpool, and Nottingham.

Table I details the lead organisations responsible for brand application in each of the 22 cities mentioned above, alongside the title of the city brand, the year of its launch, and the principal audiences being addressed. Of the 22 branding authorities, seven were public sector, forming a part of city government (Belfast, Bilbao, Madrid, Lyon Rotterdam, Stockholm and The Hague). All the rest were public-private partnerships (PPPs). Of these, four were to all intents and purposes the local tourist board (Glasgow, Gothenburg, Nottingham, and Riga), and four were integrated city marketing agencies (Birmingham, Cardiff, Dresden, and Leeds). Another PPP was responsible for Liverpool's overarching social and economic strategy. The remaining six PPPs comprised bespoke branding agencies set up specifically to co-ordinate development and implementation of the city brand (viz. Amsterdam, Berlin, Hamburg, Copenhagen, Edinburgh, and Maastricht).

The PPP organisational format reflects the need both to attract private sector commitment and funding, and to take forward brand implementation in a co-ordinated and networked manner. The importance of a shared and inclusive stakeholder approach to implementing city branding as opposed to autocratic, top-down initiatives is stressed by Dinnie (op.cit. p. 4). One of the first cities in Europe to attempt such a stakeholder approach was Marketing Hamburg – see Table 1 and Figure 2. This organisation was set up in 2004 to introduce and guide the subsequent implementation of the official Hamburg city brand. Its management board was chaired by the Mayor of Hamburg, providing a mix of local authority and chamber of commerce representatives. Another example,

Amsterdam Partners, was also established in the same year as the city branding authority for the metropolitan area. Constituted as an independent PPP foundation, its five- strong management board was chaired by the then head of corporate affairs for the Schiphol Group. The other members were senior level appointments drawn from Wolters Kluwer, the Amsterdam Chamber of Commerce, and the city councils of Amsterdam and Almere. Reporting to the management board was a team of twelve employees who on a day-to-day basis were charged with taking forward the *IAmsterdam* city brand. It should be noted that the Amsterdam Partners organisation has lately become part of a multi-purpose, integrated city marketing agency entitled Marketing Amsterdam which is inter alia responsible for the city brand, as well as destination marketing, inward investment and event promotion (Diender, 2011).

A British example, the Destination Edinburgh Marketing Alliance (DEMA), was established in 2000, and its activities were overseen by a 16 strong steering group chaired by the Leader of Edinburgh City Council, and included representatives from higher education, events and the arts, tourism, science, and the private sector (www.edinburghbrand.com). A management board directed implementation of the *Edinburgh Inspiring Capital* city brand, while day-to-day management of the project rested with four permanent, full-time staff. As in Amsterdam, the work of DEMA is now subsumed under an integrated city marketing agency called Marketing Edinburgh. Interestingly, the latter organisation's first chief executive was obliged to resign in December 2012 in the wake of ill-judged attempts to replace *Edinburgh Inspiring Capital* with a new *Incredinburgh* city brand.

As custodian of the brand, the activities of a branding authority embraces 'policing' of the brand; city dressing; a proactive approach to brand adoption; execution of marketing campaigns and the production of supporting marketing materials; market intelligence to track the impact of the brand; and the maintenance of ambassador networks.

Table 1: City branding campaigns in 22 European cities, 2000-2010

City	Brand Title	Launch	Brand Authority	Visitors	Residents	Investors/ Businesses	Students
Amsterdam	I Amsterdam	2004	Amsterdam Partners	✓	✓	✓	✗
Birmingham	The Birmingham b	2003	Marketing Birmingham	✓	✓	✓	✓
Berlin	be Berlin	2008	Berlin Partners	✓	✓	✓	✗
Belfast	The Belfast B	2008	Belfast City Council	✓	✓	✓	✗
Bilbao	Bilbao B	2003	Bilbao City Council	✓	✓	✓	
Cardiff	The Cardiff brand	2008	Cardiff & Co	✓	✓	✓	✓
Copenhagen	Copenhagen: open for you	2009	Copenhagen Brand Secretariat	✓	✓	✓	✗
Dresden	The Dresden D	2009	Dresden Marketing Board	✓	✓	✓	✗
Edinburgh	Edinburgh Inspiring Capital	2005	Destination Edinburgh Marketing Alliance	✓	✓	✓	✓
Glasgow	Glasgow: Scotland with style	2004	Glasgow City Marketing Bureau	✓	✓	✓	✗
Gothenburg	The Gothenburg brand	2009	Gothenburg & Co	✓	✓	✓	✓
Hamburg	The Hamburg brand	2004	Hamburg GmbH	✓	✓	✓	✗
Leeds	Leeds: live it, love it	2005	Marketing Leeds	✓	✓	✓	✗
Liverpool	The Liverpool brand	2009	Liverpool Vision	✓	✓	✓	✗
Lyon	Only Lyon	2007	Lyon Area Development Agency	✓	✓	✓	✓
Maastricht	Everything points to the Maastricht region – to work, to live, and to love	2008	Maastricht Region Branding Foundation	✓	✓	✓	✓
Madrid	The Madrid brand	2005	City of Madrid	✓	✓	✓	✓
Nottingham	The Nottingham N	2005	Experience Nottinghamshire	✓	✓	✓	✓
Riga	Live Riga	2009	Riga Tourism Development Bureau	✓	✓	✓	✗
Rotterdam	Rotterdam:world port, world city	2008	Rotterdam City Marketing Office	✓	✓	✓	✗
Stockholm	Stockholm: the capital of Scandinavia	2008	Stockholm Visitors Board Stockholm Business Region Development	✓	✗	✓	✗
The Hague	International city of peace and justice	2006	Hague City Council Marketing Office	✓	✓	✓	✓

The structure of city brands – the brand platform

All city brands have a more or less similar structure, henceforth referred to as the brand platform. One of the weaker facets of the academic literature on city branding is the lack of attention afforded to the seven components or building blocks of a city brand, viz. core values, logo, straplines, font, language, colour palette, and signature shots. Together, these elements comprise the brand platform. They are literally the 'bricks and mortar' of a consciously created place identity.

 The first aspect of the brand platform - **core values** – is a central part of corporate and product brands, and is sometimes referred to as brand essence. For example, the Volvo brand is underpinned by values of quality, safety and environmental care, while its Boots counterpart stands for trust and staff knowledge. In the case of some city brands, defining core values may prove to be elusive and go by default, mainly due to the difficulty of achieving consensus as to what core values should be uppermost. This, in turn, reflects the complexity and pluralistic nature of cities. In most instances, however, core values are explicitly defined. For example, the core values identified in the *Edinburgh Inspiring Capital* place branding programme were made up of three clusters:

♦   inventive visionary, rich diversity;

♦   striving for excellence, understated;

♦   sincere warmth.

Homing in on a past redolent with passion and a future which is focused, the core values of the Madrid city brand were reduced to 'focused passion' (**Seisdedos and Vaggione** 2005). In contrast, the Belfast city brand comprised an abundance of core values, ranging from 'witty' and 'genuine' through to 'determined', 'vibrant', and 'inspiring' (www.belfastcity.gov.uk).

Frequently and unsurprisingly, the core values identified for city branding initiatives are those deemed to be rooted in the people past and present of the city. For the *Nottingham N* this meant 'genuine', 'independent' and 'ambitious'. The starting point for the *IAmsterdam* city brand was three core values held to be characteristic of Amsterdammers, viz. 'creativity', 'innovation' and 'spirit of enterprise'. *Glasgow: Scotland with style* is noteworthy as a city brand for being underpinned by a single core value (**Clark** 2006, pp 1-81). The iconic symbol of the style core value was the Glasgow born architect, painter and designer Charles Rennie Mackintosh (1868 – 1928). Ambitious claims were made at the time of the brand's launch in 2004 that what Gaudi had done for Barcelona, Rennie Mackintosh could do for Glasgow. Arriving at this particular core value was the end-product of meticulous content analysis of travel reviews which indicated a Glasgow competitive advantage clustered around style. A travel piece published in Time magazine, for instance, had portrayed the city as follows: 'Brimming with style and culture, Scotland's biggest city is a revelation.' In the event, reducing the city to a single core value invited criticism of *Glasgow: Scotland with style* from launch onwards, and such a limitation was being frankly acknowledged by the branding authority (Glasgow City Marketing Bureau) ahead of the brand's replacement in 2013:

> "The word 'style' meant that the brand was perceived by many as being biased in favour of retail, anchored as it was in Mackintosh and the associated 'Glasgow style'. The *Glasgow: Scotland with style* brand was also construed as being too heavily focussed on the work of our Bureau – tourism, major events and conventions - sense of place in that context. So while the brand served the Glasgow City Marketing Bureau well, it didn't in the end really reach sectors like financial services who are now looking for a city brand to be developed which is something a bit more specific to their sector. Even the universities and colleges, who in the past utilised *Glasgow: Scotland with style* to communicate the advantages of Glasgow as a place in which to study, are nowadays calling for something which is more clearly a differentiator for their particular sector. So as far as 'Glasgow: Scotland with style' is concerned at this particular point in time (January 2013), it is a case of 'the brand is dead, long live the brand' " (Rice, 2013).

In June 2013, Glasgow City Marketing Bureau therefore launched *People make Glasgow*.

Components two and three of the city brand platform – **logo** and **slogan** - are the highly visible parts of a city brand. Figure 3 is the logo and slogan associated with the *Edinburgh Inspiring Capital* city brand. Usually the logos (or marques) are reinforced by slogans (or straplines, mottos or taglines).

Figure 3: The logo and strapline associated with the current city branding programme in Edinburgh.

Lyon cleverly uses an anagram of Lyon to come up with an *Only Lyon* strapline. The place brand for Copenhagen has the strapline *Copenhagen – open for you*, intended to emphasise the diverse opportunities available in the Danish capital. Sub-sets of the main strapline follow such as 'open for dialogue', 'open for science' and 'open for inspiration' – see 'open for meetings' in Figure 4. The Hague logo – dubbed 'the kite' by the city's residents – is remarkable for the absence of slogan.

Figure 4: The Copenhagen logo and strapline

As the visible end of the city brand 'iceberg', logo and slogan are critical to its success or otherwise. If they are not well received, then self-evidently the marketing subsequently undertaken by the branding authority is compromised and weakened, and local organisations will be wary of adopting the city brand, so that its usage across both alignment and sub-branding becomes fitful. The potential for logo and slogan to engender controversy lies in part on the mistaken, but nonetheless widely held belief that they represent the entire cost of the city branding campaign. In fact, the cost of these items is usually a marginal one. More importantly, it reflects the intrinsic difficulty of collapsing a city and its people, with all its facets and achievements, into one symbol and a handful of words. For these reasons, city logos and slogans at and around their launches are nearly always lambasted for being costly and/or bland. For instance, the launch of the Liverpool place brand platform in March 2009 led to criticisms from some residents that the city skyline logo was predictable, simplistic and a waste of money. Similarly, the *be Berlin* city branding exercise was castigated for the allegedly large amounts of money being used to come up with just two words. Overcoming criticism such as this and achieving visibility - in formats ranging from aeroplane fuselages, websites, and posters, through to lapel badges and carrier bags, and across fields as diverse as community, tourism, business, events and cityscape - represents no mean challenge.

If the logo and strapline are the visible tip of the branding iceberg, then font, language, colour palette and signature shots are its less recognised and equally misunderstood underbelly!

Font, **language**, and **colour palette** build on core values and logo/straplines so that the city brand becomes ever more coherent, substantial, recognisable and distinctive. In the case of *Edinburgh Inspiring Capital*, for instance, the font or typeface is Myriad Roman to facilitate communication which is 'clean, modern, and stylish'. The language – the words and the associated tone to be used in marketing materials - links to the three clusters of core values referred to above, and is meant to be 'imaginative, vibrant', 'determined',' authentic' and 'confident'. Finally, there are 10 colours forming the palette, half of them 'warm and rich' and the remainder 'lively and vibrant'.

The final and usually most expensive element of the place brand platform is the stock of **signature shots**. For the *Edinburgh Inspiring Capital* brand campaign, there is an image library containing such photographs grouped under seven headings, viz. abstract, buildings and skyline, people and lifestyle, festivals and events, study, and business/investment. Figure 5 provides an *Edinburgh Inspiring Capital* signature shot which is part of the 'people and lifestyle' category.

Figure 5: The 'giggle' signature shot from the 'Edinburgh Inspiring Capital' campaign.

Signature shots are meant to reflect core values and home in on competitive strengths, so presumably the 'giggle' image is designed to counter the negative perception that Edinburgh's residents are somewhat reserved and stuffy! Unsurprisingly, signature shots figure prominently in marketing materials produced by the brand authority and - more fitfully - they are used by brand adopters. Media and other communicators are also encouraged to utilise such imagery.

All seven elements of the city brand platform are usually brought together by the brand authority in guidelines to facilitate extensive and high quality adoption of the city brand. A link to the Edinburgh brand guidelines is provided through www.edinburghbrand.com

Once each of the above elements have been constructed as a brand platform and codified in guidelines, the city brand itself can then be introduced. Having examined the structure of city branding, it is to the process that we now turn.

City branding as a process – development, launch and application

As a process, city branding comprises three distinct phases – development, launch and implementation.

As we have seen, the **development** of a city brand platform requires significant resourcing and budgets vary widely: development costs for the *Edinburgh Inspiring Capital* and *Nottingham N* city brands were £800,000 and £115,000 respectively. The development phase invariably begins with the issuing of a brief-to-tender. Preparation of the latter is itself a challenge. All too easily, its scope and content may become diluted and parochial, influenced by 'the sensibilities of a multitude of stakeholders, to embrace vast compendia of previous strategic background and be informed by every imaginable study, relevant or not, conducted over the past five years' (Whitfield, 2005).

For the *Nottingham N* city brand, a local design agency, Purple Circle, was appointed to advise the branding authority, Experience Nottinghamshire. This ushered in a 16 month period of research, design, and refinement. Experience Nottinghamshire, an independent public/private partnership with a tourism remit, managed that process, guiding and coordinating all the relevant parties and players. To this end, it established an Image and Branding Panel drawing upon communications specialists from the local authorities, universities, local media and the private sector. The Chief Executive of Nottingham City Council and the Managing Director of the local newspaper – the Nottingham Evening Post (NEM) – also sat on the Panel. The Panel reviewed the various aspects of the brand platform put forward by the design agency, including the *Nottingham N* logo (Figure 6) which as we shall see later turned out to be so controversial.

Figure 6: Nottinghamshire's N logo

Both the Panel and the board of directors of Experience Nottinghamshire gave wholehearted and enthusiastic 'sign-off' to the new city brand for Nottingham in February 2005. So when the brand was formally launched in the following month – see below – substantial support and 'buy in' had notionally been secured across the local public and private sectors. In particular, great care had been taken to ensure that the new brand, especially its logo, was acceptable to both the political leadership and senior management of Nottingham City Council. Ironically, in view of its Managing Director having participated in the deliberations of the Image and Branding Panel, NEM orchestrated an intense campaign of opposition to the *Nottingham N*.

The second stage in the life-cycle of a city brand is its formal **launch** of the city brand. Self evidently, the intent here is to create an initial wave of awareness and acceptance. The usual format is to stage a high profile event, to which the branding authority invites stakeholders and – crucially – media. For example, for the launch of the *IAmsterdam brand* on 23rd September 2004 the 'good and great' of the city and assorted media assembled at the Amsterdam Concert Hall where they listened to presentations (the Mayor of the city delivered a keynote address), perusing the brand website **www.iamsterdam.com** and an exhibition featuring specially commissioned photographs of the city. All attendees were issued with a commemorative book.

Launch events are often fronted by radio and TV personalities as well as locally born 'celebrity' backers of the new brand. While widespread awareness and acceptance might be the intent, in practice this is seldom achieved. In particular, media are prone to focus on 'negative' aspects of the brand, notably:

♦ Its cost to local residents

♦ The alleged banality of the logo and strapline

♦ Characteristics of the place overlooked or underemphasised in the new brand

Three cases instanced below exemplify how the launch of a city brand may result in ambiguous media coverage.

The launch of *Glasgow: Scotland with style* in March 2004 used Scottish television personality Sarah Heaney and Glasgow born actor Billy Boyd. More or less coinciding with the launch, statistics were published showing Glasgow had the highest per capita murder rates in Europe, and no less than 8 homicides were subsequently recorded in the city in the month following the launch of *Glasgow: Scotland with style*. Extensive media reportage of the 'Glasgow is Europe's murder capital' variety spotlighted how a rising tide of homicides stood awkwardly by the side of a campaign which was reducing the essence of the city to 'style'. In so doing, the reportage conjured up the very 'No Mean City' images of gang violence that city leaders had been assiduously seeking to eradicate over the past thirty or so years.

For the launch of *Leeds: live it, love* it in September 2005 a champagne party was organised by Marketing Leeds, the branding authority, along with a film in which Leeds-born celebrities eulogised their city. Local media coverage focused on the superficiality of the slogan, the fact that Hong Kong was already using a similar one, and the high cost of the launch event (reputedly £15,000). Confronted by all of this, the Chief Executive of Marketing Leeds was obliged to resign.

A final example is provided by the launch of the *Nottingham N* city brand. This was staged at Newstead Abbey – the ancestral home of Lord Byron – in March 2005. Press and PR coverage of the launch was extensive and, unusually for a city brand, was national as well as local. BBC Radio 5 Live conducted five separate interviews, syndicated across BBC Radios 2, 3 and 4. Radio 4 featured the brand launch on its morning news programme 'Today', and BBC1 organised 4 live feeds on its UK breakfast television show. Newspapers from the Daily Telegraph to the Sun reported on the launch. Two days later the media interest became international – from CBS Radio to the Tawain News. The coverage - local, national and international - was mainly critical, coalescing around the view that the former Robin Hood-based brand was to be displaced by an N. Successive features in the Nottingham Evening Post called for the discontinuation of the new place brand platform (Figure 7).

The third phase – **implementation** – lies at the heart of city branding as a process. Co-ordinated by whoever is the branding authority, an integrated programme of brand applications is introduced. The applications themselves fall into two main categories. The first is city dressing and other infrastructure aiming to create a 'sense of place' for residents, and for visitors, students and inward investors alike, as exemplified in Figure 8 taken in Glasgow in 2004 at the time of the launch of *Glasgow: Scotland with style*. City dressing and other infrastructural applications are expensive, and typically consist of banners, pennants, posters and billboards, screens, bus backs and sides, and floral displays. The second group of applications comprises marketing materials such as brochures, guides, videos/DVDs and websites, fact sheets, image libraries, 'pop-up' stands and branded car stickers, t-shirts, pens and badges. An example – again drawn from *Glasgow: Scotland with style* – is shown in Figure 9.

Figure 7: The Evening Post's reactions to the N logo

Figure 8: City dressing in Glasgow, 2004

Figure 9: Marketing materials, Glasgow, 2004

The marketing materials mentioned above are used to support marketing campaigns internal and external to the city. These are of varying degrees of intensity and sophistication, conditioned inevitably by the level of financial resource available and the degree of professionalism and creativity to be found in the branding authority. Following the launch of *Glasgow: Scotland with style*, for instance, the Glasgow Marketing Bureau mounted a £1.5 million campaign over a two and half year period which included city dressing, local and national advertising, and PR activity designed to secure international media exposure. In the case of *Only Lyon*, an annual promotional budget of approximately £1.3 million was identified for use on a range of applications, including a 5,000 strong ambassador network of brand supporters and an *Only Lyon* award scheme.

The brand-related marketing undertaken by Amsterdam Partners soon acquired a reputation for creativity and innovation. For instance, one campaign sought to exploit the annual Queen's Day holiday by inviting residents and visitors to 'party' in the city, utilising posters depicting world leaders seemingly representing Amsterdam, e.g. the then American Secretary of State Hilary Clinton sporting an orange afro wig! Extensive *Iamsterdam* bannering in the city accompanied three dimensional *IAmsterdam* letters which became an integral part of the tourist beaten treck. By 2008, a range of eye-catching *IAmsterdam* merchandising was generating sales in the region of £500,000 per annum, *IAmsterdam* stewards were greeting visitors at the Central Station, and 'Iambassadors' (recruited from the ranks of journalists and the creative industries) were penning their online tributes to the city. The *I Amsterdam* city brand was figuring prominently at major events both in and outside of the Netherlands, especially festivals, congresses and sporting championships. In this respect, forty events were linked to 'I Amsterdam' in 2008, including Amsterdam International Fashion Week and Dream Amsterdam. By that time, Amsterdam Partners was concentrating its international communications and marketing activities on eleven cities - New York, San Francisco, Los Angeles, Boston, Berlin, Barcelona, Bombay, Beijing, Shanghai, Guangzhou, and Tokyo - aiming to position the city region as an ideal location for companies to base their European headquarters. To that end, a glossy 'quality of life' magazine *Proud* was being distributed to opinion formers and decision makers, alongside themed media campaigns such as 'good ideas grow big in Amsterdam'.

To achieve maximum impact for a city brand, the branding authority invariably seeks to reinforce campaign activities by seeking partners from across the public, private and voluntary sectors, encouraging them to become brand adopters. The latter arise in three main ways. First, city leaders and residents are encouraged by the branding authority to wear or otherwise display the logos and straplines in the form of badges, stickers, t-shirts and the like. Secondly, local organisations with a citywide remit are invited by the branding authority to become fully-fledged sub-brands of the city brand. The promotional brochure in Figure 10 shows how the Vision Nottingham inward investment agency adopted the *Nottingham N* as its own corporate identity, thus becoming a sub-brand.

Figure 10: Brand adoption in Nottingham

Thirdly, local councils, companies, and voluntary bodies can be persuaded to align themselves to the city brand by carrying the logo/straplines and other aspects of brand architecture without diluting their own corporate identities. Alignment typically occurs in departments and sections of the city council, as well as individual operators from the tourism, retail, transport, festivals, real estate, education and other sectors. Figure 12 shows the home page of the Nottingham Trent University website, carrying the *Nottingham N* logo as well as two brand signature shots. Two years after its launch, Experience Nottinghamshire reported a total of just one sub-brand and over 150 alignments. The Copenhagen *Open for you* city brand secured a more impressive early range of brand adopters, ranging from the city government and the Confederation of Danish Industries through to leading companies, retailers, hotel chains, and transport providers, as well as the University of Copenhagen and the Microsoft Development Centre. Opposite the iconic Little Mermaid statue, the cruise port authority had emblazoned the B&W building with a huge "Open for you" banner, while rolling stock carried the slogan on the city's underground system.

Figure 11: The home page of the Nottingham Trent University website

When set against the universe of possible adopters and of potential adoptions, however, the extent of sub-branding and alignment tends at best to be relatively small. Indeed, across many of the twenty one cities surveyed in this review, sub-branding and alignment tends in the main to be slight and to fade out post-launch – part of a wider 'fizzling out' symptomatic of city branding as a process. Even where the branding authority is proactive, the number of sub-brands is usually small because city organisations are generally reluctant to give up their own corporate identities. Alignment typically flounders on the absence of a widespread awareness of the city brand amongst city organisations and of a genuine commitment to it.

The *IAmsterdam city brand* is exceptional for the degree of sub-branding and alignment it has attained. A second version of the **www.Iamsterdam.com** site went live in 2008, representing a remarkable partnership achievement in that it embodied and combined the strengths of six 'sectoral' marketing organisations:

♦   the Amsterdam Tourism and Convention Board

♦   the Amsterdam Uit Bureau (**citywide event calendar and ticketing**)

♦   Amsterdam Top City (a clearing house and facilitator of inter-agency collaboration)

♦   Amsterdam in Business (the city region investment board)

♦   Expat Centre (the regional service bureau for expats and foreign residents)

♦   the Communications Department of the municipality

Effectively each of these organisations became a sub-brand of *IAmsterdam*, giving an impressively joined up 'look and feel' throughout their various marketing endeavours. The portal in its first full year of operation received monthly in the region of 200,000 unique visits. Arguably even more impressively, brand adoption is nowadays strikingly evident within the municipal authority. Amsterdam City Council systematically employs the *IAmsterdam* brand to fashion a uniform housestyle across forty four urban districts and forty five municipal departments - from museums to tax offices. As a result, *IAmsterdam* is 'officially' visible on trams, vans, signage, posters, stationery, brochures, presentations and factsheets.

In the case of *IAmsterdam*, there is also a significant degree of alignment taking place, and this also merits consideration. A small, but important portion of Amsterdam Partner's marketing budget (4%) comprises networking expenses. This activity is co-ordinated by the organisation's Network Project Manager who seeks through meetings, an annual outing, and other informal contacts to maximise partner commitment to the city brand. In part, this is about maintaining and expanding the local authority subventions, as well as the 'bite size' funding contributions from companies and other institutions referred to above. Equally, if not more importantly, it is about strengthening relationships with the various partners so as to deliver additional 'off the balance sheet' activity in support of the *IAmsterdam brand*. Networking encourages public and private sector partners to themselves utilise the city brand in their own media and marketing activities. Alignment by partners takes many forms: deploying the logo and brand images on canal boats and screens at Amsterdam airport, in JCDecaux outdoor display cases, and at high profile venues such as the Amsterdam Arena and the Ajax football ground. It leads Heineken to align its Amstel 'One

Dam Good Beer' advertising campaign to the city brand. In this particular co-operation, the *IAmsterdam* logo appeared prominently in commercials and at the New York product launch for Amstel which took place on Amsterdam Avenue. Through alignment such as this, the city brand becomes ever more impactful at no or little cost to Amsterdam Partners. Effectively, it enables Amsterdam Partners to expand marketing activity beyond that expensed from within its own finite and ultimately modest budgets.

In contrast to Amsterdam, the difficulties of sustaining a city brand post-launch are well exemplified by the *Birmingham b* and the *Nottingham N* city brand platforms.

The 'Birmingham b' brand was launched in 2003 as a key element of a new approach to promoting the city spearheaded by a public/private partnership, Marketing Birmingham, established in the previous year. The brand platform had been produced by a local design agency, Boxer, and was premised on core values held to be reflective of the city past, present and future. Local media were equivocal about the likely impact of the *Birmingham b*, but nonetheless in the aftermath of its launch the new city brand achieved a high degree of visibility locally on posters, billboards, taxis, and bannering. However, a proactive process of adoption locally and an external marketing campaign failed to materialise, so that inertia soon came to surround the brand platform. By 2007 Birmingham City Council's Director of Public Affairs was minded to remark that more needed to be done to brand Britain's second city. To this day, the *Birmingham b* has not been revised or replaced. It survives not as a city brand, but only as the corporate brand of Marketing Birmingham and a municipal offshoot - the Birmingham City Centre Partnership. In terms of an engineered city brand, Birmingham is nowadays effectively 'brandless'.

Similarly, following its launch in 2005, the *Nottingham N* city brand achieved a significant amount of local visibility in terms of city dressing as well as alignment and sub-branding, all of it made possible by post-launch grant funding. The new brand was widely commended by marketing professionals for the quality and flexibility of its platform, and study visits were made by UK and continental cities. Its prospects of medium to long-term success, however, were compromised both by the time-limited nature of the initial, 'pump-priming' resourcing, and by the persistence of the view that the logo should have majored on the city's legendary icon, Robin Hood. As we have shown already, this view was held strongly and vocally by the local newspaper, which referred pejoratively to the logo as the 'wonky' or 'slanty' N. The Nottingham Evening Post mounted a sustained campaign for the brand platform to be 'binned' and be replaced by one based on Robin Hood. Eventually, a small number of local business persons and politicians came to hold similar sentiments, albeit expressed mostly in private. This undercurrent of 'anti Nottingham N'/ 'pro Robin Hood' feeling existed despite the failure of previous attempts to brand the city on the back of Robin Hood (reference the *Our style is legendary* place brand 1997-2003) and the fact that important city institutions were opposed to the idea of a one-dimensional brand platform centred upon Robin Hood. With grant funding for the brand progressively reducing from 2006/7 onwards, and after three and a half years of having 'officially' supported the *Nottingham N* place brand, Nottingham City Council announced in November 2008 that it would be withdrawing its support of the city brand. The NEM front page headline pithily said: 'The End'. The Council committed itself to the introduction of a new Robin Hood city brand spearheaded by a commission to be chaired by the Sheriff of Nottingham. The new brand platform has yet to be introduced, so that six years on this Midlands city, too, remains brandless.

Having examined the process of city branding - with all its pitfalls - the next section discusses the outcomes and impacts of city branding initiatives.

City branding – assessing the outcomes and impacts

City branding projects everywhere are premised on delivering two main sets of benefits. First, they can act as a reference and rallying point for a city's companies, institutions and people. Secondly, brands are introduced to heighten awareness of a city's advantages in key audiences and to subsequently generate sales and other conversions, leading to economic benefit. As we have seen – see Figure 1 and Table 1 - for a city brand the key audiences typically addressed are student, resident, inward investor and tourist ones. Unsurprisingly, city branding projects are often described by the official branding authority as being successful. For example, the Destination Edinburgh Marketing Alliance was soon reporting that its *Edinburgh Inspiring Capital* brand was 'now well established and..... delivering impressive results.' Three years on from the launch of the *Glasgow: Scotland with Style* campaign, the branding authority - the Glasgow Marketing Bureau - was citing impressive benefits:

- 359,000 additional overnight visitors, generating nearly £42 million of local economic benefit.
- A 3% growth in hotel occupancy rates.
- Positive media coverage worth £48million in terms of advertising equivalence.

The Bureau's Chief Executive suggested that in just three years the brand had 'more than proved its worth' (www.seeglasgow.com).

Figures such as those above recording a growth in the volume and value of tourism, however, are not the same as measuring the success of individual campaigns – be they brand campaigns or sectoral ones. As various commentators have pointed out, the evaluation criteria for city branding projects is either non-existent or at best unstandardised and vague (**Murray** 2001). As discussed directly below, there is a requirement both for greater critical appraisal and for the establishment of meaningful key performance indicators (**Henderson** 2007).

Systematic arrangements to monitor the number of sub-brands and alignments secured by the branding authority are infrequently put in place, despite the fact that this is an indicator of the success or otherwise of a city brand as a rallying point. The development of key performance indicators tracking increased awareness and conversions from the implementation of a city branding campaign are constrained by the costs of undertaking such research across the four principal audiences and – more importantly – by the methodological problem of how to isolate marketing cause and effect in respect of the city brand in question. The latter point – the difficulty of disentangling and then quantifying the effects of the city brand from the various other marketing influences – is compounded when account is taken of the wider city marketing context within which city branding exercises are executed.

For the reasons set out above, it remains the case that the impacts of city branding programmes remain resistant to authoritative measurement and evaluation.

Conclusions – whither city branding in Western Europe?

Despite its topicality, city branding as it is currently being undertaken in Europe is a quintessentially marginal and problematic affair. Indeed, one can go as far as saying that many cities are still unsure as to how to use city branding in an effective manner to drive forward economic development (**Levy** 2005, pp. 328-338). As we have seen, only a tiny minority of cities have explicit, engineered campaigns in place. Either consciously or by default, most cities do not perceive themselves as needing to create a city brand. Since 2010, few cities can be added to the roll-call of the 22 listed in Table 1. Though Innsbruck, Kiev (*The city where it all starts*) and Dundee (*One city, many discoveries*) have put in place city branding projects, a bandwagon effect is still far from evident.

Moreover, amongst the still relatively small number of cities who have elected to go down the city branding route, none can demonstrate proven levels of success, with the possible exception of *IAmsterdam*. It remains the case that little empirical work has been done to assess how far city branding demonstrably 'makes a difference' to the development and prosperity of cities. ROI is not easily captured and measured, with cause and effect being difficult to disentangle and assess. Intuitively, the magnitude of the constraints surrounding city branding means that the outputs and outcomes from such initiatives are likely to be limited. Analogies with what can be achieved through corporate branding exercises in the private sector fall down in the face of a lack of control and influence evident on the part of the branding authorities. In short, there is a great danger in expecting too much of city branding.

Having reviewed what has been achieved in the early years of the new Millennium, one can characterise city branding as still being very much in its infancy. As we have seen, good progress has been made in developing brand platforms which are flexible and multi-dimensional, enabling a range of audiences to be addressed. City branding is no longer confined to simple logo and slogan-led advertising campaigns of the *Glasgow's Miles Better* variety. In contrast to the growing sophistication of the brand platform, however, the implementation of city branding strategies do not follow 'tried and tested' procedures and are rarely evaluated systematically and meaningfully. It is at the crucial applications stage that city branding initiatives typically falter: budgets are small; stakeholders remain aloof or semi-detached; local media ignore or disown the city brand; for most residents the city brand is peripheral to their everyday concerns; and the relationship of city branding to the remainder of the wider city marketing enterprise remains weak. As a consequence, city branding exercises tend to lose momentum and have a short lifespan. Of the 22 city brands identified in Table 1, the bulk have either been replaced (e.g. *Glasgow: Scotland with style*), become defunct (The Hague's *International city of peace and justice*) or are 'fizzling out' (e.g. *the Belfast B*). In Europe, only the brands of Amsterdam, Berlin, Bilbao, Copenhagen and Lyon boast small, but significant levels of visibility and audience reach. Of these, only *IAmsterdam* is beginning to show other cities a 'way forward' – financially, creatively, and operationally.

Tantalisingly, *IAmsterdam* is hinting that city branding can really be made to work, and for that reason alone, I think it would be a shame were city branding to come to be seen as an irrelevance, and in so doing fall completely off the agenda of urban planning and management. In spite of its limitations – inherent and contrived – city branding holds out three enormous potential gains:

◆ It is one of only a few techniques that can be used by cities to differentiate themselves in what is an increasingly homogenised, urban world.

◆ It provides a rare, apolitical opportunity for the coming together of business, governance, and residents.

◆ It enables city marketing to become more 'joined up', through the processes of alignment and sub-branding.

For these three reasons, the survival of city branding for the remainder of the 21st century is probably assured, with the caveat that the starting point for any such project must be an awareness of its likely limitations and pitfalls. Ghandi, when asked what he thought about western civilisation, allegedly remarked that it would be " a good idea". City branding is rather like that!

References

Anholt, S. (2007) *Competitive Identity: the new brand management for nations, cities and regions*, Palgrave Macmillan, Basingstoke.

Ashworth, G. (2011) Should we brand places?, *Journal of Town and City Management*, **1** (3), 248-253.

Baker, B. (2007) *Destination Branding for Small Cities: the essentials for successful place branding*, Creative Leap Books, Oregon.

Bendel, P.R. (2011) Branding New York City – the saga of I Love New York, in Dinnie, K. (ed.) *City Branding: Theory and Cases*, Palgrave Macmillan, Basingstoke, pp.179-183.

Clark, G. (2006) City marketing and economic development, paper submitted to the *International City Marketing Summit*, Madrid,pp.1-81. http://www.gregclark.net/papers/Greg%20Clark%20Global%20City%20Marketing%20Summit%20Madrid%20.pdf

Diender, S. (2011) City tourism or city marketing – the integrated approach, presentation by the Chief Executive of Amsterdam Tourism and Conventions delivered at *the Annual Meeting of the Chief Executives of Capital and Major Cities* held in Vienna under the auspices European Cities Marketing.

Dinnie, K. (ed.) (2011) *City branding: theory and cases*, Palgrave Macmillan, Basingstoke.

Govers, R. and Go, F. (2009) *Place Branding: global, virtual and physical identities constructed and experienced*, Palgrave Macmillan, Basingstoke.

Grupp, J. (2010) The Berlin Partner organisation and the 'be Berlin' city marketing campaign, Powerpoint presentation delivered at *European Cities Marketing Autumn Meeting*, Uppsala, Sweden.

Hankinson, G.A. (2001) Location branding: a study of the branding practices of 12 English cities, *Journal of Branding Management*, **9**(2), 127-142.

Heeley, J. (1987) A tale of two cities and tourism, *Fraser of Allander Institute Quarterly Economic Commentary*, **11** (4), 49-54.

Heeley, J. (2011) *Inside City Tourism: a European perspective*, Bristol, Channel View Publications.

Hospers, G. (2011) City branding and the tourist gaze, in Dinnie, K. (ed.) *City Branding: Theory and Cases*, Palgrave Macmillan, Basingstoke, pp.27-35..

Henderson, J. C. (2007) Uniquely Singapore? A case study of destination branding, in *Journal of Vacation Marketing*, **13** (3), 261-274.

Kavaratzis, M. and Ashworth, G. J. (2005) City Branding: an effective assertion of identity or a transitory marketing trick?, *Tijdschrift voor Economischeen Sociale Geografie*, **96** (5), 506-514.

Levy, S. E., Blain, C. and Ritchie, J. R. B. (2005) Destination branding: Insights and practices from destination marketing organisations, *Journal of Travel Research*, **43** (4), 328-338.

Matson, W. (1994) Can cities market themselves like Coke and Pepsi do?, *International Journal of Public Sector Management*, **7** (2), 35-41.

Moilanen T. and Rainistro, S. (2008) *How to Brand Nations, Cities and Destinations: a planning book for place branding*, Palgrave Macmillan, Basingstoke.

Monclus, J. and Guardia, M. (eds.) (2006) *Culture, Urbanism and Planning*, Ashgate, Farnham.

Morgan, N., Pritchard, A. and Pride P. (eds.) (2004) *Destination Branding: creating the unique destination proposition*, Butterworth-Heinemann, Oxford.

Murray, C. (2001) *Making Sense of Place: New approaches to place marketing*, Comedia, Cheltenham.

Olins, W. (1994) *Corporate Identity*, Thames and Hudson, London.

Olins, W. (2008) *Wally Olins: the brand handbook*, Thames & Hudson, London.

Pike, S. (2008) *Destination Marketing: an integrated marketing communications approach*, Butterworth-Heinemann, Oxford.

Rice, T. Interview with the Head of Communications and Marketing, *Glasgow City Marketing Bureau*, 9 January 2013.

Seisdedos, G. and Vaggione, P. (2005) The city branding process: the case of Madrid, paper submitted to the 41st Congress of the International Society of City and Regional Planners, pp. 1-10.

Steden, P. and Holtgrewe, S. (2013) Berlin Partner GmbH and Business Development in the Capital Region, presentation delivered to the *UBC Business Commission*.

Walton, J.K. (1983) *The English Seaside Resort: a social history*, Leicester, Leicester University Press.

Whitfield G. (2005) Mountains don't smile back, *DMO World e-newsletter*, Issue 2, January.

Glossary

1988 Glasgow Garden Festival: Held between April and September 1988, the festival was the third of the UK's National Garden Festivals and attracted 4.3 million visitors to Pacific Quay on the River Clyde. The National Garden Festivals were part of the regeneration of neglected and derelict land in Britain's industrial cities, the five festivals were held in Liverpool, Stoke-on-Trent, Glasgow, Gateshead and Ebbow Vale.

1990 European Capital of Culture: Glasgow was the European Capital of Culture in 1990. The designation is now European City of Culture. A city (or cities) in the European Union is designated as such for one calendar year in which it showcases cultural life, often using it to transform and regenerate the city, both culturally and in terms of National, European and international reputation.

Amsterdam Partners: www.iamsterdam.com

Barcelona Metropolis website: Website based on Information and thoughts on the city of Barcelona. www.barcelonametropolis.cat/en/page.asp?id=22&ui=305

Berlin Partners: Organisation that provides support for investors in Berlin and also Berlin based companies who want to invest in foreign markets in order to forward and strengthen the city's brand. http://www.berlin-partner.de/

'Birmingham b': The brand of the city of Birmingham, UK. It has gradually become less and less used, though it still being used by Marketing Birmingham

Brand: "The name, symbol, term, design or any combination of these used to differentiate products or services from those competitors." (R. Teare and J. Costa, in J Jafari (2003), *Encyclopaedia of Tourism*, Taylor & Francis)This could refer to an individual product or complete product line. Branding refers to the process in which companies decide what they should offer and how it will be represented.

Burrell Collection (1983): The collection gifted by Sir William Burrell and his wife Lady Burrell in 1944 contained over 9,000 works of art. The collection is housed at Pollok Country Park. The building it is housed in was designed by Barry Gasson in collaboration with Brit Andresen and was opened by the Queen in 1983.

City branding: 'The self-conscious application of branding to places as an instrument of urban planning and management' (p 507). It creates a city brand, such as 'Nottingham 'the big N', 'Coventry inspires' and the 'Birmingham B' (link to definitions)

City Brands Index: Developed by Simon Anholt in 2006 the index measures the image and reputation of the world's cities. The index ranks 40 world cities on the dimensions:

Presence - Based on the city's international status and standing and the global familiarity/knowledge of the city. It also measures the city's global contribution in science, culture and governance.

Place - Exploring people's perceptions about the physical aspect of each city in terms of pleasantness of climate, cleanliness of environment and how attractive its buildings and parks are.

Pre-requisites - Determines how people perceive the basic qualities of the city; whether they are satisfactory, affordable and accommodating, as well as the standard of public amenities such as schools, hospitals, transportation and sports facilities.

People - Reveals whether the inhabitants of the city are perceived as warm and welcoming, whether respondents think it would be easy for them to find and fit into a community that shares their language and culture and whether they would feel safe.

Pulse - Measures the perception that there are interesting things to fill free time with and how exciting the city is perceived to be in regard to new things to discover.

Potential - Measures the perception of economic and educational opportunities within the city, such as how easy it might be to find a job, whether it's a good place to do business or pursue a higher education.

www.gfkamerica.com/practice_areas/roper_pam/placebranding/cbi/index.en.html

Core values: The main ideals of an organisation

'Coventry Inspires': The former brand of the city of Coventry, UK. Launched as the city brand in May 1999 used in the promotion of the city.

Destination Edinburgh Marketing Alliance: A public/private body that facilitates the promotion of the city of Edinburgh, Scotland. It was established in 2009 and l brings together "leading businesses and organisations to promote the city through fresh co-ordinated planning and to enhance Edinburgh's reputation as a place to visit, invest, live, work and study."In 2011, DEMA, the Edinburgh Convention Bureau, and the film location office for the Scottish capital are to be merged into a single organisation to be called Marketing Edinburgh.

www.edinburghbrand.com/about_the_brand.aspx

European Cities Marketing network: "European Cities Marketing is a network of City Tourist Offices and Convention Bureaux for sharing expertise, working together on an operational level, and creating business opportunities." The objective of the network, "is to increase visitors to city destinations through effective tourism and convention marketing."

www.europeancitiesmarketing.com/

Font, language, and colour palette: Elements that go into creating a logo. Font is the style of lettering. Language is the words chosen and used in the logo. A colour palette is a fixed set of colours used in digital images.

Glasgow Royal Concert Hall (1990): Constructed in the 1980s and opened in 1990 as part of Glasgow's status as City of Culture that year. The Hall was seen as a symbol of the regeneration of the city.

'Glasgow's Miles Better': Launched in 1983 the campaign attempted to change the image of the city from its 'No Mean City' image. The campaign featured the image of Mr Happy to put across a positive image of the city. The campaign ended in 1989.

Global village : Associated with Marshall McLuhan, the term refers to the idea that through technology the world has been contracted into a village. The greater awareness of the world through technology and the immediate transfer of information across the globe has been accelerated by the spread of the Internet across the world.

Hamburg Marketing GmbH: Develops and steers the Hamburg brand within the city, nationally and internationally aiming to portray the city as a positive location and boost awareness and attractiveness of the region through promotion and marketing.
www.marketing.hamburg.de/Hamburg-Marketing-GmbH.home.0.html?L=1

Interbrand: A brand consultancy specializing in brand services and activities. It is the largest brand consultancy in the world with 40 offices worldwide. /www.interbrand.com/

Landor: Landor is a brand and creative design consultancy based in San Francisco and with 21 global offices. www.landor.com/

Logos: An image used by organisations to represent themselves. The image often includes the name of the company or organisation and aims to be instantly recognisable to the public.

Lyon Area Development Agency: A body that promotes the city of Lyon, France. It aims to promote Lyon as a recognised economic force, but generally to get Lyon recognised around the world creating a brand for the city so it is "visible, clear, easy to identify and remember". www.onlylyon.com

Nottingham 'the big N': The brand of the city of Nottingham, UK. The brand was unveiled in 2005 used in the promotion of the city through leaflets, advertising and road signs. The brand has lately been discontinued and there are plans by Nottingham City Council to introduce a new one.

Place branding: The branding (link to Brand definition) of a nation, city or region

Procter and Gamble: An American multinational corporation that manufacture consumer goods.

Repositioning: The process of changing the identity of a product or a brand to occupy a different position in the market and eyes of the consumer. In effect changing the product identity in order for it to fit more effectively into the market.

Return on investment: A measure of performance of investments.

Scottish Conference and Exhibition Centre (1985): Supported by the Scottish Development Agency and built on the derelict Queens Dock site at Finnieston, Glasgow. The SECC is Scotland's largest exhibition centre.

'Sheffield Shines': The former brand of the city of Sheffield, UK

Straplines: The sentence or phrase attached to a brand. This emphasises the image of the brand and how the company wants to promote itself and its brand.